Mathematics

A REVISION AND REFERENCE GUIDE
FOR FIRST EXAMINATIONS

Also available from Stanley Thornes

A. Greer   A COMPLETE GCSE MATHEMATICS — GENERAL COURSE

A. Greer   A COMPLETE GCSE MATHEMATICS — BASIC COURSE

A. Greer   A COMPLETE GCSE MATHEMATICS — HIGHER COURSE

J. M. Hankin   MATHEMATICS FOR GCSE — A WORKBOOK APPROACH

P. Sherran   ESSENTIAL CALCULATOR PRACTICE FOR FIRST EXAMINATIONS

Mathematics

A REVISION AND REFERENCE GUIDE FOR FIRST EXAMINATIONS

G Godfrey

Head of Mathematics, Maiden Erlegh School, Reading

S Llewellyn

Stanley Thornes (Publishers) Ltd

First published in 1987 by:
Stanley Thornes (Publishers) Ltd
Old Station Drive
Leckhampton
CHELTENHAM GL53 0DN
England

British Library Cataloguing in Publication Data

Godfrey, G.
Mathematics: a revision and reference
guide for first examinations.
1. Mathematics—Examinations, questions, etc.
I. Title   II. Llewellyn, S.
510'.76   QA43

ISBN 0-85950-587-1

Typeset by Profile Filmsetters Ltd, Salisbury
in 10/12 Century Schoolbook
Printed and bound in Great Britain at the Bath Press, Avon

CONTENTS

INTRODUCTION

This book aims to provide mathematics students approaching their first public examination with a textbook that is not only a revision course, but is also a reference manual.

The text begins with a *glossary*, where terms, symbols and vocabulary are explained concisely, but reference to the given page will provide further explanation or examples of application. In Section II, theory is quoted and explained under numbered topic headings. This allows for flexibility of use in that either one complete topic can be revised or an individual item can be found when only a quick reminder of its meaning is required.

Using the book for revision, topic by topic

First study the notes and examples under your chosen topic heading in Section II. Check your understanding and knowledge by working through questions on this topic in Section III, where the questions are similar to the worked examples in Section II.

Then go on to the questions on the same topic in Section IV. If you are aiming at the higher levels of the examination, continue on to the questions in Section V.

When you have revised all the topics covered in your syllabus, work through the Papers in Section VI: for the lower levels of the examination work as far as Paper 3 Test A; for the middle levels work as far as Paper 4; for the higher levels work as far as Paper 5.

We hope that you will not only benefit from the ease with which you can refer to theory, but will also find there is an ample supply of practice questions which will enable you to gain both a greater understanding and appreciation of mathematics and a commendable examination grade.

Our thanks are due to the Examining Groups and in particular to the Southern Regional Examinations Board and the University of London School Examinations Board for permission to reproduce questions from past examination papers—in Sections IV and V respectively. We accept responsibility for the accuracy of the given answers.

G Godfrey
S Llewellyn

SECTION I

LIST OF SYMBOLS. UNITS. GLOSSARY.

LIST OF SYMBOLS

$\therefore$	therefore
$=$	is equal to
$\equiv$	is equivalent to
$\neq$	is not equal to
$>$	is greater than
$<$	is less than
$\geqslant$	is greater than or equal to
$\leqslant$	is less than or equal to
$\ngtr$	is not greater than
$\nless$	is not less than
$\Rightarrow$	implies
$\Leftrightarrow$	implies and is implied by
$\Leftarrow$	is implied by
$\approx$	is approximately equal to
$\propto$	varies directly as, is proportional to
$/$	solidus, e.g. $5\,\text{cm/s}$ (5 centimetres per second)
$\{a, b, c\}$	the set of elements a, b, c
$:$	such that, e.g. $A = \{x : x \text{ is an integer}\}$
$\circ\!\!-\!\!\circ$	open interval on the number line
$\bullet\!\!-\!\!\bullet$	closed interval on the number line
$\parallel$ or $/\!/$	is parallel to

parallel lines

equal in length

equal angles

a right angle

$\cup$	union
$\cap$	intersection
$\in$	is an element of
$\notin$	is not an element of
A'	the complement of set A
$\varnothing$	the null set
$\mathscr{E}$	the universal set
$\subseteq$	is a subset of
$\supseteq$	contains as a subset
$\subset$	is a proper subset of

⊃	contains as a proper subset
⊄̸	is not a subset of
⊄	is not a proper subset of
⊅̸	does not contain as a subset
⊅	does not contain as a proper subset
$n(A)$	the number of elements in set A
$\sqrt{}$	square root sign
$|x|$	the modulus or absolute value of x
$\overrightarrow{AB}$ **a**	vectors
↔	is in one-to-one correspondence with
π	pi ≈ 3.142
∞	infinity
△	i) triangle ii) symbol to represent an operation iii) symmetric difference sets
f: $A \mapsto B$	f is a function mapping set A into set B
f(A)	$\{f(x): x \in A\}$
f: $x \mapsto y$	f maps x to y
f(x)	the image of x under function f
$\mathbf{M}^{-1}$	the inverse of matrix **M**
$\mathbf{M}^T$	the transpose of matrix **M**
$p(A)$	probability of event A
ℕ	the set of natural numbers $\{1, 2, \ldots\}$
ℤ	the set of integers $\{0, \pm 1, \pm 2, \pm 3\}$
ℚ	the set of rational numbers
ℝ	the set of real numbers
+ ve	positive
− ve	negative
±	plus or minus
arcsin x $\sin^{-1} x$	the angle whose sine is x
→	approaches, tends to (in limits)

UNITS

METRIC   IMPERIAL

Length

10 mm = 1 cm

100 cm = 1 metre

1000 m = 1 km

12 inches (in) = 1 foot

3 ft = 1 yard

1760 yd = 1 mile

Square measure

$100 \, \text{m}^2$ = 1 are

$10\,000 \, \text{m}^2$ = 1 hectare

$1 \, \text{km}^2$ = 100 hectares

4840 sq yd = 1 acre

640 acres = 1 sq mile

Weight

1000 mg = 1 gram

1000 g = 1 kg

1000 kg = 1 tonne

16 ounces (oz) = 1 pound

14 lb = 1 stone

2240 lb = 1 ton

Capacity

1000 ml = 1 litre (l)

8 pints (pt) = 1 gallon (gal)

CONVERSIONS

Length

1 in ≈ 2.54 cm

1 m ≈ 39.37 in

Square measure

1 acre ≈ 0.405 hectares

1 hectare ≈ 2.47 acres

Weight

1 lb ≈ 0.454 kg

1 kg ≈ 2.2 lb

Capacity

1 gallon ≈ 4.51 l

1 litre ≈ 0.22 gal

GLOSSARY

Entries in capital letters are the chapter headings of topics in Section II.

Some entries in the glossary are given for reference only.

Acceleration	rate of change of velocity	96
Acute angle	$< 90°$	108

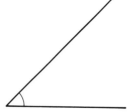

Addition	process of achieving a sum or total	
ALGEBRA		35
Allied angles		109

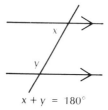

$$x + y = 180°$$

Alternate angles		109

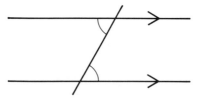

Altitude	perpendicular height	
Angle	$\hat{ABC}$ or $\angle ABC$	118

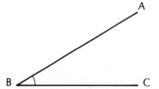

Approximate value	nearly the same, written as $\approx$, e.g. $47 \approx 50$ to the nearest 10	
Arc	i) part of a curve	83

ii) line joining 2 vertices, e.g. here there are 3 arcs   129

iii) arcsin x means 'The angle whose sin is x' and can also be written as $\sin^{-1} x$. Similarly for arccos x and arctan x

AREA AND VOLUME   64

Area	the surface enclosed, measured in square units	
Area factor	if the scale factor is s, then the area factor for similar figures is s^2	72
Arrowhead		110

Associative	$a * (b * c) = (a * b) * c$ for all a, b, c belonging to the given set	140
Average	mean, median and mode	100
Average speed	$\dfrac{\text{Total distance}}{\text{Total time taken}}$	95
Axes		85

Bar chart	a graph on which the frequency is represented by the height of the bar	101
Base	the number which, when raised to consecutive powers, gives the column headings of a system of counting, e.g. base 10: 10^3 10^2 10^1 units $10^{-1}\ldots$ base 2: 2^3 2^2 2^1 units $2^{-1}\ldots$	

Base vectors	$\begin{pmatrix} 1 \\ 0 \end{pmatrix}$ and $\begin{pmatrix} 0 \\ 1 \end{pmatrix}$, denoted by **i** and **j**	
Bearing	direction measured clockwise from North	80

Binary	to base two	
Binary operation	$+$, $\times$, $\div$, $-$ or some specially defined operation combining 2 elements	
Bisect	'cut in half'	120
Block graph	bar chart	
Boundary	i) end value in a class of grouped statistical data ii) border	102
Calculate	'work out'	
Cancel	divide top and bottom of a fraction by common factors, e.g. $\dfrac{\not{6}^1}{\not{8}_4} \times \dfrac{\not{2}^1}{\not{6}_1}$	53
Capacity	volume	
Chord	a line joining 2 points on a curve AB is a chord of the circle	82, 116

CIRCLES		82
Circle formulae	$C = 2\pi r = \pi d$ $\qquad A = \pi r^2$	
CIRCLE GEOMETRY		115
Circumference	perimeter of a circle, $C = \pi d$ or $2\pi r$	
Class	a group of statistical data	102
Class interval	the range of values included in a class (highest boundary minus lowest boundary)	102
Closed	a set is closed if the result of a binary operation between members of the set is always a member of the given set	
Coefficient	the number multiplying the variable, e.g. consider $\quad 8x - 3y$ $\qquad\qquad$ 8 is the coefficient of x $\qquad\qquad$ -3 is the coefficient of y	
Column matrix	$\begin{pmatrix} x \\ x \\ x \end{pmatrix}$	127

Commutative $a * b = b * a$ for all a, b belonging to a given set   140

Complement   the set of those 'not in',   146
e.g.   if $\mathscr{E} = \{$children in a class$\}$
    and $B = \{$boys in the class$\}$
then the complement of B,
       $B' = \{$girls in the class$\}$

Composite functions   a combination of functions,   156
e.g.   fg or gf

Compound interest   interest added to the principal, also earning interest   56

Concentric

with a common centre,
e.g.   concentric circles

Concurrent

passing through a common point,
e.g.   concurrent lines

Cone

3-dimensional solid with a circular   67
base, tapering to a point
$V = \frac{1}{3}\pi r^2 h$

Congruent   'same size and shape'   70
e.g.   these triangles are congruent

Consecutive numbers   following in order,
e.g.   16, 17, 18

Constant   a number with a fixed value
e.g.   3 and 5 in $3y + 5$

Constant term   a term that contains only a constant and/or a letter with a
fixed value
e.g.   5 in $3y + 5$
      c in $y = mx + c$ given that when $x = 0$, $y = 4$

Continuous variable	a variable which can take any real value in an interval, e.g. a person's height	102
Conversion	change	91
Coordinates	give the position of a point	84

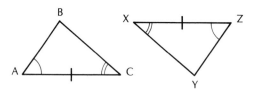

Corresponding	in the same position on similar figures e.g. AC corresponds to ZX	

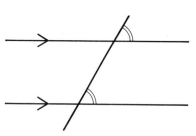

Corresponding angles		109

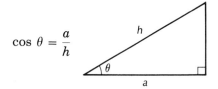

Cosine (cos)		73

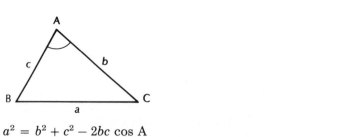

$$\cos \theta = \frac{a}{h}$$

Cosine rule		76

$$a^2 = b^2 + c^2 - 2bc \cos A$$

Counting numbers	$\{1, 2, 3, 4, \ldots\}$	
Cube	a three-dimensional figure with six congruent square faces	113

Cuboid	rectangular prism	66, 113

Cumulative frequency	'running total'	104
Curve	the graphs of quadratic and other powers of x (apart from 0 and 1) are curved	89
Cyclic quadrilateral (or concyclic points)	a circle passes through all the vertices	115

Cylinder	a three-dimensional solid with uniform circular cross-section	66

$$V = \pi r^2 L$$

DECIMALS		50
Decimal places	the number of figures after the decimal point, e.g. 8.37 has 2 decimal places (usually abbreviated to dec.pl. or d.p.)	50
Denary	to base ten	
Denominator	$\text{Fraction} = \dfrac{\text{Numerator}}{\text{Denominator}}$	52
Density	$\dfrac{\text{Mass}}{\text{Volume}}$	

Depression—angle of	Angle of depression	80

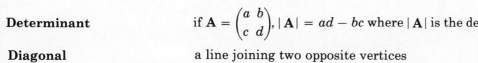

Determinant	if $\mathbf{A} = \begin{pmatrix} a & b \\ c & d \end{pmatrix}$, $|\mathbf{A}| = ad - bc$ where $|\mathbf{A}|$ is the determinant	128
Diagonal	a line joining two opposite vertices	

Diameter	a chord passing through the centre of a circle	82

$$d = \frac{C}{\pi}$$

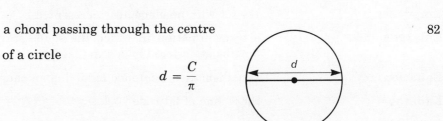

Differentiation	the process of calculating the rate of change of one variable with respect to another	
Digits	the figures 0, 1, 2, 3, 4, 5, 6, 7, 8, 9	
DIRECTED NUMBERS		49
Direction		139

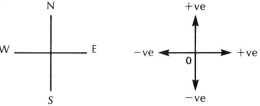

Directly variable	$y \propto x \Rightarrow y = cx$	97
Discount	reduction	
Discrete variable	a variable which can take only specific values, e.g. shoe sizes	102
Distance	measurement of the space between 2 points	
Distributive	$a * (b \triangle c) = (a * b) \triangle (a * c)$ for all a, b, c belonging to the given set	140
Division	the process of finding a quotient	

$$a \div b = \frac{a}{b}$$

Dodecahedron	a polyhedron with 12 pentagonal faces	114
Domain	for f(x), the set of values of x	152
Edges	lines where faces meet	114

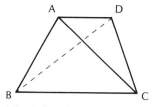

AB, AC, AD, BC, BD, CD are the edges of this solid

Element	an individual member of a set or matrix	127, 146
Elevation	view of the front or side of a model	
Elevation—angle of		80

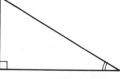

Angle of elevation

Empty set	the set with no elements, represented by { } or $\varnothing$	146
Enlargement	a transformation in which the shape stays the same and lengths are altered by a scale factor	69, 132, 135
Equation	a mathematical sentence involving an equals sign	37
Equator	the 0° line of latitude	
Equidistant	'the same distance from'	121

12

Equilateral triangle

Equivalent — the same as, even though expressed differently, written as ≡

ERROR

Error — the difference between the true value and an approximate value

Euler's theorem

two-dimensional	three-dimensional
$R + V - A = 2$	$F + V - E = 2$
regions + vertices − arcs = 2	faces + vertices − edges = 2

Evaluate — calculate

EVERYDAY ARITHMETIC

Expand — multiply out,
e.g. $(x + 2)(x + 3) = x^2 + 5x + 6$

Extend — continue,
e.g.

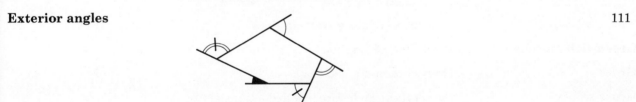

XY has been extended to W

Exterior angles

Faces — flat surfaces of three-dimensional solids

Factor of a whole number — will divide into the number exactly,
e.g. 5 is a factor of 15

Factor theorem — $(x - a)$ is a factor of f(x) if f$(a) = 0$

Fibonacci numbers — the next term in the sequence is the sum of the two preceding terms,
e.g. 1, 1, 2, 3, 5, 8, 13, . . .

FLOW CHARTS

Formula — an algebraic relationship,
e.g. $V = \frac{4}{3}\pi r^3$
or $C = 2\pi r$

FRACTIONS

Fraction	$\dfrac{a}{b} = a \div b = a/b$	44, 52
Frequency	number of times	100
Function	a one-to-one or many-to-one mapping, e.g. f: $x \mapsto 3x + 7$	152
GEOMETRY		108
Gradient		92

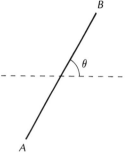

slope, direction, gradient of AB $= \tan \theta$
If $y = mx + c$, then gradient of the line $= m$

Gradient of a curve   the gradient at a point on a curve is the gradient of the tangent at that point

GRAPHS		84
Graph		

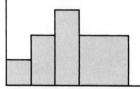

Cartesian   Polar

a means of relating two variables

Greenwich meridian	the 0° line of longitude	
Gross	twelve dozen	
Gross salary	the total salary before any deductions are made	
Grouped frequency	the frequency of an interval class	104
Groups	sets with certain properties	
HCF	highest common factor	48
Hectare	unit of area; 1 hectare $= 10\,000\ \text{m}^2$	
Hexagon	a six-sided polygon	110
Histogram	a vertical bar chart with the area of each bar representing the frequency	101

Horizontal	flat, perpendicular to the vertical	
Hypotenuse		

the side opposite the right angle in a right-angled triangle

Icosahedron a polyhedron with 20 triangular faces   114

Identity element when combined with the identity element by means of a binary operation, all other elements are unaltered,
e.g. 1 for the set of integers with respect to multiplication
$1 \times 8 = 8 \times 1 = 8$

Identity matrix $\begin{pmatrix} 1 & 0 \\ 0 & 1 \end{pmatrix}$ for 2 by 2 matrices, $\begin{pmatrix} 1 & 0 & 0 \\ 0 & 1 & 0 \\ 0 & 0 & 1 \end{pmatrix}$ for 3 by 3 matrices   132

with respect to matrix multiplication

Identity transformation leaves shapes unchanged   132

Image i) $f(x)$ is the image of x under function f   152
ii) the result of the transformation of a shape

Implies gives as a logical deduction, written $\Rightarrow$

Improper fraction greater than 1, where numerator $>$ denominator,
e.g. $\frac{8}{3}$

Incidence matrices these show the contact properties of a network,   131
e.g. which arcs and nodes touch, or which arcs and regions
are in contact

Index the power to which a number is to be raised,   47
e.g. in x^3, 3 is the index (plural *indices*)

Inequalities   41
$>$ greater than
$<$ less than
$\geqslant$ greater than or equal to
$\leqslant$ less than or equal to

Infinity an immeasurably large number, written ∞

Integer a positive or negative whole number or zero,
$\{\ldots -3, -2, -1, 0, 1, 2, 3, 4, \ldots\}$ is the set of integers

Integration the reverse of differentiation; the integral of $f(x)$ with respect to x is written as $\int f(x)\,dx$

Intercept for $y = mx + c$, c is the intercept on the y-axis   93

Interest	see **Simple interest** and **Compound interest**	
Interior angles	inside angles	110

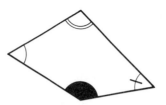

Intersect	'meet'	
Intersection		146

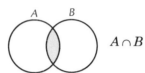

$$A \cap B$$

e.g. $\{2, 5, 7\} \cap \{2, 3, 4, 5\} = \{2, 5\}$

Into	set A maps into set B under function f if $f(A) \subset B$	154

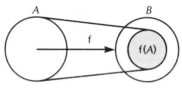

Invariant	unchanging	136
Inverse	if $A * B$ equals the identity, then B is the inverse of A and A is the inverse of B	155
Inverse matrix	for $\begin{pmatrix} a & b \\ c & d \end{pmatrix}$ the inverse matrix is $\dfrac{1}{ad - bc}\begin{pmatrix} d & -b \\ -c & a \end{pmatrix}$	129
Inversely proportional	$y \propto \dfrac{1}{x} \Rightarrow y = \dfrac{c}{x}$	98
Irrational number	cannot be expressed as a fraction in which numerator and denominator are integers, e.g. $\sqrt{2}, \pi$	
Isosceles triangle		109

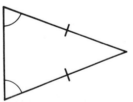

Jointly variable	$y \propto xv \Rightarrow y = cxv$, i.e. y is proportional to both x and to v	99
Kilo	'kilo' means a thousand 1 kilogram (kg) = 1000 grams (g) 1 kilometre (km) = 1000 metres (m)	
Kite		110

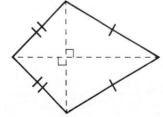

Knot	a speed of 1 nautical mile per hour	
Latitude, line of	a circle on the Earth's surface parallel to the equator; the equator has a latitude of $0°$; the North Pole is at $90°$N	
LCM	lowest common multiple	48
Like terms	terms which contain the same variables, e.g. $6xy$ and $3xy$ or $8x^2$ and $-4x^2$	35
Line		85, 94

180°

Line of best fit	the 'best' line that can be drawn through a set of points	

Linear equation	the equation of a straight line, $y = mx + c$, e.g. $y = 3x + 4$	37
Linear programming	method of solving an equation together with inequalities to give the 'best' solution	87
Litre	unit of volume, 1 litre $= 1000\,\text{cm}^3$	
LOCI		121
Locus	the path followed by a point moving under certain conditions	
Logarithm	the logarithm of a number is the power to which the base must be raised to give the number, e.g. since $10000 = 10^4$ then $\log_{10} 10000 = 4$	
Longitude, line of	a circle on the Earth's surface passing through the North and South pole; the Greenwich meridian has a longitude of $0°$	
Magnitude	size, $\lvert \overrightarrow{AB} \rvert = \sqrt{x^2 + y^2}$	138

Mapping	a relation between two sets, covering the whole of the first set, e.g. g: $x \mapsto 2x + 1$ where x is a real number; the arrow means 'maps to'	152
Mass	amount of matter, units are g, lb, ...	

Matrix	a rectangular array of numbers	
Maximum	highest value or point	

Highest ✕ Maximum point

Mean	the total divided by the number of values	100
Median	i) the middle value or mean of the two middle values when arranged in ascending (or descending) order ii) the line from the vertex of a triangle to the middle of the opposite side	100
Member	an element of a set, e.g. a is a member of $\{a, b, c\}$ written as $a \in \{a, b, c\}$	146
Meridian	a semicircle along the Earth's surface starting and ending at the North and South Poles	
Metre	unit of length, $1000\,m = 1\,km$ $100\,cm = 1\,m$	

Metric units		kilo	hecto	deca		deci	centi	milli	51
	Mass:	kg	hg	dag	g	dg	cg	mg	
	Length:	km	hm	dam	m	dm	cm	mm	

Minimum	lowest value or point	

Lowest ✕ Minimum point

Mixed number	part whole number, part fraction, e.g. $3\frac{3}{8}$	52
Mode	the most frequent value	100
Modular arithmetic	'clock' arithmetic	
Modulus	$\lvert x \rvert = x$ if x is positive and $\lvert x \rvert = -x$ if x is negative	
Multiple	the result of multiplying the given number by an integer e.g. 35 is a multiple of 5	47
Multiplication	the process of obtaining a product, e.g. 3×4, $5x$	
N.B.	*Nota bene* meaning 'note well'	
Natural numbers	$\{1, 2, 3, 4, \ldots\}$	
Nautical mile	the distance subtended at the equator by an angle of 1 minute ($\frac{1}{60}$ of a degree) at the centre of the earth	
Negative	$-$ve; with a value less than zero	49
Net	a plane figure which can be folded to form a three-dimensional model	115
Net salary	the amount left after deductions have been made	

Network   a diagram consisting of nodes, arcs and regions not depen-   129
                       dent on size or shape but on position in relation to each
                       other, e.g.

Node   vertex, junction,   129
                       e.g.   A, B, C, D are nodes in this network

NUMBERS   46

Number line   49

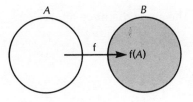

Numerator $\text{Fraction} = \dfrac{\text{Numerator}}{\text{Denominator}}$ 52

Obtuse angle $90° < \text{angle} < 180°$ 108

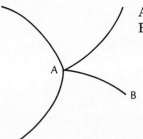

Octagon   eight-sided polygon   110

On to   set A maps on to set B under the function f if $\text{f}(A) = B$ 154

Operation   instruction,   44
                       e.g.   ×, square, +
                       A **binary** operation combines **two** elements

Order of a matrix the number of rows × the number of columns,   127
                       e.g. $\begin{pmatrix} \text{x x x} \\ \text{x x x} \end{pmatrix}$ has order 2 × 3

Order of a node   the number of arcs meeting at the point,
                       e.g.

A has order four
B has order one

Order of rotational symmetry	the number of times a shape will fit on top of itself in one complete turn	125

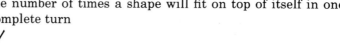

e.g. this figure has order three

Origin	beginning

Parabola	a U-shaped curve representing a quadratic equation e.g.

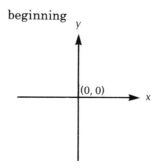

Parallel lines	lines always the same distance apart

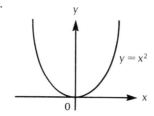

Parallel of latitude	a circle on the surface of the earth connecting points with the same angle of latitude

Parallelogram		64, 109

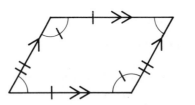

Pascal's triangle	1	145
	1 1	
	1 2 1	
	1 3 3 1	
	1 4 6 4 1	
	etc.	

Pentagon	5-sided polygon	110
Percentage	%, out of 100	

PERCENTAGES

Percentage error $\dfrac{\text{Error}}{\text{True value}} \times 100\%$

Percentage profit $\dfrac{\text{Profit}}{\text{Cost price}} \times 100\%$

Perimeter   total distance round   83

Perpendicular   lines meet at a right angle

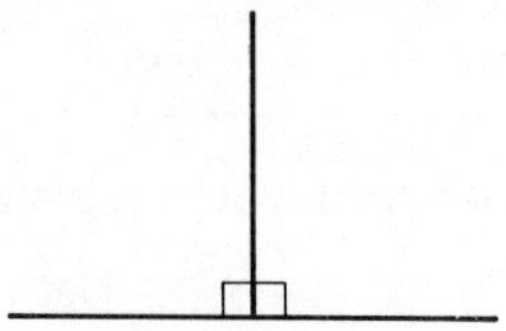

Pi $\pi \approx 3.14$ or $\frac{22}{7}$ 82

Pictogram   the use of a number of symbols or pictures to represent the frequency of data   101

Pie chart   a circle with sectors representing sizes of groups   105

Plan   the view of an object from above

Plane   flat surface   79

Point   84

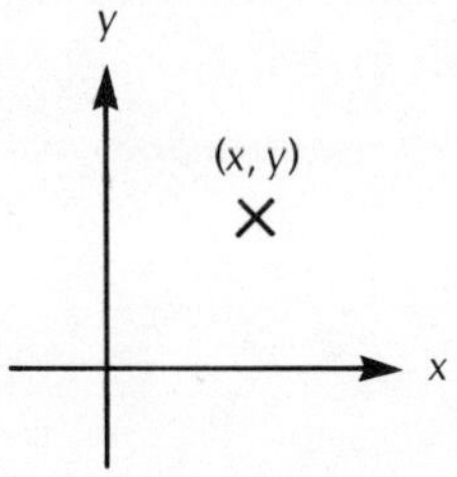

Polar coordinates $P = (r, \theta)$ 91

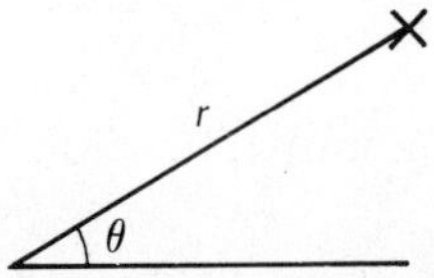

Polygon   a plane closed figure with straight sides   110

Polyhedron   a 3-dimensional solid with plane faces and straight edges only
e.g.   cube, pyramid   113

Polynomial   an expression such as $2x^3 + 3x^2 + 5x + 10$

Position vector   140

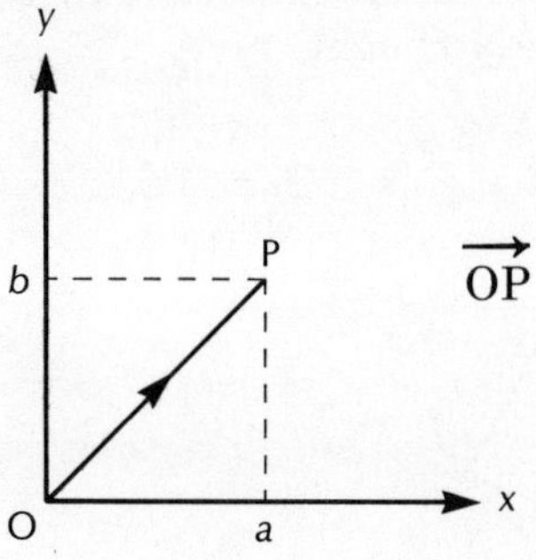

$$\overrightarrow{OP} = \begin{pmatrix} a \\ b \end{pmatrix}$$

SECTION I

21

Positive	+ ve; with a value greater than zero	49
Power	the result of raising a base to an index, e.g. 3^4 is the fourth power of 3 and equals $3 \times 3 \times 3 \times 3$	47
Premium	one year payment for insurance	
Prime number	a number divisible only by itself and one, e.g. 2, 3, 5, 7, 11, 13... (1 is not a prime number)	47
Principal	amount of money invested or borrowed	56

Prism 3-dimensional solid with uniform polygonal cross-section, e.g. 66, 114

V = area of end × length

PROBABILITY 142

Probability the likelihood of an outcome occurring, given as a fraction between 0 and 1

Produced extended in the direction given, e.g. AB produced to C

C

B

A

Product	the result of a multiplication	
Profit	Selling price – Cost price	55
Proper subset	a subset not equal to the original set	
Proportional	varies as, e.g. $y \propto x$ or $y = cx$	97

Pyramid a polyhedron which tapers uniformly to a point 66, 114
$V = \frac{1}{3}$ Area of base × Height

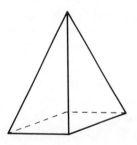

Pythagoras' theorem	for a right-angled triangle $h^2 = a^2 + b^2$	73, 111

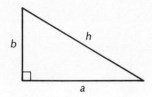

Quadratic equation	an equation which can be put into the form $ax^2 + bx + c = 0$, e.g. $x^2 + 3x - 4 = 0$	40

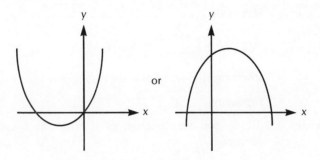

or

are graphs of quadratic equations

Quadrilateral	a 4-sided polygon	109
Quotient	the answer in a division	
Radian measure	the angle subtended at the centre of a circle by an arc equal in length to the radius of the circle; one radian is written as 1^c so $\pi^c = 180°$	
Radius	half the diameter of a circle	82

Range	i) for f(x), the set of values of f(x)	152
	ii) Maximum value − Minimum value of data in statistics	104
Rate	the percentage interest charged per annum	
Rateable value	the value given to property for the purpose of assessing rates to be paid	
Rates	payment to council calculated by Rateable value of property × Rate in the pound	
RATIO		59
Ratio	a comparison of quantities, written as $a:b$	
Rational number	can be written as a fraction	
Real numbers	set of numbers that can be put on the number line	46

Reciprocal	the result when a fraction is 'turned upside down', e.g. reciprocal of $\frac{3}{4} = \frac{4}{3}$ reciprocal of $3 = \frac{1}{3}$	
Rectangle	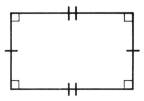	64, 109
Rectangular numbers	can be expressed as a product of two whole numbers greater than one, e.g. $12 = \frac{\text{xxxxxx}}{\text{xxxxxx}} = 6 \times 2$ Rectangular numbers are non-prime	46
Recurring	repeating	
Reduce to lowest terms	divide top and bottom of a fraction by all the common factors, e.g. $\frac{8}{16} = \frac{1}{2}$	
Reflection	mirror image	132, 133
Reflex angle	$> 180°$ 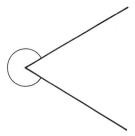	108
Region	space, area e.g. 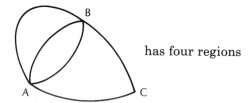 has four regions The outside is counted as a region	86, 129
Regular polygon	all sides are equal and all angles are equal	110
Relation	connection between two sets, e.g. 'is a multiple of'	151
RELATIONS, MAPPINGS AND FUNCTIONS		151
Remainder theorem	if $f(x) \div (x - a)$ then $f(a) = $ Remainder	45
Revolution	one revolution is a complete turn through $360°$	

24

Rhombus	quadrilateral with four equal sides	109

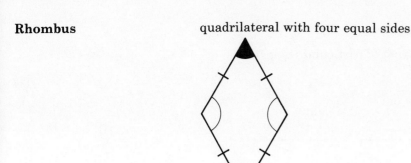

Right angle		108

90°

Ring		83

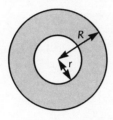

$$\text{Area} = \pi R^2 - \pi r^2$$
$$= \pi(R - r)(R + r)$$

Root	i) $\sqrt{}$ square root,	47

e.g. $\sqrt{16} = +4$ or -4

$\sqrt[3]{}$ cube root,

e.g. $\sqrt[3]{8} = 2$

ii) solution of an equation,

e.g. $x^2 - 6x = 0$ has roots 0 and 6

Rotation	turning	132, 134
Row matrix	(x x x x x)	127
Scalar	a real number	139
Scale	ratio of reduced (or enlarged) to real measurement	60
Scale factor	ratio of corresponding sides of similar figures	69, 132
Scientific notation	**see Standard form**	
Second degree equation	of the form $y = ax^2 + bx + c$	
Sector	'slice' of a circle	82, 83

O

Segment	part of a circle cut off by a chord	82, 116

Semicircle	half a circle	
Set	a collection of particular things	
SETS		
Sharing	dividing out	
Shear	'push',	

e.g.

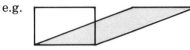

Significant figures the digits in the highest-value columns being used,

e.g. $3.18 = 3.2$ to 2 s.f.

$6172 = 6170$ to 3 s.f.

Similar figures 'same shape',

e.g.

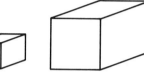

i) if the scale factor is s
then the area factor is s^2
and the volume factor is s^3

ii) if the ratio of the lengths is $x:y$ then the ratio of areas is
$x^2:y^2$ and the ratio of volumes is $x^3:y^3$

Similar triangles equal angles, fixed ratio of corresponding lengths

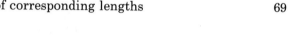

SIMILARITY		
Simple interest	the money paid for use of a loan	
Simplify	write in a shorter and more convenient way	
Simultaneously	at the same time	

Sine (sin)

$$\sin \theta = \frac{b}{h}$$

Sine rule

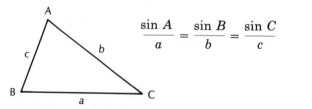

$$\frac{\sin A}{a} = \frac{\sin B}{b} = \frac{\sin C}{c}$$

Singular matrix matrix with no inverse, determinant $= 0$

Slope	gradient	
Solution	answer	
Solution set	the set of values satisfying a given equation,	94
	e.g. for $(x - 3)(x + 5) = 0$ the solution set is $\{3, -5\}$	

SPEED AND DISTANCE 95

Speed	$\dfrac{\text{Distance}}{\text{Time}}$; units might be km/h or m/s	
Sphere	Surface area $= 4\pi r^2$	67
	Volume $= \frac{4}{3}\pi r^3$	
Square	a regular quadrilateral	109

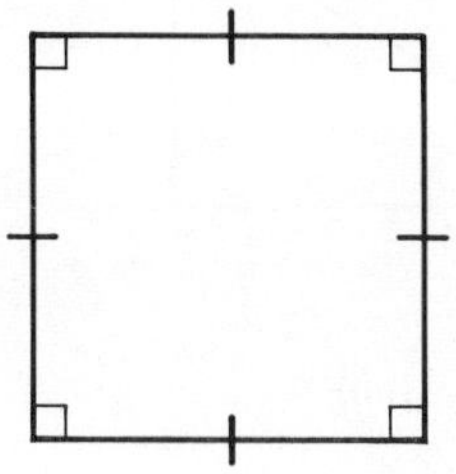

Squared	'multiplied by itself',	47
	e.g. $8^2 = 8 \times 8$	
	$\quad\;\; = 64$	
Standard form	$a \times 10^n$ where $1 \leqslant a < 10$ and n is an integer,	48
	e.g. $0.0032 = 3.2 \times 10^{-3}$ in standard form	
Stationary points	points where the gradient of the curve is zero	

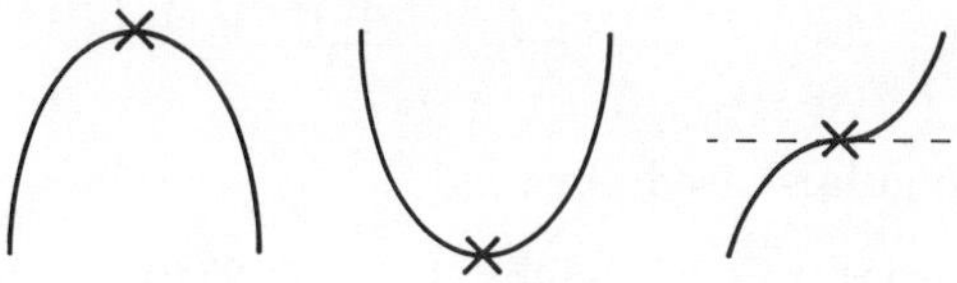

STATISTICS 100

STRAIGHT LINES 92

Stretch	shape is transformed by enlarging in one direction	132, 136
Subject	the variable 'on its own', usually on the left-hand side,	43
	e.g. in $y = 4x + 7$	
	y is the subject	
Subset	a set which is contained in another set,	146
	e.g. $\{1, 2\} \subset \{1, 2, 3, 4\}$.	
Substitution	the act of replacing a variable with a constant	36
Subtended		115

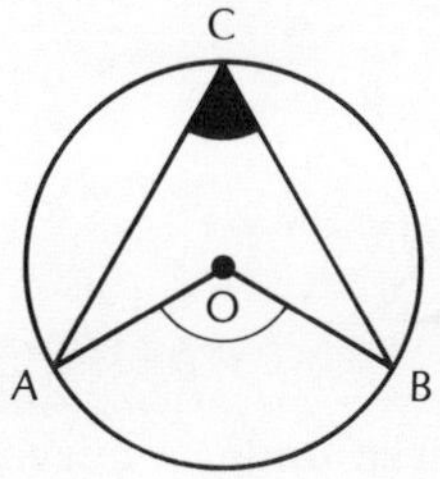

an angle is subtended by an arc; $A\hat{O}B$ is subtended at the centre by AB; $A\hat{C}B$ is subtended at the circumference by AB

27

Subtraction	the process of obtaining a difference, e.g. $6 - 4$, $x - y$	
Sum	the result of an addition	
Surd	a number in surd form is one containing root signs, e.g. $\sqrt{2}$, $2\sqrt{3}$ in which the root is irrational and so can only be expressed approximately in its simplest form	

Tally	method of recording frequency, e.g. $\cancel{||||}\,|||$ represents 8	100
Tangent (tan)		73

$$\tan\theta = \frac{b}{a}$$

Tangent	a line which touches a curve	116
Term	one item in an algebraic sum, e.g. $3x$, $-4x^2$, $+2xy$	35
Tessellation	a repeated pattern which covers an area, e.g. a tessellation of	113

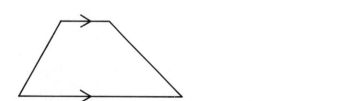

Tetrahedron	triangular-based pyramid	114
Ton	Imperial unit of weight, 1 ton = 2240 lb	
Tonne	metric unit of weight, 1 tonne = 1000 kg	

Translation	displacement described by a vector $\begin{pmatrix} x \\ y \end{pmatrix}$	133
Transpose of a matrix	rows become columns, e.g. transpose of $\begin{pmatrix} 1 & 2 \\ 3 & 4 \end{pmatrix} = \begin{pmatrix} 1 & 3 \\ 2 & 4 \end{pmatrix}$	129
Trapezium		64, 109

Trapezium rule	a method of finding the area under a curve	90

Traversable   can be traced without repetition and without
                       taking pen from paper

e.g.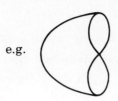

Tree diagram   an aid to solving probability problems   144

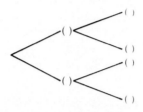

Triangle   a 3-sided polygon   64, 109
                       Sum of angles = 180°

Triangular numbers

     x
   x   x   1, 3, 6, 10, 15, 21, 28, ...
 x   x   x
x   x   x   x

TRIGONOMETRY   73

Turn   one complete revolution

Turning point

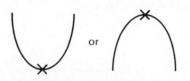

Union   146

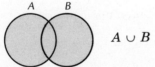

$A \cup B$

e.g. $\{2, 3\} \cup \{1, 3, 4\} = \{1, 2, 3, 4\}$

Unit vector   i) a vector of unit length

ii)

i represents $\begin{pmatrix} 1 \\ 0 \end{pmatrix}$

j represents $\begin{pmatrix} 0 \\ 1 \end{pmatrix}$

Universal set	$\mathscr{E}$, {all elements being considered}	146
Variable	a quantity represented by a letter, subject to change, e.g. in $y = 3x$, x and y are variables, 3 is a constant	
VARIATION		97
Vector	a vector quantity has magnitude and direction and can be expressed as	

$$\overrightarrow{AB},$$

or

VECTORS		138
Velocity	speed in a given direction	
Venn diagram	representation of sets, e.g.	147

Vertical	upright, perpendicular to the horizontal	
Vertically opposite angles		109

Vertices (plural of vertex)	points where arcs meet or end	114, 129

A, B, C are vertices

Volume	amount of space taken up, measured in cubic units	
Volume factor	if the scale factor is s, then the volume factor for similar figures is s^3	72

SECTION II

NOTES AND WORKED EXAMPLES

HINTS FOR MATHEMATICS EXAMINATION CANDIDATES

1. Check your geometry instruments and the batteries in your calculator before the examination.

2. Read the instructions carefully.

3. Do **not** write out the question.

4. **You** may be able to read your own writing, but make sure that the examiner can as well.

5. If given a choice attempt your 'best' question first.

6. When given a choice of questions, it is not to your advantage to attempt all of them.

7. **Show all working**: particularly in an arithmetic question in which a calculator is being used.

8. Draw sketch diagrams to help find solutions.

9. Make sure that you answer the question actually asked.

10. Check that you have answered all parts of the question.

11. Spend time proportional to the marks for the question.

12. Use your common sense; all answers will be 'sensible', e.g. a train will not stop in 2.1 mm.

13. Take care with **units**.

14. Graph scales will always fit on the paper provided.

15. Check that an answer is possible, e.g. Probability $\leqslant 1$ so Probability $= 7/5$ **must** be wrong; perhaps it should be 5/7?

16. Don't round off numbers too soon. If an answer to three decimal places is asked for, then only the *final* answer should be corrected to three decimal places.

17. When asked to approximate, work out one more figure than required, e.g. for three decimal places, actually work out to four decimal places then approximate.

18. The examiners are trying to find out what you know, not to trick you into making errors. Take every opportunity to show the examiners that you do understand the question, can think out a logical, sensible method, do know relevant facts, and can calculate accurately.

19. 'Panic' loses marks, so **do not panic!**

20. Answer **every** question in the multiple choice paper, even if some have to be guessed.

21. Do **not** cross anything out until you have actually written down the correction.

22. If you have difficulty with a question, do not waste too much time; go on to the next question.

23. If you finish early go back and **check your answers.**

1 ALGEBRA

In algebra, letters are used in place of numbers because either

i) the value of the number is originally unknown, but can be found using the given information to form and solve equations;

or

ii) the problem has been generalised, i.e. the letter represents any number.

TERMS

A term is a group of numbers and letters,

Examples

$6x, \quad -4y^2, \quad \dfrac{3x}{2y}, \quad \dfrac{3}{x+y}$

The number, e.g. 6, -4, is the *coefficient*; the letter is the *variable*.

Only like terms, i.e. those containing the same variables, can be added or subtracted to give a single term.

Examples

a) $x + 3x = 4x$

b) $x^2 - 5x^2 = -4x^2$

c) $xy - 5yx + 3xy = -xy$

Neither $5x + 3y$ nor $x + 8x^2$ may be added to give a single term since they do not contain like terms.

SIMPLIFICATION

Expressions, i.e. a collection of terms, can often be simplified. This involves writing the expression in a shorter or more convenient way without altering its meaning or value.

Examples

a) $4x + 3x + 2y = 7x + 2y$

b) $5ab + 6a - 2ab - 4a = 3ab + 2a$

c) $2x \times 4x = 8x^2$

d) $6ab \times 2a \times 3 = 36a^2b$

e) $\dfrac{4xy}{2x} = 2y$

f) $\dfrac{3x^4y}{12xy^7} = \dfrac{x^3}{4y^6}$

g) $\dfrac{x^2 - x - 2}{x^2 + 4x + 3} = \dfrac{(x+1)(x-2)}{(x+1)(x+3)}$ (if $x \neq -1$)

$\qquad\qquad = \dfrac{x-2}{x+3}$

SUBSTITUTION

If the values of the letters are given then they can be substituted in place of the letters and the instructions contained in the expression can be carried out in order to find a numerical answer.

Examples

When $t = 2$, $w = -5$, $x = 3$, $y = 4$

a) $3y^2 = 3 \times 4 \times 4$

$= 48$

b) $5t + 4w = 5 \times 2 + 4 \times -5$

$= 10 - 20$

$= -10$

c) $\dfrac{3(x + y)}{2} = \dfrac{3(3 + 4)}{2}$

$= \dfrac{3 \times 7}{2}$

$= 10\frac{1}{2}$

EXPANSION

Each term inside the bracket is multiplied by each term outside the bracket.

Examples

a) $2(x + y) = 2x + 2y$

b) $3(2x + 4y) = 6x + 12y$

c) $-4(3a + 2b) = -12a - 8b$ Note the change of sign.

d) $2x(3x - 4y) = 6x^2 - 8xy$

e) $(x + 2)(x + 4) = x^2 + 2x + 4x + 8$ i.e. $(x + 2)(x + 4)$: multiply the

$= x^2 + 6x + 8$ terms connected by the loops

f) $(2x - 3)(3x - 4) = 6x^2 - 9x - 8x + 12$

$= 6x^2 - 17x + 12$

g) $-(x - y) = -1(x - y) = -x + y$

h) $(a - b)(a + b) = a^2 - b^2$

i) $(a + b)(a + b) = a^2 + 2ab + b^2$

FACTORISATION

This is the opposite of expansion, in which the expression is written as the product of factors.

Examples

a) $2x + 2y = 2(x + y)$ i.e. 2 is a factor common to both terms

b) $6x + 12y = 6(x + 2y)$

c) $-12a - 8b = -4(3a + 2b)$ i.e. find the highest common factor

d) $6x^2 - 8xy = 2x(3x - 4y)$

e) $x^2 + 6x + 8 = (x + 2)(x + 4)$

f) $6x^2 - 17x + 12 = (2x - 3)(3x - 4)$

g) $x^2 - y^2 = (x - y)(x + y)$ 'the difference of two squares'

h) $ax + bx + ay + by = (a + b)x + (a + b)y$

$$= (a + b)(x + y) \qquad \text{'factorisation by grouping'}$$

i) $8x^2 - 18y^2 = 2(4x^2 - 9y^2)$

$$= 2(2x + 3y)(2x - 3y)$$

j) $x^2 - y^2 - x + y = (x - y)(x + y) - (x - y)$

$$= (x - y)(x + y - 1)$$

EQUATIONS

An equation is a mathematical sentence which contains an equals sign. Solving the equation means finding the value of the variable.

Solving linear equations containing only one unknown

Examples

a) $x + 1 = 6$

$x = 6 - 1$

$x = 5$

b) $x - 1 = 6$

$x = 6 + 1$

$x = 7$

c) $6x = 5$

$x = \frac{5}{6}$

d) $4 = \dfrac{x}{2}$

$4 \times 2 = x$

$8 = x$

$x = 8$

e) $4x + 1 = 6 + 2x$

$4x - 2x = 6 - 1$

$2x = 5$

$x = \frac{5}{2}$

$x = 2\frac{1}{2}$

f) $3(5x + 1) = 27$

$5x + 1 = 9$

$5x = 8$

$x = \frac{8}{5}$

$x = 1\frac{3}{5}$

g) $5(x + 3) = 2(1 - x)$ expand the brackets first

$5x + 15 = 2 - 2x$

$7x = -13$

$x = -1\frac{6}{7}$

h) $\dfrac{2}{3x - 1} = 4$

$2 = 4(3x - 1)$

$2 = 12x - 4$

$12x = 6$

$x = \frac{1}{2}$

Solving using 'flow charts'

First, flow chart the expression. The value of x is found by replacing the operations 'add', 'multiply by', 'divide by', 'take from', etc. in a second flow chart underneath (working from right to left) by the inverse operation.

The inverse of 'multiply by' is 'divide by'
            "   'divide by' is 'multiply by'
            "   'add' is 'subtract'
            "   'subtract' is 'add'
            "   'divide into' is 'divide into'
            "   'take from' is 'take from'

Example

$\frac{1}{2}(3 - 2x) = 9$

So $x = \dfrac{-15}{2}$

$\qquad = -7\frac{1}{2}$

Solving pairs of linear equations containing two unknowns (simultaneous equations)

Examples

a) $2x + y = \ \ 7 \qquad$ add

$\underline{3x - y = \ \ 4}$

$\qquad 5x = 11$

$\qquad x = \frac{11}{5}$

$\qquad = 2\frac{1}{5}$

Substituting into $\quad 2x + y = 7$

$\qquad\qquad\qquad\qquad\quad 4\frac{2}{5} + y = 7$

$\qquad\qquad\qquad\qquad\qquad\quad y = 2\frac{3}{5}$

So $x = 2\frac{1}{5}, \ y = 2\frac{3}{5}$

b) $\quad 5x + \ \ 3y = -3 \qquad$ multiply by two

$\underline{\quad 2x + \ \ 5y = \ \ 14} \qquad$ multiply by five

$10x + \ \ 6y = -6 \qquad$ Subtract

$\underline{10x + 25y = \ \ 70}$

$\qquad -19y = -76$

$\qquad\quad y = \dfrac{-76}{-19}$

$\qquad\qquad = 4$

Substituting into $5x + 3y = -3y$

$\qquad\qquad 5x + 12 = -3$

$\qquad\qquad\qquad 5x = -15$

$\qquad\qquad\qquad\quad x = -3$

So $x = -3, \quad y = 4$

c) Solving pairs of linear equations by the matrix method: Write the equation in matrix form. Premultiply both sides by the inverse matrix.

38

$$\begin{aligned} 3x + 2y = -2 \\ 5x - 6y = 27 \end{aligned} \equiv \begin{pmatrix} 3 & 2 \\ 5 & -6 \end{pmatrix}\begin{pmatrix} x \\ y \end{pmatrix} = \begin{pmatrix} -2 \\ 27 \end{pmatrix}$$

$$\frac{1}{-28}\begin{pmatrix} -6 & -2 \\ -5 & 3 \end{pmatrix}\begin{pmatrix} 3 & 2 \\ 5 & -6 \end{pmatrix}\begin{pmatrix} x \\ y \end{pmatrix} = \frac{1}{-28}\begin{pmatrix} -6 & -2 \\ -5 & 3 \end{pmatrix}\begin{pmatrix} -2 \\ 27 \end{pmatrix}$$

$$\begin{pmatrix} 1 & 0 \\ 0 & 1 \end{pmatrix}\begin{pmatrix} x \\ y \end{pmatrix} = \frac{1}{-28}\begin{pmatrix} -42 \\ 91 \end{pmatrix}$$

$$\begin{pmatrix} x \\ y \end{pmatrix} = \begin{pmatrix} 1\frac{1}{2} \\ -3\frac{1}{4} \end{pmatrix}$$

$$x = 1\tfrac{1}{2}, \quad y = -3\tfrac{1}{4}$$

d) Simplified version of the matrix method leaving the determinant until the end:

$$\begin{aligned} 3x + 2y = -2 \\ 5x - 6y = 27 \end{aligned} \equiv \begin{pmatrix} 3 & 2 \\ 5 & -6 \end{pmatrix}\begin{pmatrix} x \\ y \end{pmatrix} = \begin{pmatrix} -2 \\ 27 \end{pmatrix}$$

$$\begin{pmatrix} -6 & -2 \\ -5 & 3 \end{pmatrix}\begin{pmatrix} 3 & 2 \\ 5 & -6 \end{pmatrix}\begin{pmatrix} x \\ y \end{pmatrix} = \begin{pmatrix} -6 & -2 \\ -5 & 3 \end{pmatrix}\begin{pmatrix} -2 \\ 27 \end{pmatrix}$$

$$\begin{pmatrix} -28 & 0 \\ 0 & -28 \end{pmatrix}\begin{pmatrix} x \\ y \end{pmatrix} = \begin{pmatrix} -42 \\ 91 \end{pmatrix}$$

$$\begin{pmatrix} -28x \\ -28y \end{pmatrix} = \begin{pmatrix} -42 \\ 91 \end{pmatrix}$$

$$\begin{pmatrix} x \\ y \end{pmatrix} = \begin{pmatrix} -42/-28 \\ 91/-28 \end{pmatrix}$$

$$\begin{pmatrix} x \\ y \end{pmatrix} = \begin{pmatrix} 1\frac{1}{2} \\ -3\frac{1}{4} \end{pmatrix}$$

$$x = 1\tfrac{1}{2}, \quad y = -3\tfrac{1}{4}$$

Solving simultaneous equations, one linear, one of the second degree

Example

$$2x + y = 0 \qquad\qquad [1]$$
$$y = 3x^2 - 7x + 2 \qquad [2]$$

Rearrange [1]　　　$y = -2x$

Substitute in [2]　　$-2x = 3x^2 - 7x + 2$

$$3x^2 - 5x + 2 = 0$$

$$(3x - 2)(x - 1) = 0$$

$$3x - 2 = 0 \quad \text{or} \quad x - 1 = 0$$

$$x = \tfrac{2}{3} \quad \text{or} \quad x = 1$$

Substitute for x in [1]

where $x = \tfrac{2}{3}$, $y = -\tfrac{4}{3}$ and when $x = 1$, $y = -2$

So $x = \tfrac{2}{3}$, $y = -\tfrac{4}{3}$ or $x = 1$, $y = -2$

39

Solving quadratic equations

1) Before solving a **quadratic** equation by factorising, it should be written in the form $ax^2 + bx + c = 0$.

Examples

a) $x^2 + 4x - 12 = 0$

$(x + 6)(x - 2) = 0$

$x + 6 = 0$ or $x - 2 = 0$

$x = -6$ or $x = 2$

N.B.   If $xy = 0$
then $x = 0$ or $y = 0$

b) $x^2 - 6x = 0$

$x(x - 6) = 0$

$x = 0$ or $x - 6 = 0$

$x = 0$ or $x = 6$

c) $(x - 6)(x - 3) = 28$

$x^2 - 9x + 18 = 28$

$x^2 - 9x - 10 = 0$

$(x - 10)(x + 1) = 0$

$x = 10$ or $x = -1$

2) Equating squares.

Examples

a) $(x + 1)^2 = 4$

$x + 1 = 2$ or $x + 1 = -2$

$x = 1$ or $x = -3$

b) Solve $x^2 + 10x + 19 = 0$ by the method of completing the square.

$x^2 + 10x = -19$

$x^2 + 10x + 25 = -19 + 25$ adding (half the coefficient of x)^2 to both sides to make the left-hand side a perfect square

$(x + 5)^2 = 6$

$x + 5 = \pm\sqrt{6}$

$x = -5 + \sqrt{6}$ or $-5 - \sqrt{6}$

$= -2.55$ or -7.45 (to 3 s.f.)

N.B. $\pm$ means plus or minus.

3) Using the formula to solve $ax^2 + bx + c = 0$

$$x = \frac{-b \pm \sqrt{b^2 - 4ac}}{2a}$$

Example

Solve $\quad 3x^2 - 4x - 2 = 0$

$a = 3$

$b = -4$

$c = -2$

Let $a = 3$, $b = -4$ and $c = -2$

Then $2a = 6$, $\quad b^2 = 16 \quad$ and $\quad 4ac = -24$

$$x = \frac{-b \pm \sqrt{b^2 - 4ac}}{2a}$$

$$= \frac{-(-4) \pm \sqrt{16 - (-24)}}{6}$$

$$= \frac{4 \pm \sqrt{16 + 24}}{6}$$

$$= \frac{4 \pm \sqrt{40}}{6}$$

$$x = \frac{4 + \sqrt{40}}{6} \quad \text{or} \quad \frac{4 - \sqrt{40}}{6}$$

$$= 1.72 \quad \text{or} \quad -0.39 \quad \text{(to 2 d.p.)}$$

N.B. *It is sensible to check equations by substituting the solution back into the given equation.*

INEQUALITIES

An inequality relates sizes when one quantity is greater or smaller than the other. The signs used are

$>$ meaning 'is greater than'
$\geqslant$ meaning 'is greater than or equal to'
$<$ meaning 'is less than'
$\leqslant$ meaning 'is less than or equal to'

Shown on a number line

A black dot means x can take the value. A white circle means x cannot actually take the value shown.

Examples

a) shows $\quad x \leqslant 4$
  0 1 2 3 4 5

b) shows $\quad x > -1$
  −2 −1 0 1 2

c) shows $\quad 0 < x \leqslant 4$
  0 1 2 3 4

41

Solving linear inequalities

Use methods similar to those used in solving equations

Examples

a) If $2 < x$

then $x > 2$

shown as ⊸━━━━━━ on the number line.

0 1 2 3 4

b) If $-x > 3$

then $x < -3$

shown as ════⊸ on the number line.

−4 −3 −2 −1 0

c) If $x - 2 \geqslant 3$

then $x \geqslant 3 + 2$

$x \geqslant 5$

shown as ━━●━━━━━ on the number line.

3 4 5 6 7

d) $5 \geqslant 3 - x$

$5 - 3 \geqslant -x$

$2 \geqslant -x$

$-x \leqslant 2$

$x \geqslant -2$

shown as ━━●━━━━━ on the number line.

−3 −2 −1 0 1

Solving quadratic inequalities

Examples

a) $x^2 - 6x + 8 > 0$

$(x - 4)(x - 2) > 0$

Since the product of two factors is positive either both factors are positive or both are negative.

$\therefore$ either $x - 4 > 0$ and $x - 2 > 0$

$\Rightarrow x > 4$ and $x > 2$

$\Rightarrow x > 4$

or $x - 4 < 0$ and $x - 2 < 0$

$\Rightarrow x < 4$ and $x < 2$

$\Rightarrow x < 2$

$\therefore x < 2$ or $x > 4$ which is shown by

════⊸ ⊸━━━ on the number line.

0 1 2 3 4 5

b) If $x^2 - 6x + 8 < 0$

$(x - 4)(x - 2) < 0$

Since the product of two factors is negative one factor must be positive and the other negative.

$\therefore$ either $x - 4 > 0$ and $x - 2 < 0$

$\Rightarrow$ $x > 4$ and $x < 2$ (impossible)

or

$x - 4 < 0$ and $x - 2 > 0$

$\Rightarrow$ $x < 4$ and $x > 2$

$\therefore$ $2 < x < 4$ which is shown by

on the number line.

FORMULAE

The subject of a formula is the variable which is 'on its own',

In $\qquad A = \pi r^2 \qquad\qquad\qquad$ A is the subject of the formula

$\Rightarrow \qquad r - \sqrt{\dfrac{A}{\pi}} \qquad\qquad$ r is now the subject of the formula

To rearrange formulae follow the same steps as for solving equations.

Examples

Make t the subject of each formula:

a) $\qquad x = a + t$

$\Rightarrow \quad t = x - a$

b) $\qquad \dfrac{x}{t} = a$

$\Rightarrow \quad at = x$

$\Rightarrow \quad t = \dfrac{x}{a}$

c) $\qquad y(x + t) = a$

$\Rightarrow \quad xy + ty = a$

$\Rightarrow \qquad ty = (a - xy)$

$\Rightarrow \qquad t = \dfrac{(a - xy)}{y}$

d) $\qquad y(x + t) = a(p + t)$

$xy + ty = ap + at$

$\Rightarrow \quad ty - at = ap - xy$

$\Rightarrow \quad t(y - a) = ap - xy$

$\Rightarrow \qquad t = \dfrac{ap - xy}{(y - a)}$

e) $4x + at^2 = y$

$\Rightarrow \quad at^2 = (y - 4x)$

$\Rightarrow \quad t^2 = \dfrac{(y - 4x)}{a}$

$\Rightarrow \quad t = \pm\sqrt{\dfrac{y - 4x}{a}}$

43

ALGEBRAIC FRACTIONS

Apply the same rules as for arithmetic fractions.

Examples

a) $\dfrac{2}{x} + \dfrac{3}{x} = \dfrac{5}{x}$

b) $\dfrac{8}{x} + \dfrac{3}{y} = \dfrac{8y + 3x}{xy}$

c) $\dfrac{4}{(x + y)} + \dfrac{2}{(x - y)} = \dfrac{4(x - y) + 2(x + y)}{(x + y)(x - y)}$

$$= \dfrac{4x - 4y + 2x + 2y}{(x + y)(x - y)}$$

$$= \dfrac{6x - 2y}{(x + y)(x - y)}$$

d) $\dfrac{x + 3}{x - 2} - \dfrac{x + 2}{x} = \dfrac{x(x + 3) - (x - 2)(x + 2)}{x(x - 2)}$

$$= \dfrac{x^2 + 3x - x^2 + 4}{x(x - 2)}$$

$$= \dfrac{3x + 4}{x(x - 2)}$$

OPERATIONS

If $\triangle$ denotes an operation, e.g. $+$, $-$, $\times$, $\div$, then the operation, $\triangle$, is:

Commutative if $A \triangle B = B \triangle A$ for all A, B belonging to the set under consideration.

Addition and multiplication are commutative for all real numbers, e.g.

$$7 + 6 = 6 + 7$$

$$7 \times 6 = 6 \times 7$$

$$x + y = y + x$$

$$xy = yx$$

Subtraction and division are *not commutative*, because

$$7 - 6 \neq 6 - 7$$

and

$$7 \div 6 \neq 6 \div 7$$

N.B. $\neq$ means 'does not equal'.

Associative if $A \triangle (B \triangle C) = (A \triangle B) \triangle C$ for all A, B, C belonging to the set under consideration.

Addition and multiplication are associative for real numbers.

$$x + (y + z) = (x + y) + z = x + y + z$$

$$x(yz) \quad = \quad (xy)z \quad = \quad xyz$$

Subtraction and division are *not associative* because

$$x - (y - z) \neq (x - y) - z$$

and

$$x \div (y \div z) \neq (x \div y) \div z$$

Brackets have to be used to avoid ambiguity.

If $\triangle$ and $\triangledown$ denote operations then the operation, $\triangle$, is

Distributive over operation, $\triangledown$, if $A \triangle (B \triangledown C) = (A \triangle B) \triangledown (A \triangle C)$ for all A, B, C belonging to the set under consideration.

Multiplication is distributive over addition on the set of real numbers. This means

$$x(y + z) = xy + xz$$

REMAINDER THEOREM

Expressions such as $x^3 + 2x^2 - 10x + 1$ or $x^4 - 2x^3 + 3x + 14$ are called *polynomials*.

The remainder theorem states that if a polynomial, f(x), is divided by $(x - a)$ the remainder is f(a).

Let g(x) be another polynomial such that

$$f(x) = (x - a)g(x) + \text{Remainder}$$

When $x = a$

f(a) = Remainder   (since $(x - a)$ and thus $(x - a)$g(x) will both be zero).

Example

Find the remainder when $x^3 - 7x^2 + 3x + 4$ is divided by $(x - 2)$.

Let $f(x) = x^3 - 7x^2 + 3x + 4$

$f(2) = 8 - 28 + 6 + 4$

$= -10$

$\therefore$ Remainder $= -10$ by the remainder theorem.

FACTOR THEOREM

The factor theorem states that if $(x - a)$ is a factor of the polynomial f(x) then f(a) = 0.

Suppose $(x - a)$ is a factor of f(x) and g(x) is another polynomial such that f(x) = $(x - a)$g(x).

When $x = a$

f(a) = 0

45

a) State whether $(x - 2)$ is a factor of $x^2 + 3x - 10$.

Let $f(x) = x^2 + 3x - 10$

$f(2) = 4 + 6 - 10$

$\quad = 0$

So $(x - 2)$ is a factor.

b) Factorise $x^3 + 3x^2 - 4x - 12$.

By trial and error, using the factor theorem:

$f(1) = 1 + 3 - 4 - 12 \neq 0 \quad$ so $(x - 1)$ *is not* a factor.

$f(2) = 8 + 12 - 8 - 12 = 0 \quad$ so $(x - 2)$ *is* a factor.

$f(-2) = -8 + 12 + 8 - 12 = 0 \quad$ so $(x + 2)$ *is* a factor.

$f(3) = 27 + 27 - 12 - 12 \neq 0 \quad$ so $(x - 3)$ *is not* a factor.

$f(-3) = -27 + 27 + 12 - 12 = 0 \quad$ so $(x + 3)$ *is* a factor.

$\therefore \quad x^3 + 3x^2 - 4x - 12 = (x - 2)(x + 2)(x + 3)$.

2   NUMBERS

REAL NUMBERS

Natural numbers (counting numbers)

$\quad$ 1, 2, 3, 4, ...

Integers (whole numbers)

$\quad$ ... −3, −2, −1, 0, 1, 2, 3, ...

Rational numbers are numbers which can be written in the form of a fraction $\dfrac{a}{b}$, where a and b are both integers ($b \neq 0$),

Examples

$\frac{3}{4}$, 7, $\frac{347}{28}$, 0.1   (Note: $7 = \frac{7}{1}$ and $0.1 = \frac{1}{10}$)

Irrational numbers are numbers which cannot be written in the form of such a fraction, e.g. $\sqrt{2}$, π.

RECTANGULAR (COMPOSITE) NUMBERS

Can be written as the *product* of two whole numbers greater than 1,

Example

12 since it is 4×3

$\quad$ x x x x

$\quad$ x x x x

$\quad$ x x x x

TRIANGULAR NUMBERS

Can be arranged as a triangle,

Examples

1, 3, 6, 10, 15, 21   (add 3, then 4 then 5, ...)

```
x        x        x              x
      x x      x x          x x
            x x x        x x x
                      x x x x
```

SQUARE NUMBERS

The result of multiplying a number by itself.

Example

49 since it is 7×7

All square numbers, except 1, are also rectangular.

PRIME NUMBERS

A number that can only be divided by itself and 1.

Examples

2, 3, 5, 7, 11, 13, 17, 19, 23

(1 is not considered to be a prime number.)

FACTOR

A number that will divide into another number without leaving a remainder.

Example

3 is a factor of 12

MULTIPLE

A multiple of a number is exactly divisible by the number.

Example

12 is a multiple of 3

POWERS

x^a means $x \times x \times x \ldots$ a times

$x^a \times x^b = x^{a+b}$ x is the *base*, a and b are *indices*

$$\frac{x^a}{x^b} = x^{a-b}$$

$x^0 = 1$ $x^{1/a} = \sqrt[a]{x}$

$$\frac{1}{x^a} = x^{-a}$$ $x^{b/a} = (\sqrt[a]{x})^b$

ROOTS

The *square root* of a number when multiplied by itself gives the number.

Examples

$$\sqrt{16} = 4 \text{ or } -4 \qquad \sqrt{20} \approx \pm 4.47$$

N.B. $x^{\frac{1}{2}} = \sqrt{x}$

$(x^{\frac{1}{2}})^2 = x$

STANDARD FORM (SCIENTIFIC NOTATION)

Expressing a number in the form $a \times 10^n$, where a is a number greater than or equal to one and less than ten, and n is an integer.

Examples

$$4500 = 4.5 \times 10^3 \qquad 0.0008 = 8 \times 10^{-4}$$

Miscellaneous Number Examples

a) Write down the next two terms in each sequence:

    i) 4, 7, 10, 13, ...   16, 19

    ii) $2^3, 2^2, 2^1, \ldots$ $2^0, 2^{-1}$

    iii) 1, 2, 3, 5, 8, 13, 21, ...   34, 55
                                      (The *Fibonacci* numbers: each term is the sum of the two preceding terms.)

    iv) Write down the line of Pascal's triangle that contains 6 numbers: 1, 5, 10, 10, 5, 1

b) {2, 3, 4, 5, 6, 7, 8}
From this set write down

    i) a square number   4

    ii) a rectangular number   4 (or 6 or 8)

    iii) a multiple of 3   3 (or 6)

    iv) the factors of 12   2, 3, 4, 6

c) List all the factors of 24:   1, 2, 3, 4, 6, 8, 12, 24

d) Express 36 as a product of prime numbers.

$$\begin{array}{r|r} 2 & 36 \\ 2 & 18 \\ 3 & 9 \\ 3 & 3 \\ & 1 \end{array}$$

$$36 = 2 \times 2 \times 3 \times 3$$
$$= 2^2 \times 3^2$$

e) Find a) the lowest common multiple (LCM) b) the highest common factor (HCF) of 12 and 32.

$$\begin{array}{r|r} 2 & 12 \\ 2 & 6 \\ 3 & 3 \\ & 1 \end{array} \qquad\qquad \begin{array}{r|r} 2 & 32 \\ 2 & 16 \\ 2 & 8 \\ 2 & 4 \\ 2 & 2 \\ & 1 \end{array}$$

$$12 = 2 \times 2 \times 3 \qquad\qquad 32 = 2 \times 2 \times 2 \times 2 \times 2$$
$$= 2^2 \times 3 \qquad\qquad\qquad = 2^5$$

LCM $= 2 \times 2 \times 2 \times 2 \times 2 \times 3$ (the smallest number divisible by 12 and by 32)

      $= 96$

HCF $= 2 \times 2$

      $= 4$ (the largest number that will divide into both 12 and 32)

f) Write in standard form

    i) $8000 = 8 \times 10^3$
    ii) $38\,000 = 3.8 \times 10^4$
    iii) $0.002\,76 = 2.76 \times 10^{-3}$

g) Write in standard form and then as a single number

    i) $0.003 \times 400 = 3 \times 10^{-3} \times 4 \times 10^2 = 12 \times 10^{-1}$

$$= 1.2$$

    ii) $\dfrac{500 \times 0.04}{0.2 \times 200} = \dfrac{5 \times 10^2 \times 4 \times 10^{-2}}{2 \times 10^{-1} \times 2 \times 10^2} = \dfrac{20 \times 10^0}{4 \times 10^1}$

$$= 5 \times 10^{-1}$$

$$= 0.5$$

3 DIRECTED NUMBERS

A number greater than 0 is *positive*.

A number less than 0 is *negative*.

A number line can be used to simplify the addition and subtraction of directed numbers.

To add, move up the line, to subtract, move down the line.

If there are two signs in front of a number then

change into one sign using
$\left. \begin{array}{l} + \ + \ = \ + \\ - \ - \ = \ + \end{array} \right\}$ two the same gives +

$\left. \begin{array}{l} + \ - \ = \ - \\ - \ + \ = \ - \end{array} \right\}$ two different gives −

If there is **no** sign in front of a number then it is positive.

```
 ─ 5
 ─ 4
 ─ 3
 ─ 2
 ─ 1
 ─ 0
 ─ −1
 ─ −2
 ─ −3
 ─ −4
 ─ −5
```

Examples

    a) $2 - 3 + 5 - 4 - 2 + 1 = 8 - 9$ (Altogether 8 have been added and 9 have been subtracted; go up 8 from 0 then down 9.)

$$= -1$$

    b) $3 - -4 + -2 - +3 = +3 + 4 - 2 - 3$

$$= 2$$

49

The same rules apply when multiplying or dividing directed numbers:

$$+ \times + = + \qquad\qquad + \div + = +$$
$$- \times - = + \qquad\qquad - \div - = +$$
$$- \times + = - \qquad\qquad - \div + = -$$
$$+ \times - = - \qquad\qquad + \div - = -$$

Examples

a) $-3 \times +2 = -6$ **b)** $-3 \times -2 = +6$

c) $\dfrac{-12}{+2} = -6$ **d)** $\dfrac{-12}{-2} = +6$

e) $-2 \times -2 \times -2 = -8$

N.B.   The square of a negative number is positive.
The square root of a number can be positive or negative.

Example

$$3^2 = 9 \qquad (-3)^2 = 9$$

and $\sqrt{9} = 3$ or -3

4   DECIMALS

PLACE VALUE

$\ldots$ Th H T Units . $\frac{1}{10}$ $\frac{1}{100}$ $\frac{1}{1000}$ $\cdots$,

Example

$$21.45 = 2 \text{ tens 1 unit 4 tenths 5 hundredths}$$
$$= 2 \text{ tens 1 unit 45 hundredths}$$

DECIMAL PLACES

Number of figures after the point.

Examples

a) $21.38 = 21.4$ to 1 d.p.
b) $0.0027 = 0.003$ to 3 d.p.
c) $9.99 = 10.0$ to 1 d.p.

TO ADD (OR SUBTRACT)

Write down the numbers with the decimal points lined up and with only one figure in each column.

Examples

a) $42.7 + 1.23 =$
$$\begin{array}{r} 42.7 \\ +\ 1.23 \\ \hline 43.93 \\ \hline \end{array}$$

b) $42.7 - 1.23 =$
$$\begin{array}{r} 42.70 \\ -\ 1.23 \\ \hline 41.47 \\ \hline \end{array}$$
Always check by adding these two lines.

TO MULTIPLY

Multiply as for whole numbers, then place the decimal point in the answer so that there are as many figures after the point in the answer as there are after the points in the question.

a)
$$
\begin{array}{r}
21.3 \\
\times\ \ 14 \\
\hline
852 \\
213 \\
\hline
29.82
\end{array}
$$

b)
$$
\begin{array}{r}
21.3 \\
\times\ 1.4 \\
\hline
29.82
\end{array}
$$

c)
$$
\begin{array}{r}
0.213 \\
\times\ 0.14 \\
\hline
0.02982
\end{array}
$$
five figures after the points

0.02982 — five figures after the point in the answer

TO DIVIDE

Write as a fraction, then change the denominator into a whole number by multiplying the top and bottom of the fraction by the same power of 10.

Examples

a) $21.4 \div 2 = \dfrac{21.4}{2}$

$= 10.7$

b) $21.4 \div 0.2 = \dfrac{21.4}{0.2}$

$= \dfrac{214}{2}$

$= 107$

c) $21.4 \div 0.002 = \dfrac{21.4}{0.002}$

$= \dfrac{21\,400}{2}$

$= 10\,700$

METRIC SYSTEM

LENGTH	km	*hm	*dam	m	*dm	cm	mm
WEIGHT	kg	*hg	*dag	g	*dg	*cg	mg

*not in common use.

1 kg = 1000 g
1 g = 1000 mg

1 km = 1000 m
1 m = 100 cm
1 cm = 10 mm

1 litre = 1000 cm^3

SIGNIFICANT FIGURES

The most '*significant*' figure in any number is the first non-zero digit on the left-hand side since this must have the highest value of all the figures.

To round off to significant figures start at the first non-zero digit and count along the required number of figures—from left to right. If the *next* digit is less than five then it and all other figures can be crossed off as being too small to be considered; if the next digit is five or more then the last significant figure must be increased by one.

It is sometimes necessary to follow (or precede) the required number of significant figures with zeros in order to indicate the position of the decimal point.

Examples

a) $4.281 = 4.3$ to 2 s.f.

b) $9137 = 9100$ to 2 s.f.

c) $0.002\,971\,2 = 0.003$ to 1 s.f.

d) $0.304\,73 = 0.305$ to 3 s.f.

STANDARD FORM

See **NUMBERS.**

5 FRACTIONS

EQUIVALENT Different ways of expressing the same fraction.

Examples

a) $\dfrac{2}{3} = \dfrac{2 \times 4}{3 \times 4}$

$\quad = \dfrac{8}{12}$

b) $\dfrac{20}{80} = \dfrac{20 \div 20}{80 \div 20}$

$\quad = \dfrac{1}{4}$

The numerator (top) and the denominator (bottom) of the fraction can *both* be multiplied or divided by the same number, without altering the value of the fraction.

TO ADD (OR SUBTRACT)

The denominator of both (or all) fractions to be added or subtracted *must* be the same.

Examples

a) $\dfrac{2}{7} + \dfrac{3}{7} = \dfrac{5}{7}$

b) $\dfrac{5}{9} + \dfrac{3}{4} = \dfrac{5 \times 4}{9 \times 4} + \dfrac{3 \times 9}{4 \times 9}$

$\quad = \dfrac{20}{36} + \dfrac{27}{36}$

$\quad = \dfrac{47}{36}$

$\quad = 1\dfrac{11}{36}$

c) $\dfrac{8}{x} + \dfrac{2}{y} = \dfrac{8y}{xy} + \dfrac{2x}{xy}$

$\quad = \dfrac{8y + 2x}{xy}$

d) $2\dfrac{2}{7} - 1\dfrac{1}{5} = 1\dfrac{10}{35} - \dfrac{7}{35}$

$\quad = 1\dfrac{3}{35}$

e) $2\dfrac{1}{3} - 1\dfrac{7}{9} = 1\dfrac{3}{9} - \dfrac{7}{9}$

$\quad = \dfrac{12}{9} - \dfrac{7}{9}$

$\quad = \dfrac{5}{9}$

or

$\dfrac{7}{3} - \dfrac{16}{9} = \dfrac{21}{9} - \dfrac{16}{9}$

$\quad = \dfrac{5}{9}$

MIXED NUMBERS Part whole number, part fraction.

Examples

a) $\dfrac{4}{3} = 4 \div 3$

$\quad = 1\dfrac{1}{3}$

b) $\dfrac{42}{5} = 42 \div 5$

$\quad = 8\dfrac{2}{5}$

c) $1\dfrac{1}{2} = \dfrac{3}{2}$

d) $2\dfrac{7}{8} = (2 \times 8 + 7)$ eighths

$\quad = \dfrac{23}{8}$

TO MULTIPLY

Mixed numbers *must* be changed into fractions. Cancel if possible.

Examples

a) $\dfrac{3}{4} \times \dfrac{5}{7} = \dfrac{15}{28}$

b) $\dfrac{3}{4} \times \dfrac{8}{9} = \dfrac{\cancel{3}^1}{\cancel{4}_1} \times \dfrac{\cancel{8}^2}{\cancel{9}_3}$

$\qquad\qquad = \dfrac{2}{3}$

c) $1\dfrac{1}{2} \times \dfrac{5}{6} \times 2\dfrac{2}{5} = \dfrac{3}{\cancel{2}_1} \times \dfrac{\cancel{5}^1}{\cancel{6}_1} \times \dfrac{\cancel{12}^1}{\cancel{5}_1}$

$\qquad\qquad\qquad = 3$

TO DIVIDE

Turn the last fraction upside down and multiply.

Examples

a) $\dfrac{3}{4} \div \dfrac{5}{7} = \dfrac{3}{4} \times \dfrac{7}{5}$

$\qquad = \dfrac{21}{20}$

$\qquad = 1\dfrac{1}{20}$

b) $6 \div 1\dfrac{1}{2} = 6 \div \dfrac{3}{2}$

$\qquad\qquad = {}^2\cancel{6} \times \dfrac{2}{\cancel{3}_1}$

$\qquad\qquad = 4$

c) $\dfrac{8}{9} \div 4 = \dfrac{8}{9} \times \dfrac{1}{4}$

$\qquad = \dfrac{{}^2\cancel{8}}{9} \times \dfrac{1}{\cancel{4}_1}$

$\qquad = \dfrac{2}{9}$

d) $3\dfrac{1}{3} \div 2\dfrac{1}{2} = \dfrac{10}{3} \div \dfrac{5}{2}$

$\qquad\qquad = \dfrac{\cancel{10}^2}{3} \times \dfrac{2}{\cancel{5}_1}$

$\qquad\qquad = \dfrac{4}{3}$

$\qquad\qquad = 1\dfrac{1}{3}$

TO CONVERT TO A DECIMAL

Divide the numerator by the denominator.

Examples

a) $\dfrac{3}{8} = 3 \div 8$ $\qquad 8\overline{\left)3.000\right.}$
$\qquad\qquad\qquad\qquad\quad 0.375$

$\quad = 0.375$

b) $\dfrac{4}{7} = 4 \div 7$ $\qquad 7\overline{\left)4.0000\right.}$
$\qquad\qquad\qquad\qquad\quad 0.5714$

$\quad = 0.571 \quad \text{(to 3 d.p.)}$

6 PERCENTAGES

%—per cent—means 'out of 100'.

A percentage can be written as a fraction with a denominator of 100 and then dealt with as any fraction.

Examples

a) $60\% = \dfrac{60}{100}$

$= \dfrac{3}{5}$

b) $12\frac{1}{2}\% = \dfrac{12\frac{1}{2}}{100}$

$= \dfrac{25}{200}$

$= \dfrac{1}{8}$

c) $175\% = \dfrac{175}{100}$

$= 1\dfrac{3}{4}$

Certain percentages should be learned:

$$1\% = \frac{1}{100} \qquad 5\% = \frac{1}{20} \qquad 10\% = \frac{1}{10} \qquad 20\% = \frac{1}{5} \qquad 25\% = \frac{1}{4}$$

$$12\frac{1}{2}\% = \frac{1}{8} \qquad 33\frac{1}{3}\% = \frac{1}{3} \qquad 66\frac{2}{3}\% = \frac{2}{3} \qquad 50\% = \frac{1}{2} \qquad 75\% = \frac{3}{4}$$

$$100\% = 1 \qquad 200\% = 2$$

TO CONVERT A FRACTION TO A PERCENTAGE

Multiply the fraction by 100%.

Examples

a) $\dfrac{2}{5} = \dfrac{2}{5} \times 100\%$

$= 40\%$

b) $\dfrac{4}{9} = \dfrac{4}{9} \times 100\%$

$= \dfrac{400}{9}\%$

$= 44\frac{4}{9}\%$

c) $2\frac{3}{5} = 2\frac{3}{5} \times 100\%$

$= \frac{13}{5} \times 100\%$

$= 260\%$

TO FIND A PERCENTAGE OF A QUANTITY

Change the percentage to a fraction and multiply.
N.B.   'of' means 'multiplied by'

Examples

a) 6% of £400 $= \dfrac{6}{100} \times £400$

$= £24$

b) 106% of 400 cm $= \dfrac{106}{100} \times 400$ cm

$= 424$ cm

c) Since 1% of £1 $= 1$ p

then 1% of £2.40 $= 2.40$ p

9% of £2.40 $= 2.40$ p $\times 9$

$= 21.6$ p

$= 22$ p to the nearest penny

TO EXPRESS ONE QUANTITY AS A PERCENTAGE OF ANOTHER

Write as a fraction, then multiply by 100% to convert to a percentage.

Examples

a) Express £84 as a percentage of £400.

$$\frac{£84}{£400} \times 100\%$$

$$= 21\%$$

b) Express 80 p as a percentage of £1.20.

$$\frac{80\,\text{p}}{£1.20} \times 100\%$$

$$= \frac{80}{120} \times 100\%$$

$$= 66\tfrac{2}{3}\%$$

PROFIT

If the selling price of an article is greater than the cost price then

Profit = Selling price − Cost price

If the selling price of an article is less than the cost price then

Loss = Cost price − Selling price

If the profit is given as a percentage then it is a percentage of the Cost price.

$$\text{Percentage profit} = \frac{\text{Profit}}{\text{Cost price}} \times 100\%$$

$$\text{Profit} = \frac{\text{Percentage profit}}{100\%} \times \text{Cost price}$$

Examples

a) If the cost price is £60 and the selling price is £66 what is the percentage profit?

$$\text{Profit} = £66 - £60$$

$$= £6$$

$$\text{Percentage profit} = \frac{£6}{£60} \times 100\%$$

$$= 10\%$$

b) If the cost price is £60 and the percentage profit is 10% what is the selling price?

$$\text{Profit} = 10\% \text{ of the Cost price}$$

$$= \frac{10}{100} \times £60$$

$$= £6$$

So   Selling price = £60 + £6

$$= £66$$

c) If the selling price is £66 and the profit is 10% find the cost price.

$$\text{Profit} = 10\% \text{ of the cost price}$$

$$\text{Selling price} = \text{Cost price} + \text{Profit}$$

$$= \text{Cost price} + 10\% \text{ of the cost price}$$

So

$$£66 = 110\% \text{ of the cost price}$$

$$= \frac{110}{100} \times \text{Cost price}$$

$$\text{Cost price} = £66 \times \frac{100}{110}$$

$$= £60$$

SIMPLE INTEREST

$$\text{Simple interest} = \frac{\text{Principal} \times \text{Rate} \times \text{Time}}{100}$$

$$I = \frac{PRT}{100}$$

£P is the amount borrowed (or lent) for T years with an interest rate per annum of $R\%$.

COMPOUND INTEREST

Interest for each year is added to the principal before interest for the next year is calculated,

Examples

a) £450 invested for 3 years at 8% simple interest per annum:

$$\text{Simple interest} = \frac{£450 \times 8 \times 3}{100}$$

$$= £108$$

b) £450 invested for 3 years at 8% compound interest per annum.

Principal for first year = £450	1% of £450 = £4.50
Interest for first year = £ 36	8% of £450 = £4.50 × 8
Principal for second year = £486	1% of £486 = £4.86
Interest for second year = £ 38.88	8% of £486 = £4.86 × 8
Principal for third year = £524.88	1% of £524.88 = £5.2488
Interest for third year = £ 41.99	8% of £524.88 = 5.2488 × 8
£566.87	

$$\text{Interest gained} = £566.87 - £450$$

$$= £116.87$$

When using a calculator to find compound interest it is much quicker to use the formula

$$A = P\left(1 + \frac{R}{100}\right)^n$$

where £A is the final amount, £P is the principal, $R\%$ is the annual rate of interest, and n is the number of years.

Example

Find the compound interest if £720 is invested for 5 years at a rate of 6%.

$$A = £720\left(1 + \frac{6}{100}\right)^5$$

$$\text{Interest} = A - P$$

$$= £720\left(1 + \frac{6}{100}\right)^5 - £720$$

$$= £243.52 \quad \text{to the nearest penny}$$

VAT

At present VAT (value added tax) is 15%. A manufacturer must add 15% to his goods before they are sold (unless they are exempt from tax), and a service bill (hotel, garage) must have 15% added before being totalled.

Example

A garage bill for labour and parts is £25.

$$\text{VAT} = 15\% \text{ of } £25 \qquad 1\% \text{ of } £25 = 25\,\text{p}$$

$$15\% = 15 \times 25\,\text{p}$$

$$= £3.75$$

$$\text{Total bill} = £25$$
$$+£\ 3.75$$
$$\overline{£28.75}$$

TAX

The amount to be paid in tax is calculated as a percentage of the tax-payer's taxable income. The percentage varies from a basic rate of 30% (at present) to higher rates for those with high incomes. The *taxable income* is calculated by deducting allowances, e.g. personal allowance, marriage allowance, various expenses, pension contributions, etc. from the tax-payer's *gross (total) income*.

Example

A man earning £14 000 per annum has allowances totalling £3450 and pays tax at the basic rate of 30%. How much tax does he pay each year?

$$\text{Gross salary} = £14\,000$$

$$\text{Allowances} = £3450$$

So

$$\text{Taxable income} = \pounds 14\,000 - \pounds 3450$$
$$= \pounds 10\,550$$
$$\text{Tax to be paid} = 30\% \text{ of } \pounds 10\,550$$
$$= \pounds 3165$$

CAR INSURANCE

Every car owner must pay an annual *premium* to insure his car. If the owner drives without accident for the whole year then the insurance company gives a *no-claims* bonus (or discount) which reduces the next year's payment. Further reductions are made for each year when no claims are made against the insurance.

The no-claims bonus is quoted as a percentage by which the full premium will be reduced.

Example

An insurance company gives a no-claims bonus of

> 30% after one year
>
> 40% after two years
>
> 50% after three years
>
> 60% after four years
>
> 60% after each additional year

A motorist's full premium is £180 but she drives without accident for six years. How much does she pay each year? The payment is made at the beginning of each year.

$$\text{Payment for first year} = \pounds 180$$

Payment for second year = £180 − 30% of £180 (She has driven without accident for one year.)

$$= 70\% \text{ of } \pounds 180$$
$$= \pounds 126$$

$$\text{Payment for third year} = \pounds 180 - 40\% \text{ of } \pounds 180$$
$$= 60\% \text{ of } \pounds 180$$
$$= \pounds 108$$

$$\text{Payment for fourth year} = \pounds 180 - 50\% \text{ of } \pounds 180$$
$$= 50\% \text{ of } \pounds 180$$
$$= \pounds 90$$

$$\text{Payment for fifth year} = \pounds 180 - 60\% \text{ of } \pounds 180$$
$$= 40\% \text{ of } \pounds 180$$
$$= \pounds 72$$

$$\text{Payment for sixth year} = \pounds 72$$

7 RATIO

Examples

a)

$$AB:CD = 2\,\text{cm}:3\,\text{cm}$$
$$= 2:3$$

A ——— 2 cm ——— B

C ——— 3 cm ——— D

A *ratio* is a comparison between two or more quantities and is written as

> The first quantity : The second quantity.

This means that for every two units of length in AB there are three in CD.

b)

$$EF:GH = 6\,\text{cm}:9\,\text{cm}$$
$$= 6:9$$
$$= 2:3$$

E ——————— 6 cm ——————— F

G ——————— 9 cm ——————— H

Again, for every two units of length in EF there are three in GH.

A ratio can be simplified if there is a factor common to all the parts of the ratio: if as in a fraction, it is possible to divide all parts of the ratio by the same number.

Examples

a) $10:15 = 2:3$ (since each number can be divided by five.)

b) $8:12:4 = 2:3:1$ (since each number can be divided by four.)

N.B. Here *three* quantities have been compared.

Before quantities can be cancelled they must be in the same units.

c) $40\,\text{p}:£2 = 40\,\text{p}:200\,\text{p}$ **d)** $100\,\text{g}:1\,\text{kg} = 100\,\text{g}:1000\,\text{g}$
$$= 1:5 \qquad\qquad\qquad\qquad = 1:10$$

FRACTION

A ratio can also be written as a fraction.

Examples

Express the ratio **a)** $£5:£10$ **b)** $40\,\text{p}:£2$ as a fraction.

a) $£5:£10 = 1:2$ **b)** $40\,\text{p}:£2 = 40\,\text{p}:200\,\text{p}$
$$= \tfrac{1}{2} \qquad\qquad\qquad = 1:5$$
$$\qquad\qquad\qquad\qquad = \tfrac{1}{5}$$

'SHARING'

A ratio can be used to describe the way in which sharing must be carried out, for example 'share in the ratio $a:b$' means for every a given to the first, b are given to the second.

If, for every £4 given to A, £6 is given to B, the ratio of A's share to B's share is $4:6 = 2:3$ but the ratio of B's share to A's share is $6:4 = 3:2$.

SECTION II

59

To share out a quantity add the numbers in the ratio to find the total number of shares, then form the fraction to be given for each part.

Examples

a) Share £96 between A, B and C in the ratio $5:4:3$.

$$\text{Total number of shares} = 5 + 4 + 3$$
$$= 12$$
$$\text{A receives } \tfrac{5}{12} \text{ of £96} = £40$$
$$\text{B receives } \tfrac{4}{12} \text{ of £96} = £32$$
$$\text{C receives } \tfrac{3}{12} \text{ of £96} = \underline{£24}$$
$$£96 \quad \text{(check that the total is correct)}$$

or

$$\text{Total of 12 shares, so one share} = \frac{£96}{12}$$
$$= £8$$
$$\text{A has five shares} = 5 \times £8$$
$$= £40$$
$$\text{B has four shares} = 4 \times £8$$
$$= £32$$
$$\text{C has three shares} = 3 \times £8$$
$$= £24$$

b) If D and E share a sum of money in the ratio $2:3$ and E receives £24 how much does D receive?

$$\text{D's share} : \text{E's share} = 2:3$$

so D gets $\tfrac{2}{5}$ and E gets $\tfrac{3}{5}$ of the total.

Since E gets £24 then $\tfrac{3}{5}$ of the total $= £24$

$$\Rightarrow \quad \text{the total} = £24 \times \tfrac{5}{3}$$
$$= £40$$
$$\therefore \quad \text{D receives } \tfrac{2}{5} \text{ of £40} = £16$$

SCALE

Scales can be expressed as ratios giving the comparison between the model or reduced form and the full or real size.

If each length on a model car is $\frac{1}{100}$ times the length on the full-sized car then the scale used is $1:100$.

On a map a scale of $1:10\,000$ would indicate that a length of 1 cm on the map would really be a distance of $10\,000$ cm. This would mean that a distance of d cm on the map would indicate a real distance of $d \times 10\,000$ cm.

Example

7 cm on the map represents a real distance of

$$7 \times 10\,000 \text{ cm} = 70\,000 \text{ cm}$$
$$= 700 \text{ m}$$
$$= 0.7 \text{ km}$$

8 ERROR

If a quantity is approximated, e.g. to one decimal place or to two significant figures, then any calculations involving this quantity may involve an error.

Examples

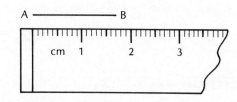

a) Given that the length of AB, when measured to the nearest centimetre, is 2 cm then AB can lie anywhere between 1.5 and 2.5 cm.

Maximum length < 2.5 cm
(AB ≠ 2.5 since this would be rounded up to 3 cm.)

Minimum length = 1.5 cm
So   1.5 cm ⩽ AB < 2.5 cm

b) If CD = 16.8 to 1 d.p. then 16.75 ⩽ CD < 16.85

c) If XY = 950 to the nearest 10 then 945 ⩽ XY < 955

PRODUCT OF APPROXIMATIONS

The maximum and minimum possible values for each quantity should be found.

The largest possible product   = one maximum × the other maximum

The smallest possible product = one minimum × the other minimum

Example

$$AB = 1.2 \text{ cm} \quad \text{to 1 d.p.} \Rightarrow 1.15 \leqslant AB < 1.25$$

$$AD = 2.4 \text{ cm} \quad \text{to 1 d.p.} \Rightarrow 2.35 \leqslant AD < 2.45$$

Area of rectangle = AB × AD

Largest possible area   = 1.25 × 2.45 cm²

                = 3.0625 cm²

Smallest possible area = 1.15 × 2.35 cm²

                = 2.7025 cm²

So   2.7025 cm² ⩽ Area < 3.0625 cm²

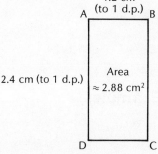

N.B.   When using a calculator, approximate only the final answer.

ERROR

When an approximation is made the difference between the true value and the approximate value is the *error*.

When an approximation is given it is not possible to find the true value, but a range in which it lies can be defined.

Example

When corrected to 2 d.p. a length = 2.98 cm.

This gives $2.975 \leqslant$ true length < 2.985 cm which can be written as 2.98 ± 0.005, meaning that the true value lies between $(2.98 + 0.005)$ cm and $(2.98 - 0.005)$ cm.

Hence the maximum possible error is 0.005 cm.

PERCENTAGE ERROR

Percentage error gives an indication of the extent of the error in comparison to the true value.

$$\text{Percentage error} = \frac{\text{Error}}{\text{True value}} \times 100\%$$

Example

What is the percentage error when £432 is rounded off to the nearest £100?

$$\text{True value} = £432$$
$$\text{Approximated value} = £400$$

So
$$\text{Error} = £432 - £400$$
$$= £32$$
$$\text{Percentage error} = \frac{£32}{£432} \times 100\%$$
$$\approx 7.4\%$$

9 EVERYDAY ARITHMETIC

Everyday Arithmetic may be described as the mathematics anyone may want to use in daily life. It is mainly concerned with money calculations, and although some knowledge is required the appropriate method is decided by the use of common sense.

Examples

a) Rolls cost 18 p each. Find the cost of half a dozen.

$$\text{Cost} = 6 \times 18 \text{ p}$$
$$= 108 \text{ p}$$
$$= £1.08$$

b) 200 bottles each holding $\frac{3}{5}$ litre are filled from a container holding 300 litres. How much is left in the container?

$$\text{Amount taken} = 200 \times \tfrac{3}{5} \text{ litres}$$

$$= 120 \text{ litres}$$

$$\text{Amount left} = (300 - 120) \text{ litres}$$

$$= 180 \text{ litres}$$

c) Mrs. Brown's daughter plays in the Youth Orchestra. Mrs. Brown took her three sons to the concert. They all had refreshments and she bought a programme. Refreshments were provided free to members of the orchestra. Mrs. Brown gave her daughter money to buy a record. Find out how much Mrs. Brown spent on the evening out.

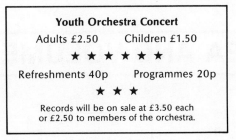

Tickets	$= £2.50 + 3 \times £1.50$	$= £7$
Refreshments	$= 4 \times 40\,\text{p}$	$= £1.60$
Programme		$= £0.20$
Record		$= £2.50$
	Total spent	$= £11.30$

d) A computer engineer works a basic 40 hour week at £8.10 per hour and $3\frac{1}{2}$ hours overtime at the weekend at time and a half. Copy the payslip shown below and on it complete the following:

    i) his basic pay
    ii) his overtime pay
    iii) his gross pay for the week
    iv) his National Insurance given that it is 9% of gross pay
    v) his taxable income if he has a weekly tax allowance of £53
    vi) his income tax if he pays 30 p in the £ on taxable income
    vii) his net pay for the week

PAYSLIP		WESTONS		S. GREENFIELD	A/2/409
National Insurance Number YH4035D				Computer Engineer	
Hours		Payments		Deductions	
Basic @ $1\frac{1}{2}$ @ $1\frac{3}{4}$		Basic £324 Overtime £42.52		Nat. Ins. £32.99 Income Tax £94.06	
40 $3\frac{1}{2}$ —		Gross £366.52		Total £127.05	

Year 1986
   Month ending
   April 30th
				Net Pay £239.47	

i) The computer engineer's Basic pay = 40 × £8.10 = £324

ii) Overtime = $3\frac{1}{2} \times 1\frac{1}{2} \times$ £8.10   = £42.52

iii) Gross pay = £324 + £42.52   = £366.52

iv) National Insurance = $\frac{9}{100} \times$ £366.52   = £32.99

v) Taxable income = £366.52 − £53   = £313.52

vi) Income Tax = 30 × 313.52 p   = £94.06

vii) Net Pay = Gross pay − Deductions

         = £366.52 − £32.99 − £94.06   = £239.47

10   AREA AND VOLUME

RECTANGLE

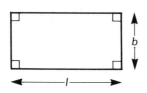

Area = Length × Width

$A = lb$

PARALLELOGRAM

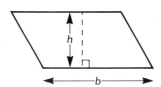

Area = Base × Perpendicular height

$A = bh$

TRAPEZIUM

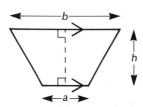

Area = $\frac{1}{2}$ × Sum of the parallel sides
           × Perpendicular height

$A = \frac{1}{2}(a + b)h$

TRIANGLE

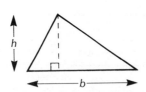

Area = $\frac{1}{2}$ Base × Height

$A = \frac{1}{2}bh$

CIRCLE

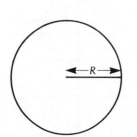

Area = π × Radius × Radius

$A = \pi R^2$

Examples

a)

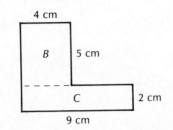

$$\text{Area} = \tfrac{1}{2} \times 4 \times 9 \text{ cm}^2$$
$$= 18 \text{ cm}^2$$

b)

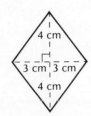

$$\text{Area } B = 4 \times 5 = 20 \text{ cm}^2$$
$$\text{Area } C = 2 \times 9 = \underline{18 \text{ cm}^2}$$
$$\text{Area} = \overline{38 \text{ cm}^2}$$

c)

$$\text{Area top } \triangle \quad = \tfrac{1}{2} \times 6 \times 4 \text{ cm}^2$$
$$= 12 \text{ cm}^2$$
$$\text{Area rhombus} = \text{top } \triangle + \text{bottom } \triangle$$
$$= (12 + 12) \text{ cm}^2$$
$$= 24 \text{ cm}^2$$

d)

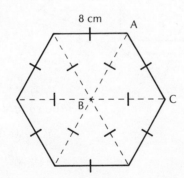 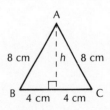

By Pythagoras $h^2 = 8^2 - 4^2$

$$h = \sqrt{48}$$

$$\text{Area } \triangle \text{ABC} = \tfrac{1}{2} \times 8 \times \sqrt{48} \text{ cm}^2$$

Area of regular hexagon $= 6 \times$ area of equilateral $\triangle \text{ABC}$

$$= 6 \times 4\sqrt{48} \text{ cm}^2$$

$$= 24\sqrt{48} \text{ cm}^2$$

$$= 166 \text{ cm}^2 \text{ (to 3 s.f.)}$$

CUBOID

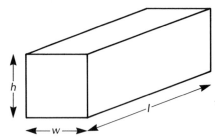

Volume = Length × Width × Height

$$V = lwh$$

PRISM

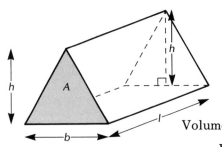

(a solid with uniform cross-section)

Volume = Area of cross-section × Length

$$V = A \times l$$

For the *triangular prism* shown

$$V = (\tfrac{1}{2}bh) \times l$$
$$= \tfrac{1}{2}bhl$$

PYRAMID

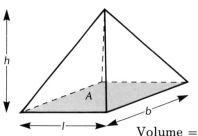

(a solid which tapers to a point)

Volume = $\tfrac{1}{3}$ Area of base × Perpendicular height

$$V = \tfrac{1}{3}A \times h$$

For the *square-based pyramid* shown

$$V = \tfrac{1}{3}(lb) \times h$$
$$V = \tfrac{1}{3}lbh$$

CYLINDER

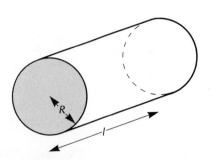

(a circular prism)

Volume = Area of end × Length

$$V = \pi R^2 l$$

Surface area $= 2\pi Rl + 2\pi R^2$
$$= 2\pi R(l + R)$$

CONE

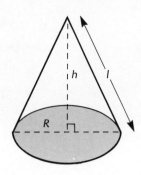

(a circular-based pyramid)

Volume $= \frac{1}{3}$ Area of base $\times$ Height

$$V = \frac{1}{3}\pi R^2 h$$

Curved surface area $= \pi R l$

SPHERE

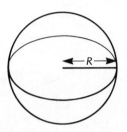

Volume $= \frac{4}{3}\pi \times$ Radius^3

$$V = \frac{4}{3}\pi R^3$$

Surface area $= 4\pi R^2$

Examples

a)

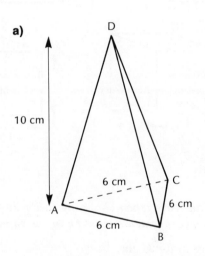

Volume $= \frac{1}{3}$ Base $\times$ Height

$\qquad = \frac{1}{3}$ Area of $\triangle$ABC $\times$ Height

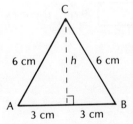

Working:

By Pythagoras

$$h^2 = 6^2 - 3^2$$

$$= 27$$

$$h = \sqrt{27}$$

Area of $\triangle$ABC $= \frac{1}{2} \times 6 \times \sqrt{27}$

$\qquad\qquad = 3\sqrt{27}$ cm^2

Volume $= \frac{1}{3} \times 3\sqrt{27} \times 10$

$\qquad\quad = 10\sqrt{27}$ cm^3

$\qquad\quad = 52.0$ cm^3 (to 3 s.f.)

b)

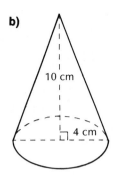

$$V = \tfrac{1}{3}\pi R^2 h$$
$$= \tfrac{1}{3}\pi \times 4^2 \times 10$$
$$= \tfrac{160}{3}\pi$$
$$= 167 \text{ cm}^3 \quad \text{(to 3 s.f.)}$$

UNITS

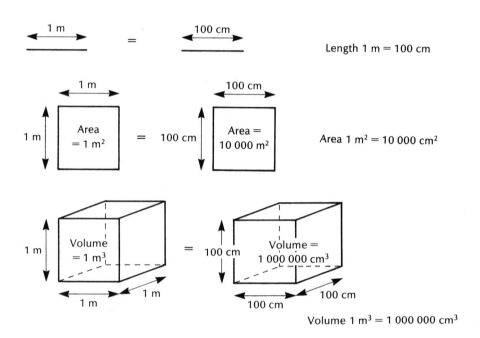

Length 1 m = 100 cm

Area 1 m² = 10 000 cm²

Volume 1 m³ = 1 000 000 cm³

N.B. *Take care when changing units. Before an area or volume is calculated all measurements must be in the same units.*

Changing units to cm

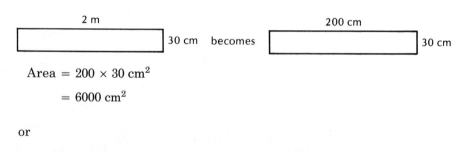

Area = 200 × 30 cm²

= 6000 cm²

or

changing units to m

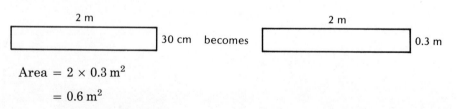

Area = 2 × 0.3 m²

= 0.6 m²

11   SIMILARITY

Figures are *similar* if they are the same shape, i.e. if

i) all angles of one are equal to angles of the other

ii) all the lengths of corresponding sides are in the same ratio

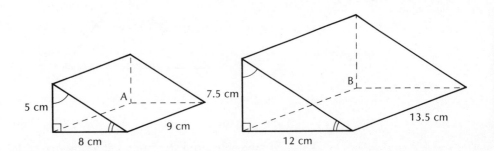

Shape B is an *enlargement* of shape A with *scale factor* 1.5 (all lengths on shape B are 1.5 times the corresponding lengths on shape A).

N.B.   Mathematically 'enlargement' may mean either an increase or a decrease in size.

SIMILAR TRIANGLES

Triangles are similar if all the angles of one are equal to the corresponding angles of the other.

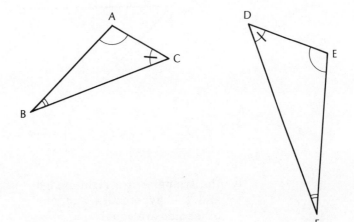

These triangles are similar since $A = E$, $B = F$ and $C = D$.

Triangle EFD is an enlargement of triangle ABC.

When triangles are similar,

a) corresponding sides are equal, or

b) one triangle is larger than the other

a) If the angles and corresponding sides are equal then the triangles are the same size and shape and are *congruent*. Triangles can be proved to be congruent, identical in every respect, by showing that

i) three sides are equal

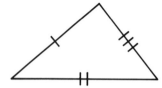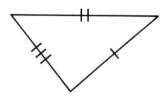

ii) two sides and the included angle are equal

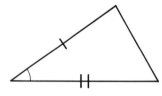

iii) two angles and a corresponding side are equal

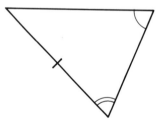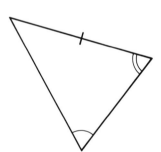

iv) the triangles are right-angled and the hypotenuse and one other side are equal

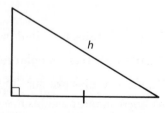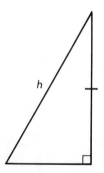

b) If one triangle is larger than the other then the corresponding sides are in the same ratio and this ratio is the scale factor.

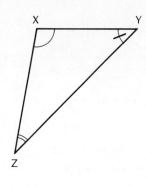
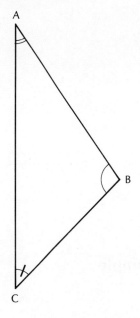

$$\text{Scale factor} = \frac{AB}{XZ} = \frac{AC}{YZ} = \frac{BC}{XY}$$

N.B △ABC is an enlargement of △XYZ with scale factor AB/XZ, but △XYZ is an enlargement of △ABC with scale factor XZ/AB.

Example

If the triangles are as shown find c and z.

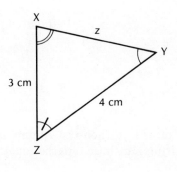
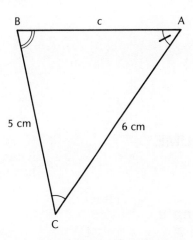

Since $Y = C$, $X = B$ and $Z = A$ the triangles are similar.

$$\frac{AC}{YZ} = \frac{AB}{XZ}$$

$$\frac{6}{4} = \frac{c}{3}$$

$$c = \frac{6 \times 3}{4} = \frac{18}{4} \text{ cm}$$

$$= 4\tfrac{1}{2} \text{ cm}$$

and

$$\frac{AC}{YZ} = \frac{BC}{XY}$$

$$\frac{6}{4} = \frac{5}{z}$$

$$z = \frac{5 \times 4}{6} \text{ cm}$$

$$= 3\tfrac{1}{3} \text{ cm}$$

71

AREA

Triangles ABC and XYZ are as shown with scale factor s.

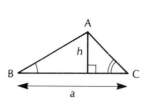 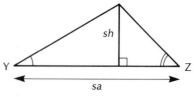

Area of ABC $= \frac{1}{2}ah$

Area of XYZ $= \frac{1}{2}sa \times sh$

$= \frac{1}{2}ah \times s^2$

The areas of the similar triangles are in the ratio

$\frac{1}{2}ah : \frac{1}{2}ahs^2 = 1 : s^2$

For *all* similar figures if the ratio of the lengths is $1 : s$ then the ratio of corresponding areas is $1 : s^2$, i.e. if lengths are multiplied by a scale factor then areas are multiplied by an area factor which is (Scale factor)^2.

Example

Suppose A and B are similar shapes as shown below. The area of A is 20 cm^2. Find the area of B.

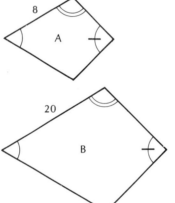

Scale factor $= \frac{20}{8}$

$= \frac{5}{2}$

Area factor $=$ (Scale factor)^2

$= \left(\frac{5}{2}\right)^2$

$= \frac{25}{4}$

If the area of A $= 20 \text{ cm}^2$ then

Area of B $= 20 \times$ (Scale factor)^2 cm^2

$= 20 \times \frac{25}{4} \text{ cm}^2$

$= 125 \text{ cm}^2$

VOLUME

If the scale factor is s, then the volume factor is s^3, since the volume is found by multiplying three lengths together, and each has been multiplied by the scale factor.

Example

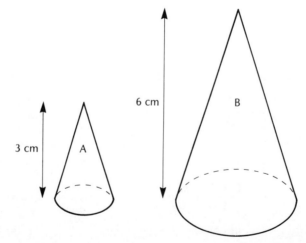

A and B are similar cones. The volume of A is 5 cm^3. Find the volume of B.

Scale factor $= 2$

Volume factor $=$ (Scale factor)^3

$= 2^3$

The volume of B (the enlargement of A with scale factor two),

$= 5 \times 2^3 \text{ cm}^3$

$= 5 \times 8 \text{ cm}^3$

$= 40 \text{ cm}^3$

12 TRIGONOMETRY

PYTHAGORAS

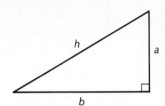

By Pythagoras

$$h^2 = a^2 + b^2$$
$$\Rightarrow a^2 = h^2 - b^2$$
$$\Rightarrow b^2 = h^2 - a^2$$

The hypotenuse is the longest side of a right-angled triangle and is opposite the right-angle.

Examples

a)

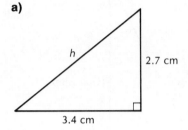

$$h^2 = 2.7^2 + 3.4^2$$
$$h = \sqrt{2.7^2 + 3.4^2}$$
$$h = 4.3 \, \text{cm} \quad \text{(to 1 d.p.)}$$

b)

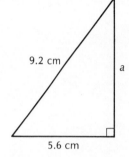

$$a^2 = 9.2^2 - 5.6^2$$
$$a = \sqrt{9.2^2 - 5.6^2}$$
$$a = 7.3 \, \text{cm} \quad \text{(to 1 d.p.)}$$

SIN, COS AND TAN

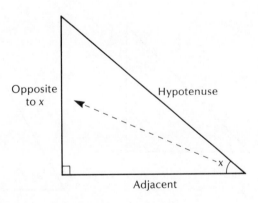

$$\sin x = \frac{\text{Opposite}}{\text{Hypotenuse}}$$

$$\cos x = \frac{\text{Adjacent}}{\text{Hypotenuse}}$$

$$\tan x = \frac{\text{Opposite}}{\text{Adjacent}}$$

Examples

a)

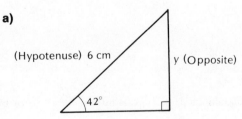

$$\sin 42° = \frac{y}{6}$$
$$y = 6 \times \sin 42°$$
$$y = 4.0 \, \text{cm} \quad \text{(to 1 d.p.)}$$

b)

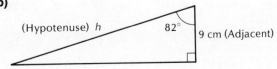

$$\cos 82° = \frac{9}{h}$$
$$h = \frac{9}{\cos 82°}$$
$$h = 64.7 \, \text{cm} \quad \text{(to 1 d.p.)}$$

c)

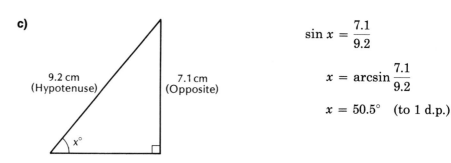

$$\sin x = \frac{7.1}{9.2}$$

$$x = \arcsin \frac{7.1}{9.2}$$

$$x = 50.5° \quad \text{(to 1 d.p.)}$$

d)

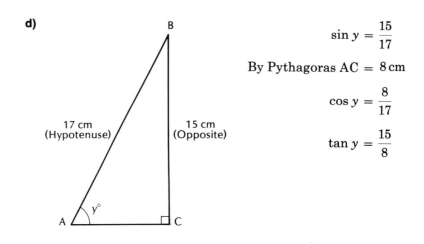

$$\sin y = \frac{15}{17}$$

By Pythagoras $AC = 8\,\text{cm}$

$$\cos y = \frac{8}{17}$$

$$\tan y = \frac{15}{8}$$

Some trigonometrical values can be found without the use of tables.

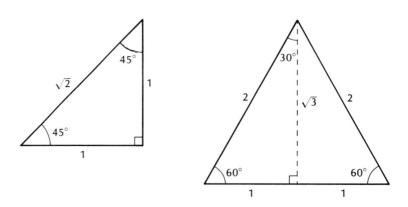

$$\sin 45° = \frac{1}{\sqrt{2}} \qquad \sin 30° = \frac{1}{2} \qquad \sin 60° = \frac{\sqrt{3}}{2}$$

$$\cos 45° = \frac{1}{\sqrt{2}} \qquad \cos 30° = \frac{\sqrt{3}}{2} \qquad \cos 60° = \frac{1}{2}$$

$$\tan 45° = 1 \qquad \tan 30° = \frac{1}{\sqrt{3}} \qquad \tan 60° = \sqrt{3}$$

$$\sin 0° = 0 \qquad \cos 0° = 1 \qquad \tan 0° = 0$$

$$\sin 90° = 1 \qquad \cos 90° = 0 \qquad \tan 90° = \infty \text{ (infinity)}$$

ANGLES GREATER THAN 90°

Rotate the radius, OR, of a circle, centre the origin, radius 1 unit, in a positive (anticlockwise) direction. Let θ be the angle described.

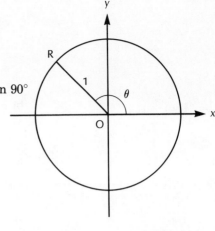

By definition, for angles greater than 90°

$$\sin \theta = y \text{ coordinate of R}$$

$$\cos \theta = x \text{ coordinate of R}$$

$$\tan \theta = \frac{y \text{ coordinate of R}}{x \text{ coordinate of R}}$$

$$= \frac{\sin \theta}{\cos \theta}$$

This definition is consistent with the usual definitions of sin, cos and tan for acute angles:

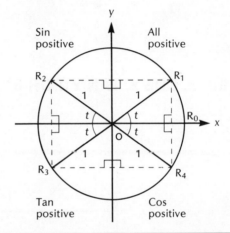

	Initial	First quadrant	Second quadrant	Third quadrant	Fourth quadrant
Position of radius	OR_0	OR_1	OR_2	OR_3	OR_4
Angle turned from positive horizontal	0	t	$180° - t$	$180° + t$	$360° - t$
Sine of angle turned = y coordinate of R	0	$\sin t$	$\sin(180° - t) =$ $\sin t$	$\sin(180° + t) =$ $-\sin t$	$\sin(360° - t) =$ $-\sin t$
Cosine of angle turned = x coordinate of R	1	$\cos t$	$\cos(180° - t) =$ $-\cos t$	$\cos(180° + t) =$ $-\cos t$	$\cos(360° - t) =$ $\cos t$
Tangent of angle turned = sin/cos	0	$\tan t$	$\tan(180° - t) =$ $-\tan t$	$\tan(180° + t) =$ $\tan t$	$\tan(360° - t) =$ $-\tan t$
		All positive	sin positive	tan positive	cos positive

The value of the ratio is found by using the appropriate sign with the sin, cos or tan of the appropriate acute angle.

Examples

a)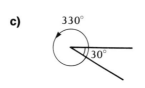

$$\tan 150° = \tan(180 - 30)°$$
$$= -\tan 30°$$
$$= -\frac{1}{\sqrt{3}}$$

b)

$$\sin 240° = \sin(180 + 60)°$$
$$= -\sin 60°$$
$$= -\frac{\sqrt{3}}{2}$$

c)

$$\cos 330° = \cos(360 - 30)°$$
$$= \cos 30°$$
$$= \frac{\sqrt{3}}{2}$$

GRAPHS OF SIN x, COS x, TAN x (FOR 0° ≤ x ≤ 360°)

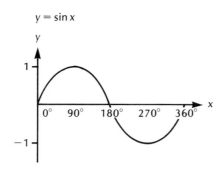

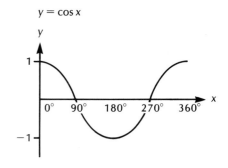

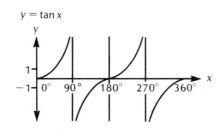

The values of sin x, cos x and tan x for $x > 90°$ can also be found by using the symmetry properties of these graphs.

THE SINE AND COSINE RULES

These rules are used for finding unknown sides or angles of any triangles that are not right-angled.

Triangle ABC is labelled as shown in the diagram:

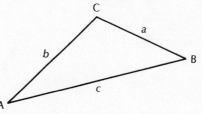

SINE RULE $\quad \dfrac{a}{\sin A} = \dfrac{b}{\sin B} = \dfrac{c}{\sin C}$

or

$$\dfrac{\sin A}{a} = \dfrac{\sin B}{b} = \dfrac{\sin C}{c}$$

COSINE RULE $\quad c^2 = a^2 + b^2 - 2ab \cos C$

or

$$\cos C = \dfrac{a^2 + b^2 - c^2}{2ab}$$

Example (sine rule)

For triangle LMN as shown find **a)** M **b)** n correct to 4 s.f.

Using the sine rule

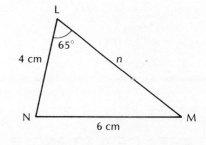

a) $\dfrac{\sin M}{4} = \dfrac{\sin 65°}{6}$

$\sin M = \dfrac{4 \sin 65°}{6}$

$M = \arcsin\left(\dfrac{4}{6} \times \sin 65°\right)$

$= 37.17°$ (to 4 s.f.)

b) $\dfrac{n}{\sin N} = \dfrac{6}{\sin 65°}$

But $\quad N = 77.83°$ (angle sum of a triangle)

$n = \dfrac{6 \times \sin 77.83°}{\sin 65°}$

$= 6.471\,\text{cm}$ (to 4 s.f.)

Example (cosine rule)

For triangle PQR as shown find **a)** Q **b)** P **c)** R (to 2 s.f.)

Using the cosine rule,

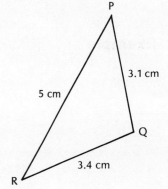

$\cos Q = \dfrac{3.1^2 + 3.4^2 - 5^2}{2 \times 3.1 \times 3.4}$

$\cos Q = -0.1817$

$Q = 100°$ (to 2 s.f.)

Now using the sine rule,

$$\frac{\sin P}{3.4} = \frac{\sin 100°}{5}$$

$$P = \arcsin\left(\frac{3.4}{5} \times \sin 100°\right)$$

$$= 42° \quad \text{(to 2 s.f.)}$$

$$R = 180° - (100 + 42)° \quad \text{(angle sum of a triangle)}$$

$$= 38° \quad \text{(to 2 s.f.)}$$

Example (cosine rule)

For triangle XYZ find z correct to 3 significant figures.

Using the cosine rule,

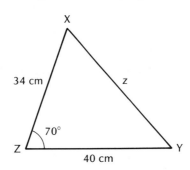

$$z^2 = 34^2 + 40^2 - 2 \times 34 \times 40 \times \cos 70°$$

$$= 1156 + 1600 - 2720 \times \cos 70°$$

$$\approx 1826$$

$$z \approx \sqrt{1826}$$

$$z = 42.7 \quad \text{(to 3 s.f.)}$$

AREA OF A TRIANGLE

For triangle ABC labelled as shown

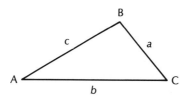

$$\text{Area} = \tfrac{1}{2}bc \sin A = \tfrac{1}{2}ac \sin B = \tfrac{1}{2}ab \sin C$$

Example

Using the formula,

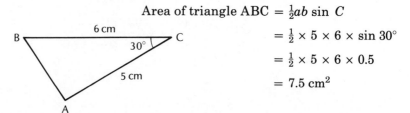

$$\text{Area of triangle ABC} = \tfrac{1}{2}ab \sin C$$

$$= \tfrac{1}{2} \times 5 \times 6 \times \sin 30°$$

$$= \tfrac{1}{2} \times 5 \times 6 \times 0.5$$

$$= 7.5 \text{ cm}^2$$

THREE-DIMENSIONAL TRIGONOMETRY

1) Suppose line LM intersects the plane P as shown.

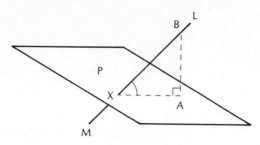

If a perpendicular is dropped from a point, B in line LM, so that it cuts the plane at A, and if X is the point of intersection between the line and the plane, then $\hat{AXB}$ is called the *angle between the line and the plane*.

2) Suppose two planes meet as shown. Their intersection is a straight line.

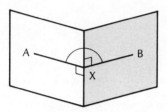

Let X be a point on this line and let AX be perpendicular to the line, with A being a point in one of the planes. If line XB is such that B is a point in the other plane, and XB is perpendicular to the line of intersection of the two planes, then $\hat{AXB}$ is known as the *angle between the two planes*.

Example

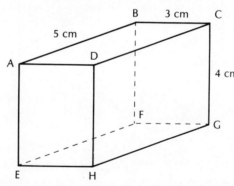

ABCDEFGH is a rectangular box with AB = 5 cm, BC = 3 cm and CG = 4 cm. Find

i) the angle between BH and the plane EFGH
ii) the angle between planes ABCD and ABGH.

i) The required angle is $\hat{BHF}$. FH is in right-angled triangles FGH and HFB.

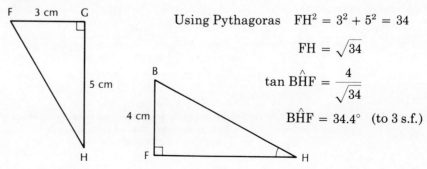

Using Pythagoras $FH^2 = 3^2 + 5^2 = 34$

$$FH = \sqrt{34}$$

$$\tan \hat{BHF} = \frac{4}{\sqrt{34}}$$

$$\hat{BHF} = 34.4° \quad \text{(to 3 s.f.)}$$

ii) The required angle is HÂD.

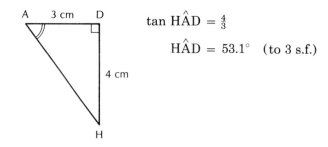

$$\tan \text{H}\hat{\text{A}}\text{D} = \tfrac{4}{3}$$

$$\text{H}\hat{\text{A}}\text{D} = 53.1° \quad \text{(to 3 s.f.)}$$

BEARINGS

A *bearing* is a direction expressed as the angle turned through clockwise from North. To avoid errors, three figures are always used to describe the angle.

Examples

a) An angle of 5° from North would be a bearing of 005°.
An angle of 20° would be a bearing of 020°.

b) Diagrams to show bearings of 150°, 300° and 050° respectively:

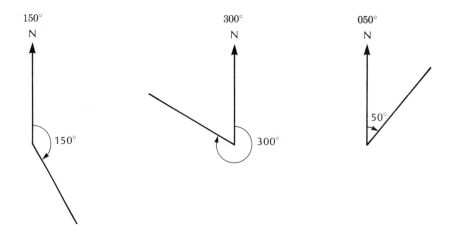

Angle of elevation (up):

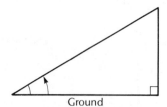

the angle between the horizontal and the line made with the highest point being looked at, i.e. the angle looked up.

Angle of depression (down):

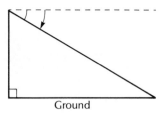

the angle between the horizontal and the lowest point being looked at, i.e. the angle looked down.

Example

A, B and C are three points on the ground. The bearing of C from A is 150° and B from A is 060°. From A the angle of elevation of the top of a tower at C is 30°; from B the angle of elevation is 17°. If the distance BC is 2 km, calculate

i) the height of the tower
ii) the distance AC
iii) the bearing of B from C

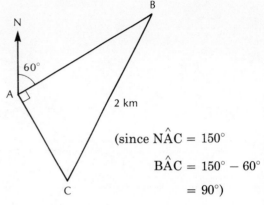

$$(\text{since } N\hat{A}C = 150°$$
$$B\hat{A}C = 150° - 60°$$
$$= 90°)$$

i) $\tan 17° = \dfrac{h}{2}$

$h = 2\tan 17°$ km

$= 0.61$ km (to 2 d.p.)

The height of the tower $= 0.61$ km (to 2 d.p.)

ii) $\tan 30° = \dfrac{0.61}{AC}$

$AC = \dfrac{0.61}{\tan 30°}$ km

$= 1.06$ km (to 2 d.p.)

iii) $\sin A\hat{B}C = \dfrac{1.06}{2}$

$A\hat{B}C = 32°$

$\therefore \ A\hat{C}B = 180° - 90° - 32°$

$= 58°$

But $A\hat{C}B = x + y$ and $x = 30°$ ($N\hat{A}C = 150°$)

$\Rightarrow \quad y = 28°$

$\Rightarrow \quad$ Bearing of B from C $= 028°$

13   CIRCLES

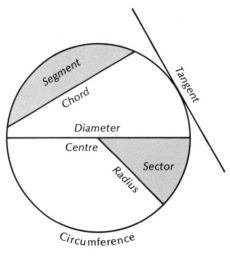

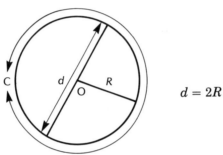

$$d = 2R$$

π is an irrational number.
$\pi \approx 3.142$ or $\frac{22}{7}$

CIRCUMFERENCE

The circumference is the boundary of a circle and its length is

$$C = \pi d$$

$$= 2\pi R$$

$$\therefore \quad d = \frac{C}{\pi}$$

$$\text{and } R = \frac{C}{2\pi}$$

AREA

The area of a circle is

$$A = \pi R^2$$

$$\Rightarrow \quad R^2 = \frac{A}{\pi}$$

$$R = \sqrt{\frac{A}{\pi}}$$

SECTOR

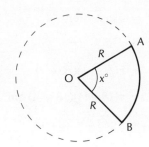

The length of arc AB is a fraction of the circumference of the circle. Since the angle at the centre of a circle is $360°$, this fraction is $\dfrac{x}{360}$.

$$AB = \dfrac{x}{360} \times 2\pi R$$

The area of sector ABO is a fraction of the area of the circle. The fraction is again $\dfrac{x}{360}$.

$$\text{Area of sector ABO} = \dfrac{x}{360} \times \pi R^2$$

Example

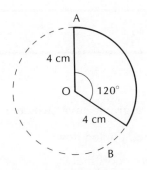

$$\begin{aligned}
\text{Length of arc AB} &= \tfrac{120}{360} \times 2\pi R \text{ cm} \\
&\approx \tfrac{1}{3} \times 2 \times \tfrac{22}{7} \times 4 \text{ cm} \\
&\approx \tfrac{176}{21} \text{ cm} \\
&\approx 8\tfrac{8}{21} \text{ cm}
\end{aligned}$$

PERIMETER

The total distance round the outside of a shape. This may involve both straight sides and curves.

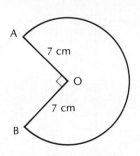

$$\begin{aligned}
\text{Perimeter} &= \text{AO} + \text{BO} + \text{arc AB} \\
&= 7 + 7 + \tfrac{3}{4} \times 2\pi \times 7 \text{ cm} \\
&\approx 14 + \tfrac{3}{4} \times 2 \times \tfrac{22}{7} \times 7 \text{ cm} \\
&\approx 47 \text{ cm}
\end{aligned}$$

RINGS

Area of ring = Area of outer circle − Area of inner circle

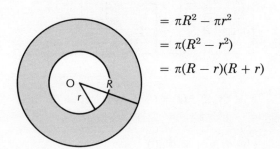

$$\begin{aligned}
&= \pi R^2 - \pi r^2 \\
&= \pi(R^2 - r^2) \\
&= \pi(R - r)(R + r)
\end{aligned}$$

Example

If $R = 18$ cm and $r = 4$ cm, then

$$\text{Area of ring} = \pi R^2 - \pi r^2$$
$$= \pi(R - r)(R + r)$$
$$= \pi(18 - 4)(18 + 4) \text{ cm}^2$$
$$= \pi \times 14 \times 22 \text{ cm}^2$$
$$= 308\pi \text{ cm}^2$$
$$= 967.6 \text{ cm}^2 \quad \text{(to 1 d.p.)}$$

14 GRAPHS

POINTS

Points plotted on a graph have two coordinates.

(x, y) (along, up and down)

These are *Cartesian* coordinates.

Examples

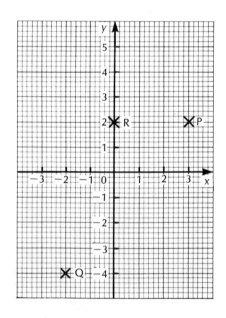

P = (3, 2)   Q = (−2, −4)   R = (0, 2)

The origin = (0, 0).

LINES

Lines on a graph are described by equations.

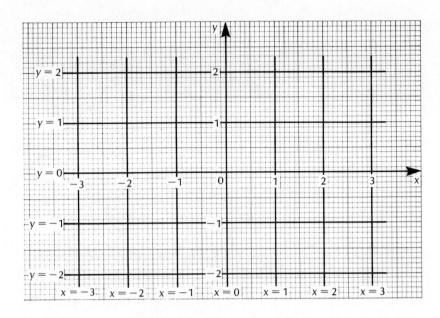

The x-axis is also described by $y = 0$ since all the points on it have a y coordinate of 0.

The y-axis is also described by $x = 0$.

N.B.   Instead of the x and y-axis some problems will refer to the x and $f(x)$ axis.

To draw a line on a graph calculate the coordinates of a number of points which satisfy the equation.

Examples

a) If $y = 2x + 3$

x	-3	-2	-1	0	1	2	3
y	-3	-1	1	3	5	7	9

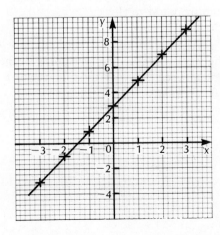

b) $x + y = 7$

x	0	1	2	3	4	5	6	7
y	7	6	5	4	3	2	1	0

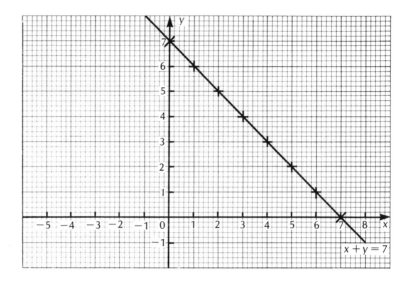

REGIONS

Regions on a graph are described by inequalities. $>$ means greater than, $\geqslant$ greater than or equal to, $<$ less than, $\leqslant$ less than or equal to.

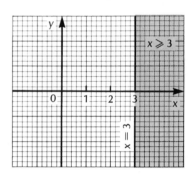

The boundary for $\geqslant$ or $\leqslant$ is a *solid* line.
The boundary for $>$ or $<$ is a *dotted* line.
The x coordinates of points on the line $x = 3$ or to the right are greater than or equal to three.

The y coordinates of every point in the shaded area are less than or equal to -3.

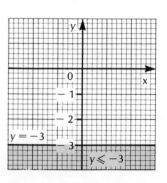

The y coordinates are all less than -3.

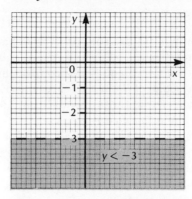

If the x and y coordinates of points in the shaded area are added the result is greater than or equal to four.

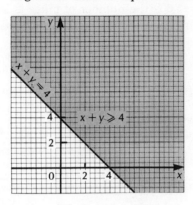

LINEAR PROGRAMMING

Linear programming is a technique used to combine inequalities when certain conditions must occur together. This is done by representing all the conditions on the same axes and (usually) shading out the regions which do not apply. It is particularly useful when solving problems concerned with maximising business profits while at the same time minimising costs.

Example

A market gardener stocks two collections of young conifers. The Supreme collection consists of three pines and five firs, whereas the Major collection consists of four pines and two firs.

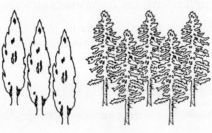

Supreme

Major

There is only room for 60 pines and 50 firs.

Suppose x Supreme and y Major collections are sold.

a) How many pines are sold (in terms of x and y)?
b) How many firs are sold (in terms of x and y)?
c) Write down two inequalities connecting x and y.
d) Using a scale of 1 cm to represent five trees on each axis draw a diagram to show these inequalities, together with $x \geqslant 0$ and $y \geqslant 0$, shading the *unwanted* regions.
e) If a profit of £2 is made on the Supreme collection and a profit of £1 is made on the Major collection, find the coordinates of the point which gives the greatest profit and write down what this profit is.

a) He sells $3x + 4y$ pines.

b) He sells $5x + 2y$ firs.

c) $3x + 4y \leqslant 60$ (the number of pines is less than or equal to 60)
$5x + 2y \leqslant 50$ (the number of firs is less than or equal to 50)

d)

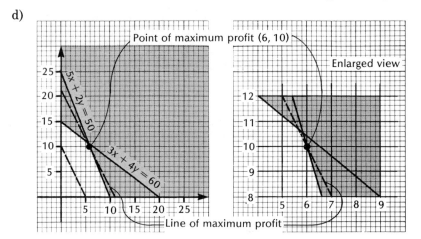

e) Let the profit be £p.

Since x collections at £2 and y collections at £1 profit are sold

$$2x + y = p \quad \text{(This is called the } profit\ equation.\text{)}$$

The line

$$2x + y = 10$$

is called a *profit line* and represents a profit of £10. ($p = 10$ was chosen for convenience because it gives a line across the region as shown, but any value could be chosen.)

All profit lines are parallel to this including the *maximum profit line* which is farthest from the origin yet still in the unshaded region.

The best integral point nearest the line of maximum profit is (6, 10) (x and y must be whole numbers).

$$\therefore \quad x = 6, \quad y = 10 \quad \text{and} \quad 2x + y = 22$$

The maximum profit is £22.

Check, by testing adjacent points, that this is correct,

e.g. if $x = 5$, $y = 11$ then $p = 21$ which is less than 22.

CURVES

An equation of the form $y = ax^2 + bx + c$ gives a graph in the shape of a curve. This U shape is a parabola. The equation is called an equation of the second degree.

Example

Plot the curve represented by $y = x^2$.

x	-3	-2	-1	0	1	2	3
y	9	4	1	0	1	4	9

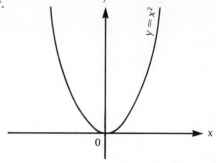

N.B. *Every* number squared is positive.

To solve a quadratic equation using a graph, rearrange the equation if necessary, to give the x^2, x and constant terms of the graph equation on one side of the equals sign and all other terms on the other side. This then indicates where to look on the graph for the solutions.

Example

Draw the graph of $y = x^2 - 3x + 2$ where $-3 \leqslant x \leqslant 3$ and then use it to solve

i) $x^2 - 3x + 2 = 0$ \qquad ii) $x^2 = 3x - 1$

$-3 \leqslant x \leqslant 3$ means between $x = -3$ and $x = 3$

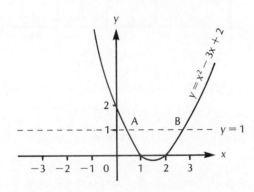

x	-3	-2	-1	0	1	2	3	$1\frac{1}{2}$
x^2	9	4	1	0	1	4	9	$2\frac{1}{4}$
$-3x$	$+9$	$+6$	$+3$	0	-3	-6	-9	$-4\frac{1}{2}$
$+2$	$+2$	$+2$	$+2$	$+2$	$+2$	$+2$	$+2$	$+2$
y	20	12	6	2	0	0	2	$-\frac{1}{4}$

$(x = 1\frac{1}{2}$ has been included at the end of the table because, since $x = 1$ and $x = 2$ both give $y = 0$, it is obvious that more information is needed about this part of the curve.)

i) When $y = 0$, $x = 1$ or $x = 2$.

89

ii) $x^2 = 3x - 1$. So, rearranging this equation,

$$x^2 - 3x = -1$$

$$\Rightarrow \quad x^2 - 3x + 2 = -1 + 2$$

$$\Rightarrow \quad x^2 - 3x + 2 = 1$$

The graph is of $x^2 - 3x + 2 = y$.

The equation can be solved from the graph by making $y = 1$.

On the graph draw the line $y = 1$. This cuts the curve at A and B, so the x coordinates of A and B will be the roots (the solutions) of the equation.

At A, $x \approx 0.38$ and at B, $x \approx 2.62$.

AREA UNDER CURVES: THE TRAPEZIUM RULE

To find the total area under a curve, cut the area into small parts, which are approximately trapeziums, by means of vertical lines.

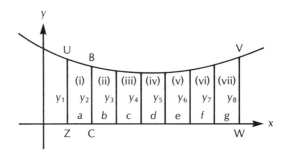

Area UVWZ = Areas (i) + (ii) + (iii) + (iv)

$$+ \text{ (v)} + \text{ (vi)} + \text{ (vii)}$$

$$= \tfrac{1}{2}(y_1 + y_2)a + \tfrac{1}{2}(y_2 + y_3)b$$

$$+ \tfrac{1}{2}(y_3 + y_4)c + \tfrac{1}{2}(y_4 + y_5)d$$

$$+ \tfrac{1}{2}(y_5 + y_6)e + \tfrac{1}{2}(y_6 + y_7)f$$

$$+ \tfrac{1}{2}(y_7 + y_8)g$$

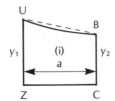

If a is very small then UB is approximately a straight line

$$\text{Area (i)} \approx \tfrac{1}{2}(y_1 + y_2)a$$

By making $a = b = c = d = e = f = g$

Area UVWZ $\approx \tfrac{1}{2}a(y_1 + 2y_2 + 2y_3 + 2y_4 + 2y_5 + 2y_6 + 2y_7 + y_8)$

POLAR COORDINATES

Polar coordinates give details of position in reference to the origin and the positive x-axis, as a distance R and an angle θ.

The distance R is measured from the origin O.

The angle θ is measured from the positive x-axis in an anticlockwise direction.

Example

All points on a circle with centre O are the same distance from O and *all* points on a radius are at the same angle from the initial direction.

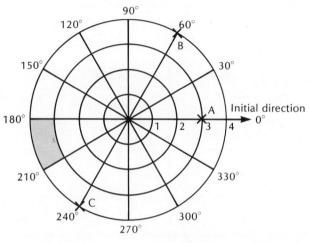

$$A = (3, 0°) \qquad B = (4, 60°) \qquad C = (4, 240°)$$

In the shaded area $3 \leqslant R \leqslant 4$ and $180° \leqslant \theta \leqslant 210°$.

CONVERSION GRAPHS

Each axis represents one of the quantities being compared.

For a comparison between two proportional units the graph will be a straight line, so if two conversions are known then the graph can be drawn.

Example

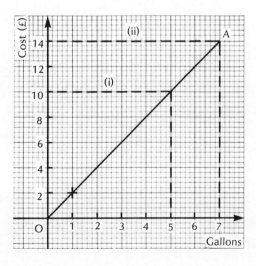

One gallon of petrol costs £2
  0 gallons of petrol cost £0

By plotting the points (0,0) and (1, 2) and joining them, the line OA on the graph now joins *all* points which compare a number of gallons with their price,

line (i) 5 gallons cost £10
line (ii) £14 would buy 7 gallons.

15 STRAIGHT LINES

When the points whose coordinates satisfy an equation of the form $y = mx + c$ are plotted, the resulting graph is a straight line,

Example

$$y = 2x - 1 \qquad \text{(To find } y \text{, double the } x \text{ then subtract 1.)}$$

x	$-\frac{1}{2}$	0	$\frac{1}{2}$	1	$1\frac{1}{2}$
y	-2	-1	0	1	2

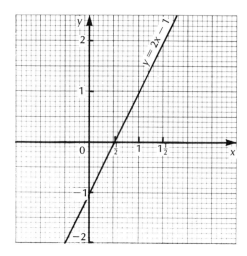

GRADIENT OF A LINE

The gradient of a line compares the distance the line has gone up (or down) with the distance it has gone along.

Since a line does not alter direction any two points can be used to find the gradient.

$$\text{Gradient AB} = \frac{AD}{BD}$$

$$= \tan \theta$$

$$= \frac{y_A - y_B}{x_A - x_B}$$

Gradient of a line =

Difference between the y coordinates of any two points
Difference between the x coordinates of the same two points

92

Examples

a) Gradient $= \dfrac{6-3}{7-2}$

$= \dfrac{3}{5}$

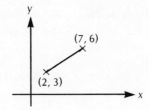

b) Gradient $= \dfrac{5-2}{-4-3}$

$= -\dfrac{3}{7}$

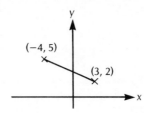

A line sloping this way

has a positive gradient

A line sloping this way

has a negative gradient

When the equation is in the form $y = mx + c$

m represents the *gradient* (the 'slope') of the line
c represents the *intercept* on the y-axis (the value of y where the line cuts the y-axis).

Examples

a) $y = 2x - 1$

Gradient $m = 2$

Intercept $c = -1$

b) $y + 4x = 7$

$y = -4x + 7$

Gradient $m = -4$

Intercept $c = 7$

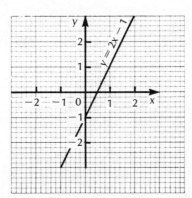

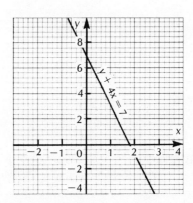

c) $2y = 5x - 1$

$y = \frac{5}{2}x - \frac{1}{2}$

Gradient $m = \frac{5}{2}$

Intercept $c = -\frac{1}{2}$

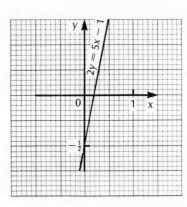

EQUATION OF A LINE

If the gradient and the intercept are known then the equation can be found by substituting into $y = mx + c$,

Examples

a) $m = 3$ and $c = 2$

$\Rightarrow \quad y = 3x + 2$

b) $m = -\frac{3}{2}$ and $c = -4$

$\Rightarrow \quad y = -\frac{3}{2}x - 4$

$\Rightarrow \quad 2y = -3x - 8$

$\Rightarrow \quad 2y + 3x + 8 = 0$

If two points are known then the equation can be found by substituting in the x and y coordinates of each point and solving simultaneously to find m and c.

Example

If A = (1, 2) and B = (5, 8), find the equation of AB.

$y = mx + c$

At A $\qquad 2 = 1m + c$
At B $\qquad 8 = 5m + c$ $\Bigg\}$ Solve simultaneously.

Subtract $6 = 4m$

$\qquad m = \frac{6}{4}$

$\qquad \quad = \frac{3}{2}$

But $\qquad 2 = m + c$

$\qquad 2 = \frac{3}{2} + c$

$\qquad c = \frac{1}{2}$

Since $m = \frac{3}{2}$ and $c = \frac{1}{2}$ the equation of AB is

$\qquad y = \frac{3}{2}x + \frac{1}{2}$

$\Rightarrow \quad 2y = 3x + 1$

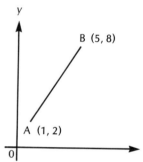

Examples

A pair of linear equations may be a) consistent, b) contradictory, c) basically the same equation.

a) The equations

$\qquad 5x + 3y = -1$

$\qquad 2x - y = 4$

have one solution,

$\qquad x = 1, y = -2$

The solution set contains one member, $(1, -2)$.

There is one point of intersection.

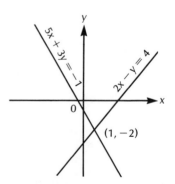

94

b) The equations

$$5x + 3y = -1$$

$$5x + 3y = 3$$

have no solution.
The solution set is the null set.
There are no points of intersection.

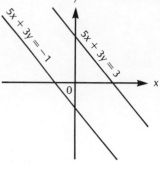

c) The equations

$$5x + 3y = -1$$

$$10x + 6y = -2$$

have an infinity of solutions. The solution set is

$$\{(x, y): 5x + 3y = -1\}$$

Both equations are represented by the same line on the graph.

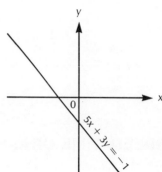

16   SPEED AND DISTANCE

$$\text{Average speed} = \frac{\text{Distance travelled}}{\text{Time taken}}$$

Units: cm/s
km/h   etc.

$$\text{Distance travelled} = \text{Average speed} \times \text{Time taken}$$

$$\text{Time taken} = \frac{\text{Distance travelled}}{\text{Average speed}}$$

Example

To travel 390 km at an average speed of 60 km/h.

$$\text{Time taken} = \frac{390 \text{ km}}{60 \text{ km/h}}$$

$$= \frac{390}{60} \text{ h}$$

$$= 6\tfrac{1}{2} \text{ h}$$

AVERAGE SPEED

$$\text{Average speed for a journey} = \frac{\text{Total distance travelled}}{\text{Total time taken}}$$

95

Example

A man sets out from home and walks 4 km to the station in 30 minutes. He then waits 15 minutes for a train which takes him 156 km in $1\frac{1}{4}$ hours. What is the average speed for his journey?

$$\text{Total distance travelled} = (4 + 156) \text{ km}$$

$$= 160 \text{ km}$$

$$\text{Total time taken} = 30 \text{ min} + 15 \text{ min} + 1\frac{1}{4} \text{ h}$$

$$= (\tfrac{1}{2} + \tfrac{1}{4} + 1\tfrac{1}{4}) \text{ h}$$

$$= 2 \text{ h}$$

$$\text{Average speed} = \frac{160}{2} \text{ km/h}$$

$$= 80 \text{ km/h}$$

SPEED–TIME GRAPH

The area underneath a speed–time graph equals the distance travelled.

Example

This graph shows a journey in which the speed increases from 0 to 30 km/h in the first hour, then stays at 30 km/h for two hours before slowing down to 'stop' during the next two hours.

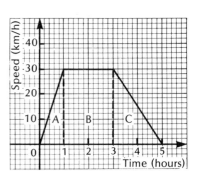

$$\text{Distance travelled} = \text{Area A} + \text{Area B} + \text{Area C}$$

$$= (\tfrac{1}{2} \times 1 \times 30) + (2 \times 30) + (\tfrac{1}{2} \times 2 \times 30) \text{ km}$$

$$= 15 + 60 + 30 \text{ km}$$

$$= 105 \text{ km}$$

The gradient of each line on a speed–time graph gives the acceleration for that part of the journey.

$$\text{Gradient during first hour} = \frac{30}{1} \text{ km/h}^2$$

$$= 30 \text{ km/h}^2$$

$$\text{Gradient during next two hours} = 0 \text{ km/h}^2$$

$$\text{Gradient during last two hours} = -\frac{30}{2} \text{ km/h}^2$$

$$= -15 \text{ km/h}^2$$

There is a deceleration during the last two hours and so the acceleration is negative.

DISTANCE–TIME GRAPH

The gradient of each line on the graph gives the speed of that part of the journey.

Example

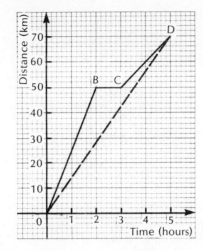

$$\text{Gradient OB} = \frac{\text{Distance}}{\text{Time}}$$

$$= \frac{50}{2}\,\text{km/h} = 25\,\text{km/h}$$

$$\text{Gradient BC} = 0\,\text{km/h}$$

$$\text{Gradient CD} = \frac{20}{2}\,\text{km/h} = 10\,\text{km/h}$$

Average speed for the journey = Gradient OD

$$= \tfrac{70}{5}\,\text{km/h} = 14\,\text{km/h}$$

17 VARIATION

DIRECTLY VARIABLE (OR PROPORTIONAL)

If one variable (y) is directly proportional to another variable (x) then for all values of x and y the ratio $y:x$ is constant.

This means that $y/x:1$ is constant so y/x is a constant.

$$\frac{y}{x} = c \quad \text{where } c \text{ is a constant}$$

$$y = cx$$

'is proportional to' is written as $\propto$ so $y \propto x$ means that $y = cx$, where c is a constant.

Since a straight line graph, passing through the origin, has an equation $y = cx$, this graph indicates that $y \propto x$, and that if y is multiplied by any factor then x is multiplied by the same factor.

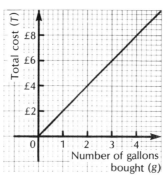

This can be illustrated by a graph of the cost of petrol.

$$T \propto g$$

$$\Rightarrow \quad T = cg \text{ where } c \text{ is the cost of } 1 \text{ gallon.}$$

Examples

a) If $y \propto x$ and $x = 2$ when $y = 5$ find an equation relating x and y.

Since $\qquad y \propto x$

then $\qquad y = cx$ where c is a constant

When $x = 2, y = 5$ so $5 = c \times 2$

$$\Rightarrow \quad c = \tfrac{5}{2}$$

$\therefore$ an equation relating x and y is $y = \tfrac{5}{2}x$

$$\Rightarrow \quad 2y = 5x$$

b) If y varies directly as x^2 and $x = 2$ when $y = 5$, find an equation relating x and y.

Since $\quad y \propto x^2$

then $\quad y = cx^2$ where c is a constant.

When $x = 2, y = 5$, so $5 = c \times 2^2$

$$\Rightarrow \quad c = \tfrac{5}{4}$$

An equation relating x and y is $y = \tfrac{5}{4}x^2$

$$\Rightarrow \quad 4y = 5x^2$$

c) If the radius of a circle is multiplied by three what happens to the area?

The area (A) of a circle of radius R is given by

$$A = \pi R^2$$

$$\Rightarrow \quad A \propto R^2 \quad \text{since } \pi \text{ is a constant.}$$

So if R is multiplied by 3 then A is multiplied by 3^2.

So the area of the circle is multiplied by 9.

INVERSELY PROPORTIONAL

If y is inversely proportional to x then y is proportional to the reciprocal of x. (The reciprocal of x is $1/x$.)

Since $\quad y \propto \dfrac{1}{x}$

then $\quad y = c\left(\dfrac{1}{x}\right)$ where c is a constant

$$\Rightarrow \quad y = \dfrac{c}{x}$$

$$\Rightarrow \quad xy = c$$

This means that as x increases, y decreases and as x decreases, y increases.

On a graph:

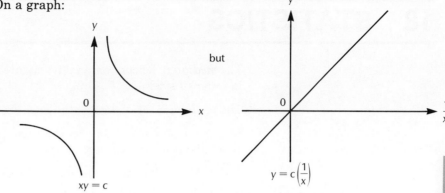

but

$xy = c$

$y = c\left(\dfrac{1}{x}\right)$

Example

If y is inversely proportional to x and $x = 3$ when $y = 2$ find x when $y = 5$.

Since $\qquad y \propto \dfrac{1}{x}$

then $\qquad y = \dfrac{c}{x}$

When $x = 3$, $y = 2$, so $\quad 2 = \dfrac{c}{3}$

$\Rightarrow \quad c = 6$

$\therefore \quad y = \dfrac{6}{x}$

When $y = 5$, $\quad 5 = \dfrac{6}{x}$

$\therefore \quad x = \frac{6}{5}$

$\qquad = 1\frac{1}{5}$

JOINTLY VARIABLE

Joint variation occurs when one variable is proportional to the product of two or more other variables.

Example

If w, x and y are variable and y varies jointly with w and x, so that when $x = 5$, $w = 3$ and $y = 4$, find x when $w = 2$ and $y = 3$.

Since $\qquad y \propto wx$

then $\qquad y = cwx \quad$ where c is a constant.

If $x = 5$, $w = 3$ and $y = 4$ then $4 = c \times 3 \times 5$

$\Rightarrow \quad c = \frac{4}{15}$

So when $w = 2$ and $y = 3$ and $y = cwx$

then $\qquad 3 = \frac{4}{15} \times 2 \times x$

$\Rightarrow \quad x = \dfrac{3 \times 15}{4 \times 2} = \dfrac{45}{8}$

$\Rightarrow \quad x = 5\frac{5}{8}$

18 STATISTICS

The *median* of a set of data is the middle value when all have been placed in order of size.

The *mode* of a set of data is the most frequent value.

The *mean* of a set of data is the result of collecting together and then sharing out all the values.

Although median, mode and mean are all averages, if only 'the average' is asked for the mean is required.

Example

$$9,\ 3,\ 3,\ 7,\ 4,\ 3,\ 4,\ 8,\ 1$$

Median of $1, 3, 3, 3, 4, 4, 7, 8, 9 = 4$

Mode $= 3$

$$\textbf{Mean} = \frac{9 + 3 + 3 + 7 + 4 + 3 + 4 + 8 + 1}{9}$$

$$= \frac{42}{9} = 4\tfrac{6}{9} = 4\tfrac{2}{3}$$

N.B.   Mean × Number of values = Total of all the values.

FREQUENCY

The number of times a result occurs.

Example

25 children are given a test marked out of 5 and their marks are

0	3	5	0	4
1	4	2	1	5
2	1	3	2	3
1	0	3	2	2
1	2	1	3	2

Mark	Tally	Frequency
0	111	3
1	⧸⧸⧸⧸ 1	6
2	⧸⧸⧸⧸ 11	7
3	⧸⧸⧸⧸	5
4	11	2
5	11	2
	Total:	25

Mode = 2 (the most frequent result)

Arranging the marks in ascending order

0, 0, 0, 1, 1, 1, 1, 1, 1, 2, 2, 2, 2, 2, 2, 2, 3, 3, 3, 3, 3, 4, 4, 5, 5

Median = 2 (the 13th mark when placed in order)

$$\text{Mean} = \frac{\text{Total marks given}}{\text{Total number of children}}$$

$$= \frac{(3 \times 0) + (6 \times 1) + (7 \times 2) + (5 \times 3) + (2 \times 4) + (2 \times 5)}{25}$$

$$= 2.12$$

PICTOGRAM

A pictogram uses a picture or symbol to represent the data and is a simple and interesting way of giving information.

Example

 represents 100 deciduous trees

 represents 100 evergreen trees

If there are 390 deciduous and 530 evergreen trees in a forest this can be shown as

(390 is rounded up to 400.)

(530 is rounded up to 550.)

BAR CHARTS

A graph on which 'bars' are used to represent the frequency distribution of data. The height of each bar represents the frequency.

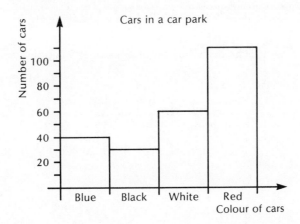

represents

	Blue	Black	White	Red
	40	30	60	110

(The bars are sometimes drawn horizontally.)

HISTOGRAM

A histogram looks similar to a bar chart (with vertical bars), but the **area** of each bar represents the frequency. If the widths of each bar are equal then the height of the bar is proportional to the frequency and the vertical axis can be labelled as the frequency; the width of each bar is considered as one unit.

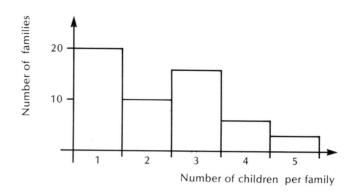

shows

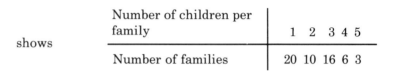

Number of children per family	1	2	3	4	5
Number of families	20	10	16	6	3

This is an example of a *discrete variable* distribution, since the measurements can only take specific values, i.e. the number of children is 1, 2, 3, 4 or 5; it cannot be a non-integral value.

A *continuous variable* distribution is one in which the measurements can have any value within the limits of two given values, e.g. ages, weights, heights.

If a large number of measurements covering a wide range are to be represented then the data are grouped into *classes* or *intervals*. The largest and smallest measurements in each class are the *boundaries* and the range of values the *class interval*.

Example

The distribution of ages of 100 people living in a street may be shown by

Table 1

Years	0–9	10–19	20–29	30–39	40–49	50–59	60–70
Frequency	6	13	12	24	20	21	4

The boundaries are 0, 10, 20, 30, 40, 50, 60, 70.

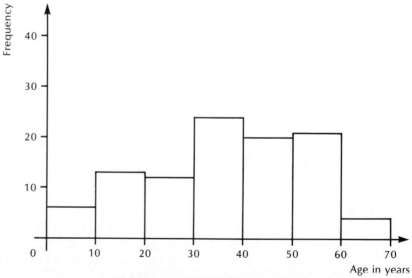

The histogram showing the ages in Table 1

The class interval for each class is ten years.

There is not really a gap between the end of one class and the beginning of the next because a person giving his age always gives the age reached on his last birthday. A boy who says he is nine may be only one day away from his tenth birthday.

Since the class intervals are equal the vertical axis can be labelled as the frequency.

Data are not always grouped into equal class intervals, although they usually are.

Example

The weights of 250 children are

	A	B	C	D
Weight (kg)	30–35	36–45	46–55	56–60
Frequency	60	100	50	40

In the context of this information weights have been corrected to the nearest kilogram.

This means that those in:

Class interval

class A have true weight	$29\frac{1}{2}$ kg $\leqslant$ true weight $< 35\frac{1}{2}$ kg	6 kg
class B have true weight	$35\frac{1}{2}$ kg $\leqslant$ true weight $< 45\frac{1}{2}$ kg	10 kg
class C have true weight	$45\frac{1}{2}$ kg $\leqslant$ true weight $< 55\frac{1}{2}$ kg	10 kg
class D have true weight	$55\frac{1}{2}$ kg $\leqslant$ true weight $< 60\frac{1}{2}$ kg	5 kg

The class intervals vary, and so the vertical scale must represent Frequency/Class interval. Thus the area of each bar will represent the frequency.

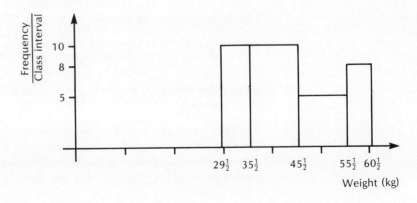

103

THE MEAN OF GROUPED DATA

When the total frequency is high and the range of values is large the data may be grouped into intervals.

The mean of grouped data

$$= \frac{\text{(Middle of each interval} \times \text{Frequency) summed over the intervals}}{\text{Total number}}$$

Example

For the distribution of ages of 100 people, shown in Table 1 on page 103.

Mean age

$$= \frac{(5 \times 6) + (15 \times 13) + (25 \times 12) + (35 \times 24) + (45 \times 20) + (55 \times 21) + (65 \times 4)}{100}$$

$$= 36.8 \text{ years}$$

CUMULATIVE FREQUENCY

This is the number of times results occur up to a specific value.

Example

From Table 1:

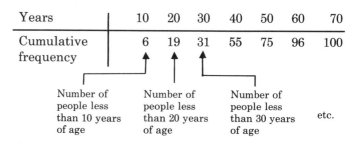

Years	10	20	30	40	50	60	70
Cumulative frequency	6	19	31	55	75	96	100

Number of people less than 10 years of age

Number of people less than 20 years of age

Number of people less than 30 years of age

etc.

CUMULATIVE FREQUENCY GRAPH

Since the data on a cumulative frequency graph are arranged in order of size, this graph can be used to find

(i) the median: the middle value of the data
(ii) the upper quartile: the value above which lies one quarter of the data
(iii) the lower quartile: the value below which lies one quarter of the data.

These values are found by using the appropriate value of the cumulative frequency as the vertical coordinate and reading off the corresponding horizontal coordinate. The interquartile range is the difference between the two quartile values, and the semi-interquartile range is half that difference.

Example

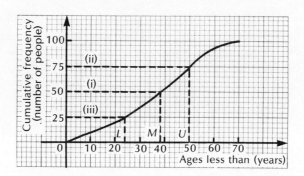

a) Upper quartile (from line (ii)): $U = 50$ years

b) Median (from line (i)): $M = 38$ years

c) Lower quartile (from line (iii)): $L = 24$ years

d) Interquartile range: $U - L = 50{-}24$ years

e) Semi-interquartile range: $\dfrac{U - L}{2} = 13$ years

PIE CHART

The total frequency is represented by a circle. Groups are represented by sectors ('slices') of the circle.

Example

In a car park there are 240 cars, 40 are blue, 30 are black, 60 are white and the rest are red.

Total frequency = 240 cars.　　　Total angle = 360°.

One car is represented by $\dfrac{360°}{240} = \dfrac{3°}{2}$

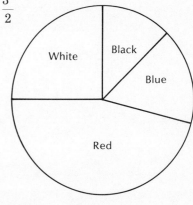

Blue cars　　$40 \times \dfrac{3°}{2} = 60°$

Black cars　　$30 \times \dfrac{3°}{2} = 45°$

White cars　　$60 \times \dfrac{3°}{2} = 90°$

Red cars　　$110 \times \dfrac{3°}{2} = \dfrac{165°}{360°}$　(check that total = 360°)

MATHEMATICS IN THE MEDIA

Increasing use is made of mathematical statements on television, in the newspapers and on radio; for example 'the number of unsolved crimes is rising but not so rapidly as in the previous twelve months', or 'prices soar'. (The first statement in this paragraph is such an example). Graphs can be helpful in making their meaning clear.

Words such as 'plummet', 'drop', 'soar', 'rise', 'rocket' indicate whether the graph goes up or down and may give an indication of the steepness.

Examples

'Prices rose slowly but steadily in the first half of 1980 but then soared away.'

'There was a rapid drop in the number of unsolved crimes during the period 1980–1982 but this tailed off in 1983.'

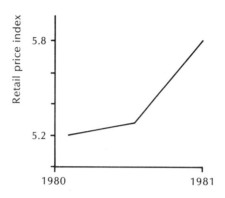 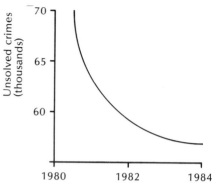

The *rate of increase* or *rate of decrease* is shown by the *gradient* of the graph.

The shape of the graph illustrates the meaning of the following:

Examples

a) 'Days lost have reached a plateau'

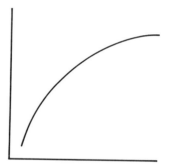

b) 'A marked jump in the number of assaults on the elderly'

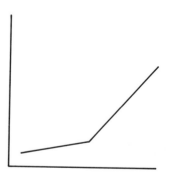

c) 'The rate of inflation eases' (or the rate of inflation is falling)

Note here that although inflation is still rising the *rate* (slope) is decreasing

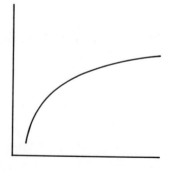

d) 'Steady increase in wages'

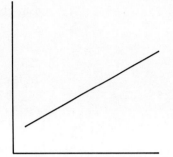

e) 'Steady drop in prices'

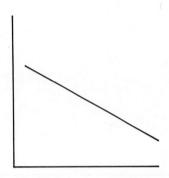

f) 'Employment soars more rapidly each year'

The shape of the graph shows that unemployment is *not* increasing steadily.

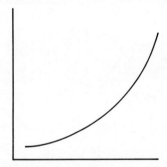

By looking at the values given in the graph it is possible to determine percentage increase or decrease but care must be taken. The first graph shows a 25% increase but the second does not.

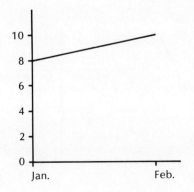

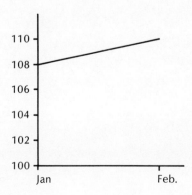

Bar charts are a particularly good way of showing percentage increase or decrease if the scales start at zero, e.g.

'25% increase in road accidents in the second half of the year'

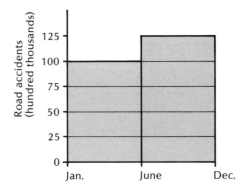

'Export sales slump by 20% in just one month'

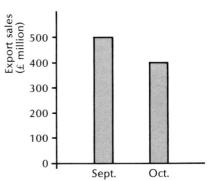

19 GEOMETRY

ANGLES

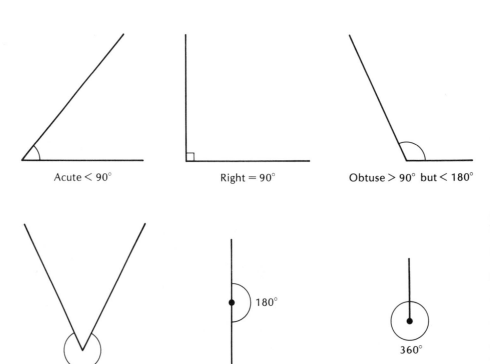

Acute < 90°   Right = 90°   Obtuse > 90° but < 180°

Reflex > 180°   180°   360°

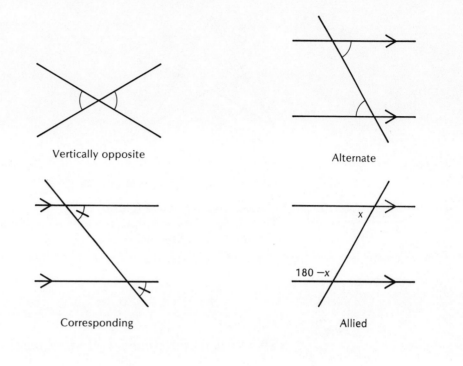

Vertically opposite

Alternate

Corresponding

Allied

TRIANGLES

Sum of the angles = 180°

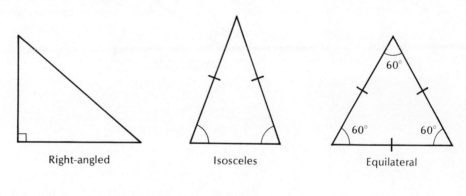

Right-angled

Isosceles

Equilateral

QUADRILATERALS

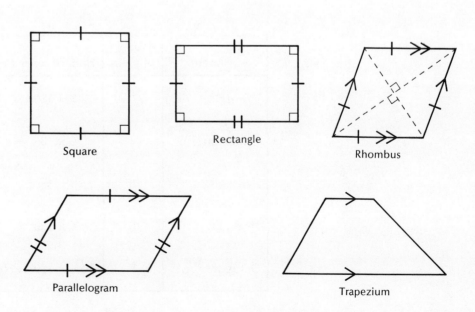

Square

Rectangle

Rhombus

Parallelogram

Trapezium

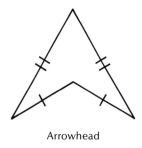

Arrowhead

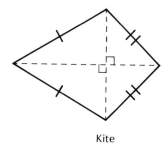

Kite

POLYGONS

Pentagon: five-sided figure
Hexagon: six-sided figure
Octagon: eight-sided figure

A *regular* polygon is a plane (flat) figure with all its sides equal and all its angles equal.

The sum of the *interior angles* of a polygon with N sides $= (N - 2) \times 180°$.

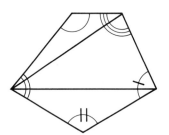

Since a pentagon can be 'cut up' into three triangles, the sum of the interior angles $= 3 \times 180°$
$= 540°$

The size of each angle of a *regular* polygon with N sides $= \dfrac{(N - 2) \times 180°}{N}$.

Shape	Number of sides	Sum of interior angles	Size of each angle of a *regular* shape
Triangle	3	$1 \times 180° = 180°$	$\dfrac{180°}{3} = 60°$
Quadrilateral	4	$2 \times 180° = 360°$	$\dfrac{360°}{4} = 90°$
Pentagon	5	$3 \times 180° = 540°$	$\dfrac{540°}{5} = 108°$
Hexagon	6	$4 \times 180° = 720°$	$\dfrac{720°}{6} = 120°$
Octagon	8	$6 \times 180° = 1080°$	$\dfrac{1080°}{8} = 135°$

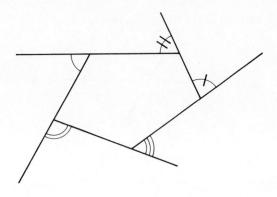

Exterior angles are formed when each side of the polygon is extended in turn.

Sum of the exterior angles of any polygon = 360°.

At each vertex: Exterior angle + Interior angle = 180°.

PYTHAGORAS

$h^2 = a^2 + b^2$

$a^2 = h^2 - b^2$

$b^2 = h^2 - a^2$

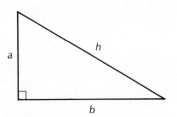

Examples

a) Calculate the lettered angles.

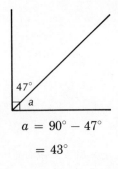

$$a = 90° - 47°$$
$$= 43°$$

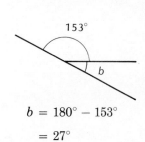

$$b = 180° - 153°$$
$$= 27°$$

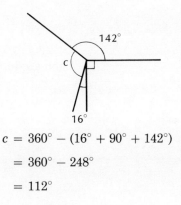

$$c = 360° - (16° + 90° + 142°)$$
$$= 360° - 248°$$
$$= 112°$$

111

b) Calculate the unknown angles.

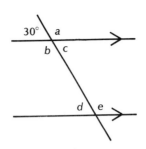

i) $a = 150°$ (angles on a straight line)

$b = 150°$ (angles on a straight line)

$c = 30°$ (vertically opposite angles)

$d = 30°$ (alternate angles)

$e = 150°$ (angles on a straight line)

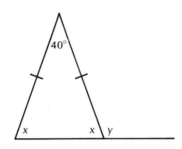

ii) $40° + 2x = 180°$

$2x = 140°$

$x = 70°$

$y = 180° - 70°$ (angles on a straight line)

$y = 110°$

c) Calculate each angle of a regular hexagon.

Sum of angles $= (6 - 2) \times 180°$

$= 4 \times 180°$

$= 720°$

Each angle $= \dfrac{720°}{6}$

$= 120°$

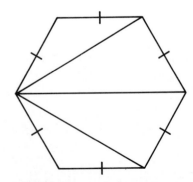

d) Calculate x.

By Pythagoras

$$9.3^2 = 4.2^2 + x^2$$
$$x^2 = 9.3^2 - 4.2^2$$
$$x = \sqrt{9.3^2 - 4.2^2}$$
$$x = 8.3 \quad \text{(to 1 d.p.)}$$

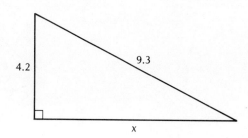

TESSELLATION

A pattern made by repeating a well-defined shape to cover a plane completely, without leaving any gaps, is a tessellation of that shape.

Examples

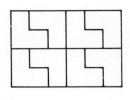 and 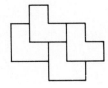 are tessellations of

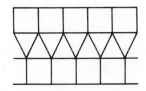 is a tessellation of and

A regular tessellation is a tessellation of regular polygons such that every vertex is identical. There are three such tessellations:

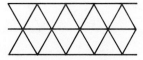

Equilateral triangles

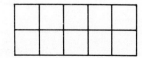

Squares

Regular hexagons

POLYHEDRON

A polyhedron is a three-dimensional solid, each face of which is a polygon.

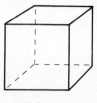

Cube

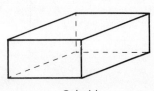

Cuboid

Tetrahedron

113

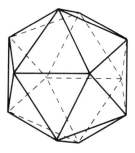
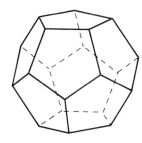

| Octahedron | Icosahedron | Dodecahedron |

The *faces* of a polyhedron are the areas enclosed by edges; the *edges* are the lines along which faces meet, i.e. the lines needed to make the skeleton of the model; and the *vertices* are the corners.

Euler's theorem states that for every polyhedron the number of (faces + vertices − edges) = 2.

Example

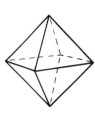

This tetrahedron has:
4 vertices: A, B, C, D
6 edges: AB, AC, AD, BC, BD, CD
4 faces: ABC, ACD, ADB, BCD

PRISM

A prism is a three-dimensional solid with uniform cross-section. If the solid is cut anywhere perpendicular to the length the front face is the same shape and size.

Examples

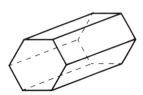
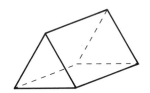

| Hexagonal prism | Triangular prism |

PYRAMID

A pyramid is a three-dimensional solid with a flat base and all other faces tapering to a point.

Examples

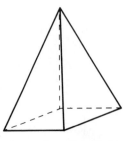
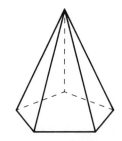
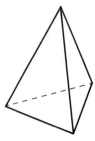

| Square-based pyramid | Pentagonal-based pyramid | Tetrahedron |

NET

A plane diagram which, when folded, will construct a three-dimensional solid.

Examples

 and 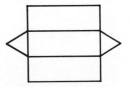 are nets of a cube

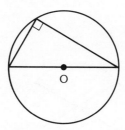

Net of a tetrahedron

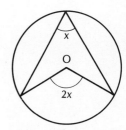

Net of a triangular prism

---

20 CIRCLE GEOMETRY

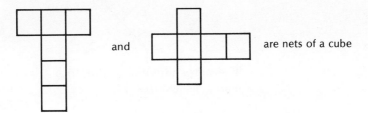

The angle in a semicircle is 90°

The angle at the centre is twice the angle at the circumference

Angles subtended by the same arc are equal

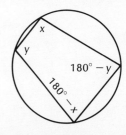

The opposite angles of a *cyclic quadrilateral* add up to 180°

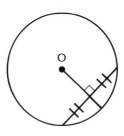

The perpendicular radius to a chord bisects the chord

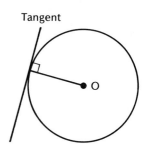

The radius is perpendicular to the tangent at the point of contact

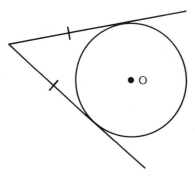

Tangents from a point are equal in length

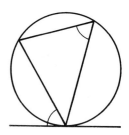

The angle in the alternate segment equals the angle between the chord and the tangent

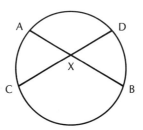

Intersecting chords
$AX \times XB = CX \times XD$

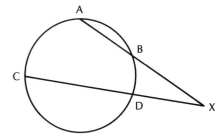

$AX \times BX = CX \times DX$

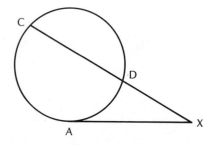

$AX^2 = CX \times DX$

Examples

a)

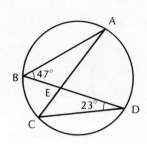

Calculate i) BÂE ii) EĈD iii) AÊB

  i) BÂE = ED̂C = 23°   (angles subtended by same arc)

  ii) EĈD = AB̂E = 47°   (angles subtended by same arc)

  iii) AÊB = 180° − 47° − 23°   (angles of a triangle)

            = 110°

b)

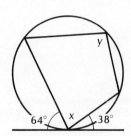

Calculate i) x ii) y

  i) $x = 180° − 64° − 38°$ (angles on a straight line)

       = 78°

  ii) $y = 180° − 78°$ (opposite angles of a cyclic quadrilateral)

        = 102°

c)

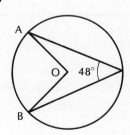

Calculate AÔB where O is the centre of the circle.

    AÔB = 2 × 48°   (angle at the centre)

         = 96°

d)

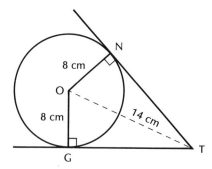

Radius of circle = 8 cm, OT = 14 cm.

What is the length of the tangent TN?

By Pythagoras $TN^2 = OT^2 - ON^2$

$$= 14^2 - 8^2 \text{ cm}$$

$$TN = 11.49 \text{ cm} \quad \text{(to 2 d.p.)}$$

e)

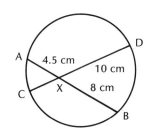

Calculate CX.

$$CX \times XD = AX \times XB$$

$$CX \times 10 = 4.5 \times 8$$

$$CX = \frac{36}{10} \text{ cm}$$

$$CX = 3.6 \text{ cm}$$

21   CONSTRUCTIONS

ANGLES

Before using a protractor, to measure angles, make an estimate of the size of the angle.

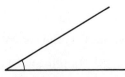

This angle is < 90°

but this angle is > 90° and < 180°

Make sure that the correct scale on the protractor is used so as to give a reading in keeping with the estimate.

When drawing angles, make sure that the angle drawn looks correct.

Since a semicircular protractor reads only up to 180°, reflex angles can be drawn (or measured) by using the fact that $\frac{1}{2}$ turn (a straight line) is 180° so only the angle under 180° need be measured.

Example

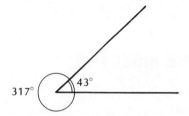

So $x = 180° + 123°$

$= 303°$

Alternatively, draw (or measure) the angle which when added to the required angle makes a complete turn of 360°.

Example

To draw 317°.
Since $360° - 317° = 43°$, draw 43°.

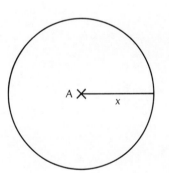

LENGTHS

A pair of compasses can be used to measure equal lengths. All points on the circle with centre A are a distance x from A.

By drawing an arc of a circle of radius R, centre X, and an arc of a circle of equal radius, centre Y, the point of intersection of the arcs, W, is the same distance from X as from Y. XWY is an isosceles triangle.

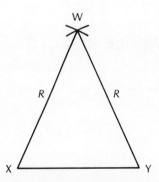

If XY is drawn to a specified length and XW and WY are given lengths, not necessarily the same, then a triangle with sides of known lengths can be drawn.

119

Examples

a) Draw △XYZ with XY = 4.8 cm, YZ = 3.5 cm and XZ = 2.6 cm.

　　i) Draw and label XY.
　　ii) With centre X and radius 2.6 cm, draw an arc.
　　iii) With centre Y and radius 3.5 cm, draw an arc to meet that drawn in ii) at Z.
　　iv) Join X to Z and Z to Y.

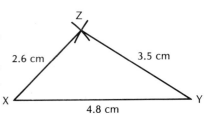

b) Draw △ABC with BC = 4 cm, B = 37° and C = 105°.

　　i) Draw BC
　　ii) Measure 37° at B
　　iii) Measure 105° at C
　　iv) Extend the lines drawn in ii) and iii) to meet at A.

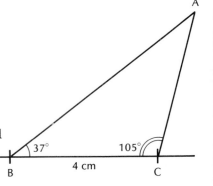

LINE BISECTOR

　　i) Place compass point on A. Draw arcs above and below the line.
　　ii) With the compasses the same distance apart place the point on B and draw arcs to cut those in i) at C and D.
　　iii) Join C and D.

　　M is then the mid-point (middle) of AB and each angle at M = 90°.

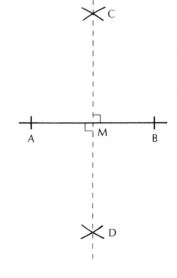

ANGLE BISECTOR

　　i) Place compass point on B and draw arcs at X and Y.
　　ii) With point on X draw an arc at W.
　　iii) With the compasses the same distance apart and the point on Y, draw an arc to cut that drawn in ii) at W.
　　iv) Join B and W.

　　BW cuts AB̂C in half.

　　AB̂W = WB̂C

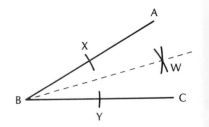

ANGLES OF 90°, 45°, 22½° . . .

i) Draw a line.
ii) Bisect the line.
iii) Bisect one of the resulting 90° angles to give two angles of 45°, i.e. $A\hat{B}C = 45°$.
iv) Bisect again for an angle of $22\frac{1}{2}°$.

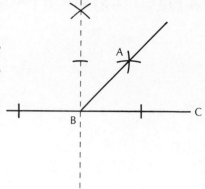

ANGLES OF 60°, 30°, 15° . . .

i) Draw a line AB.
ii) With compass points the length of AB apart, place the point on A and draw an arc.
iii) Keeping the compass points the length of AB apart, place the point on B and draw an arc to meet the first arc at C.
$C\hat{A}B = 60°$ (because ABC is an equilateral triangle).
iv) Bisect $C\hat{A}B$ for an angle of 30°.
v) Bisect again for an angle of 15°.

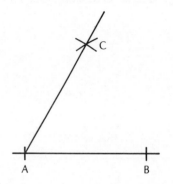

22 LOCI

The *locus* (plural *loci*) of a point P is the path that it could take if moving while satisfying certain conditions. In the examples given, P is the moving point and A, B and C are fixed points.

EQUIDISTANT FROM TWO POINTS

If PA must equal PB then P can be anywhere on QR, the perpendicular bisector of AB.

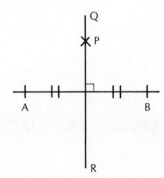

EQUIDISTANT FROM TWO LINES

If P must be equidistant from AB and BC then P can be anywhere on BQ, the bisector of the angle between AB and BC.

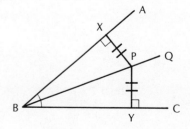

121

A FIXED DISTANCE FROM A FIXED POINT

If PA must be constant then P can be anywhere on the circumference of the circle centre A, radius PA.

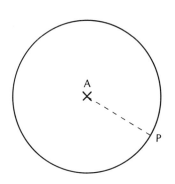

A FIXED DISTANCE FROM A FIXED LINE

If P must be a constant distance, h from line AB then P can be anywhere on a line parallel to AB and distance h from it or on a semicircle, radius h, at A, or a semicircle, radius h at B.

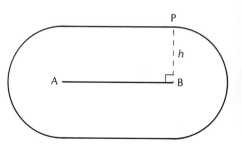

ANGLE FORMED BY JOINING TO TWO FIXED POINTS EQUALS 90°

If $A\hat{P}B$ must be 90° then P must be on the circumference of a circle, centre the mid-point of AB and radius AB/2.

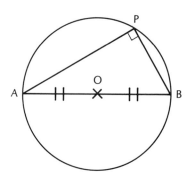

LESS THAN A FIXED DISTANCE FROM A FIXED POINT

The locus of a point may also be an area. If PA must be less than a constant, r, then P may be anywhere inside the circle, centre A radius r.

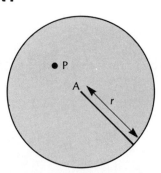

ANGLE FORMED BY JOINING THE POINT TO TWO FIXED POINTS

If $\hat{APB}$ must be a fixed angle θ then P may lie anywhere on the circumference of two circle segments which pass through A, B and P.

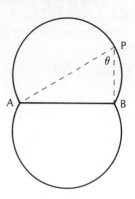

THREE-DIMENSIONAL LOCI

Examples

a) The locus of a point which moves so that it is a fixed distance from a line is a cylinder.

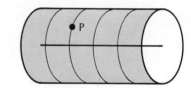

b) The locus of a point, P, which moves so that $\hat{PAB} = \theta°$ is a cone.

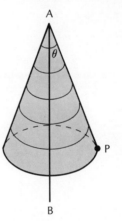

c) The locus of a point, P, which moves so that PA is a constant is a sphere.

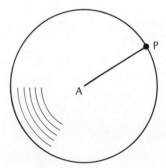

d) The locus of a point which moves so that the perpendicular distance from a plane is constant, d, is two planes parallel to the first plane and a distance d away.

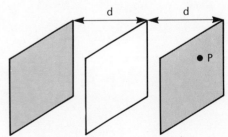

23 SYMMETRY

LINE SYMMETRY

A figure is *symmetrical* if it can be *folded* in half so that one side lies exactly on top of the other side. The fold line is the *line of symmetry*.

A square has four lines of symmetry

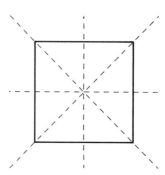

A rectangle has two lines of symmetry

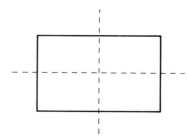

This figure has *no* lines of symmetry

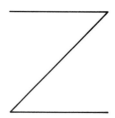

Examples

If AB is the line of symmetry complete each diagram.

a)

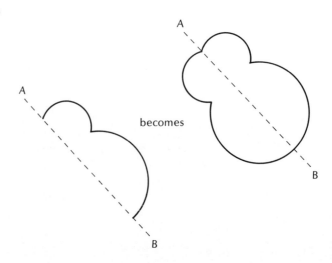

becomes

b)

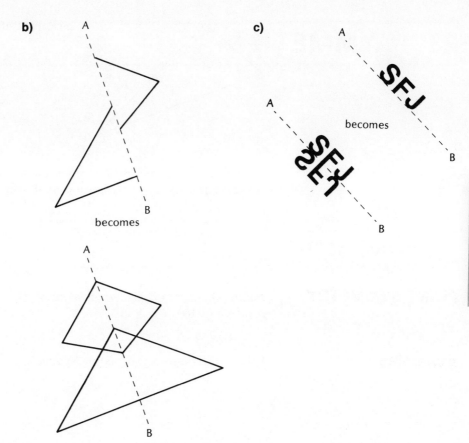

becomes

c)

becomes

ROTATIONAL SYMMETRY

A figure has *rotational symmetry* if, when rotated about a fixed point, the rotated figure looks identical to the original in at least one position before it has been rotated through a complete turn. The number of different positions giving an identical figure to the original is the *order of rotational symmetry* of the figure.

Examples

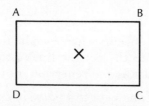

has order of rotational symmetry two

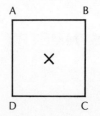

has order of rotational symmetry four

The two positions are:

The four positions are:

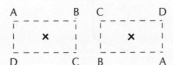

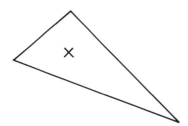

has order of rotational symmetry one.

The order *must* be at least one since a figure will always fit on top of itself. However in this case the figure is said to have *no rotational symmetry*.

POINT SYMMETRY

Point symmetry occurs when a plane shape appears the same after a rotation of 180°.

Examples

This parallelogram has point symmetry.

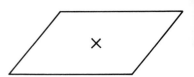

This shape also has point symmetry.

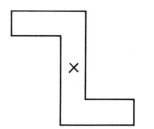

PLANE SYMMETRY

Plane symmetry occurs when a model is cut in half so that on each surface perpendicular to the cut the line of the cut acts as a line of symmetry. (Each half looks like a 'reflection' of the other half.)

The surface of each cut is a *plane of symmetry*.

Example

A cube has nine planes of symmetry.

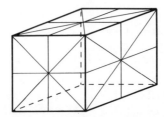

AXIS OF ROTATION

A solid figure may also have symmetry about an *axis of rotation*.

The cross-section of the solid has rotational symmetry.

24 MATRICES

A matrix is the presentation of information in an orderly manner with the *elements* arranged in *rows* ($\equiv$) and *columns* (||||).

Example

The results of a football tournament between 4 teams (A, B, C, D):

$$\begin{array}{c} \\ \text{Win} \\ \text{Lose} \\ \text{Draw} \end{array} \begin{array}{cccc} \text{A} & \text{B} & \text{C} & \text{D} \end{array} \\ \begin{pmatrix} 2 & 1 & 0 & 1 \\ 1 & 0 & 2 & 1 \\ 0 & 2 & 1 & 1 \end{pmatrix}$$

ORDER OF A MATRIX

The order of a matrix describes the arrangement of the elements. It is the number of rows × the number of columns.

Examples

a) $\begin{pmatrix} 2 & 4 \\ 6 & 1 \end{pmatrix}$ has order 2 × 2

b) $\begin{pmatrix} 1 \\ 7 \end{pmatrix}$ has order 2 × 1

c) $\begin{pmatrix} 5 & -3 & 8 & 4 \\ 7 & -4 & 9 & -6 \end{pmatrix}$ has order 2 × 4

ADDITION AND SUBTRACTION

Matrices can only be added (or subtracted) if they are of the same order. Add (or subtract) elements in corresponding positions.

Examples

a) $\begin{pmatrix} 2 & 4 \\ 6 & 1 \end{pmatrix} + \begin{pmatrix} 4 & 3 \\ 1 & 7 \end{pmatrix} = \begin{pmatrix} 6 & 7 \\ 7 & 8 \end{pmatrix}$

b) $\begin{pmatrix} 2 & 4 \\ 6 & 1 \end{pmatrix} + \begin{pmatrix} 9 & 7 & 4 \\ 2 & 3 & 6 \end{pmatrix}$ *not possible*

c) $\begin{pmatrix} 3 & 9 & 6 \\ 5 & 2 & 5 \end{pmatrix} - \begin{pmatrix} 2 & 3 & 2 \\ 1 & 5 & 6 \end{pmatrix} = \begin{pmatrix} 1 & 6 & 4 \\ 4 & -3 & -1 \end{pmatrix}$

127

MULTIPLICATION

Matrices can only be multiplied if they obey the *domino* rule.

A matrix of order $x \times y$ can only be multiplied by one of $y \times z$, i.e. the number of columns of the first matrix must equal the number of rows of the second matrix. The order of the answer will be $x \times z$.

$x \times [y \quad y] \times z$ gives an answer of order $x \times z$

Example

A matrix of order 2×3 multiplied by a matrix of order 3×4 gives a matrix of order 2×4.

$$2 \times [3 \quad 3] \times 4 \qquad\qquad \text{order of answer} = 2 \times 4$$

must be the same
for the multiplication
to be possible

When multiplying, *rows* are taken from the first matrix and *columns* are taken from the second matrix. Elements are paired off and multiplied, and the results then added.

For multiplication of 2×2 matrices

$$\begin{pmatrix} a & b \\ c & d \end{pmatrix}\begin{pmatrix} A & B \\ C & D \end{pmatrix} = \begin{pmatrix} aA + bC & aB + bD \\ cA + dC & cB + dD \end{pmatrix}$$

Examples

a) $\begin{pmatrix} 2 & 4 \\ 6 & 1 \end{pmatrix}\begin{pmatrix} 4 & 3 \\ 1 & 7 \end{pmatrix} = \begin{pmatrix} 2 \times 4 + 4 \times 1 & 2 \times 3 + 4 \times 7 \\ 6 \times 4 + 1 \times 1 & 6 \times 3 + 1 \times 7 \end{pmatrix}$

$2 \times [2 \quad 2] \times 2 = \begin{pmatrix} 12 & 34 \\ 25 & 25 \end{pmatrix}$

b) $\begin{pmatrix} 4 & 3 \\ 1 & 7 \end{pmatrix}\begin{pmatrix} 2 & 4 \\ 6 & 1 \end{pmatrix} = \begin{pmatrix} 4 \times 2 + 3 \times 6 & 4 \times 4 + 3 \times 1 \\ 1 \times 2 + 7 \times 6 & 1 \times 4 + 7 \times 1 \end{pmatrix}$

$2 \times [2 \quad 2] \times 2 = \begin{pmatrix} 26 & 19 \\ 44 & 11 \end{pmatrix}$

N.B.   When multiplying matrices, **A** and **B**, in general $\mathbf{AB} \neq \mathbf{BA}$.

c) $\begin{pmatrix} 1 & 3 & 4 & 2 \\ 1 & 7 & 9 & 4 \\ 3 & 2 & 1 & 7 \end{pmatrix}\begin{pmatrix} 2 & 9 \\ 4 & 6 \\ 1 & 2 \end{pmatrix}$ is *not possible*

$3 \times [4 \quad 3] \times 2$

DETERMINANT

$|\mathbf{A}|$ means the determinant of matrix **A** (sometimes written det **A**).

$$\text{If}\quad \mathbf{A} = \begin{pmatrix} a & b \\ c & d \end{pmatrix}\quad \text{then}\quad |\mathbf{A}| = \begin{vmatrix} a & b \\ c & d \end{vmatrix}$$

$$= ad - bc$$

Example

If $\mathbf{A} = \begin{pmatrix} 2 & 4 \\ 1 & 6 \end{pmatrix}$ then

$|\mathbf{A}| = 2 \times 6 - 1 \times 4$

$= 8$

In a transformation $|\mathbf{A}|$ is the *area factor*.

INVERSE

$\mathbf{A}^{-1}$ is the inverse of $\mathbf{A}$, where

$\mathbf{A} \times \mathbf{A}^{-1}$ = the unit (or identity) matrix

$$= \begin{pmatrix} 1 & 0 \\ 0 & 1 \end{pmatrix} \quad \text{for } 2 \times 2 \text{ matrices (usually denoted by } \mathbf{I})$$

If $|\mathbf{A}| = 0$ then the matrix is *singular* and does not have an inverse.

If $|\mathbf{A}| \neq 0$ and $\mathbf{A} = \begin{pmatrix} a & b \\ c & d \end{pmatrix}$ then $\mathbf{A}^{-1} = \dfrac{1}{ad - bc} \begin{pmatrix} d & -b \\ -c & a \end{pmatrix}$.

Example

$$\mathbf{A} = \begin{pmatrix} 2 & 4 \\ 6 & 1 \end{pmatrix}$$

$$\mathbf{A}^{-1} = \frac{1}{2 \times 1 \; - \; 4 \times 6} \begin{pmatrix} 1 & -4 \\ -6 & 2 \end{pmatrix}$$

$$= \frac{1}{-22} \begin{pmatrix} 1 & -4 \\ -6 & 2 \end{pmatrix}$$

$$= \begin{pmatrix} \dfrac{1}{-22} & \dfrac{-4}{-22} \\ \\ \dfrac{-6}{-22} & \dfrac{2}{-22} \end{pmatrix}$$

$$= \begin{pmatrix} -\dfrac{1}{22} & \dfrac{2}{11} \\ \\ \dfrac{3}{11} & -\dfrac{1}{11} \end{pmatrix}$$

Check that $\mathbf{A} \times \mathbf{A}^{-1} = \begin{pmatrix} 1 & 0 \\ 0 & 1 \end{pmatrix}$.

The inverse of a matrix can be used to solve simultaneous equations: see **Algebra** notes.

TRANSPOSE

The transpose of a matrix has the rows changed into columns and columns changed into rows.

If $\mathbf{A} = \begin{pmatrix} a & b \\ c & d \\ e & f \end{pmatrix}$ then the transpose of $\mathbf{A}$ (sometimes written $\mathbf{A}^{T}$)

is $\begin{pmatrix} a & c & e \\ b & d & f \end{pmatrix}$.

Matrices can be used to describe *networks* or *relations*.

NETWORKS

A network is a diagram described not by size or shape, but by the number of

i) nodes, junctions, vertices: the points at which arcs meet or end
ii) arcs, branches: lines joining two nodes
iii) regions: areas enclosed by arcs

N.B. The outside counts as a region.

Example

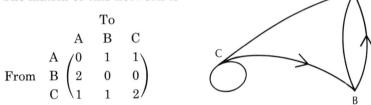

This network has

3 nodes = A, B, C
4 arcs = AB, BA, AC, BC
3 regions = area enclosed by AB and BA; area enclosed by AB, BC and AC; the outside

Euler's rule states that for every network

Number of nodes + Number of regions − Number of arcs = 2

A one-stage route matrix describes the number of direct routes between one node and another of a network. This matrix squared gives the two-stage route matrix which describes the number of routes from one node, via a second node, to another node.

Examples

a) The matrix of this network is

$$\begin{array}{c} \\ \text{From} \end{array} \begin{array}{cc} & \text{To} \\ & \begin{array}{ccc} \text{A} & \text{B} & \text{C} \end{array} \\ \begin{array}{c} \text{A} \\ \text{B} \\ \text{C} \end{array} & \left(\begin{array}{ccc} 0 & 1 & 1 \\ 2 & 0 & 0 \\ 1 & 1 & 2 \end{array}\right) \end{array}$$

N.B.   The 'ring road' at C gives two routes from C to C. The one-way route from B to A means that from A to B there is one route but from B to A there are two routes.

b)

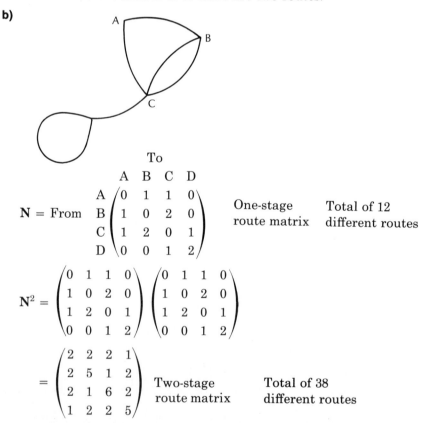

$$\mathbf{N} = \begin{array}{c} \\ \text{From} \end{array} \begin{array}{c} \begin{array}{cccc} \text{A} & \text{B} & \text{C} & \text{D} \end{array} \\ \begin{array}{c} \text{A} \\ \text{B} \\ \text{C} \\ \text{D} \end{array} \left(\begin{array}{cccc} 0 & 1 & 1 & 0 \\ 1 & 0 & 2 & 0 \\ 1 & 2 & 0 & 1 \\ 0 & 0 & 1 & 2 \end{array}\right) \end{array}$$

One-stage route matrix Total of 12 different routes

$$\mathbf{N}^2 = \left(\begin{array}{cccc} 0 & 1 & 1 & 0 \\ 1 & 0 & 2 & 0 \\ 1 & 2 & 0 & 1 \\ 0 & 0 & 1 & 2 \end{array}\right) \left(\begin{array}{cccc} 0 & 1 & 1 & 0 \\ 1 & 0 & 2 & 0 \\ 1 & 2 & 0 & 1 \\ 0 & 0 & 1 & 2 \end{array}\right)$$

$$= \left(\begin{array}{cccc} 2 & 2 & 2 & 1 \\ 2 & 5 & 1 & 2 \\ 2 & 1 & 6 & 2 \\ 1 & 2 & 2 & 5 \end{array}\right)$$

Two-stage route matrix Total of 38 different routes

The elements of $\mathbf{N}^2$ give the number of two-stage routes, but the details of the routes must be found by reference to the network. The first element of $\mathbf{N}^2$ shows that there are 2 two-stage routes from A to A, namely A to A via B and A to A via C.

INCIDENCE MATRICES

These connect two of the three properties of a matrix, e.g. they may show which nodes are in contact with which regions, or which arcs touch which nodes. If the Incidence matrix shows the connection between arcs and regions, an entry of 1 in the matrix means that an arc touches a region, and an entry of 0 means that it does not touch a region.

Examples

a) Node A is in contact with regions p and q.
Node B is in contact with regions p, q and r.
Node C is in contact with regions p, q and r.

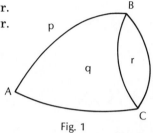

Fig. 1

For nodes incident on regions the matrix is of the form

$$\text{Nodes} \begin{pmatrix} & \text{Regions} & \\ & & \end{pmatrix}$$

The incidence matrix would be

$$\begin{array}{c} & p & q & r \\ A & \begin{pmatrix} 1 & 1 & 0 \\ B & 1 & 1 & 1 \\ C & 1 & 1 & 1 \end{pmatrix} \end{array}$$

b)

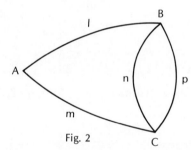

Fig. 2

Arc l touches nodes A and B.
Arc m touches nodes A and C.
Arc n touches nodes B and C.
Arc p touches nodes B and C.
For arcs incident on nodes the matrix will be of the form

$$\text{Arcs} \begin{pmatrix} & \text{Nodes} & \\ & & \end{pmatrix}$$

The incidence matrix would be

$$\begin{array}{c} & A & B & C \\ l & \begin{pmatrix} 1 & 1 & 0 \\ m & 1 & 0 & 1 \\ n & 0 & 1 & 1 \\ p & 0 & 1 & 1 \end{pmatrix} \end{array}$$

This shows which nodes each arc joins

131

TRANSFORMATIONS

Transformations can be represented by matrices. The transformed points can be found by pre-multiplying by these matrices

Transformation	Matrix	Transformation	Matrix
Reflection in x-axis	$\begin{pmatrix} 1 & 0 \\ 0 & -1 \end{pmatrix}$	Reflection in y-axis	$\begin{pmatrix} -1 & 0 \\ 0 & 1 \end{pmatrix}$
Reflection in $y = x$	$\begin{pmatrix} 0 & 1 \\ 1 & 0 \end{pmatrix}$	Reflection in $y = -x$	$\begin{pmatrix} 0 & -1 \\ -1 & 0 \end{pmatrix}$
Rotation of 90°, centre (0, 0)	$\begin{pmatrix} 0 & -1 \\ 1 & 0 \end{pmatrix}$	Rotation of 180° centre (0, 0)	$\begin{pmatrix} -1 & 0 \\ 0 & -1 \end{pmatrix}$
Rotation of −90°, centre (0, 0)	$\begin{pmatrix} 0 & -1 \\ -1 & 0 \end{pmatrix}$	Shear, invariant line the x-axis	$\begin{pmatrix} 1 & k \\ 0 & 1 \end{pmatrix}$
Enlargement, scale factor k, centre of enlargement (0, 0)	$\begin{pmatrix} k & 0 \\ 0 & k \end{pmatrix}$	Identity transformation (leaves shapes unaltered)	$\begin{pmatrix} 1 & 0 \\ 0 & 1 \end{pmatrix}$
Stretch parallel to the x-axis	$\begin{pmatrix} k & 0 \\ 0 & 1 \end{pmatrix}$		

N.B.   A positive rotation is *anticlockwise*.
A negative rotation is *clockwise*.

Example

DEFG is a rectangle with D(2, 3), E(2, 7), F(4, 7), G(4, 3).

Pre-multiply by $\begin{pmatrix} -1 & 0 \\ 0 & 1 \end{pmatrix}$ to transform to D′E′F′G′.

$$\begin{pmatrix} -1 & 0 \\ 0 & 1 \end{pmatrix}\begin{pmatrix} 2 & 2 & 4 & 4 \\ 3 & 7 & 7 & 3 \end{pmatrix} = \begin{pmatrix} -2 & -2 & -4 & -4 \\ 3 & 7 & 7 & 3 \end{pmatrix}$$

So D′ has coordinates (−2, 3), E′(−2, 7), F′(−4, 7) and G′(−4, 3).

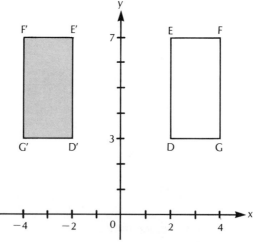

The inverse transformation is given by the inverse of $\begin{pmatrix} -1 & 0 \\ 0 & 1 \end{pmatrix}$ which (since *all* reflections are self-inverse) is also $\begin{pmatrix} -1 & 0 \\ 0 & 1 \end{pmatrix}$.

Check: $\begin{pmatrix} -1 & 0 \\ 0 & 1 \end{pmatrix}\begin{pmatrix} -1 & 0 \\ 0 & 1 \end{pmatrix} = \begin{pmatrix} 1 & 0 \\ 0 & 1 \end{pmatrix}$

25 TRANSFORMATIONS

In the following transformations, the figure can be moved by moving the vertices first and then joining them to complete the figure.

TRANSLATION (SLIDE)

No change in size or shape. Instruction for movement is given in a vector $\begin{pmatrix} a \\ b \end{pmatrix}$ where a is the distance to move along, and b is the distance to move up or down.

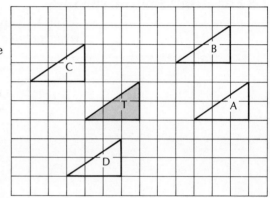

Examples

If T is the original triangle,

the translation to A is $\begin{pmatrix} 6 \\ 0 \end{pmatrix}$

the translation to B is $\begin{pmatrix} 5 \\ 3 \end{pmatrix}$

the translation to C is $\begin{pmatrix} -3 \\ 2 \end{pmatrix}$

the translation to D is $\begin{pmatrix} -1 \\ -3 \end{pmatrix}$

REFLECTION (MIRROR IMAGE)

No change in size or shape.

Instruction for movement is given by the equation of the mirror line.

The image is as far away on one side of the mirror line as the object is on the other.

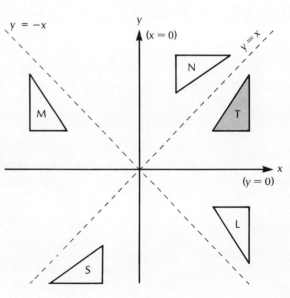

Examples

If T is the original triangle,

the reflection in the x-axis (the line $y = 0$) is L

the reflection in the y-axis (the line $x = 0$) is M

the reflection in the line $y = x$ is N

the reflection in the line $y = -x$ is S

To construct the mirror line

Join AA′ and construct the perpendicular bisector of this line (see *constructions* notes).

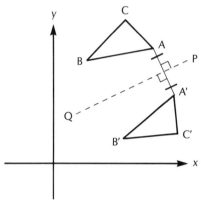

PQ is the mirror line.

ROTATION (TURN)

No change in size or shape.

Instructions for movement are given by the centre of rotation, and the angle of turn.

Example

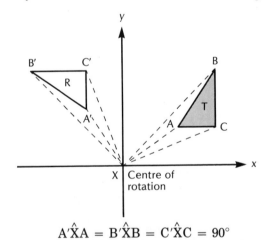

$$A'\hat{X}A = B'\hat{X}B = C'\hat{X}C = 90°$$

N.B.   an *anticlockwise* turn is positive, and a *clockwise* turn is negative.

If T is the original triangle then the image of T after a rotation of 90° about the centre of rotation X is R.

To draw R join A to X and turn AX through 90° anticlockwise for the position of A′X, so that $A\hat{X}A' = 90°$ and A′X = AX. Repeat for B and C, to rotate BX and CX on to B′X and C′X.

To find the centre of rotation

Construct the perpendicular bisectors of AA′ and BB′. The centre of rotation is the point at which these lines intersect.

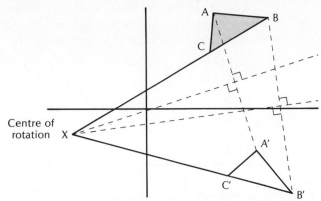

The angle of rotation is then $A\hat{X}A'$ or $B\hat{X}B'$ or $C\hat{X}C'$. All three angles are equal.

ENLARGEMENT (SIMILAR FIGURES)

The shape remains the same, but each length is multiplied by the scale factor. The enlargement is *similar* to the original.

N.B. The angles remain the same.

To decrease the size, the scale factor will be between zero and one.

A negative scale factor means that all vertices will be moved to the other side of the centre away from their original position.

Instructions for movement are given as a centre of enlargement and a scale factor.

Examples

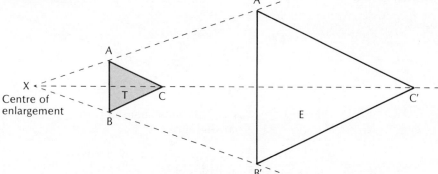

If T is the original triangle, the enlargement, scale factor 3, with centre of enlargement X will be E.

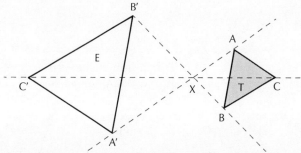

If T is the original triangle, the enlargement, scale factor −2, with centre of enlargement X, will be E.

The area factor of an enlargement is (the scale factor)^2.

STRETCH (PULL)

The shape is pulled out in only one direction.

Instructions for movement are an invariant line and a stretch factor.

The *invariant line* undergoes no change during the transformation, and the stretch factor is the number by which lengths are multiplied in a direction parallel to the invariant line.

Examples

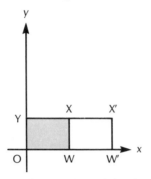

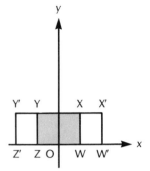

OYXW is the original figure.

OY is the invariant line, the stretch factor is 2, the transformed figure is OW′X′Y.

OYXW is the original figure.

OW is the invariant line, the stretch factor is 2, the transformed figure is OWX′Y′.

XYZW is the original figure.

The y-axis is the invariant line, the stretch factor is 2, the transformed figure is X′Y′Z′W′.

SHEAR (PUSH OVER)

The shape is altered, but the area remains the same.

A line is invariant and the rest of the figure is 'pushed' in a direction parallel to this line.

Examples

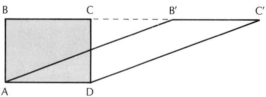

AD is the invariant line. The image of B is B′. The image of C is C′.

A rectangle is sheared into a parallelogram.

(Imagine a pack of cards being pushed over).

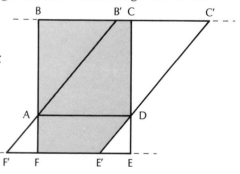

A triangle is sheared into a triangle.

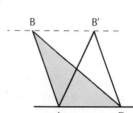

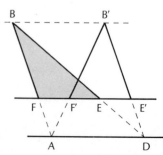

TRANSFORMATION MATRICES

Some transformations such as rotation, reflection, enlargement, shear and stretch can be described by 2×2 matrices (see notes on **Matrices**). Translation is described by a vector (a 2×1 matrix).

The *inverse* transformation (which will move shapes back to the original shape, size and position) is described by the inverse of the given matrix.

If a figure is transformed to a point or a line then the matrix has no inverse. This will be shown by the matrix having a determinant of zero. The matrix is then said to be *singular*.

Example

$$\mathbf{M} = \begin{pmatrix} 3 & 6 \\ 2 & 4 \end{pmatrix}$$

$$|\mathbf{M}| = 3 \times 4 - 6 \times 2$$

$$= 0$$

$\mathbf{M}$ has no inverse and so is a singular matrix.

AREA FACTOR

If a figure is transformed by the matrix $\mathbf{M}$, then the determinant of $\mathbf{M}$ is the area factor.

$$\text{Area of transformed figure} = |\mathbf{M}| \times \text{Area of original figure.}$$

COMBINED TRANSFORMATIONS

If $\mathbf{M}$ and $\mathbf{N}$ are the matrices representing different transformations then the transformation represented by $\mathbf{MN}$ means transform by $\mathbf{N}$ first and then by $\mathbf{M}$.

The inverse of $\mathbf{MN} = (\mathbf{MN})^{-1}$

$$= \mathbf{N}^{-1}\mathbf{M}^{-1}$$

Transform by the inverse of $\mathbf{M}$ first then by the inverse of $\mathbf{N}$ to move back to the original figure.

Example

$$\mathbf{M} = \begin{pmatrix} 2 & 1 \\ 4 & 3 \end{pmatrix}, \qquad \mathbf{N} = \begin{pmatrix} 2 & 0 \\ 0 & 2 \end{pmatrix} \qquad \text{So} \qquad \mathbf{MN} = \begin{pmatrix} 2 & 1 \\ 4 & 3 \end{pmatrix}\begin{pmatrix} 2 & 0 \\ 0 & 2 \end{pmatrix}$$

$$\mathbf{M}^{-1} = \frac{1}{2}\begin{pmatrix} 3 & -1 \\ -4 & 2 \end{pmatrix}, \quad \mathbf{N}^{-1} = \begin{pmatrix} \frac{1}{2} & 0 \\ 0 & \frac{1}{2} \end{pmatrix} \qquad\qquad = \begin{pmatrix} 4 & 2 \\ 8 & 6 \end{pmatrix}$$

$$= \begin{pmatrix} 1\frac{1}{2} & -\frac{1}{2} \\ -2 & 1 \end{pmatrix}$$

So $(\mathbf{MN})^{-1} = \mathbf{N}^{-1}\mathbf{M}^{-1}$

$$= \begin{pmatrix} \frac{1}{2} & 0 \\ 0 & \frac{1}{2} \end{pmatrix}\begin{pmatrix} 1\frac{1}{2} & -\frac{1}{2} \\ -2 & 1 \end{pmatrix}$$

$$= \begin{pmatrix} \frac{3}{4} & -\frac{1}{4} \\ -1 & \frac{1}{2} \end{pmatrix}$$

Check that $(\mathbf{MN}) \times (\mathbf{MN})^{-1} = \begin{pmatrix} 1 & 0 \\ 0 & 1 \end{pmatrix}$.

26 VECTORS

A *vector* is a quantity with magnitude (length) and direction.

AB means the distance from A to B.

$\overrightarrow{AB}$ or **a** is a vector. It could represent the *journey* from A to B, or a *force* acting along the line AB or any other quantity with direction and size.

When the direction is reversed the vector changes sign.

$$\overrightarrow{BA} = -\overrightarrow{AB} = -\mathbf{a}$$

A vector can be expressed as a 2×1 matrix, with the top number representing distance along and the bottom number representing distance up or down.

Examples

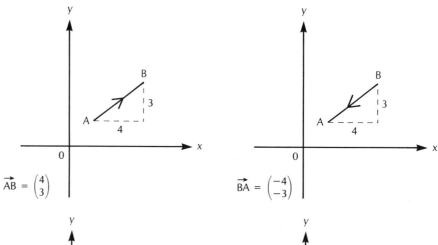

$$\overrightarrow{AB} = \begin{pmatrix} 4 \\ 3 \end{pmatrix} \qquad\qquad \overrightarrow{BA} = \begin{pmatrix} -4 \\ -3 \end{pmatrix}$$

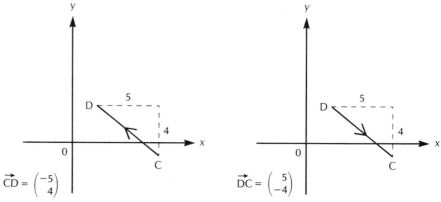

$$\overrightarrow{CD} = \begin{pmatrix} -5 \\ 4 \end{pmatrix} \qquad\qquad \overrightarrow{DC} = \begin{pmatrix} 5 \\ -4 \end{pmatrix}$$

The *magnitude* is the length of the vector and is written as $|\overrightarrow{AB}|$.

If $\overrightarrow{AB}$ is $\begin{pmatrix} a \\ b \end{pmatrix}$ then the magnitude (by Pythagoras) is

$$|\overrightarrow{AB}| = \sqrt{a^2 + b^2}$$

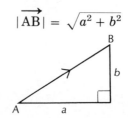

Example

$$\overrightarrow{AB} = \begin{pmatrix} 3 \\ 4 \end{pmatrix}$$

$$|\overrightarrow{AB}| = \sqrt{3^2 + 4^2}$$

$$= \sqrt{25}$$

$$= 5$$

$$|\overrightarrow{AB}| = |\overrightarrow{BA}|$$

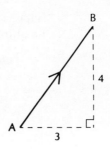

The *direction* is defined as the angle that the vector makes with the positive horizontal.

Examples

$$\overrightarrow{AB} = \begin{pmatrix} 3 \\ 4 \end{pmatrix}$$

Direction = a

$$= \arctan \tfrac{4}{3}$$

$$\approx 53°$$

$$\overrightarrow{CD} = \begin{pmatrix} -3 \\ 4 \end{pmatrix}$$

Direction = d

$$= 180° - c$$

$$= 180° - \arctan \tfrac{4}{3}$$

$$\approx 180° - 53°$$

$$= 127°$$

Equal vectors are equal in length and parallel.

Multiplication by a scalar (by a number) alters the length of the vector. If the number is positive, the direction is the same. If it is negative, the direction is reversed

Examples

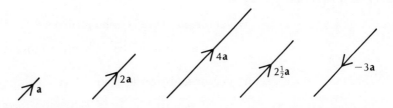

ADDITION AND SUBTRACTION

Suppose ABCD is a parallelogram with $\overrightarrow{AB} = \mathbf{a}$ and $\overrightarrow{AD} = \mathbf{b}$. Since opposite sides are equal and parallel $\overrightarrow{DC} = \mathbf{a}$ and $\overrightarrow{BC} = \mathbf{b}$.

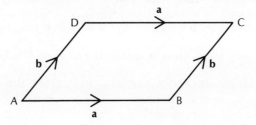

139

Suppose the vectors represented journeys. The journey starting at A and finishing at C could be A to C direct, or A to C via B, or A to C via D.

Hence $\overrightarrow{AC} = \overrightarrow{AB} + \overrightarrow{BC}$ and $\overrightarrow{AC} = \overrightarrow{AD} + \overrightarrow{DC}$

$\overrightarrow{AC} = \mathbf{a} + \mathbf{b}$ and $\overrightarrow{AC} = \mathbf{b} + \mathbf{a}$

$\therefore \quad \mathbf{a} + \mathbf{b} = \mathbf{b} + \mathbf{a}$

$\overrightarrow{DB} = \overrightarrow{DA} + \overrightarrow{AB}$ an $\overrightarrow{DB} = \overrightarrow{DC} + \overrightarrow{CB}$

$\overrightarrow{DB} = -\mathbf{b} + \mathbf{a}$ and $\overrightarrow{DB} = \mathbf{a} - \mathbf{b}$

A *position vector* is a vector that starts at the origin.

Example

If P is the point (3, 4) the position vector $\overrightarrow{OP}$ is represented by $\begin{pmatrix} 3 \\ 4 \end{pmatrix}$. $\overrightarrow{OQ}$ is the position vector $\begin{pmatrix} -2 \\ 5 \end{pmatrix}$ if Q has coordinates $(-2, 5)$.

$\overrightarrow{PQ} = \overrightarrow{PO} + \overrightarrow{OQ}$

$= \begin{pmatrix} -3 \\ -4 \end{pmatrix} + \begin{pmatrix} -2 \\ 5 \end{pmatrix}$

$= \begin{pmatrix} -5 \\ 1 \end{pmatrix}$

PROPERTIES OF VECTORS

i) vector addition is commutative

$\mathbf{a} + \mathbf{b} = \mathbf{b} + \mathbf{a}$ for all vectors **a** and **b**.

ii) vector addition is associative

$\mathbf{a} + (\mathbf{b} + \mathbf{c}) = (\mathbf{a} + \mathbf{b}) + \mathbf{c}$ for all vectors **a**, **b** and **c**.

iii) scalar multiplication is distributive over addition

$2(\mathbf{a} + \mathbf{b}) = 2\mathbf{a} + 2\mathbf{b}$

$\frac{1}{3}(\mathbf{c} + 2\mathbf{d}) = \frac{1}{3}\mathbf{c} + \frac{2}{3}\mathbf{d}$

iv) $\mathbf{a} = \mathbf{b} \Rightarrow |\mathbf{a}| = |\mathbf{b}|$ and **a** is a parallel to **b**.

v) $h\mathbf{a} = k\mathbf{b} \Rightarrow$ **a** is parallel to **b** or $h = 0$ and $k = 0$.

N.B. iv) and v) can be used to prove lines are equal in length or parallel and to show whether points occupy the same position (are coincident).

Examples

a) i)

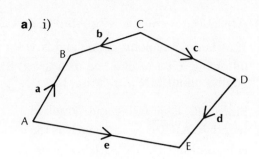

$$\overrightarrow{AE} = \overrightarrow{AB} + \overrightarrow{BC} + \overrightarrow{CD} + \overrightarrow{DE}$$

$$e = a - b + c + d$$

ii)

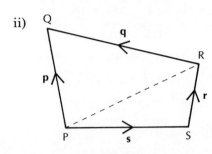

$$\overrightarrow{PR} = p - q$$
$$= s + r$$

b) Find $\overrightarrow{AD}$ if $\overrightarrow{AB} = \begin{pmatrix} 2 \\ 6 \end{pmatrix}$, $\overrightarrow{BC} = \begin{pmatrix} -2 \\ 3 \end{pmatrix}$, $\overrightarrow{DC} = \begin{pmatrix} 1 \\ -2 \end{pmatrix}$.

$$\overrightarrow{AD} = \overrightarrow{AB} + \overrightarrow{BC} + \overrightarrow{CD} \quad \text{but} \quad \overrightarrow{CD} = -\overrightarrow{DC} = \begin{pmatrix} -1 \\ 2 \end{pmatrix}$$

$$\overrightarrow{AD} = \begin{pmatrix} 2 \\ 6 \end{pmatrix} + \begin{pmatrix} -2 \\ 3 \end{pmatrix} + \begin{pmatrix} -1 \\ 2 \end{pmatrix}$$

$$= \begin{pmatrix} -1 \\ 11 \end{pmatrix}$$

c) If $\overrightarrow{OA} = a$, $\overrightarrow{OB} = b$, $\overrightarrow{OC} = c$ and $\overrightarrow{OD} = d$ express the following in terms of **a**, **b**, **c** and **d**   i) $\overrightarrow{DB}$ ii) $\overrightarrow{AD}$ iii) $\overrightarrow{BC}$

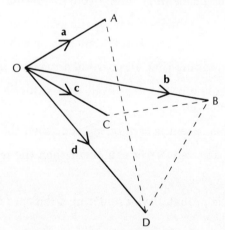

i) $\overrightarrow{DB} = -d + b = b - d$

ii) $\overrightarrow{AD} = -a + d = d - a$

iii) $\overrightarrow{BC} = -b + c = c - b$

d) If $\overrightarrow{OA} = a$, $\overrightarrow{OB} = b$, $\overrightarrow{OC} = 2a$, and $\overrightarrow{OD} = 3b$ find, in terms of **a** and **b**
i) $\overrightarrow{DB}$ ii) $\overrightarrow{AD}$ iii) $\overrightarrow{BO}$.

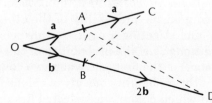

i) $\overrightarrow{DB} = -2b$

ii) $\overrightarrow{AD} = -a + 3b$

iii) $\overrightarrow{BC} = -b + 2a$

141

e) ABCD is a rectangle with $\overrightarrow{AB} = \mathbf{a}$, and $\overrightarrow{BC} = \mathbf{b}$.

If M is the mid-point of AD and N is the mid-point of CD express the following in terms of $\mathbf{a}$ and $\mathbf{b}$: i) $\overrightarrow{BN}$ ii) $\overrightarrow{BM}$ iii) $\overrightarrow{MN}$, and say what this implies about MN in relation to AC:

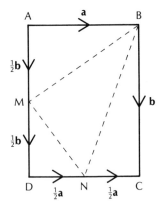

Since DC is parallel and equal in length to AB, $\overrightarrow{DC} = \mathbf{a}$. Since N is the mid-point of CD, $\overrightarrow{DN} = \overrightarrow{NC} = \frac{1}{2}\mathbf{a}$. Similarly $\overrightarrow{AM} = \overrightarrow{MD} = \frac{1}{2}\mathbf{b}$.

i) $\overrightarrow{BN} = \overrightarrow{BC} = \overrightarrow{CN}$

$\qquad = \mathbf{b} - \frac{1}{2}\mathbf{a}$

ii) $\overrightarrow{BM} = \overrightarrow{BA} = \overrightarrow{AM}$

$\qquad = -\mathbf{a} + \frac{1}{2}\mathbf{b}$

iii) $\overrightarrow{MN} = \overrightarrow{MD} + \overrightarrow{DN}$

$\qquad = \frac{1}{2}\mathbf{b} + \frac{1}{2}\mathbf{a}$

$\qquad = \frac{1}{2}(\mathbf{a} + \mathbf{b})$

$\overrightarrow{AC} = \overrightarrow{AB} + \overrightarrow{BC}$

$\qquad = \mathbf{a} + \mathbf{b}$

$\therefore \ \overrightarrow{MN} = \frac{1}{2}\overrightarrow{AC} \ \Rightarrow \ MN = \frac{1}{2}AC$ and MN is parallel to AC.

27 PROBABILITY

'Choosing a king' or 'Throwing a six' are examples of *events*.

The probability of an event occurring

$$= \frac{\text{Number of ways the event can occur successfully}}{\text{Total number of possible outcomes}}$$

providing that all possible outcomes are equally likely.

Probability is expressed as a value between one and zero, usually as a fraction.

If an event is *certain* to occur then the probability is 1.

If an event *never* can occur then the probability is 0.

Example

The probability of selecting a red card from a normal pack $= \dfrac{26}{52}$

$$= \frac{1}{2}$$

Events are *independent* if the probability of one event occurring has no bearing on the probability of the other event occurring, e.g. throwing a dice and selecting a card are independent events. Otherwise events are *conditional*, i.e. the probability of the second event is conditional on the outcome of the first, e.g. when two counters are selected without replacement the probability of a given colour for the second counter is conditional on which colour was selected first.

'OR'

If A and B are independent events then the probability of A *or* B occurring is given by

$$p(A \text{ OR } B) = p(A) + p(B),$$

Example

Out of 6 red, 2 blue and 8 green counters, what is the probability of selecting a red or a green one?

$$p(\text{red}) = \frac{6}{16} \qquad p(\text{green}) = \frac{8}{16}$$

$$p(\text{red or green}) = \frac{6}{16} + \frac{8}{16}$$

$$= \frac{14}{16}$$

$$= \frac{7}{8}$$

'AND'

If A and B are independent events then the probability of A *and* B occurring is given by

$$p(A \text{ AND } B) = p(A) \times p(B)$$

Example

If a coin is tossed and a die is thrown what is the probability of getting a head and a 4?

$$p(\text{Head}) = \frac{1}{2} \qquad p(4) = \frac{1}{6}$$

$$p(\text{Head and a 4}) = \frac{1}{2} \times \frac{1}{6}$$

$$= \frac{1}{12}$$

This can be shown on a graph.

```
Die   6 |  x     x
      5 |  x     x
      4 |  x     x
      3 |  x     x
      2 | (x)    x
      1 |  x     x
        |_____
         head  tail   Coin
```

Only one result out of the 12 possible gives a head and a 4.

REPRESENTATION OF RESULTS ON A GRAPH

As shown above for two independent events the possible results for each event can be represented on the axes of a graph.

Example

A red die and a blue die are thrown. What is the probability of scoring
  i) 1 on the red and 6 on the blue?
 ii) an even number on both dice?
iii) a total of 7?

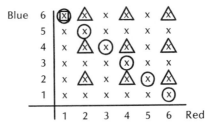

each x represents a possible score

For i) the possible score is enclosed by a $\square$, probability $= \dfrac{1}{36}$

For ii) the possible score is enclosed by a $\triangle$, probability $= \dfrac{9}{36}$

$$= \dfrac{1}{4}$$

For iii) the possible score is enclosed by a $\bigcirc$, probability $= \dfrac{6}{36}$

$$= \dfrac{1}{6}$$

TREE DIAGRAMS

A tree diagram is a means of showing the probabilities of a series of events. The events may be independent or conditional. The probability of a particular outcome occurring is found by multiplying the probabilities on each branch followed to reach that outcome.

Examples

a) a coin is tossed 3 times

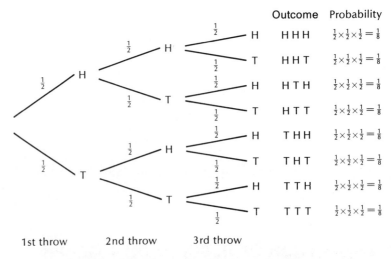

The outcome in throwing the coin the first time has no effect on the outcomes in the second and third throws (the events are independent).

144

b) 3 tins of soup (S), 2 tins of meat (M), and 1 tin of beans (B) are in a cupboard. Show on a tree diagram the ways in which 2 tins can be selected at random.

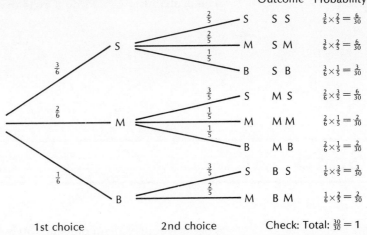

| | Outcome | Probability |

1st choice   2nd choice   Check: Total: $\frac{30}{30} = 1$

If the tin of beans is taken first then there are only soup and meat left to choose from. The outcome of the second choice is affected by the first choice, because the first tin is not replaced (the events are conditional).

i) The probability of 2 tins the same = SS + MM = $\frac{6}{30} + \frac{2}{30} = \frac{8}{30}$

ii) The probability of at least 1 tin of meat =
SM + MS + MM + MB + BM = $\frac{18}{30}$

PASCAL'S TRIANGLE

Total in each row

$$
\begin{array}{c}
1 \\
1\ 1 \\
1\ 2\ 1 \\
1\ 3\ 3\ 1 \\
1\ 4\ 6\ 4\ 1
\end{array}
\qquad
\begin{array}{l}
1 = 2^0 \\
2 = 2^1 \\
4 = 2^2 \\
8 = 2^3 \\
16 = 2^4
\end{array}
$$

. . . .

The first and last numbers of each row are 1. The other numbers are found by adding together the two numbers immediately above,

e.g. $\begin{smallmatrix} 1 & & 3 \\ & 4 & \end{smallmatrix}$

Pascal's triangle can be used to find the probability of a given outcome when repeating an experiment, such as tossing a coin, which has only two possible outcomes.

Example

The row   1   4   6   4   1   Total outcomes = 16

shows the possible outcomes of tossing four coins:

HHHH	HHHT	HHTT	TTTH	TTTT
	HHTH	HTHT	TTHT	
	HTHH	HTTH	THTT	
	THHH	THHT	HTTT	
		THTH		
		TTHH		

$$p(3\ \text{Heads}) = \frac{4}{16}$$
$$= \frac{1}{4}$$

This method could be applied to other situations.

Example

The probability of finding 3 girls in a family of 4 children is

$$p(3 \text{ girls}) = \frac{4}{16}$$

$$= \frac{1}{4}$$

28 SETS

A set is a collection of objects. Curly brackets, { }, mean 'the set of' and these contain either a description of the set or a list of the objects in the set. The individual objects are the members or *elements* of the set.

Examples

$$\{\text{natural numbers} \leqslant 5\} = \{1, 2, 3, 4, 5\}$$
$$\{\text{factors of } 12\} = \{1, 2, 3, 4, 6, 12\}$$

SYMBOLS AND THEIR MEANING

$\mathscr{E}$	the universal set	the set of all elements being considered
$\varnothing$ or { }	the empty set	a set with no members
$\in$	'is an element (or member) of'	$d \in \{a, b, c, d, e\}$
$\notin$	'is *not* an element of'	$x \notin \{a, b, c, d, e\}$
$\subset$	'is a subset of'	$\{d, f\} \subset \{b, c, d, e, f\}$
$\not\subset$	'is *not* a subset of'	$\{a, f\} \not\subset \{b, c, d, e, f\}$
$\supset$	'contains'	$\{b, c, d, e, f\} \supset \{d, f\}$
$\not\supset$	'does *not* contain'	$\{b, c, d, e, f\} \not\supset \{a, f\}$
A'	the *complement* of set A	the set of all elements in $\mathscr{E}$ which are *not* in A
$n(A)$	the number of elements in A	if $A = \{d, f, h, m, p\}$ then $n(A) = 5$
$A \cup B$	the *union* of sets A and B	the set of all elements in A or B or both
		If $A = \{d, e\}$ and $B = \{a, d, f\}$ then $A \cup B = \{a, d, e, f\}$
$A \cap B$	the *intersection* of A and B	the set of all elements which are common to both A and B
		If $A = \{d, e\}$ and $B = \{a, d, f\}$ then $A \cap B = \{d\}$

VENN DIAGRAMS

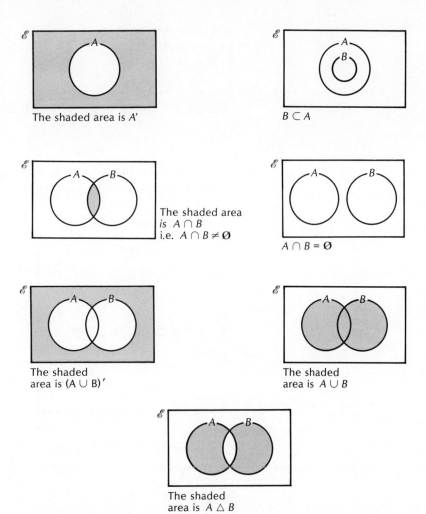

The shaded area is A'

$B \subset A$

The shaded area is $A \cap B$
i.e. $A \cap B \neq \varnothing$

$A \cap B = \varnothing$

The shaded area is $(A \cup B)'$

The shaded area is $A \cup B$

The shaded area is $A \triangle B$

The symbol $\triangle$ is sometimes used to represent 'symmetric difference'. $A \triangle B$ is the set of elements *only* in A together with those *only* in B.

Examples

a) In this example the letters shown in each region are the *elements in the set* represented by the region.

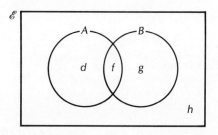

d is *only* in A,
i.e. in A and not in B $d \in A \cap B'$

f is in *both* A and B,
i.e. f is common to both
sets $f \in A \cap B$

g is *only* in B,
i.e. in B and not in A $g \in A' \cap B$

h is in *neither* set,
i.e. not in A and not $h \in A' \cap B'$
in B

$\mathscr{E} = \{d, f, g, h\}$

$A = \{d, f\}$ $B = \{f, g\}$ $A \cup B = \{d, f, g\}$ $(A \cup B)' = \{h\}$

b) In this example the numbers in each region are the *number of elements in the set* represented by that region.

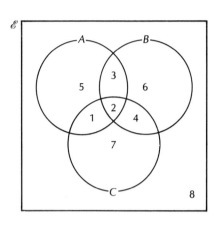

$n(\mathscr{E}) = 1 + 2 + 3 + 4 + 5 + 6 + 7 + 8$

$= 36$

Number in *all* three sets $= n(A \cap B \cap C) = 2$

Number in A *and* B only $= n(A \cap B \cap C') = 3$ (i.e. in A and B but not in C)

Number in A *and* $B = n(A \cap B) = 3 + 2$ (i.e. could be in C as well)

$= 5$

Number in $A = n(A) = 1 + 2 + 3 + 5$ (i.e. total of all elements $= 11$ everywhere in the A circle)

Number in *none* of the sets $= n(A \cup B \cup C)' = 8$

N.B.   Examples a) and b) show two different uses of Venn diagrams.

When completing a Venn diagram try to start with the central region, i.e. with the elements in *all* three sets, and then with the regions for elements in two sets and then with the regions for elements in only one set.

The number of elements in the universal set must equal the total number of elements in all the regions of the rectangle.

Examples

a) A sports club has 120 members all of whom play football or tennis or both. If 97 play tennis and 78 play football, how many play both?

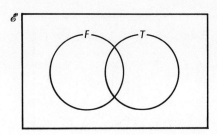

From the information given $n(\mathscr{E}) = 120$
$$n(T \cup F)' = 0$$
(those who play neither game is zero)

$$n(T) = 97$$
$$\underline{n(F) = 78}$$

Total $= 175$ (but the number playing both has been counted twice)

Since $n(\mathscr{E}) = 120$ then the number playing both $= 175 - 120$

$$= 55$$

Therefore the number who play football *only* $= 78 - 55$

$$= 23$$

and the number who play tennis *only* $= 97 - 55$

$$= 42$$

$n(\mathscr{E}) = 120$

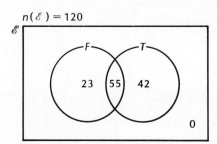

Check on the diagram that $23 + 55 + 42 + 0$ does equal $n(\mathscr{E})$.

In some problems it may not be possible to calculate the required number, in which case an algebraic solution may be necessary, so let any unknown number be x.

b) A sports club has 330 members all of whom play football or tennis or darts. 30 play darts and tennis but *not* football. 120 play football and tennis (NB this means that some of them play darts as well). 125 play football and darts. If 192 altogether play tennis, 186 play darts and 27 play *only* football, then how many play all three games?

149

Let the number who play all three games be x.

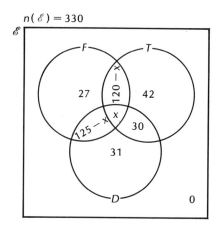

$n(\mathcal{E}) = 330$

$n(D \cap T \cap F') = 30$

$$n(F \cap T) = 120 \Rightarrow n(F \cap T \cap D') = 120 - x$$

$$n(F \cap D) = 125 \Rightarrow n(F \cap D \cap T') = 125 - x$$

$$n(T) = 192 \Rightarrow n(T \cap F' \cap D') = 192 - 30 - x - (120 - x)$$

$$= 42 \quad \text{(number in } T \text{ only)}$$

$$n(D) = 186 \Rightarrow n(D \cap F' \cap T') = 186 - 30 - x - (125 - x)$$

$$= 31 \quad \text{(number in } D \text{ only)}$$

$n(F \cap T' \cap D') = 27 \quad$ (number in F only)

$n(F \cup T \cup D)' = 0 \quad$ (since everybody plays at least one game)

Since $n(\mathcal{E}) = 330$

$$27 + 120 - x + x + 125 - x + 31 + 30 + 42 = 330$$

$$375 - x = 330$$

$$x = 45$$

Therefore the number who play all three games = 45.

Filling in the Venn diagram:

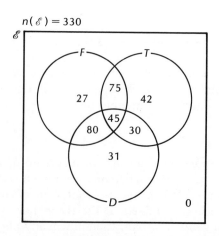

$n(\mathcal{E}) = 330$

29 RELATIONS, MAPPINGS AND FUNCTIONS

Let {Ben, William, John} be the set of three children in a family. 'is the brother of' is an example of a relation between the members of the set. This can be shown by an *arrow diagram*.

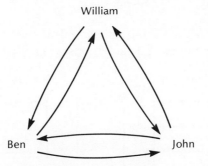

or by a diagram like this:

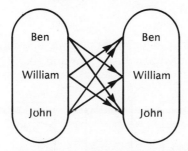

The arrow stands for 'is the brother of'. This is a *many-to-many* relation because more than one arrow leaves at least one element of the set {Ben, William, John} and more than one arrow arrives at one member, at least, of the other set {Ben, William, John}. In fact two arrows leave and two arrive at each member of the set.

The relation 'is three times' between the members of the sets {1, 2, 3, 4} and {3, 6, 9, 12} is a *one-to-one* relation.

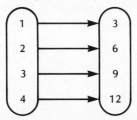

The relation 'is a multiple of' between {3, 6, 9, 10} and {3, 4, 5} is a *many-to-one* relation.

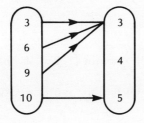

151

The relation 'is a factor of' between $\{2, 3\}$ and $\{4, 8, 9, 15\}$ is a *one-to-many* relation.

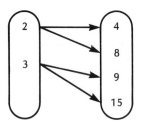

A *mapping* is a relation in which at least one arrow leaves *every member of the starting set*. The starting set is called the *domain*.

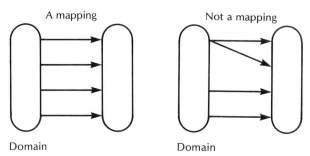

A *function* is a *one-to-one* or *many-to-one* mapping. One and only one arrow leaves each member of the starting set.

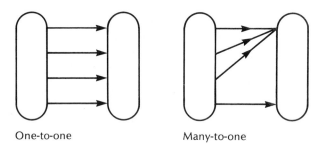

Each element maps to its corresponding *image*.

For the function f: $x \mapsto 3x$ (f maps x on to $3x$), where x and f(x) are real numbers, the image of 1 would be 3, the image of 2 would be 6 and so on. The image of x is f(x). The set of images is called the *range*.

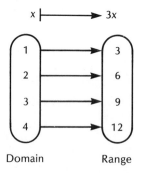

Examples

a) For f: $x \mapsto 3x$ with domain $\{1, 2, 3, 4\}$ the range is $\{3, 6, 9, 12\}$

b) For g: $x \mapsto \sin x$ with domain $0° \leqslant x \leqslant 360°$ the range is $-1 \leqslant g(x) \leqslant 1$.

Functions may be represented in different ways:

Examples

i) using function notation

$$f: x \mapsto 3x$$

ii) by means of a mapping diagram

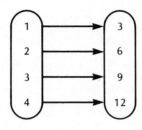   or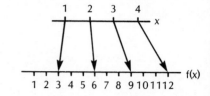

iii) as a set of ordered pairs

(1, 3) (2, 6) (3, 9) (4, 12)

iv) on a graph where $y = f(x)$

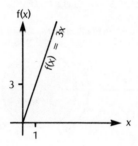

Note that the graphs shown below do not represent functions because there is not just one y corresponding to each x.

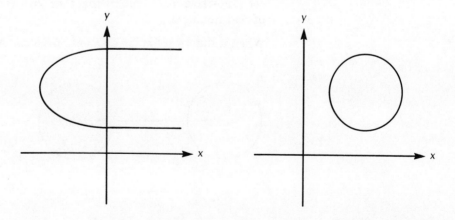

When only one y corresponds to each x in an equation, function notation may be used. $f(x)$, $g(x)$ or $h(x)$, etc. are written in place of y.

153

Examples

a) $f(x) = 2x + 3$ **b)** $g(x) = \dfrac{2x - 1}{3}$

$f(1) = 2 \times 1 + 3$ $g(-4) = \dfrac{2 \times (-4) - 1}{3}$

$= 5$ $= -3$

c) The notation $x \mapsto$ which means 'x maps on to' can be used

$$f: x \mapsto 2(x + 3)$$

So $f(1) = 2(1 + 3)$

$= 8$

This function can be shown using a *flow chart*

Mappings are *from* one set either *into* or *on to* another set (it may be the same set).

Suppose a function f maps elements from set A to set B.

The set of images of elements of A under the mapping is denoted by $f(A)$.

If f maps A *into* B then $f(A) \subset B$

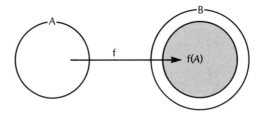

Example

The function f: $x \mapsto x^2$ with domain the set of real numbers has range the set of positive real numbers together with zero, which is a subset of the set of real numbers.

When a function f maps elements from set A *on to* set B then $f(A) = B$.

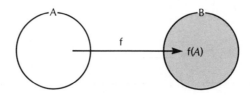

Example

If A and B are the set of real numbers then the function f: $x \mapsto 2x + 4$ has domain A and range B.

THE INVERSE FUNCTION

If function f represents a one-to-one mapping then an inverse function, f^{-1}, will exist. If f maps set A on to set B then f^{-1} will map set B on to set A.

If $f(x) = y$ then $f^{-1}(y) = x$

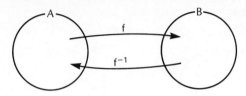

Example

$f(4) = 9 \qquad f^{-1}(9) = 4$

To find the inverse, reverse the flow chart of f, replacing

'multiply by'	by	'divide by'		'subtract'	by	'add'
'divide by'	by	'multiply by'		'divide into'	by	'divide into'
'add'	by	'subtract'		'take from'	by	'take from'

Examples

a) Find f^{-1} when $f: x \mapsto 2x + 1$.
If $f: x \mapsto 2x + 1$

```
 x →  [Multiply by two]  → 2x →  [Add one]  → 2x + 1
```

```
 (x-1)/2 ←  [Divide by two]  ← x - 1 ←  [Subtract one]  ← x
```

$$f^{-1}: x \mapsto \frac{x-1}{2},$$

b) $g(x) = 1 - \dfrac{x}{3}$

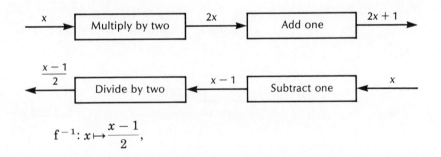

$$g^{-1}(x) = 3(1 - x)$$

155

THE COMPOSITE FUNCTION

If f and g are both functions then there exists a *composite function* gf, obtained by carrying out the function f first and then g.

If $f: x \mapsto f(x)$ and $g: x \mapsto g(x)$ then $gf: x \mapsto g(f(x)) = gf(x)$.

Suppose f maps set A into set B and g maps set B into set C. Then gf will map set A into set C.

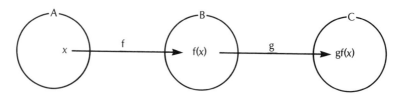

Note that the letters are reversed.

Example

If $f: x \mapsto 2x + 1$ and $g: x \mapsto x - 2$ find i) gf(4) and fg(4) ii) gf and fg in the form $gf: x \mapsto$ and $fg: x \mapsto$.

i) $gf(4) = g(f(4))$ $fg(4) = f(g(4))$

$\quad\quad = g(9)$ $\quad\quad = f(2)$

$\quad\quad = 7$ $\quad\quad = 5$

ii) Since gf means 'do f first then g'

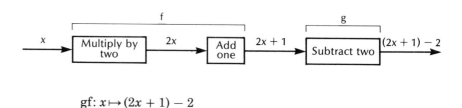

$\quad gf: x \mapsto (2x + 1) - 2$

$\quad\quad\quad = 2x - 1$

fg means 'do g first then f'

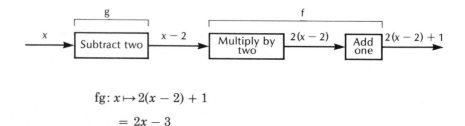

$\quad fg: x \mapsto 2(x - 2) + 1$

$\quad\quad\quad = 2x - 3$

N.B.   In general the function gf is *not* the same as the function fg.

156

EXPONENTIAL FUNCTION

$f: x \mapsto a^x$ where a is a constant is an *exponential function*. The shape of the graph of such a function is shown below.

N.B. $a^0 = 1$ for all values of a.

Example

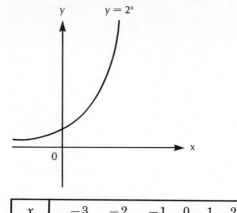

x	-3	-2	-1	0	1	2	3
y	$\frac{1}{8}$	$\frac{1}{4}$	$\frac{1}{2}$	1	2	4	8

ABSOLUTE FUNCTION

$f: x \mapsto |x|$ is called the *absolute function*.

$|x|$ means the *absolute* value of x, i.e. x if x is positive and $-x$ if x is negative. Thus $|x| \geqslant 0$.

Examples

$$|2| = 2$$
$$|-3| = 3$$

30   FLOW CHARTS

A flow chart is a means of giving instructions which have to be carried out in a specified order.

The order in which the instructions must be carried out is indicated by

An instruction is written in a rectangular box.

$$\boxed{X = X + 2}$$ means increase X by 2

A question is written in a rhombic box.

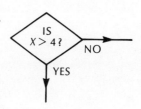

157

The next step depends on the answer to the question.

Example

Start with $X = 1$

Y is 1 more than X

Add X and Y and let the answer be Z

Stop when $X = 10$

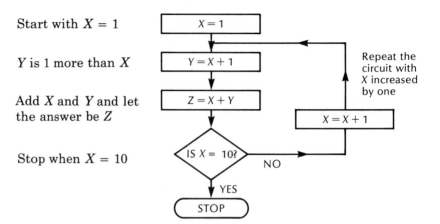

Results

X	Y	Z
1	2	3
2	3	5
3	4	7
4	5	9
5	6	11
6	7	13
7	8	15
8	9	17
9	10	19
10	11	21

This flow chart gives instructions for adding two consecutive numbers, the smallest being one and the largest eleven.

SECTION III

QUESTIONS

1 ALGEBRA Questions

1. Simplify

a) $2x + 3y + 4x + 2y$

b) $12def + 3ef - 4def$

c) $5a \times 2a \times 6$

d) $\dfrac{12ab}{4a}$

e) $5x^2 + 2x - x^2 - x$

f) $\dfrac{6x^2y^4}{2x^6y^2}$

g) $\dfrac{6x + 2y}{9x + 3y}$

h) $\dfrac{ax^2 + axy}{2x + 2y}$

i) $\dfrac{(x + 3)(x - 7)}{(x - 7)(x + 4)}$

j) $\dfrac{12x^4y^2}{6x^3y^7}$

g) $-16x - 12y$

h) $8a^2 - 32g^2$

i) $3x + 3y + x^2 - y^2$

j) $8t - 4xt + 6y - 3xy$

k) $5x^2 - 15x + 10$

l) $x^2 - 16x + 64$

2. Substitute $a = 2, d = 5, f = 7$.

a) $3d^2$

b) $2f - 3a$

c) $d(3f - a^2)$

d) $\dfrac{6a - f}{d}$

e) $af + ad + df$

If $g = -1, h = 4, k = -2$, find the values of

f) $h - 2k$

g) $3g^2 + 7$

h) $\dfrac{3(h + g)}{k^2}$

i) $(k - g)(k + g)$

j) $4k - 2h + 3g$

3. Expand

a) $4(2a + 3b)$

b) $3x(2x - 4y)$

c) $(x + 3)(x + 5)$

d) $(x - 3)(x - 2)$

e) $(2x + 1)(x + 3)$

f) $(x - 4)(x + 4)$

g) $-3(2d - g)$

h) $(3 + y)(2 + 4y)$

i) $(5a - 2)(2a + 5)$

j) $(2f - 3)(2f + 3)$

4. Factorise

a) $6y + 6t$

b) $9xy + 6ay$

c) $12ab - 8a^2$

d) $x^2 + 7x + 12$

e) $x^2 - 3x - 10$

f) $2y^2 + 11y + 12$

5. Solve

a) $2x + 3 = 11$

b) $5x + 2 = 3x + 7$

c) $3(2y + 1) = 21$

d) $\frac{2}{3}x = 12$

e) $\frac{1}{4}(3x - 2) = 3$

f) $3(2a - 4) = 5(3a - 1)$

g) $\dfrac{3}{2y + 3} = 5$

h) $\dfrac{3x - 2}{x + 1} = \dfrac{2}{3}$

i) $\frac{1}{3}(2 - 5x) = 4$

j) $6t = 2(1 - 3t) + 4$

k) $3x + \dfrac{1}{8} = \dfrac{7}{8}$

l) $\dfrac{x}{5} + \dfrac{x}{2} = 14$

6. Solve

a) $x + y = 5$
$2x - y = 4$

b) $4x + y = 11$
$2x + y = 5$

c) $2x + 3y = -2$
$4x - y = 3$

d) $5x + 3y = 12$
$2x + 2y = 7$

e) $2x - 5y = 3$
$3x + 4y = 4$

f) $x - y = 0$
$x = y^2 - y + 1$

g) $x + y = 6$
$x^2 = y$

h) $2x - 3y = 4$
$4x + y^2 = 8$

i) $\begin{pmatrix} 3 & -1 \\ -2 & 4 \end{pmatrix}\begin{pmatrix} x \\ y \end{pmatrix} = \begin{pmatrix} 2 \\ 1 \end{pmatrix}$

7. Solve (to two decimal places where necessary)

a) $x^2 + 6x + 8 = 0$

b) $x^2 - 9x + 14 = 0$

c) $x^2 - 8x = 20$

d) $x^2 - 3x = 0$

e) $x^2 - 6x + 9 = 0$

f) $x^2 - 9 = 0$

g) $(x + 3)^2 = 25$

h) $(x - 1)^2 = 17$

i) $x^2 - 4x - 6 = 0$

j) $5x^2 - 13x + 1 = 0$

k) $3x - 2x^2 + 4 = 0$

l) $6 - 2x^2 = 3x$

m) $4x = (x - 2)^2$

n) $2(3 - 2x) = 3x^2$

8. a) What inequalities are represented by

i)

?

ii)

?

iii)

?

b) Show the following on number lines:

  i) $3 < x \leqslant 5$ ii) $-2 \leqslant x \leqslant 2$ iii) $x > 0$

Solve

c) $x - 2 > 6$

d) $-x < 4$

e) $13 - x \leqslant 7$

f) $2x - 3 \geqslant x - 2$

g) $x^2 - 2x - 3 \geqslant 0$

h) $x^2 - 2x - 3 < 0$

i) $x^2 + 7x + 12 < 0$

j) $x^2 + 2x - 8 > 0$

9. Make x the subject of each formula.

a) $ax = t$

b) $dx + ey = p$

c) $3x^2 = y$

d) $3x + 7y = ax + dy$

e) $tx = \dfrac{a}{t}$

f) $a(x - t) = d(y - x)$

g) $\dfrac{(t + x)}{(x + y)} = 4t$

h) $3x^2 - t = 4y$

i) $t = y - ax^2$

j) $t = a(y - x^2)$

10. Simplify

a) $\dfrac{9}{y} + \dfrac{3}{y}$

b) $\dfrac{6}{5x} + \dfrac{4}{5x}$

c) $\dfrac{t}{y} + \dfrac{p}{y}$

d) $\dfrac{3}{a} - \dfrac{2}{b}$

e) $\dfrac{8}{3t} - \dfrac{9}{2y}$

f) $\dfrac{2x}{3y} + \dfrac{5y}{4t}$

g) $\dfrac{8}{(x + t)} + \dfrac{2}{(x - t)}$

h) $\dfrac{3a}{(a + 3)} - \dfrac{2a}{(a + 1)}$

i) $\dfrac{4t}{(2x + 1)} - \dfrac{3t}{(2x - 1)}$

j) $\dfrac{6 + y}{y} - \dfrac{3 - 2y}{y + 1}$

11. Write down the expression or equation given by each of the following:

a) The number of pence in £x.

b) The average of three consecutive numbers if the middle number is t.

c) The product of a number (x) and twice the number.

d) The length of a rectangle is L cm and the width is half of 2 cm less than the length. Write down the area, A, and the perimeter, P.

e) A bus has 24 passengers. If x get off at the next stop and four less than x get on, how many passengers are now on the bus?

f) Three times a son's age is the age that his father was twelve years ago.

g) Twice a number (x) is decreased by three and the result is then halved. If this answer is the same as multiplying one less than the number by four, what is the number?

h) How many minutes are there between x minutes past four and y minutes past five?

i) An apple costs 9 p and an orange costs 8 p. What is the total cost of x oranges and y apples?

j) By increasing a third of a number by four and then doubling the result, the answer arrived at is ten.

12. Where necessary, place brackets in the following to make the equation correct:

a) $24 - 4 \div 5 = 4$

b) $16 - 2 \div 5 - 3 = 7$

c) $4 + 12 \div 3 = 8$

d) $8 \times 2 - 4 \times 2 = 8$

e) $14 - 2 \times 3 = 36$

f) $2 \times 4 + 5 = 18$

g) $36 \div 4 - 2 = 7$

h) $36 \div 4 - 2 = 18$

i) $180 - 51 - 62 = 67$ **j)** $1 + 1 \div 1 + 1 \times 3 = 3$

13. Find the remainder when

a) $x^3 - 3x^2 - 2x + 7$ is divided by $(x - 3)$

b) $x^3 + 4x^2 + 8x - 2$ is divided by $(x - 1)$

c) $x^3 + x^2 - 4x - 1$ is divided by $(x + 2)$

d) $2x^3 - 3x^2 - 2x + 11$ is divided by $(x + 1)$

e) $3x^3 + 5x^2 + 5x + 2$ is divided by $(x + 1)$

f) $x^3 - 2x^2 + 3x + 2$ is divided by $(2x - 1)$

14. Factorise

a) $x^3 + 7x^2 + 14x + 8$

b) $x^3 + 5x^2 + 2x - 8$

c) $x^3 + 5x^2 - 4x - 20$

d) $x^3 - 6x^2 + 5x + 12$

e) $2x^3 - x^2 - 2x + 1$

f) $3x^3 + 5x^2 - 4x - 4$

2 NUMBERS

Questions

1. Write down the next two numbers in each sequence:

   a) $4, 2, 1, \frac{1}{2}, \ldots, \ldots$

   b) $100, 10, 1, \ldots, \ldots$

   c) $0.001, 0.02, 0.4, \ldots, \ldots$

   d) $4, 9, 16, 25, \ldots, \ldots$

   e) $26, 39, \ldots, \ldots$

2. $\{6, 7, 8, 9, 10, 11, 12, 13, 14, 15, 16, 17\}$
   Using this set of numbers, write down

   a) a square number

   b) two prime numbers

   c) a number which is a multiple of 5

   d) a number which has 4 as a factor

   e) two numbers whose product is 180

   f) three triangular numbers

3. List all the factors of

   a) 36   b) 49   c) 100   d) 56

4. Express each number as a product of prime numbers.

   a) 12   b) 18   c) 35   d) 80   e) 144

5. a) Find the LCM of each pair of numbers

      i) 12 and 15   ii) 9 and 18   iii) 22 and 21

   b) Find the HCF of each pair of numbers
      i) 36 and 32   ii) 75 and 90   iii) 42 and 70

6. Express these numbers in standard form:

   a) 40 000   b) 290   c) 0.0003

   d) 0.42   e) 3420   f) 0.0206

   g) 95 000 000   h) 0.000 000 9

   i) 0.05702   j) 63.1

7. Express as numbers

   a) 3×10^2 b) 4.2×10 c) 1.3×10^{-2}

   d) 5.6×10^{-6} e) 8×10^{-1} f) 7.03×10^3

   g) 2.1×10^{-1} h) 6.4×10^1 i) 8.2×10^8

   j) 3.9×10^{-8}

8. Simplify and give the answer in standard form.

   a) $2 \times 10^3 \times 3 \times 10^2$ b) $4 \times 10^{-2} \times 8 \times 10^4$

   c) $1.2 \times 10^1 \times 5 \times 10^2 \times 1 \times 10^{-3}$

   d) $\dfrac{8 \times 10^{-3}}{4 \times 10^1}$ e) $\dfrac{3 \times 10^8}{5 \times 10^6}$

   f) $\dfrac{4.8 \times 10^2}{1.2 \times 10^{-1}}$ g) $\dfrac{6 \times 10^3 \times 8 \times 10^{-4}}{4 \times 10^2}$

   h) $1.1 \times 10^{-2} \times 1.5 \times 10^{-4}$

   i) $\dfrac{3.6 \times 10^1 \times 6 \times 10^{-3}}{9 \times 4.8 \times 10^{-2}}$

   j) $8 \times 10^7 \times 3 \times 10^{-9} \times 2 \times 10^{-1} \times 5 \times 10^1$

9. Write in standard form and then as a single number

   a) $300\,000 \times 0.0002$

   b) $0.01 \times 200 \times 0.03$

   c) $450 \times 1000 \times 0.0002 \times 0.12$

   d) $\dfrac{1200}{0.06}$ e) $\dfrac{0.3 \times 0.8}{40}$ f) $\dfrac{6000 \times 0.004}{0.003 \times 200}$

   g) $0.05 \times 10\,000 \times 0.4 \times 60$

   h) $\dfrac{0.5 \times 4000 \times 0.12}{30 \times 20 \times 0.0002}$

   i) $8\,000\,000\,000 \times 0.000\,000\,2$

   j) $\dfrac{0.000\,012 \times 0.0015}{0.0018 \times 0.000\,002}$

10. Evaluate

    a) 2^4 b) 3^3 c) $(-1)^3$ d) 4^{-1}

    e) $\sqrt{121}$ f) $\sqrt[3]{8}$ g) $\sqrt{\dfrac{4}{9}}$ h) $\left(\dfrac{1}{2}\right)^{-3}$

    i) $\sqrt{625}$ j) $(-3)^2$

3 DIRECTED NUMBERS Questions

1. Place a $>$ or $<$ between each pair of numbers to complete a correct inequality.

a) $2 \qquad -1$

b) $-7 \qquad 3$

c) $-2 \qquad -9$

d) $-47 \qquad 0$

e) $-294 \quad -295$

f) $-1\frac{1}{2} \qquad -1\frac{1}{4}$

2. Simplify

a) $3 - 4 - 2$

b) $-2 - 7 - 3$

c) $1 - +3 - -4$

d) $8 - -4 + +1 + -6 - +4$

e) $-10 + 40 - 80 - 20$

f) $-34 + -27 - -18$

g) $-\frac{1}{2} + 3 + 4 - 8 - 1\frac{1}{2}$

h) $180 - 42 - 61 + 37 - 12$

i) $1 - -1 + -1 - +1 - -1$

j) $-437 + 923 - 291 - 48$

3. Calculate

a) -2×6

b) -8×-7

c) $\dfrac{24}{-3}$

d) -1×-1

e) $\dfrac{-16}{-4}$

f) $-3 \times 2 \times -1$

g) $\dfrac{-3 \times 4}{-2}$

h) $-3 \times -4 \times -2$

i) $\dfrac{-5 \times -20}{-4 \times 2}$

j) $\dfrac{16 \times -25 \times -6}{-100 \times 2}$

4. State the values of

a) $\sqrt{49}$

b) $(-2)^2$

c) $(-2)^3$

d) $\sqrt{12\,100}$

e) $(-3)^2 \times (+3)^2$

f) $(+5)^3$

5. If $x = 2$, $y = -1$ and $z = 5$, find the values of

a) xy

b) $z - y$

c) $3(x - z)$

d) $3y^2$

e) $5x + z + 2y$

6. If $a = 2$, $b = -4$ and $c = -10$, state the values of

a) $2a$

b) b^2

c) $4ac$

d) $-b$

e) $b^2 - 4ac$

7. Evaluate

a) $(-2 - 3) \times (3 - 4)$

b) $\dfrac{-8(2 + 4)}{-6 \times -2}$

c) $3(-6 + 9) - 2(3 - 5)$

d) $\dfrac{8}{-2 \times -4} + \dfrac{-2 \times -6}{3}$

e) $(-5)^2 - (-3)^2$

8. Simplify

a) $2x - 5x + 4x$

b) $-3a + 4y - 6y - 2a$

c) $-3x \times -4y$

d) $-2(4 - 8a)$

e) $2(a + 3y) - 4(2a - 3y)$

f) $4y + 3x - 8x + 2x - 9y + 3y$

4 DECIMALS Questions

1. Write as decimals

  a) $2\dfrac{3}{10}$ b) $\dfrac{42}{100}$ c) $6\dfrac{2}{100}$

  d) $497\dfrac{14}{1000}$ e) $10\dfrac{101}{1000}$

2. a) Correct each of the following to 1 decimal place:

    i) 2.38   ii) 0.572   iii) 64.98
    iv) 10 037.293   v) 9.98

  b) Correct each of the following to 2 decimal places:

    i) 4.328   ii) 28.2071   iii) 0.007 68
    iv) 1.0972   v) 0.004 97

3. Simplify

  a) $2.97 + 46.32 + 0.382 + 10.8$

  b) £92.34 + £1.08 + 29 p

  c) $39.72 - 14.97$

  d) £250 − £182.34

  e) $83.76 + 9.8 - 27.39 - 2.63 + 42.65$

4. Calculate

  a) 3.2×4 b) 1.3×0.7

  c) 0.4×0.9 d) 12.3×0.7

  e) 6.2×1.6 f) $0.2 \times 0.3 \times 0.4$

  g) $300 \times 0.5 \times 0.02$ h) $0.4 \times 600 \times 0.1$

  i) 0.0092×4000 j) $3.142 \times 0.5 \times 0.5$

5. a) $12.8 \div 4$ b) $0.045 \div 9$

  c) $80 \div 0.2$ d) $4.8 \div 0.3$

  e) $0.06 \div 0.003$ f) $18\,000 \div 60\,000$

  g) $2 \div 0.0005$ h) $0.01 \div 0.000\,001$

  i) $0.96 \div 0.2$ j) $240 \div 0.024$

6. Convert

  a) 2000 m to km   b) 3 kg to g

  c) 4 g to mg   d) 847 cm to m

  e) 3.27 m to cm   f) 2946 g to kg

  g) 5 mm to m   h) 0.047 km to m

  i) 2.98 litres to cm^3 j) 148 cm to km

7. Round off

  a) 2.78 to 2 s.f.   b) 16.82 to 1 s.f.

  c) 0.005 876 1 to 4 s.f.   d) 3560 to 1 s.f.

  e) 9.87 to 1 s.f.   f) 0.807 26 to 3 s.f.

  g) 2.0091 to 2 s.f.   h) 817.4236 to 1 s.f.

  i) 29.378 to 2 s.f.   j) 0.032 146 to 3 s.f.

5 FRACTIONS Questions

1. Cancel

  a) $\dfrac{8}{16}$ b) $\dfrac{24}{36}$ c) $\dfrac{14}{21}$ d) $\dfrac{9}{51}$

  e) $\dfrac{54}{81}$ f) $\dfrac{39}{52}$ g) $\dfrac{12}{15}$ h) $\dfrac{81}{243}$

  i) $\dfrac{3000}{8000}$ j) $\dfrac{6}{9}$

2. Calculate, giving each answer in its simplest form

  a) $\dfrac{8}{11} + \dfrac{2}{11}$ b) $\dfrac{5}{12} + \dfrac{7}{12}$ c) $\dfrac{4}{5} + \dfrac{1}{10}$

  d) $\dfrac{2}{9} + \dfrac{5}{18}$ e) $\dfrac{3}{7} - \dfrac{1}{3}$ f) $\dfrac{5}{6} - \dfrac{2}{5}$

  g) $2\dfrac{1}{4} - 1\dfrac{3}{5}$ h) $33\dfrac{3}{8} - 2\dfrac{1}{16}$ i) $\dfrac{3}{4} + 1\dfrac{5}{6} + \dfrac{2}{3}$

  j) $4\dfrac{1}{2} + 1\dfrac{3}{4} - \dfrac{5}{28}$

3. Change into mixed numbers

a) $\dfrac{4}{3}$ b) $\dfrac{23}{5}$ c) $\dfrac{90}{8}$ d) $\dfrac{30}{12}$

e) $\dfrac{43}{19}$ f) $\dfrac{96}{10}$ g) $\dfrac{19}{7}$ h) $\dfrac{46}{4}$

i) $\dfrac{96}{2}$ j) $\dfrac{28}{17}$

4. Change into fractions

a) $1\dfrac{2}{3}$ b) $2\dfrac{5}{6}$ c) $6\dfrac{9}{10}$ d) $1\dfrac{16}{19}$

e) $5\dfrac{2}{13}$ f) $1\dfrac{6}{53}$ g) $3\dfrac{1}{3}$ h) $9\dfrac{4}{11}$

i) $21\dfrac{3}{4}$ j) $4\dfrac{6}{7}$

5. a) $\dfrac{3}{5} \times \dfrac{4}{7}$ b) $\dfrac{8}{9} \times \dfrac{3}{4}$

c) $\dfrac{11}{12} \times \dfrac{4}{5}$ d) $\dfrac{3}{4} \times \dfrac{1}{2} \times \dfrac{12}{15}$

e) $2\dfrac{1}{4} \times 2\dfrac{2}{3}$ f) $4\dfrac{1}{2} \times \dfrac{2}{3} \times 1\dfrac{1}{4}$

g) $4 \times 4\dfrac{2}{3} \times 1\dfrac{3}{4}$ h) $3\dfrac{1}{7} \times 1\dfrac{3}{11} \times 3\dfrac{2}{3}$

6. a) $\dfrac{2}{5} \div \dfrac{3}{7}$ b) $\dfrac{5}{8} \div \dfrac{3}{4}$ c) $\dfrac{8}{11} \div \dfrac{1}{4}$

d) $\dfrac{4}{5} \div 2\dfrac{1}{2}$ e) $\dfrac{4}{5} \div 6$ f) $\dfrac{8}{9} \div 2\dfrac{2}{5}$

g) $1\dfrac{1}{2} \div 2\dfrac{3}{4}$ h) $2\dfrac{3}{4} \div 1\dfrac{1}{2}$

7. Convert into decimals (to 3 decimal places where necessary).

a) $\dfrac{4}{5}$ b) $\dfrac{7}{8}$ c) $\dfrac{19}{20}$ d) $\dfrac{3}{4}$

e) $1\dfrac{3}{8}$ f) $2\dfrac{27}{50}$ g) $\dfrac{7}{16}$ h) $\dfrac{19}{25}$

i) $\dfrac{2}{3}$ j) $\dfrac{11}{12}$

6 PERCENTAGES   Questions

1. Convert each percentage into a fraction and cancel if possible.

a) 40% b) 65% c) 12% d) $8\frac{1}{3}\%$

e) 145% f) $62\frac{1}{2}\%$ g) 275% h) 95%

i) $2\frac{1}{2}\%$ j) 44%

2. Convert each fraction into a percentage

a) $\dfrac{4}{5}$ b) $\dfrac{7}{20}$ c) $\dfrac{19}{25}$ d) $\dfrac{4}{7}$ e) 7

f) $\dfrac{5}{9}$ g) $6\dfrac{1}{2}$ h) $\dfrac{47}{50}$ i) $2\dfrac{9}{10}$ j) $\dfrac{7}{8}$

3. Calculate

a) 50% of 72 g b) 20% of £800

c) 16% of £6 d) 4% of £5.50

e) 112% of 600 cm f) 75% of 84 litres

g) $12\frac{1}{2}\%$ of £96.16 h) 38% of £12.50

i) 7% of 25 m j) 92% of £8

4. Find what percentage

a) £50 is of £200 b) 12 is of 96

c) 20 p is of £1.25 d) 2 m is of 10 m

e) 80 cm is of 1 m f) £12 is of £8

g) 8 p is of $12\frac{1}{2}$ p h) £4.20 is of £6.30

i) 90 000 is of 300 000 j) £75 is of £600

5. Fill in the missing values

	Cost price	Profit	Selling price	Percentage profit
a)	£80	£20	—	—
b)	£5	—	£8	—
c)	—	£12	—	4%
d)	—	—	£6.60	10%
e)	—	£1.50	—	20%
f)	£42	—	—	3%
g)	—	—	£287.50	15%
h)	£1.44	—	£1.56	—

6. a) Calculate the simple interest gained by investing

    i) £300 for 3 years at 11% per annum
    ii) £750 for 2 years at 16% per annum
    iii) £82 for 6 months at 10% per annum
    iv) £8000 for 8 years at 9% per annum

  b) Calculate the compound interest gained by investing

    i) £400 for 2 years at 9% per annum
    ii) £250 for 4 years at 11% per annum
    iii) £68 for 3 years at 10% per annum
    iv) £142 for 5 years at 12% per annum

7. If VAT is 15%, what amount must be added to an item costing

  a) £50   b) £7.50   c) £800

  d) £1250   e) £12   f) £1.20

8. How much tax (at the basic rate of 30%) does a man have to pay if he earns

  a) £8000 per annum and has allowances of £3500?

  b) £12,500 per annum and has allowances of £4250?

  c) £10,470 per annum and has allowances of £4020?

  d) £17,821 per annum and has allowances of £6416?

  e) £5276 per annum and has allowances of £2750?

9. A motorist drives without accident for five years, how much would he have to pay each year if his full premium is

  a) £480   b) £360   c) £600

  d) £252   e) £575

(Use the information given in the notes on Percentages.)

7 RATIO   Questions

1. Simplify each of the following:

  a) $9:12$ b) $21:14$

  c) $1000:200$ d) $32:48$

  e) $12:8:20$ f) $18:36:9$

  g) $\frac{3}{4}:\frac{1}{4}$ h) $1\frac{3}{5}:2\frac{2}{5}$

  i) $\frac{1}{2}:1\frac{1}{2}$ j) $\frac{2}{3}:\frac{5}{6}$

  k) £6:£24:£12   l) 20 p:£2

  m) 4 m:200 cm   n) 50 p:£2.50:£4

  o) £1500:£1250

2. Express these ratios as fractions:

  a) $8:16$ b) $15:18$

  c) £20:£50   d) 24 cm:60 cm

  e) 75 p:£1.50   f) $12:6$

  g) $\frac{3}{8}:\frac{5}{8}$ h) 200 km:8000 km

  i) $2\frac{1}{2}$ g:$12\frac{1}{2}$ g   j) $80:96$

3. a) Share £100 in the ratio $3:7$

  b) Share £144 in the ratio $8:4$

  c) Share £4000 in the ratio $17:3$

  d) Share £60 in the ratio $7:3:2$

  e) Share 120 km in the ratio $11:9:4$

  f) Share 96 p in the ratio $1:2:3$

4. If A and B share a sum of money in the ratio

  a) $3:4$ and B receives £8, how much does A receive?

  b) $7:3$ and B receives £600, how much does A receive?

  c) $5:6$ and A receives £120, how much does B receive?

  d) $11:3$ and B receives 48 p, how much does A receive?

  e) $2:9$ and A receives £7, how much does B receive?

5. Copy and complete the following

	Scale	Real length	Length on model
a)	1 : 20	40 m	—
b)	1 : 100	—	3 cm
c)	1 : 50	—	2 m
d)	1 : 10	60 cm	—
e)	—	1 m	20 cm
f)	1 : 10 000	—	5 cm
g)	—	4 km	2 cm
h)	1 : 50	5 m	—
i)	1 : 1000	—	8 mm
j)	—	5 km	1 m

8 ERROR — Questions

1. Give the largest and smallest possible true values if a line is given as measuring

   a) 6 cm to the nearest cm

   b) 35.6 m to 1 decimal place

   c) 870 km to the nearest 10 km

   d) 0.73 m to 2 decimal places

   e) 8000 mm to the nearest 100 mm

   f) 3.41 m to 3 significant figures

   g) 4370 cm to the nearest 10 cm

   h) 2 km to the nearest km

   i) 0.004 km to the nearest m

   j) 9.1 cm to the nearest mm

2. Calculate the maximum and minimum possible area of rectangles which have measurements of

   a) 1.5 cm and 1.2 cm to 1 decimal place

   b) 80 mm and 20 mm to the nearest 10 mm

   c) 0.42 m and 0.04 m to 2 decimal places

   d) 3 km and 0.2 km to 1 significant figure

   e) 11 m and 9 m to the nearest m

3. What is the maximum possible error when

   a) a length is given as 82.3 cm to 1 decimal place

   b) a value is given as £4000 to the nearest £100

   c) a weight is given as 0.02 kg to 1 significant figure

   d) an amount is given as 234.72 to 2 decimal places

   e) a value is given as £2.76 to the nearest penny

4. Calculate the percentage error when

   a) £275 is rounded off to the nearest £100

   b) £58 is rounded off to the nearest £10

   c) 8.4 cm is rounded off to the nearest cm

   d) 0.32 km is rounded off to 1 decimal place

   e) £1.34 is rounded off to the nearest 10 p

   f) 412 800 cm is rounded off to the nearest km

9 EVERYDAY ARITHMETIC Questions

1. List ten different ways 47p can be given in change.

For example:

$1 \times$ 20p $2 \times$ 10p

$1 \times$ 5p $1 \times$ 2p

2. Copy and complete this menu:

	£
2 coffees @ 36p each	....
4 rolls & butter @ 25p each	....
4 soups @ .... each	1.40
.... ham salads @ £1.45 each	4.35
1 chicken salad @ £1.20	....
Total (without VAT)	....
VAT @ 15%	....
Total including VAT	....

3. I go on holiday to Portugal in fifteen days time. If the date today is 23rd July what is the date of the first day of my holiday?

The flight is 3 hours 10 minutes long. It takes a further 55 minutes to reach my destination by coach. Also Portugese time is one hour ahead of our time. If the plane leaves at 11.55 a.m. what time (by Portugese time) will I arrive at my holiday apartment?

If I buy an embroidered tablecloth for 2000 escudos and the rate of exchange is 190 escudos to the pound how much will the tablecloth cost to the nearest penny?

4. A school starts at 9.10 a.m. After five minutes for registration there are four morning lessons at 35 minutes each with a 30 minute break mid-morning. Lunch break is 1 hour 20 minutes. There are three afternoon lessons each 40 minutes long with no afternoon break. Draw a timetable showing this.

a) At what time does the last lesson of the morning end?

b) At what time does the last lesson of the afternoon end?

5. Which graph illustrates the following statement 'gas bills are worked out by adding a quarterly standing charge to the number of therms used multiplied by the cost per therm'?

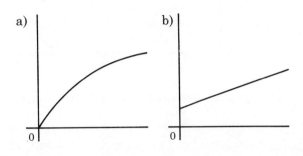

a)   b)

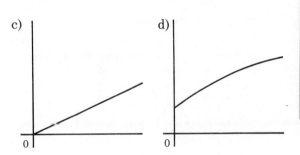

c)   d)

6. An electricity bill is calculated by multiplying the cost per unit by the number of units used and then adding a standing charge. Diagram a) shows the meter reading at the beginning of the quarter and diagram b) the reading at the end. Calculate the quarterly bill if the cost per unit is 5.17 p and the standing charge is £5.82.

a)

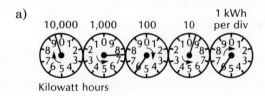

Kilowatt hours

b)

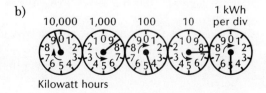

Kilowatt hours

SECTION III

169

7.

Number of days	14	14	14
Apartment	1 bedroom (2 people)	2 bedrooms (3 to 4 people)	3 bedrooms (5 to 7 people)
Low season *Mid season* *High season*	£190 £210 £280	£175 £180 £230	£145 £160 £210

The charge is per person. Airport charges and air fares are included, but there is a flight supplement for travel from Birmingham.

a) A young couple with two children aged 16 years and 11 years decide to take a holiday in Majorca. They book a 2 bedroom apartment for a fortnight in mid-season and travel from Birmingham.

There is a 10% reduction for children aged between 2 and 14 years. The flight supplement is £8.25 extra per person and insurance is £9 each.

Using the table above, calculate

i) the total cost of their holiday
ii) how much more it would have cost if they had travelled in high season
iii) the total cost if they decide instead to take another child aged 13 years with them and to go in low season. (This will mean they have to book a 3 bedroom apartment.)

b) They decide to hire a car for 5 days. Car hire is 5300 pesetas for 3 days with an additional cost of 1800 pesetas per day for each extra day. They travel 240 km using petrol at an average consumption of 10 km/litre. Petrol costs 80 pesetas per litre.

Work out

i) how much their car hire will be in pesetas for the 5 days, excluding petrol
ii) how far they travel in miles given that 5 miles equals 8 kilometres
iii) the cost in pesetas of one gallon of petrol given that 4.5 litres are equivalent to one gallon
iv) the cost, in £, of one gallon of petrol if 200 pesetas are equivalent to £1
v) the total cost, in £, of the car hire plus petrol.

8. a) A retailer takes out a £1500 loan from his bank. The interest charged is 16% per annum. The repayments are in twelve equal monthly instalments.

Calculate

i) the total amount to be repaid to the bank
ii) the amount of each instalment.

b) He sells a television for £325 cash or on hire purchase for a 12% deposit and six monthly payments of £52.

Find

i) the value of the deposit
ii) the cost of the six monthly payments
iii) the total cost of buying on hire purchase
iv) the difference between the cash price and the hire purchase price.

c) Express the difference found in your answer to b) iv) as a percentage of the cash price of the television.

9. During 1986 a motorist paid £100 road tax, £352.55 for repairs and servicing, the premium for his insurance is £180 and he has a 60% no claims discount. He travelled 6400 miles with an average petrol consumption of 32 miles to the gallon. Petrol cost on average £2.05 per gallon.

a) Calculate

i) the insurance paid
ii) how many gallons of petrol he used
iii) the cost of petrol for the year
iv) the total running cost for the year

b) The cost of spare parts was 2/5 of the cost of repairs. How much was spent on spare parts if repairs and servicing are in the ratio 7 : 4?

c) He bought the car for £7800 in January 1985 and estimated that the car depreciated in value by 20% in the first year and by 10% of its value at the beginning of the year in the second year. Calculate its value at the end of 1986.

10. a) Part of an electricity bill for the quarter December to March is shown below.

Calculate

  i) the total number of units used
  ii) the total cost (correct to the nearest penny) of the units used
  iii) the electricity bill for the quarter December to March.

b) The pie chart shows how the rates of a town are spent.

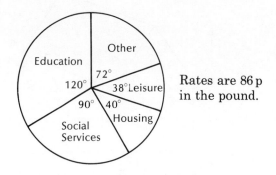

Rates are 86 p in the pound.

Calculate

  i) the rates paid by a householder who has a rateable value of £310
  ii) the amount paid by the householder towards education.

EASTSHIRE ELECTRICITY BOARD			
Mr. J. Smith 8 London Road		Ref 203/16	
		EEB	
Meter Readings		Unit rate charged	Fixed Charge
Present	Previous	5.37p	£8.75
42831	39627		

10 AREA AND VOLUME Questions

1. Calculate the areas of

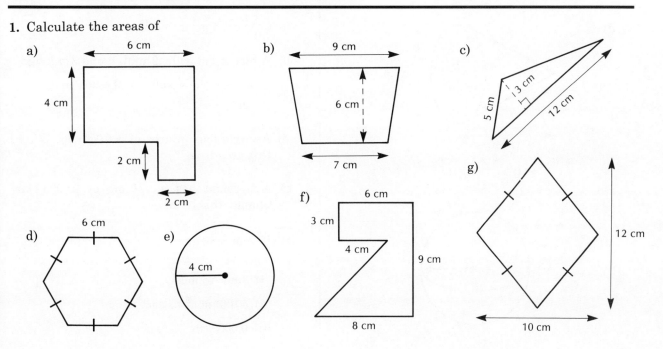

171

2. Calculate the volumes of

a)

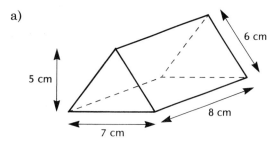

b)

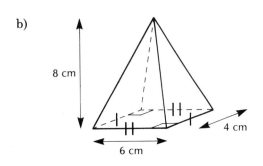

c)

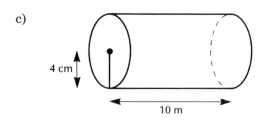

d)

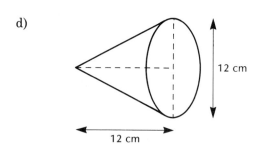

e)

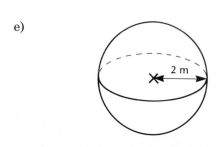

3. Calculate the surface areas of these solids:

a)

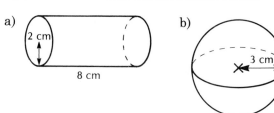

b)

c)

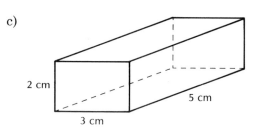

d)

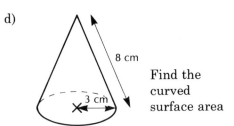

Find the curved surface area

4. a)

```
┌──────────────── 1 m ────────────────┐
│                                      │ 20 cm
└──────────────────────────────────────┘
```

Calculate this area in
i) cm²   ii) m²

b) Convert 4 m² into cm²

c) A box is 1 m wide, 2 m high and 3 m long.
Calculate the volume of the box in
i) cm³   ii) m³

d) A circle has an area of 600 000 cm². What is this area in m²?

e) A pyramid has a volume of 0.000 12 km³. Change this to m³.

f) If 1 cm = 10 mm,
convert
i) 6 cm² to mm²
ii) 50 000 mm³ to cm³
iii) 0.0008 cm² to mm²

1. Which pairs of triangles are similar?

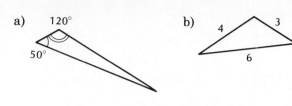

a)

b)

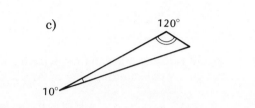

c)

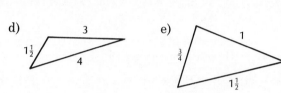

d)

e)

2. Which pairs of triangles are congruent?

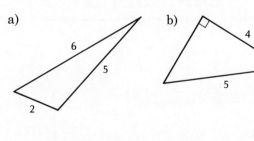

a)

b)

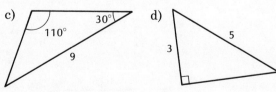

c)

d)

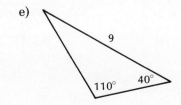

e)

3. Calculate the lengths labelled with letters.

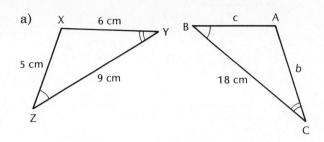

a)

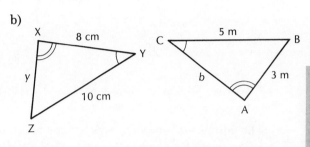

b)

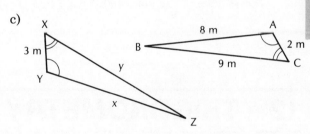

c)

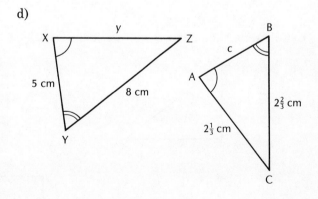

d)

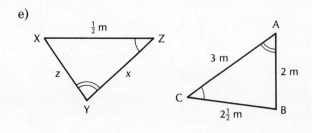

e)

4. a)

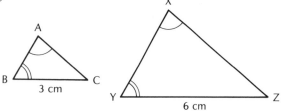

If the area of △ABC is 4 cm², find the area of △XYZ.

b)

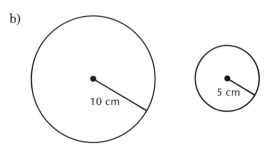

The area of the larger circle is 314.2 m². What is the area of the smaller circle?

c) The volume of a prism is 8 cm³. If the prism is enlarged with a scale factor of 3, what will be the volume of the enlarged prism?

d) A sphere with a volume of 10 m³ has a radius twice the length of a smaller sphere. What is the volume of the smaller sphere?

e)

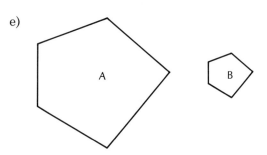

A and B are similar shapes, with each side of B $\frac{1}{3}$ the corresponding side of A.

i) If the area of A is 54 m², what is the area of B?

ii) One side of A is 4 m, what is the length of the corresponding side of B?

iii) When B has an area of 5 cm², what is the area of A?

---

12 TRIGONOMETRY   Questions

---

1. Calculate the unknown side in each triangle.

a)
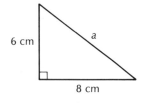

b)
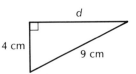

c)
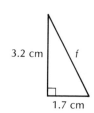

d)
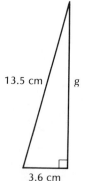

e)
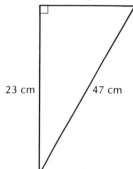

f)
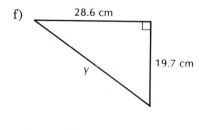

2. Calculate each length labelled with a letter.

a)

b)

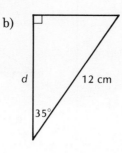

c)

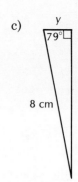

d)

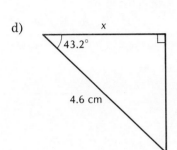

e)

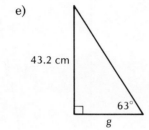

f)

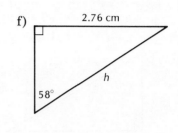

g)

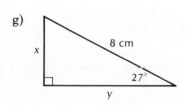

h)

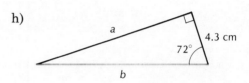

3. Find the size of the marked angle.

a)

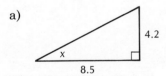

b)

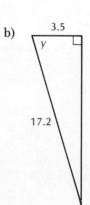

c)

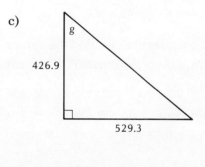

d)

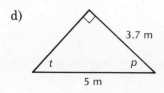

e)

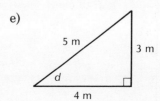

4. a)

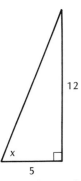

12

x

5

Write down the values of

i) tan x ii) sin x iii) cos x

b)

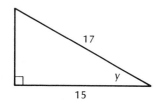

17

y

15

Write down the values of

i) cos y ii) tan y iii) sin y

c)

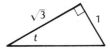

$\sqrt{3}$

1

t

Write down the values of

i) tan t ii) sin t iii) cos t

d) If cos $g = \frac{4}{5}$, what are the values of

i) tan g ii) sin g ?

5. Without using tables, find the values of

a) sin 150°   b) tan 330°   c) cos 240°

d) tan 135°   e) tan 120°   f) cos 210°

g) sin 225°   h) tan 240°   i) sin 300°

j) cos 120°

6. a)

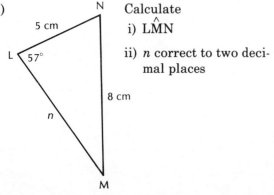

N

5 cm

L   57°

8 cm

n

M

Calculate

i) $L\hat{M}N$

ii) n correct to two decimal places

b)

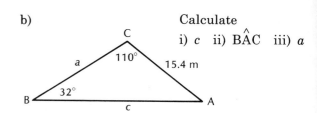

C

110°

a

15.4 m

B   32°

c

A

Calculate

i) c ii) $B\hat{A}C$ iii) a

c) In the triangle DEF, $E = 63°$, $e = 9.3\,\text{cm}$ and $D = 38°$. Calculate d and f.

d)

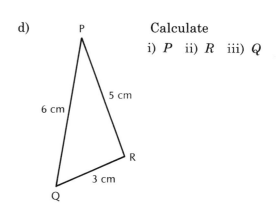

P

5 cm

6 cm

R

3 cm

Q

Calculate

i) P ii) R iii) Q

e)

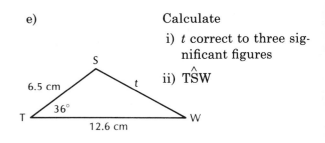

S

6.5 cm

t

36°

T

12.6 cm

W

Calculate

i) t correct to three significant figures

ii) $T\hat{S}W$

7. Calculate the area of

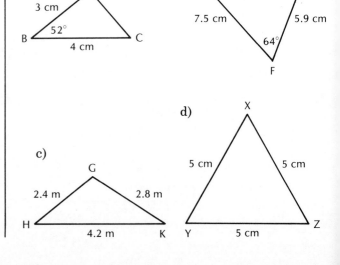

a)

A

3 cm

52°

B

4 cm

C

b)

D

47°

E

7.5 cm

5.9 cm

64°

F

c)

G

2.4 m

2.8 m

H

4.2 m

K

d)

X

5 cm

5 cm

Y

5 cm

Z

8. a)

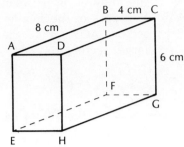

Calculate to 1 d.p.

    i) AH
   ii) EG
  iii) BH

b)

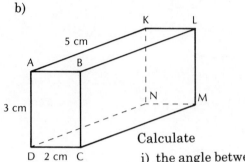

Calculate

  i) the angle between LD and ABLK
 ii) the angle between the planes KLMN and ADML

9. Sketch the bearings

  a) 170°   b) 290°   c) 020°   d) 350°

  e) 255°   f) 090°   g) 100°   h) 190°

10. P is 8 km due west of Q and R is 12 km due east of Q. S is on a bearing of 052° from P and due north of Q.

Calculate

  a) QS

  b) the bearing of S from R

11. A, B and C are three points on the same horizontal plane. $A\hat{B}C = 90°$, AB = 30 m and BC = 40 m. A point D is 80 m vertically above B.

Calculate

  a) the angle of elevation of D from A

  b) the angle of depression of C from D

12. Town X is 18 km from town W on a bearing of 052° and town Y is 20 km from X on a bearing of 322°. When an aircraft is directly above Y, the angle of elevation as seen from X is 8°. Calculate the altitude (perpendicular height) of the aircraft and the distance from W to Y.

13 CIRCLES   Questions

1. Calculate the circumference of each circle using the given value of π.

a)

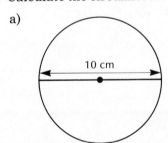

π ≈ 3.14

b)

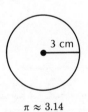

π ≈ 3.14

c)

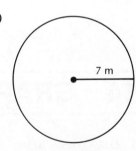

$\pi \approx \frac{22}{7}$

d)

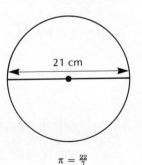

$\pi = \frac{22}{7}$

e)

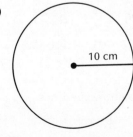

π ≈ 3.14

177

2. Calculate the area of each circle shown in Question 1, using the given value of π.

3. a)

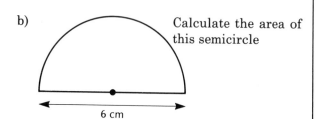

A Calculate the length of arc AB

b)

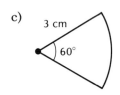

Calculate the area of this semicircle

c)

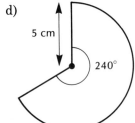

Calculate

i) the area of this sector

ii) the perimeter of this sector

d)

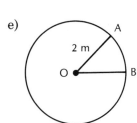

Find the perimeter and the area of this shape

e)

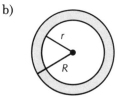

If $\overset{\wedge}{AOB} = 45°$, calculate the difference between the areas of the smaller sector AOB and the larger sector.

4. Calculate the area of each of the following rings:

a)

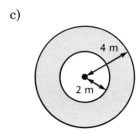

$r = 3\,\text{cm}$
$R = 7\,\text{cm}$

b)

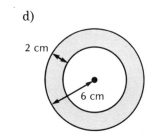

$R = 1.7\,\text{cm}$
$r = 1.3\,\text{cm}$

c)

d)

Leave your answer in terms of π

e) If the diameter of the outer circle is 24 m and the diameter of the inner circle is 16 m, what is the area of the ring between them in terms of π?

14 GRAPHS   Questions

1. Draw axes where $-4 \leqslant x \leqslant 5$ and $-5 \leqslant y \leqslant 4$.

Plot and label the points

A (2, 0)   B (0, −1)   C (−2, 4)

D (−3, −2)   E (5, −1)   F (−2, −2)

2. Sketch diagrams to show the lines

a) $y = 3$ b) $x = -2$

c) $x + y = 3$ d) $y = 3x - 1$

e) $y = 6 - x$ f) $y = 2x + 3$

g) $2y = x + 3$ h) $3y = x$

i) $y = 2(x - 1)$ j) $y = 2 - 3x$

3. On the same axes, draw the lines $y = x + 3$ and $x + y = 2$. What are the coordinates of the point where the lines intersect?

4. On separate diagrams shade the regions

a) $y < -2$ b) $x \geqslant 3$

c) $x + y < 2$ d) $y \geqslant 3x - 1$

e) $y < x + 4$ f) $y \leqslant x$

g) $y > 2x + 1$ h) $2y \leqslant x$

i) $x + y + 1 > 0$ j) $x < y - 2$

5. A shop sells bunches of flowers consisting of tulips and daffodils. The large bunch consists of 8 tulips and 12 daffodils and the small bunch of 10 tulips and 4 daffodils. The shop has a total of 120 tulips and 96 daffodils to make x large and y small bunches

a) How many tulips are sold?

b) How many daffodils are sold?

c) Write down two inequalities connecting x and y.

d) Using a scale of 1 cm to represent 2 bunches on each axis draw a diagram to show these inequalities (shading the *unwanted* region).

e) If the cost of a large bunch is £2 and of a small bunch is £1, find the greatest possible takings and the numbers of bunches which must be sold to make this amount.

6. A factory manufactures two types of machine. Machine A requires a skilled man to work for 8 hours and an unskilled man to work for 6 hours and machine B requires 5 hours work by a skilled man and 9 hours by an unskilled man. If x of machine A and y of machine B are made in a week and a skilled man cannot work more than 40 hours or an unskilled man 36 hours

a) Write down two inequalities showing the time worked by the skilled and by the unskilled man.

b) Show these inequalities on a graph, shading the *unwanted* region.

c) If £300 profit is made on machine A and £200 on machine B, what is the maximum profit that can be made in a week?

7. Complete this table and then use it to draw the graph of $f(x) = x^2 - 5x + 6$ for $-2 \leqslant x \leqslant 4$.

x	-2	-1	0	1	2	3	4
x^2					4		16
$-5x$		$+5$			-10		
$+6$			$+6$		$+6$		
$f(x)$					0		

Use the graph to solve the equations

a) $x^2 - 5x + 6 = 0$ b) $x^2 = 5x - 4$

8. Copy and complete this table and then use it to draw the graph of $y = x^2 + 3x - 4$.

x	-5	-4	-3	-2	-1	0	1	2
x^2								
$+3x$								
-4								
y								

Use the graph to solve the equations

a) $x^2 + 3x = 4$ b) $x^2 = 1 - 3x$

9. a) Use the trapezium rule to calculate the approximate area under the curve $y = x^2$ between $x = 1$ and $x = 6$

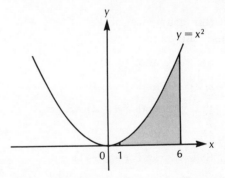

b) Calculate the shaded area.

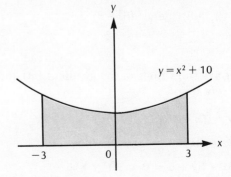

10. a) Draw a diagram to show the points

A $(2, 60°)$ B $(1, 90°)$ C $(4, 280°)$
D $(1, 170°)$ E $(2, 350°)$

b) Shade in the area where $3 \leqslant R \leqslant 4$ and $30° \leqslant \theta \leqslant 60°$.

c) Shade in the area where $0 \leqslant R \leqslant 2$ and $90° \leqslant \theta \leqslant 210°$.

11. a) £1 is worth 4.5 DM (German marks).

Draw a conversion graph to show up to £10.

From the graph, what is the value of:
i) £4 in DM?   ii) 32 DM in £?
iii) How many DM would a tourist be given for a travellers cheque worth £5?

b) Repeat part a) using the exchange rate of £1 being worth 6 DM.

---

15   STRAIGHT LINES   Questions

---

1. Draw on a graph the lines with equations

a) $y = x + 2$ b) $2y = 3x - 1$

c) $x + y = 4$ d) $y = 2x - 3$

e) $y = 6 - x$

g) $x + y = 9$ h) $5y - 2x = 3$

i) $3y = 2x$ j) $x - y = 4$

2. Find the gradients of the lines which pass through the points

a) $(3, 5)$ and $(4, 9)$

b) $(-2, 3)$ and $(8, 11)$

c) $(-1, -2)$ and $(-3, 4)$

d) $(0, 4)$ and $(5, -2)$

e) $(6, 6)$ and $(-1, -1)$

f) $(24, -18)$ and $(-6, -3)$

g) $(-2, 7)$ and $(10, 5)$

h) $(-1, -8)$ and $(6, -8)$

3. What are the values of the gradient (m) and the intercept (c) of

a) $y = 7x - 4$ b) $y = 3 + 2x$

c) $2y = 4x + 3$ d) $2x + y = 4$

e) $3x + 2y + 5 = 0$ f) $y = 6$

4. Write down the equations of the lines when

a) $m = 2, c = 3$ b) $c = -2, m = -\frac{3}{4}$

c) Gradient $= -\frac{1}{2}$ d) $m = 6, c = \frac{1}{2}$
   Intercept $= 5$

e) $m = \frac{1}{3}, c = -\frac{1}{6}$ f) Intercept $= -3$
                              Gradient $= 3$

g) $c = 1\frac{1}{2}, m = 2\frac{1}{2}$ h) $m = \frac{5}{8}, c = -2\frac{1}{4}$

5. Find the equations of the lines which pass through the points

a) $(3, 5)$ and $(4, 9)$

b) $(1, 1)$ and $(-1, 2)$

c) $(-3, 5)$ and $(-1, 7)$

d) $(-3, 2)$ and $(3, -2)$

e) $(-2, -1)$ and $(2, 2)$

f) $(8, 12)$ and $(-4, 2)$

g) $(4, 4)$ and $(-1, -1)$

h) $(-2, 9)$ and $(-2, 4)$

1. a) Calculate the speed of a car which travels 495 miles in 10 hours.

   b) How long would it take to travel 360 km at an average speed of 80 km/h?

   c) What distance can be travelled in 3 seconds by a body travelling at 8 cm/s?

   d) The average speed for a journey is 42 km/h. If the total distance travelled is 7 km, how long does the journey take?

   e) 120 cm is travelled in 1 hour at a constant speed. How far is travelled in 3 minutes?

   f) Change 72 000 km/h into km/s.

2. a) What is the average speed of a journey if 100 km is travelled in the first hour, during the next two hours the object does not move and during the next five hours the object travels 250 km?

   b) Find the average speed of the 100 mile journey from A to D if the 30 miles from A to B takes 35 minutes, the 40 miles from B to C takes 55 minutes and the journey from C to D takes 90 minutes.

   c) A train travels at 100 km/h for 25 minutes, 80 km/h for 15 minutes and at 90 km/h for 20 minutes. What is the average speed of the complete journey?

   d) A snail crawls 12 cm in 48 seconds, rests for eight seconds then crawls for another 20 cm in 40 seconds. What is its average speed for the whole journey?

3. a)   What speed is shown here?

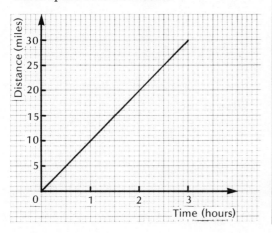

b) Calculate the total distance travelled.

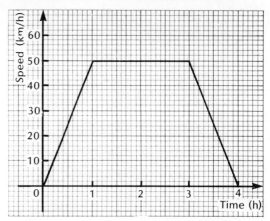

c) Calculate the total distance covered in this journey.
   What is the acceleration
      i) in the first 5 seconds?
      ii) in the next 2 seconds?
      iii) in the last 3 seconds?

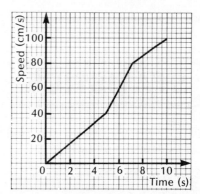

d) Draw a distance–time curve to show the journey of a boy who leaves home at 8:30 am to travel to school three miles away. He arrives at school at 9:00 am and stays until 4:00 pm when he takes one hour to return home.

e) A train leaves a station and gradually increases speed until it is travelling at 120 km/h. This takes $\frac{1}{4}$ h. It then travels at this speed for $\frac{3}{4}$ h before gradually slowing down until it stops $\frac{1}{2}$ h later. Draw a graph of this journey and use it to calculate the total distance travelled by the train.

SECTION III

17 VARIATION — Questions

1. Find the equation relating x and y if
   a) $y \propto x$ and $x = 8$ when $y = 2$
   b) $y \propto x$ and $x = \frac{1}{2}$ when $y = 6$
   c) $y \propto x^2$ and $x = 4$ when $y = 48$
   d) $y \propto x$ and $y = 36$ when $x = 9$
   e) $y \propto x^3$ and $x = 2$ when $y = 24$
   f) $y \propto x$ and $y = 8$ when $x = 16$
   g) $y \propto x$ and $y = 2\frac{1}{2}$ when $x = \frac{1}{2}$
   h) $y \propto x$ and $x = 1$ when $y = \frac{2}{3}$

2. If y is inversely proportional to x find the equation relating x and y if, when
   a) $x = 2, y = 3$
   b) $x = 5, y = 1$
   c) $y = 6, x = 4$
   d) $y = 2, x = \frac{1}{2}$
   e) $x = 3, y = \frac{2}{3}$
   f) $x = 1, y = 1$
   g) $x = \frac{1}{4}, y = \frac{1}{2}$
   h) $y = 1\frac{1}{2}, x = 6$

3. a) y is proportional to x and when $x = 4$, $y = 12$. Find y when $x = 6$.
   b) If y is proportional to x^3 and $y = 32$ when $x = 2$, find x when $y = 108$.
   c) Given that y is inversely proportional to x and that $x = 5$ when $y = 4$, what is y when $x = 10$?
   d) $y \propto x$ and when $x = \frac{1}{2}$, $y = 4\frac{1}{2}$. What is y when $x = 8$?
   e) If the radius of a circle is doubled, what happens to the area of the circle?

4. a) y varies jointly with w and x such that when $y = 24$, $w = 2$ and $x = 3$. What is w when $x = 5$ and $y = 60$?
   b) $w \propto xy$. Find x when $w = 18$ and $y = 6$ if when $x = 4$, $y = 4$ and $w = 20$.
   c) If y is jointly variable to w and x and $w = 12$ when $y = 2$ and $x = \frac{1}{2}$, find w when $x = 5$ and $y = 2\frac{1}{2}$.

18 STATISTICS — Questions

1. Calculate i) the median ii) the mode iii) the mean of each of the following:
   a) 9, 2, 7, 3, 5, 8, 2, 1, 2
   b) 82, 83, 82, 81, 85, 86, 82
   c) 17.2, 17.3, 17.2, 17.1, 17.5, 17.6, 17.2
   d) 1048, 1041, 1046, 1040, 1049, 1040
   e) 99, 102, 97, 98, 101, 103

2. a) Draw up frequency tables of the following data and use them to find the i) mode ii) median iii) mean.

1 5 3 4 5	0 1 3 4 5	52 54 55 54 53
8 2 1 5 3	2 5 0 2 0	55 53 51 50 53
8 6 1 4 1	1 4 0 1 1	54 51 51 52 55
3 4 2 6 4	3 2 1 1 4	50 50 53 50 53
	2 1 4 3 0	52 50 51 54 51
	5 5 0 1 2	
	3 1 1 4 0	
	2 2 3 1 4	

   b) Draw a block graph of each set of data.

3. Draw up a frequency table of the following data, showing the ages of 30 children attending a day nursery.

1	5	2	5	2	4
2	4	3	3	4	4
2	4	3	1	3	4
3	3	2	1	2	3
4	1	1	1	4	2

   What is the

   a) modal age

   b) median age

   c) mean age

   of the children?

4.

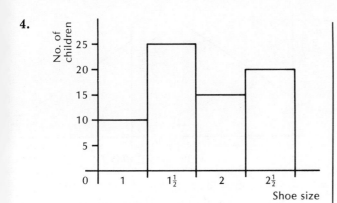

a) What is the modal shoe size?

b) What is the total number of children represented on the graph?

c) Calculate the mean shoe size per child.

5. 100 children are given a test. Write out a frequency table grouping the results 0–10, 11–20, etc. and use it to calculate the mean score.

```
38 62 53 21 87 53 29 62 92 35
47 59 82 36 72 54 51 76 41 29
29 84 75 19 94 27 65 71 83 61
51 16 68  8 38 43 29 73 27 38
58 95 59 42 42 17 28 77 27 27

 5 63 97 62 93 38 84 22 46 76
23 74 31 69 84 21 77 38 42 62
15 29 28 53 81 52 72 94 58 51
28 36 49 32 62 39 68 29 94 94
32 52 58 41 14 32 12 37 91 35
```

6.

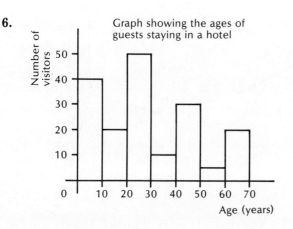

Graph showing the ages of guests staying in a hotel

a) Calculate the mean age of the guests.

b) Draw a cumulative frequency graph of this information.

c) Use the graph drawn in part b) to find the median age of the guests.

7. The number of spectators at 100 football matches played one Saturday was:

Number of spectators	Less than 2000	2000 – 3999
Number of matches	6	3

Number of spectators	4000 – 5999	6000 – 7999	8000 – 9999
Number of matches	8	12	21

Number of spectators	10 000 – 11 999	12 000 – 13 999	14 000 – 15 999
Number of matches	17	23	10

a) Show these data on a histogram

b) Calculate the mean attendance per match

c) Draw a cumulative frequency graph of this information

d) Use your graph in part c) to find
  i) the median attendance
  ii) the inter-quartile range

8. Draw a pie chart to show the following:

a) A die was thrown 180 times and the results obtained were

Score	1	2	3	4	5	6
Frequency	15	25	50	20	40	30

b) A man earns £96 a week and spends £24 on rent, £12 on food, £16 on entertainment and £44 on other expenses.

9. a) Which of the graphs below best fits this statement

'the number of muggings increased steadily in the year 1985?'

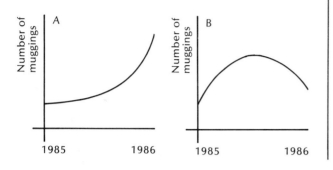

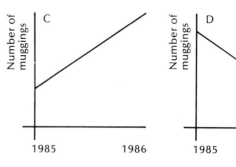

b) Sketch the shape of the graph that would illustrate the statement 'the price of new cars was rising more rapidly in April 1984 than at any time in the previous twelve months'.

19 GEOMETRY   Questions

1. Calculate the lettered angles

a)
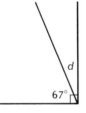

b)
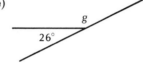

c)
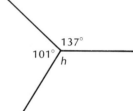

d)
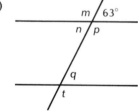

e)
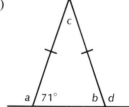

f)
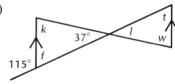

g)
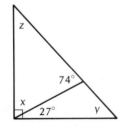

h)
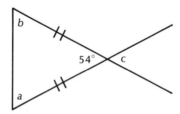

i)
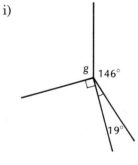

j)

2. Calculate

  a) the sum of the interior angles of a pentagon

  b) the size of each interior angle of a regular octagon

  c) the sum of the exterior angles of a hexagon

  d) the size of each exterior angle of a regular 14-sided polygon

  e) the size of each interior angle of a regular 20-sided polygon

3. Use Pythagoras' theorem to calculate the lengths of the lettered sides

a)
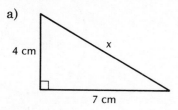

b)
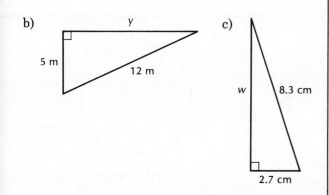
c)

d)
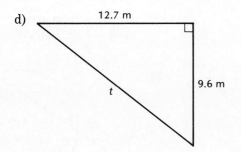

e)
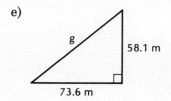

4. Draw a tessellation of

  a) squares   b)

  c) squares and equilateral triangles

  d)    e)

5. Draw a net of each of the following:

  a) a square-based pyramid

  b) a hexagonal-based prism

  c)
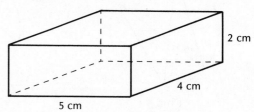

6. Sketch all the possible nets of a cube.

7. Count the number of faces, edges and vertices of a

  a) cube

  b) square based pyramid

  c) hexagonal-based prism

  d) icosahedron

  e) dodecahedron

8. a) If a solid has five faces and seven edges, how many vertices must it have?

  b) A solid has 42 edges and 24 faces. How many vertices does it have?

  c) A prism has 16 vertices and 24 edges. What type of prism is it?

1.

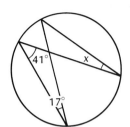

Find x

2.

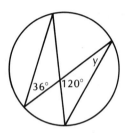

Find y

3.

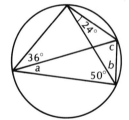

Find a, b, and c.

4.

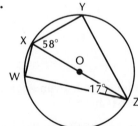

Calculate
a) $X\hat{Y}Z$ b) $X\hat{Z}Y$
c) $X\hat{W}Z$ d) $W\hat{X}Z$

5.

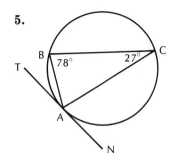

Calculate the sizes
of $T\hat{A}B$, $C\hat{A}N$ and $B\hat{A}C$.

6.

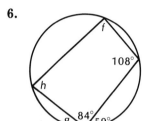

Find f, g and h.

7.

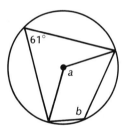

Calculate a and b.

8.

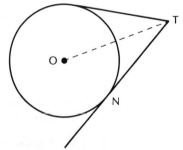

If $OT = 13$ cm and the
tangent $TN = 12$ cm.
what is the radius of the circle?

9.

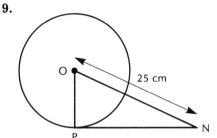

If the radius of the circle is
7 cm, calculate PN.

10.

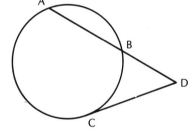

Calculate x

11.

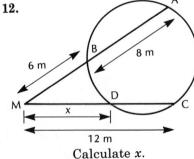

CD is a tangent to
the circle.

If $AD = 9$ cm and
$BD = 4$ cm, calculate CD.

12.

Calculate x.

1. Use a protractor to draw angles of
a) 25°   b) 95°   c) 320°   d) 225°   e) 190°
f) 117°   g) 63°   h) 273°   i) 12°   j) 345°

2. Measure these angles as accurately as possible:

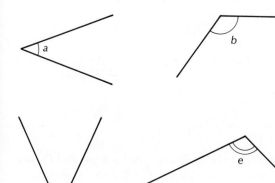

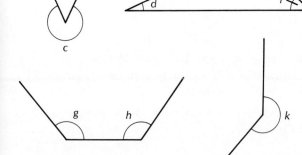

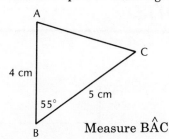

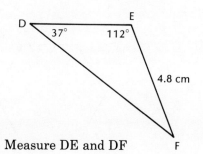

3. Draw accurate copies of these figures:
a)

Measure BÂC

b)

Measure DE and DF

c)

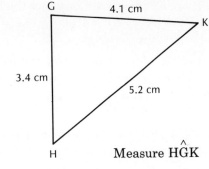

Measure HĜK

d)

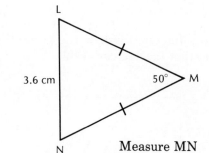

Measure MN

e)

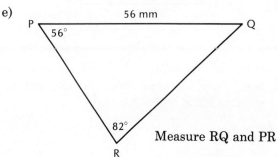

Measure RQ and PR

4. Draw triangle XYZ with XY = 10 cm, XZ = 9 cm and YZ = 8 cm.

Without using a protractor, bisect each of the three angles of △XYZ.

5. Construct an equilateral triangle of side 6 cm. Use this triangle to construct an angle of 15°.

6. Without using a protractor, or a set square, construct a square of side 7 cm.

7. Copy this diagram accurately.

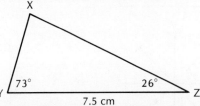

Use compasses to draw the perpendicular bisectors of XY, YZ and XZ.

SECTION III

22 LOCI   Questions

1. A and B are 8.7 cm apart. Construct the locus of a point P such that AP = PB.

2. Construct an angle of 60°. Show the locus of a point P which is equidistant from both arms of the angle.

3. A line XY is 7 cm long. Draw the locus of a point P which is at a fixed distance of 3 cm from XY.

4. A dog is tied to a post by a lead 200 cm long. Sketch a diagram to show the ground around the post that the dog can reach.

5.

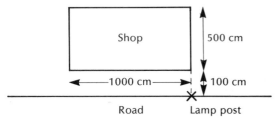

If the dog is tied to this lamppost by the same lead, show the area which the dog can reach without going on to the road.

6. Two landmarks on the coast subtend an angle of 120° at the centre of a circle 50 km in diameter. A ship sails so that the angle at the ship formed by joining it to each of the landmarks is a right angle. Construct the possible positions of the ship on a scale diagram and find the distance between the two landmarks.

7. A and B are fixed points. Describe the locus in three dimensions of a fixed point which moves so that $A\hat{P}B = 90°$.

8. Given that C and D are fixed points and $P\hat{C}D = 60°$, describe the locus of P in three dimensions.

9. XY is a straight line and the perpendicular distance of P from XY is 3 cm. Is the locus of P, in three dimensions

a) a plane   b) a cylinder   c) a sphere
d) a cone?

23 SYMMETRY   Questions

1. Draw all the lines of symmetry of each figure.

a)
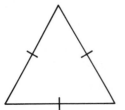

b)
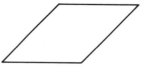

c)

d)
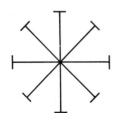

e)
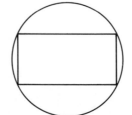

f)

2. Complete these diagrams if – – – – – – – is the line of symmetry.

a)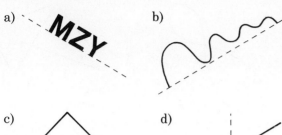

b)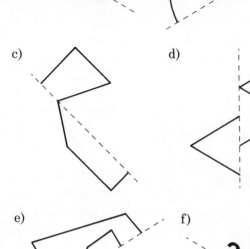

c)

d)

e)

f)

3. What is the order of rotational symmetry of each figure?

a)

b)

c)

d)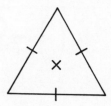

e)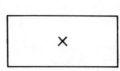

f)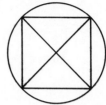

4. Draw diagrams with
a) 3 lines of symmetry
b) order of rotation 3
c) 2 lines of symmetry *and* order of rotation 2
d) 5 lines of symmetry *and* order of rotation 5
e) 2 lines of symmetry *and* order of rotation 1

5. a) What is the number of planes of symmetry of a square-based pyramid?

b) Sketch a diagram showing all the planes of symmetry of an equilateral triangular based prism.

c) How many axes of rotation does a cube have?

24 MATRICES   Questions

1. Write down the order of each of these matrices:

a) $(7 \quad 2 \quad 3)$

b) $\begin{pmatrix} 6 & -4 \\ 0 & -2 \end{pmatrix}$

c) $\begin{pmatrix} 19 & -2 & -1 \\ 4 & 6 & 0 \end{pmatrix}$

d) $\begin{pmatrix} 3 \\ -1 \\ 7 \end{pmatrix}$

e) $\begin{pmatrix} a & b \\ c & d \end{pmatrix}$

f) $\begin{pmatrix} 2 & 2 & 2 & 2 \\ 2 & 2 & 2 & 2 \\ 2 & 2 & 2 & 2 \end{pmatrix}$

2. Where possible, answer the following:

a) $\begin{pmatrix} 5 & 1 \\ 6 & 2 \end{pmatrix} + \begin{pmatrix} 3 & 4 \\ 2 & 7 \end{pmatrix}$

b) $\begin{pmatrix} 1 \\ 2 \end{pmatrix} + \begin{pmatrix} 6 \\ 5 \end{pmatrix}$

c) $(3 \quad -2) + (4 \quad -3)$

d) $\begin{pmatrix} 2 & 9 & 3 \\ 1 & 4 & 7 \end{pmatrix} - \begin{pmatrix} 1 & 6 & 1 \\ 1 & 2 & 5 \end{pmatrix}$

e) $\begin{pmatrix} 7 \\ 1 \\ 3 \end{pmatrix} + (2 \quad 5 \quad 2)$

f) $\begin{pmatrix} -2 & 1 \\ 4 & 6 \end{pmatrix} + \begin{pmatrix} 3 & -5 \\ -2 & 1 \end{pmatrix}$

g) $\begin{pmatrix} 7 & 9 \\ 4 & 0 \end{pmatrix} - \begin{pmatrix} 2 & 6 \\ 0 & 5 \end{pmatrix}$

h) $\begin{pmatrix} 5 & -1 & 2 \\ 3 & 11 & 44 \\ 0 & 1 & 4 \end{pmatrix} + \begin{pmatrix} -7 & 2 & -5 \\ 1 & 3 & 2 \\ -1 & -1 & 5 \end{pmatrix}$

3. $\mathbf{A} = \begin{pmatrix} 1 & 3 \\ 5 & 2 \end{pmatrix}$ $\quad \mathbf{B} = \begin{pmatrix} 2 & 4 \\ 3 & 4 \end{pmatrix}$ $\quad \mathbf{C} = \begin{pmatrix} 1 & -1 \\ 0 & 3 \end{pmatrix}$

$\mathbf{D} = \begin{pmatrix} -2 \\ 4 \end{pmatrix}$ $\quad \mathbf{E} = (1 \quad 3)$ $\quad \mathbf{F} = \begin{pmatrix} 4 & 2 & 0 \\ 3 & 1 & 2 \end{pmatrix}$

Where possible, calculate

a) **AB**   b) **DE**   c) **ED**   d) **AF**

e) **BC**   f) **CB**   g) **A^2**   h) **CE**

i) **FA**   j) **E^2**   k) 2**A** + **B**   l) **B** − **C**

4. Find the determinant of

a) $\begin{pmatrix} 2 & 0 \\ 0 & 2 \end{pmatrix}$ b) $\begin{pmatrix} 6 & 4 \\ 2 & 8 \end{pmatrix}$ c) $\begin{pmatrix} 2 & -1 \\ -3 & 4 \end{pmatrix}$

d) $\begin{pmatrix} 10 & 4 \\ 12 & 3 \end{pmatrix}$ e) $\begin{pmatrix} -4 & 1 \\ -2 & 3 \end{pmatrix}$ f) $\begin{pmatrix} 1 & 0 \\ 0 & -1 \end{pmatrix}$

5. Work out the inverse of each of the following:

a) $\begin{pmatrix} 3 & 4 \\ 2 & 5 \end{pmatrix}$ b) $\begin{pmatrix} 1 & 2 \\ 1 & 5 \end{pmatrix}$ c) $\begin{pmatrix} 2 & -3 \\ -2 & 5 \end{pmatrix}$

d) $\begin{pmatrix} -1 & 0 \\ 0 & -1 \end{pmatrix}$ e) $\begin{pmatrix} 5 & 0 \\ 0 & 5 \end{pmatrix}$ f) $\begin{pmatrix} -4 & 3 \\ -1 & 0 \end{pmatrix}$

6. Write down the transpose of

a) $\begin{pmatrix} 2 \\ 7 \end{pmatrix}$ b) $\begin{pmatrix} 6 & 9 \\ 2 & 1 \end{pmatrix}$ c) $\begin{pmatrix} 4 & 2 & 6 \\ -1 & 3 & 4 \end{pmatrix}$

d) $(8 \quad 2 \quad 7 \quad -1)$ e) $\begin{pmatrix} 0 & 3 \\ 3 & 0 \end{pmatrix}$

f) $\begin{pmatrix} 2 & -3 \\ -1 & 0 \\ 3 & -4 \end{pmatrix}$

7. Count the number of nodes, arcs and regions for each figure.

a) 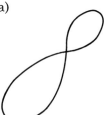   b)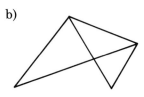

c) 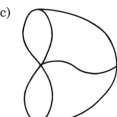   d)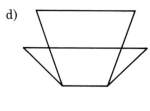

e)   f)

g)    h)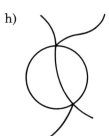

8. i) Write down the matrix, **N**, describing this network.

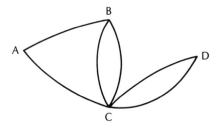

ii) Calculate **N^2**.

iii) How many two stage routes are represented by **N^2**?

190

9. Repeat Question 8 for these networks

a)

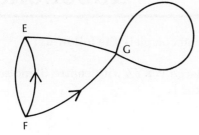

b)

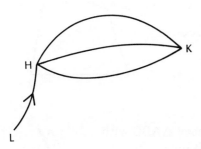

c)

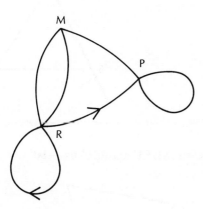

10. a)

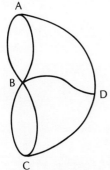

For this network, write down the incidence matrix of

  i) nodes incident on regions
 ii) arcs incident on nodes
iii) arcs incident on regions

b)

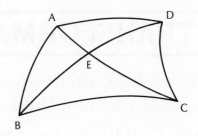

Write down the incidence matrix of

  i) regions incident on nodes
 ii) arcs incident on regions
iii) nodes incident on arcs

11. A = (1, 2), B = (4, 2), C = (4, 4), D = (1, 4).

a) Transform ABCD by the matrix $\begin{pmatrix} 0 & 1 \\ -1 & 0 \end{pmatrix}$ to $A_1B_1C_1D_1$.

b) Plot ABCD and $A_1B_1C_1D_1$ on the same axes.

c) Describe, in words, the transformation represented by the inverse of $\begin{pmatrix} 0 & 1 \\ -1 & 0 \end{pmatrix}$.

d) Express the inverse as a 2 × 2 matrix.

12. W = (3, 5), X = (2, 3), Y = (7, 3), Z = (5, 5).

a) Plot WXYZ on axes.

b) Premultiply WXYZ by $\begin{pmatrix} 1 & 0 \\ 0 & -1 \end{pmatrix}$, plot on the axes and label this image P.

c) Premultiply WXYZ by $\begin{pmatrix} -1 & 0 \\ 0 & 1 \end{pmatrix}$, plot on the axes and label this image Q.

d) Premultiply WXYZ by $\begin{pmatrix} 0 & 1 \\ 1 & 0 \end{pmatrix}$, plot on the axes and label this image R.

13. L = (1, 1), M = (6, 2), N = (2, 4).

a) Premultiply by $\begin{pmatrix} -1 & 0 \\ 0 & -1 \end{pmatrix}$ to transform LMN to $L_1M_1N_1$.

b) What is the inverse of this transformation?

c) Premultiply $L_1M_1N_1$ by $\begin{pmatrix} 0 & -1 \\ 1 & 0 \end{pmatrix}$ and label the image $L_2M_2N_2$.

d) What transformation would take $L_2M_2N_2$ back to LMN?

e) Show all these triangles on a graph.

25 TRANSFORMATIONS Questions

1. Plot A (2, 1), B (3, 1), C (4, 4), D (5, 0) on a graph.

   What vector describes the translation from

   a) B to C   b) D to A   c) A to B

   d) C to D   e) C to A ?

2. a) Plot D (1, 1), E (4, 2) and F (3, 4) on a set of axes where $-6 \leqslant x \leqslant 6$ and $-6 \leqslant y \leqslant 6$.

   b) Reflect $\triangle$DEF in the x-axis and label the image X.

   c) Reflect $\triangle$DEF in the y-axis and label the image Y.

   d) Reflect $\triangle$DEF in the line $x + y = 0$ and label the image Z.

3. a) If the triangle A (5, 4), B (4, 0), C (6, 2) is reflected to A′ $(-1, 4)$, B′ (0, 0), C′ $(-2, 2)$, where is the mirror line?

   b) Where is the mirror line which reflects F (3, 1), G (4, 3) to F′(1, 3), G′(3, 4)?

4. a) Reflect the triangle KLM where K = (3, 0), L = (5, 2) M = (4, 3) in the line $y = x + 3$. What are the coordinates of the vertices of the image?

   b) What are the coordinates of the vertices of the image when $\triangle$KLM is reflected in the line $y = -x$?

5. a) Draw and label A (1, 1), B (3, 1), C (3, 3), D (1, 3) on a set of axes.

   b) Rotate ABCD 90° about (0, 0) and label the image $A_1B_1C_1D_1$.

   c) Rotate ABCD $-90°$ about (0, 0) and label the image $A_2B_2C_2D_2$.

   d) Rotate ABCD 180° about (0, 0) and label the image $A_3B_3C_3D_3$.

6. Copy and complete the following:

   a) Enlarge WXYZ with centre C and scale factor $\frac{1}{2}$.

   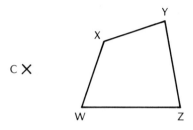

   b) Shear $\triangle$ABC with AB invariant.

   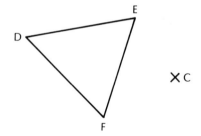

   c) Rotate $\triangle$DEF about C by $-90°$.

   d)

   Stretch OABC with OC invariant and stretch factor 2.

192

e) Enlarge △KLM with scale factor −3 and centre C.

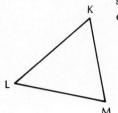

f) Find the centre of rotation which maps ABC to A′B′C′.

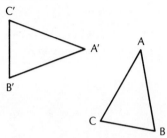

What is the angle of rotation?

g)

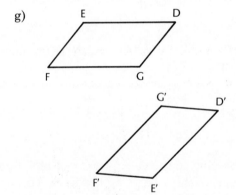

If DEFG is reflected to D′E′F′G′, where is the mirror line?

7. a) If a triangle of area $6\,\text{cm}^2$ is enlarged by a scale factor of 2, what is the area of the enlarged triangle?

b) A quadrilateral of area $2\frac{1}{2}\,\text{cm}^2$ is transformed by $\begin{pmatrix} 2 & 3 \\ 3 & 6 \end{pmatrix}$. What is the area of the transformed figure?

c) A (2, 4), B (3, 9), C (5, 9), D (4, 4) is transformed by $\begin{pmatrix} -4 & -1 \\ 2 & -3 \end{pmatrix}$ to A′B′C′D′. What is the area of A′B′C′D′?

8. a) $\mathbf{M} = \begin{pmatrix} 3 & 1 \\ 4 & 2 \end{pmatrix}$, $\mathbf{N} = \begin{pmatrix} 1 & 2 \\ 1 & 4 \end{pmatrix}$. Calculate

i) $\mathbf{MN}$ ii) $(\mathbf{MN})^{-1}$

b) If a figure is transformed by $\mathbf{MN}$ where $\mathbf{M} = \begin{pmatrix} 1 & -1 \\ -1 & 2 \end{pmatrix}$ and $\mathbf{N} = \begin{pmatrix} 0 & 3 \\ -1 & 2 \end{pmatrix}$, what matrix will represent the inverse of this transformation?

c) $\mathbf{A} = \begin{pmatrix} 0 & 1 \\ -1 & 0 \end{pmatrix}$, $\mathbf{B} = \begin{pmatrix} 2 & 0 \\ 0 & 2 \end{pmatrix}$. Calculate

i) $(\mathbf{AB})^{-1}$ ii) $(\mathbf{BA})^{-1}$

iii) Describe these transformations in words.

26 VECTORS   Questions

1. On a graph, plot the points A(2, 4), B(−2, 3), C(0, 4), D(5, 1), E(−1, −2).

Write down the column matrix of the vectors

a) $\overrightarrow{AB}$ b) $\overrightarrow{ED}$

c) $\overrightarrow{CA}$ d) $\overrightarrow{BE}$

e) $\overrightarrow{EB}$ f) $\overrightarrow{AB} + \overrightarrow{BD}$

g) $\overrightarrow{CA} + \overrightarrow{AD} + \overrightarrow{DE}$ h) $\overrightarrow{AC} + \overrightarrow{CB} + \overrightarrow{BA}$

2. Calculate the length of the vectors

a) $\begin{pmatrix} 3 \\ 4 \end{pmatrix}$ b) $\begin{pmatrix} 6 \\ 8 \end{pmatrix}$ c) $\begin{pmatrix} 5 \\ 12 \end{pmatrix}$ d) $\begin{pmatrix} 2 \\ 3 \end{pmatrix}$ e) $\begin{pmatrix} 6 \\ 4 \end{pmatrix}$

3. Find the directions of the vectors

a) $\begin{pmatrix} 1 \\ 1 \end{pmatrix}$ b) $\begin{pmatrix} 4 \\ 3 \end{pmatrix}$ c) $\begin{pmatrix} -2 \\ 2 \end{pmatrix}$

d) $\begin{pmatrix} 6 \\ -2 \end{pmatrix}$ e) $\begin{pmatrix} -3 \\ -1 \end{pmatrix}$

4. Are the following pairs of vectors parallel? If they are, what is the connection between their lengths?

a) $\overrightarrow{AB} = 3\mathbf{a}$ $\overrightarrow{CD} = \mathbf{a}$

b) $\overrightarrow{XY} = (\mathbf{a} + \mathbf{b})$ $\overrightarrow{PQ} = \frac{1}{2}(\mathbf{a} + \mathbf{b})$

c) $\overrightarrow{EF} = (2\mathbf{a} - \mathbf{b})$ $\overrightarrow{GH} = 6(\mathbf{a} - \mathbf{b})$

d) $\overrightarrow{ST} = \frac{1}{2}\mathbf{a} + \mathbf{b}$ $\overrightarrow{MN} = 4\mathbf{a} + 8\mathbf{b}$

e) $\overrightarrow{CD} = \mathbf{a} - \mathbf{b}$ $\overrightarrow{EF} = 2\mathbf{b} - 2\mathbf{a}$

5. a)

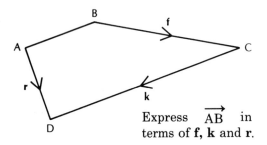

Express $\overrightarrow{AB}$ in terms of **f**, **k** and **r**.

b)

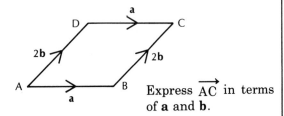

Express $\overrightarrow{AC}$ in terms of **a** and **b**.

c)

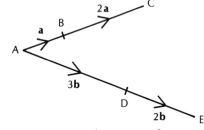

Express i) $\overrightarrow{BE}$ ii) $\overrightarrow{EC}$ iii) $\overrightarrow{DC}$ in terms of **a** and **b**.

d)

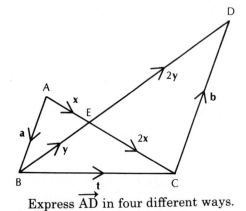

Express $\overrightarrow{AD}$ in four different ways.

6.

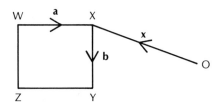

WXYZ is a square. If $\overrightarrow{OX} = \mathbf{x}$ express in terms of **a**, **b** and **x**.

a) $\overrightarrow{OY}$ b) $\overrightarrow{OZ}$ c) $\overrightarrow{WO}$

d) $\overrightarrow{WY}$ e) $\overrightarrow{MO}$ (where M is the mid-point of WZ)

7. ABCD is a rectangle with $\overrightarrow{AB} = 2\mathbf{a}$ and $\overrightarrow{BC} = 4\mathbf{b}$.

If M is the mid-point of AB and N is the mid-point of BC

a) Express $\overrightarrow{AC}$, $\overrightarrow{AN}$, $\overrightarrow{DB}$ and $\overrightarrow{DM}$ in terms of **a** and **b**

b) By referring to the vectors $\overrightarrow{AC}$ and $\overrightarrow{MN}$, find the relationships between the lines AC and MN

8. $\overrightarrow{OA} = \mathbf{a}$, $\overrightarrow{OB} = \mathbf{b}$, $\overrightarrow{OC} = 3\mathbf{b}$, and $\overrightarrow{OD} = \frac{1}{2}\mathbf{a}$

Express, in terms of **a** and **b**, $\overrightarrow{BA}$, $\overrightarrow{AC}$, $\overrightarrow{DC}$ and $\overrightarrow{DB}$.

9. $\overrightarrow{AB} = \mathbf{a}$, $\overrightarrow{AC} = -\mathbf{a}$, $\overrightarrow{AD} = -2\mathbf{b}$, $\overrightarrow{AE} = 3\mathbf{b}$.

Show this information on a diagram, and use it to find the vectors

a) $\overrightarrow{CB}$ b) $\overrightarrow{DB}$ c) $\overrightarrow{EB}$ d) $\overrightarrow{CE}$ e) $\overrightarrow{ED}$

27 PROBABILITY — Questions

1. What is the probability of

   a) throwing an odd number on a die?

   b) selecting a blue sock from a pile of three blue and two grey socks?

   c) it raining tomorrow if the probability that it will be fine is $\frac{3}{7}$?

   d) choosing a red sweet from a pocket containing 7 red and 9 green sweets?

   e) choosing a red and then a green sweet from a pocket containing 7 red and 9 green sweets?

   f) selecting a spade or a king from a pack of cards?

   g) throwing a 3 or a 2 on a die?

   h) having a head and a 6 when throwing a coin and a die?

   i) winning a game by scoring a double 6 when throwing two dice?

   j) a family of three children being all boys?

   k) scoring more than 10 when throwing two dice?

   l) selecting 2 tins of the same variety from a shelf holding 3 tins of soup and 4 tins of meat?

2. The box of chocolates that David and John are sharing contains 7 plain chocolates and 4 milk chocolates. The boys take it in turns to choose a chocolate, John taking one first. Draw a tree diagram to show how they could select one chocolate each.

   What is the probability that both boys will select the same type of chocolate?

3. In a car park there are 2 blue and 3 green cars. Each car is equally likely to leave first. Draw a tree diagram to show the ways in which the different coloured cars could leave.

   What is the probability of a blue car being the last to leave?

4. The probability that a student studies Chemistry is $\frac{2}{3}$.

   If he studies Chemistry then the probability that he also studies Physics is $\frac{9}{10}$ but if he does not study Chemistry, the probability that he studies Physics is $\frac{1}{4}$. Show this information on a tree diagram and list the possible outcomes and probabilities.

5. The probability of scoring an even number on a biased die is $\frac{2}{5}$. Draw a tree diagram to show the possible outcomes when this die is thrown three times.

   What is the probability of scoring

   a) only one even number

   b) scoring only odd numbers

   c) scoring two or more even numbers

28 SETS — Questions

1. Fill in the missing sign, e.g. $\in$, $\notin$, $\subset$, $\not\subset$, $=$, $\cap$, $\cup$, $\varnothing$.

   a) $\{2, 7\}$ ...... $\{2, 3, 4, 5, 6, 7\}$

   b) $\square$ ...... $\{\triangle, \bigcirc, \square\}$

   c) $\{A, B, C\}$ ...... $\{C, D, E\}$

   d) $\{p, q, r\}$ ...... $\{q, r, t\} = \{p, q, r, t\}$

   e) $\{9, 10, 11\}$ ...... $\{11, 12, 14\} = \{11\}$

   f) T ...... $\{D, F, S\}$

   g) $\{a\}$ ...... $\{a, b, c, d\}$

   h) $\{47, 48, 49\}$ ...... $\{48, 50, 52\} = \{48\}$

   i) $\{4, 8\} \cap \{6, 9\} = $ ......

   j)

    ...... =

195

2.

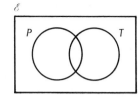

Shade in the regions represented by

a) $P \cap T$ b) $P \cap T'$ c) T'

d) $(P \cup T)'$ e) $(P \triangle T)'$

3. Write a description of each shaded area in set notation.

a)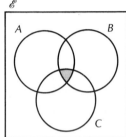
b)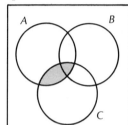

c)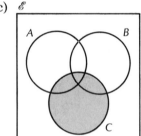
d)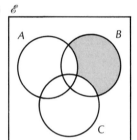

e)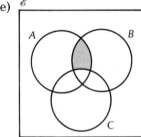
f)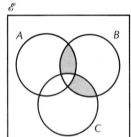

g)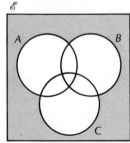
h)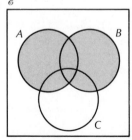

4.

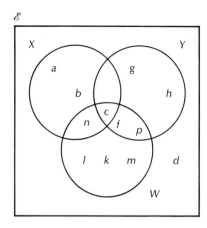

List the elements in these sets.

a) Y b) $X \cap W$ c) $X \cup Y$

d) $(X \cup Y \cup W)'$ e) $(X \cup W) \cap Y$ f) $Y \triangle W$

g) $W \cap (Y \cup X)$ h) $Y \cap X \cap W$ i) $Y' \cup X'$

j) W'

5.

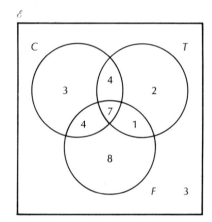

Calculate

a) $n(\mathscr{E})$

b) $n(C \cap T \cap F)$

c) $n(C \cup T \cup F)'$

d) $n(C \cap T)$

e) the number in F and T *only*

f) the number in F and T

g) the number in F but *not* in T

h) the number in F *only*

i) the number in F

j) $n(T \cap C' \cap F')$

6. Draw Venn diagrams to help answer each of the following:

a) Out of a group of 30 people, 24 could speak English and 17 could speak French. How many could speak both languages?

b) There are 40 houses in a street. 21 have gas central heating, 5 have no central heating and the remainder have oil central heating. How many have oil central heating?

c) In a class 24 children have a brother, 17 children have a sister, 11 children have both a brother and a sister and 3 have neither. How many are in the class?

d) Out of a group of 50 men, 20 are wearing black shoes; 8 are wearing black shoes, socks and ties; 13 are wearing black shoes and socks; 10 are wearing black shoes and ties; 3 are wearing only black socks, 6 are wearing only black ties and 14 are not wearing anything black. How many are wearing only black ties and socks?

e) 3 people out of a group of 32 like neither tea nor coffee. 24 like tea and 16 like coffee. How many like both tea and coffee?

7. a) Draw a Venn diagram to show that out of a class of 30, 17 are boys and that of the 23 in the class who study Physics, 12 are girls.

b) If, in addition to the information given in a), 3 girls study Chemistry as well as Physics, 4 boys also do both, 1 boy does neither and no girls do neither, then by means of a Venn diagram, find how many of the class study Chemistry.

8. Complete a Venn diagram showing the sets A, B, C and $\mathscr{E}$ such that

$n(\mathscr{E}) = 42, n(A) = 14, n(B) = 23, n(C) = 20,$

$n(A \cup B \cup C)' = 6, n(A \cap B' \cap C') = 8,$

$n(A \cap B \cap C) = 2, n(A \cap C \cap B') = 1$

What is the value of $n(A' \cap B \cap C')$?

SECTION III

29 RELATIONS, MAPPINGS AND FUNCTIONS Questions

1. Copy and complete the following:

a) $x \mapsto x + 1$

2
3
4
5

b) $x \mapsto \dfrac{x}{2}$

2 1
4 2
6 3
8 4

c) $\mapsto$ means 'is 2 more than'

13
14
15
16
17

d) $x \mapsto x^2$

−2 0
−1 1
0 2
1 3
2 4

e) $\mapsto$ means 'is a factor of'

2 8
3 9
4 10
5 11
12

f) f: $x \mapsto 2(x + 1)$

1
2
3
4

g) g: $x \mapsto \sqrt{x + 1}$

15
8
3

h) $x \mapsto 3x - 1$

$\mapsto$ 2
$\mapsto$ 8
5 $\mapsto$
$\mapsto$ 29

197

i) $h: x \mapsto 5 - x$
$$\begin{array}{c} 3 \\ 2 \\ 1 \\ 0 \\ -1 \end{array}$$

j) $x \mapsto 5x$
$$\begin{array}{c} -10 \\ -5 \\ 0 \\ 5 \\ 10 \end{array}$$

k) $\mapsto$ means 'is half of'

$-2 \mapsto$
$\mapsto -1$
$\mapsto \quad 4$
$16 \mapsto$

l) $f: x \mapsto \dfrac{12}{x}$

$$\begin{array}{c} 4 \\ 3 \\ 2 \\ 1 \\ -1 \\ -2 \end{array}$$

2. a) $h: x \mapsto 2(1 - x)$. If the domain set is $\{-1, 0, 1, 2, 3\}$, what is the range set?

b) $g: x \mapsto x + 3$. If the range set is $\{2, 4, 6, 8\}$, what is the domain set?

3. a) $f(x) = 3x - 1$. Evaluate
   i) $f(2)$ ii) $f(0)$ iii) $f(-2)$

b) $g(x) = \dfrac{2(x + 1)}{3}$. Evaluate

   i) $g(0)$ ii) $g(-4)$ iii) $g(20)$

c) $h(x) = 10 - x$. Evaluate
   i) $h(7)$ ii) $h(0)$ iii) $h(-2)$

d) $g(x) = \dfrac{18}{x}$. Evaluate

   i) $g(9)$ ii) $g(\tfrac{1}{2})$ iii) $g(18)$

e) $f(x) = (x + 3)(x + 2)$. Evaluate
   i) $f(4)$ ii) $f(y)$ iii) $f(7)$

f) $h(x) = x^2 - 1$. Evaluate
   i) $h(-3)$ ii) $h(3)$ iii) $h(2a)$

g) $h(x) = \dfrac{3(2 + x)}{4}$. Evaluate

   i) $h(2)$ ii) $h(-6)$ iii) $h(t)$

h) $f(x) = \dfrac{2 - x}{x^2}$. Evaluate

   i) $f(1)$ ii) $f(6)$ iii) $f(3)$

i) $g(x) = \dfrac{2}{2x + 1}$. Evaluate

   i) $g(3)$ ii) $g(-1)$ iii) $g(21)$

j) $f(x) = 2x^2$. Evaluate
   i) $f(2)$ ii) $f(-6)$ iii) $f(3y)$

4. Find the inverse of each of the following:
   a) $f(x) = x - 2$ b) $f: x \mapsto 6x$

   c) $f(x) = 3x - 1$ d) $f(x) = \dfrac{1}{x}$

   e) $f(x) = 2(3x + 4)$ f) $f: x \mapsto 3 - x$

   g) $f: x \mapsto \dfrac{2x}{3} + 1$ h) $f(x) = \dfrac{2}{3}\left(1 + \dfrac{x}{2}\right)$

   i) $f(x) = 2 - \dfrac{1}{x}$ j) $f(x) = \dfrac{3 - 2x}{4}$

   k) $f(x) = (x + 1)^2$ l) $f: x \mapsto 3(4 - 2x)$

5. a) $g(x) = x + 3$, $h(x) = 2x$. Calculate
   i) $gh(1)$ ii) $hg(1)$ iii) $hg(4)$

b) $g(x) = 2(x + 1)$, $h(x) = x - 2$. Calculate
   i) $gh(4)$ ii) $gh(0)$ iii) $gg(2)$

c) $g(x) = \dfrac{x}{2}$, $h(x) = 3x - 1$. Calculate

   i) $hh(2)$ ii) $gh(8)$ iii) $gh(3a)$

d) $g(x) = \dfrac{1}{x}$, $h(x) = 2x + 3$. Calculate

   i) $gh(4)$ ii) $gh(\tfrac{1}{2})$ iii) $hg(-1)$

e) $g(x) = \tfrac{1}{2}(x - 1)$, $h(x) = 1 - x$. Calculate
   i) $hh(3)$ ii) $ggz(3)$ iii) $gh(-2)$

198

6. a) $h: x \mapsto x + 3$ and $g: x \mapsto 2x$. Express

    i) $gh(x)$ ii) $hg(x)$ iii) $hh(x)$ iv) $gg(x)$

b) $f: x \mapsto x^2$ and $h: x \mapsto (x - 1)$. Express

    i) $fh(x)$ ii) $ff(x)$ iii) $hf(x)$

c) $f(x) = 2(x - 2)$, $g(x) = \dfrac{x}{2}$, $h(x) = 3x$. Express

    i) $fg(x)$ ii) $hg(x)$ iii) $fh(x)$
    iv) $hh(x)$ v) $ff(x)$ vi) $hf(x)$

d) $g(x) = \dfrac{2}{x}$, $f(x) = (1 - x)$. Express

    i) $gf(x)$ ii) $fg(x)$ iii) $ff(x)$ iv) $gg(x)$

7. Copy and complete these tables and use the results to sketch the graphs of $y = 5^x$ and $y = 10^x$ on the same axes. ('Sketch' means draw a 'rough' diagram).

a)

x	-2	-1	0	1	2	3	4
$y = 5^x$							

b)

x	-2	-1	0	1	2	3	4
$y = 10^x$							

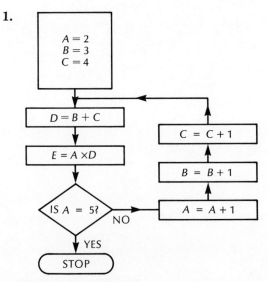

---

30   FLOW CHARTS   Questions

1.

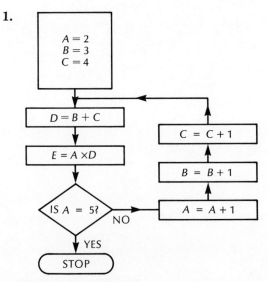

Complete this table of results.

A	B	C	D	E
2	3	4	7	14
3				

2. Draw a flow chart to show the addition of numbers from 1 to 10.

3. Draw a flow chart which will calculate powers of 2.

Use the flow chart to complete the table of results up to 2^7.

4. Draw a flow chart to find the mean of numbers, A, B and C starting with $A = 7.3$, $B = 9.2$, $C = 4.5$, where A increases by 0.5 while B increases by 0.3 and C decreases by 0.2, four times.

SECTION IV

EXAMINATION QUESTIONS (1)

1. Given that $a = 2$, $b = 3$, $c = -1$. find the value of:

  a) $3a - 2b$ (b) $a^2 - 2c^2$.

2. Solve

  a) $2x - 9 = 7$ b) $x^2 - 25 = 0$
  c) $x^2 + 3x - 4 = 0$ d) $1 - 3x \geqslant 4$

3. Write the inequalities which represent the shaded regions, including boundaries.

  a)

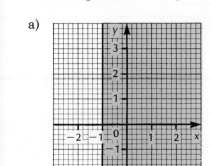

  b)

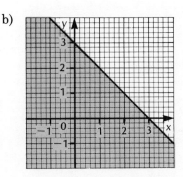

4. a) If $3x^2 + bx - 1 = (3x - 1)(x + 1)$ for all values of x, find the value of b.

  b) Factorise $3x^2 - 7x - 6$.

5. Find the values of x and y which satisfy both of these equations.

$$3x - y = 10$$
$$x + 2y = 1$$

6. $3k = kx + 7$.

  a) Calculate x when $k = 4$.

  b) Express x in terms of k.

7. a) If $y = x^2 + 3x - 4$, find the value of y when $x = 3$.

  b) i) Factorise $x^2 + 3x - 4$, given that one factor is $(x - 1)$.
   ii) Find two values of x such that $x^2 + 3x - 4 = 0$.

8. In triangle ABC, AB $= (2x - 1)$ cm, BC $= (x - 2)$ cm and AC $= 2$BC.

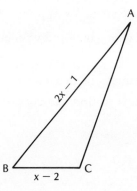

Find

  a) the length of AC in terms of x,

  b) the perimeter of triangle ABC in terms of x (answer in simplest form),

  c) the value of x if the perimeter of triangle ABC is 33 cm.

9. The diagram shows the plan of a room. The central area represents a rectangular carpet measuring x metres by $(x + 2)$ metres. The carpet is surrounded by a tiled border 0.5 metres wide.

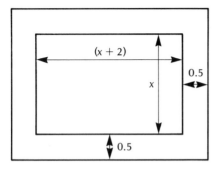

a) Give an expression for the area of the carpet in terms of x.

b) i) Write down the length and width of the room in terms of x.
    ii) Give an expression for the area of the room in terms of x.

c) If $x = 2$

   i) What is the area of the tiled border?
   ii) If the tiles cost £7.50 per m², how much does it cost to tile the border?

a) Express in terms of x the lengths 'd' in each of the following cases. *Give your answers in their simplest form.*

i)

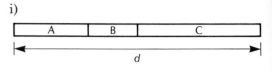

ii)

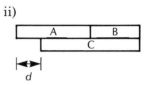

iii)

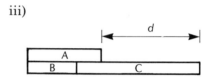

iv)

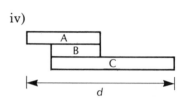

v)

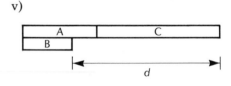

10. A boy is sent to buy 3 biros and 2 pencils which would have cost altogether 34 p. By mistake he bought 2 biros and 3 pencils for 31 p.

If x pence is the cost of one biro and y pence the cost of one pencil,

a) write down two equations in x and y,

b) solve the equations to find the cost of one biro.

11. *The diagrams in this question have not been drawn to scale.*

Three rods A, B and C have lengths of x, $(x - 1)$ and $(x + 2)$ cm respectively, as shown.

 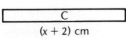

b) Rod A is used as a template to make a square, as shown.

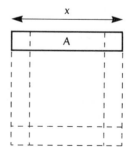

State, in terms of x, in its simplest form,

i) the perimeter,
ii) the area of the square of side x cm.

c) Rods B and C used as templates to make a rectangle, as shown.

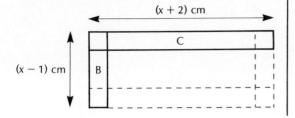

State, in terms of x, the area of the rectangle formed, with length $(x + 2)$ cm and breadth $(x - 1)$ cm.

d) If the area of the rectangle is equal to the area of the square, calculate the value of x.

2–5 NUMBER Examination Questions (1)

1. The digits 1, 2, 3, 4 are written on separate pieces of paper.

    | 1 | | 2 | | 3 | | 4 |

   a) Using each *once* only, arrange the digits to form

      i) the largest four figure number,
      ii) the smallest four figure *odd* number,
      iii) the largest four figure number exactly divisible by 4.

   b) In how many different ways can the digits be arranged to form a four figure number beginning with 4?

2. a) Add 2.97, 0.643 and 42.065

   b) Write the number 627.0583

      i) correct to 2 decimal places,
      ii) correct to 2 significant figures.

3. Given that 80 g of jelly babies cost 18 p, how much would 360 g cost?

4. Work out:

   a) 0.7×0.2 b) $0.9 \div 0.03$

   c) $2\frac{3}{5} - 1\frac{3}{4}$ d) $1\frac{1}{9} \div 1\frac{2}{3}$

5. a) Write 584 000 in standard form, $a \times 10^n$ (where 'a' is a number between 1 and 10 and 'n' is any integer).

   b) Write 497 682 correct to 3 significant figures.

6. State the value of n in each of the following equations:

   a) $7^n = 49$,   b) $3^n = 1$,

   c) $0.025 = 2.5 \times 10^n$

7. Calculate $2 \times 10^{-2} \times 5.8 \times 10^3$ and write your answer in standard form.

8. Jason is paid at an hourly rate of £2.50 and works a basic 40 hour week. Overtime is paid at time and a half.

   a) What is Jason's basic wage for a 40 hour week?

   b) The table below shows the number of hours worked in a certain week.

Day	Mon	Tues	Wed	Thurs	Fri	Sat
Hours	9	$8\frac{1}{4}$	8	$8\frac{3}{4}$	$8\frac{1}{2}$	$5\frac{1}{2}$

   i) How many hours overtime did Jason work?
   ii) Calculate his total wage for the week.

9. Calculate:

a) $2^3 + 3^2$

b) $27^{\frac{2}{3}}$

10. A colour T.V. costs £220 cash or £88 deposit and 24 payments of £7.33. What is the difference between the cash and the hire purchase prices?

11. All parts of the question refer to this list of numbers:

$$3 \quad 6 \quad 10 \quad 15 \quad 21$$

a) The numbers form a sequence. Write down the next number.

b) Write down the prime number.

c) Write down the number which is a multiple of 7.

d) Three of the numbers add up to 24. Write down these three numbers.

12. Find the value of 'n' in each of the following:

a) $12^6 \times 12^n = 12^9$ b) $2^8 \div 2^4 = 2^n$

c) $37\,500 = 3.75 \times 10^n$

13. Simplify:

a) $\dfrac{1}{12} + \dfrac{5}{6}$ b) $\dfrac{3}{4} \div \dfrac{7}{12}$

14.

A	1	2	3	4	5	6	7
B	2	4	6	8	10	12	14
C	3	6	9	12	15	18	21
D	4	8	12	16	20	24	28
E	5	10	15	20	25	30	35
F	6	12	18	24	30	36	42
G	7	14	21	28	35	42	49

a) Use the table above to find the next two numbers in the sequence 3, 8, 15, *, *.

b) Write down the two largest perfect square numbers in the table.

c) If $S =$ sum of the numbers in Row A, what is the value of S?

d) What is the sum of the numbers in the following *in terms of S*?

   i) Row B.
   ii) Row G.
   iii) The whole table.

e) Write down the square root of the sum of the numbers in the whole table.

6–9 PERCENTAGES
Examination Questions (1)

1. In a survey 25 000 people were asked which television channel they liked best.

   10 000 chose ITV.
   1000 said they did not have TV.

a) What fraction chose ITV? (Give your answer in the lowest terms.)

b) What percentage did not have a TV?

2. a) Share £350 in the ratio 3 : 4.

b) In a sale, a washing machine marked at £160 is sold at a discount of 20%. What is the sale price?

3. a) An article costs a shopkeeper 80 p. He sells it to make a profit of 30% on his cost price. What is his selling price?

b) The shopkeeper then takes 4 p off his selling price. What is his percentage profit now?

4. How much water must be added to 6 ml of alcohol so that the final solution contains 25% alcohol?

5.

SIMPLEX ELECTRIC COOKER
CASH PRICE £230

a) The cooker can be bought on hire purchase by paying a deposit of $12\frac{1}{2}\%$ of the cash price and 156 weekly payments of £1.65.

How much is

  i) the deposit,
  ii) the total of the weekly payments,
  iii) the total hire purchase price.

b) The cooker can also be purchased by taking out a bank loan for £230, to which the bank adds interest equivalent to 20% of the loan.

  i) How much interest is charged?
  ii) What is the total cost by this method?
  iii) The bank loan plus interest has to be repaid by 12 equal monthly payments, how much is repaid each month?

c) The cash price of the cooker includes 15% VAT. How much of the cooker's price is the VAT?

d) In a sale the cash price of the cooker is reduced by 5%. Calculate how much VAT is paid on the cooker in the sale.

6. a) 15% of a sum of money is £75. What is the sum of money?

b) A video tape-recorder was increased in price from £475 to £494. What was the percentage increase on the original price?

7. a) The Rateable Value of a town is £115 476 000 and for the financial year 1986/7 the local council charges a general rate of 80 p in the £.

  i) How much is raised by a penny rate?
  ii) How much is paid in *rates* by a householder whose property has a Rateable Value of £226?

  iii) Another householder pays £156 in *rates*, what is the Rateable Value of his property?
  iv) The cost of education is 52 p *in the £* of the Rateable Value. What percentage of the *rates* is spent on education?

b) The council decide to support public amenity schemes with a monthly lottery. Each month 36 000 tickets are sold at 25 p each and prizes are distributed as follows:

1st prize	£1000
2nd prize	£250
2 prizes of	£150
8 prizes of	£50
348 prizes of	£5

Calculate for one month

  i) how much is collected from the sale of tickets?
  ii) how much is paid out in prize money?
  iii) how much profit is made, if in addition to prize money overheads amount to 7 p per ticket?
  iv) what percentage of takings is paid out in prize money?

8. Susan, Mary and John are given £2000 to be shared between them in the ratio 2 : 3 : 5.

a) How much do Susan and Mary each receive?

Susan invested £300 of her money in a Building Society Account giving an annual rate of 9% interest. She took out the interest gained at the end of 12 months and spent it.

b) How much money did she spend?

Mary puts £300 of her money into the same Building Society at the same rate of annual interest. She decided not to touch *any* of this money until the end of 3 years when she withdrew her £300 and the interest it had gained.

c) i) How much interest did she earn during the *second* year?
  ii) How much interest did she earn during the *third* year?
  iii) What was the total amount of money Mary withdrew from the Building Society at the end of the third year?

207

9. The bar chart shown below represents the various costs involved in the manufacture of a particular make of colour television.

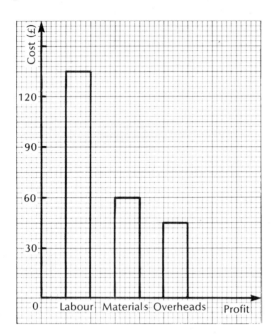

a) Calculate the total cost of manufacturing a colour television.

b) What is the ratio of *Labour* to *Overheads*? *Give your answer in its simplest form.*

c) What percentage of the manufacturer's costs is spent on materials?

d) The manufacturer adds $12\frac{1}{2}\%$ to his total costs, as profit, before selling to the retailer.

   i) Calculate the manufacturer's profit.
   ii) Draw a bar on the chart to represent the manufacturer's profit.
   iii) Calculate the price paid for the television by the retailer.

e) The retailer adds on 30% of the price he pays for the television as profit, and then adds 15% VAT to this total price before selling the television to a customer.

   Calculate

   i) the retailer's profit,
   ii) the VAT payable,
   iii) the total price paid by the customer.

f) Calculate the cost of materials as a percentage of the final selling price. *Give your answer to the nearest whole number.*

10.

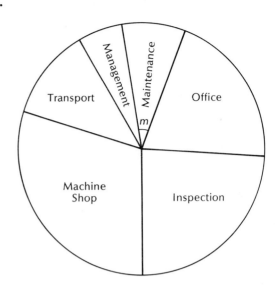

The pie chart above is not drawn to scale.

A firm employs 720 people. The pie chart represents the numbers of employees in the six departments.

a) Complete the items missed out from the table below, using the information given:

Department	Number Employed	Information
Maintenance	....	$m = 30°$
Office	....	20% of work force
	Total 204	

b) The remainder of the work force is divided up among Machine Shop, Inspection, Transport and Management in the ratio $5 : 4 : 2 : 1$ respectively. How many would be employed in Transport?

c) A decision to reduce the work force by 10% in all departments is made. How many would now be employed in Maintenance?

d) Consider whether the size of the angle m would have to be changed when the work force is reduced by 10%. What would its value now be?

10 AREA AND VOLUME
Examination Questions (1)

1. A square has an area of 81 cm². Calculate its perimeter.

2. How many cubic blocks of wood of side 2 cm can be made to fit into a cubic box of side 10 cm measured internally?

3.

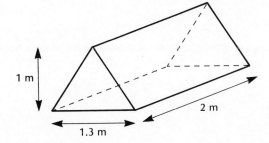

The diagram shows a hiker's small ridge tent, 2 m long, 1.3 m wide and 1 m in height. What is the volume inside the tent in m³?

4.

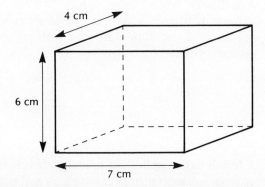

Calculate the volume of the rectangular box shown, in cm³.

5.

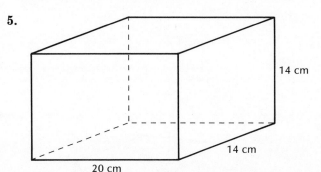

The diagram represents a rectangular block of wood, 20 cm long, with a square end of side 14 cm. Find, in cm³, the volume of the largest solid cylinder which can be cut from this block. ($\pi \approx 3\frac{1}{7}$.)

6. The diagram shows a rectangular swimming pool 2.3 m deep at the shallow end and 4.7 m deep at the deep end. The pool is 20 m long and 15 m wide. Builders are contracted to tile the pool (walls and bottom).

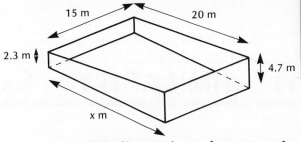

This diagram is not drawn to scale.

Calculate
a) the value of x,
b) the area to be covered,
c) the cost if tiles of area 1 m² cost £1.80.

The pool is filled with water to 1 m *below the top*.

Calculate
d) the volume of water in the pool,
e) the mass of this water in kilogrammes.

(1000 litres = 1 m³. The mass of 1 litre of water is one kilogramme.)

7.

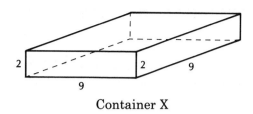

Container X

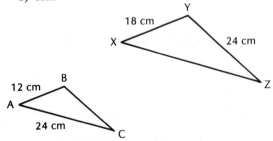

Container Y

A container X has a square lid of side 9 cm and a depth of 2 cm.

a) Calculate its volume in cm³.

Another container Y has a regular hexagonal lid of side 6 cm and a depth of 2 cm. O is the middle point of the diagonal Ed. OB is drawn perpendicular to AC.

b) Calculate the size of angle OAC.

c) Calculate the length of the straight line OB.

d) If the area of triangle OAC ≈ 15.6 cm², what is the volume of container Y in cm³?

e) If the total area of the four vertical faces of container X = P, and the total area of the six vertical faces of container Y = Q, which *one* of the statements below is true?

   i) $P = Q$ ii) $P > Q$ iii) $P < Q$

---

11 SIMILARITY   Examination Questions (1)

1. ABC and XYZ are similar triangles. Calculate

  a) BC,

  b) XZ.

The diagrams are not drawn to scale.

2. A cylinder whose base radius is 1 cm has a volume of 10 cm³. A similar cylinder has a base radius of 2 cm. Calculate the volume of the second cylinder.

3. A beach ball is spherical in shape. If it is blown up from a diameter of 25 cm to 50 cm and remains spherical, how many times greater is its surface area?

4. The Scalebox Toy Company decide to make a king-size scale model of a new Euro-Container lorry on a scale of 1 : 20.

Complete the following table.

	Model	Euro-container lorry
Length	a)	30 m
Volume of cargo	0.1 m³	b)
Number of wheels	16	c)

5. In the triangle ADE, BC is parallel to DE, and AC = CE.

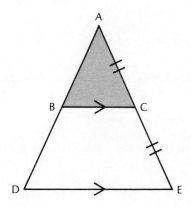

What fraction of the triangle ADE is shaded?

6. Work out the value of *x* (the length YB).

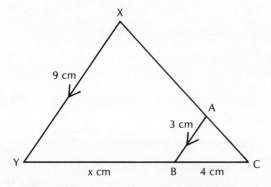

The diagram is not drawn to scale.

7. A toy manufacturer decides to make a new plastic shape for making patterns, as shown.

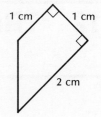

a) What is the area of the shape?

b) Draw *three different* sketches to show how *two* of these shapes can be placed together to form each of the following figures:

   i) a rectangle,
   ii) a parallelogram,
   iii) an isosceles trapezium.

c) *Eight* of the shapes are used to form a rectangle 4 cm by 3 cm, sketch *two* different ways in which the shapes can be arranged.

d) The shapes can also be used to form a square of side 3 cm. How many of the shapes are needed?

e) A larger *similar* shape is made, as shown.

   i) How many of the small shapes are needed to make one large shape?
   ii) What is the area of the larger shape?

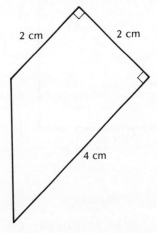

f) The manufacturer produces each shape in 6 different colours and packs them in sets, so that each set has twice as many small shapes as large shapes and contains at least 4 of each size and colour.

What is the *minimum* number of shapes in a set?

1.

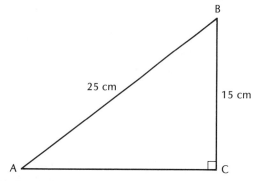

In the right-angled triangle ABC

a) find the value of

   i) sine A,
   ii) angle A.

b) Calculate the length of AC in cm.

2. The farm gate shown in the diagram is not drawn to scale. The gate is 2.4 m wide and the diagonal bar is 3 m. Calculate angle x.

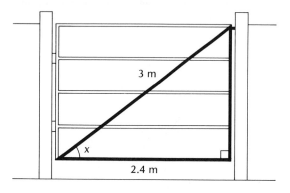

3.

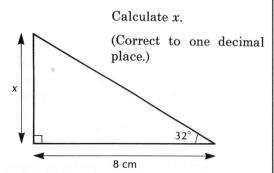

Calculate x.

(Correct to one decimal place.)

This diagram is not drawn to scale.

4. The diagram shows an iron gate made with thin tubing. What length of iron tube is required to build it?

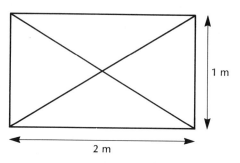

This diagram is not drawn to scale.

5. The triangle ABC is isosceles AB = AC = 10 cm and BC = 8 cm

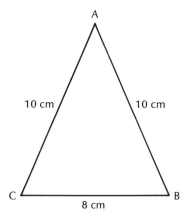

a) E is a point on BC such that angle $\hat{AEC}$ = 90°.
   Show accurately the point E on the diagram.

b) Calculate the length AE.

c) i) State cos C as a fraction.
    ii) Use your values of cos C to calculate the size of angle C.

6. A triangle has sides of length x, $x + 1$ and 7 cm as shown in the diagram. It is right angled as indicated.

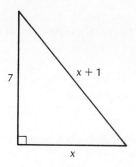

7

$x + 1$

x

a) State the perimeter in terms of x. (Simplify as much as possible).

b) State the area in terms of x.

c) Use Pythagoras' theorem to complete this equation:

$$(x + 1)^2 = \ldots\ldots\ldots$$

Now solve this equation.

7. ABCD is a trapezium with AB parallel to DC.

BE is perpendicular to CD.

EX is perpendicular to BC, and AD is perpendicular to CD.

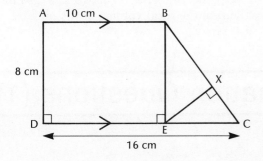

A   10 cm   B

8 cm

X

D   E   C

16 cm

a) Write down the lengths of the following sides:

i) EC,   ii) BE.

b) Calculate the length of BC.

c) Calculate the area of the trapezium ABCD.

d) Calculate the size of angle BCE.

e) Calculate the length of EX.

8. In triangle ABC (not drawn to scale) AB = 10 cm and angle B = 72.5°.

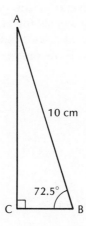

A

10 cm

72.5°

C   B

a) Using the extract from 3 figure tables,* calculate the length of AC.

* Extract from 3 figure tables

	Degrees	.0	.1	.2	.3	.4
Sin	72	.951	952	952	953	953
Cos	72	.309	307	306	304	302
Tan	72	3.078	096	115	133	152

	Degrees	.5	.6	.7	.8	.9
Sin	72	954	954	955	955	956
Cos	72	301	299	297	296	294
Tan	72	172	191	211	231	251

b) Given that BC is approximately 3 cm calculate the area of the triangle correct to 3 significant figures.

213

9.

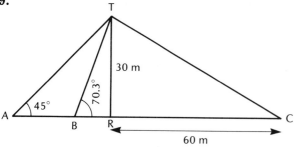

In the above diagram (which is not drawn to scale), AC is a horizontal straight line at ground level. TR is a vertical tower 30 metres high; RC = 60 metres. From a point A the angle of elevation of T is 45°. At a point B the angle of elevation is 70.3°.

Calculate

a) angle ATR,

b) the length of AR in metres,

c) angle BTR,

d) the length of BR in metres,

e) the angle of elevation of T from C.

10. *The diagrams in this question have not been drawn to scale.*

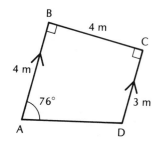

AB is parallel to DC

$\hat{ABC} = \hat{DCB} = 90°$

a) Calculate angle ADC.

b) Calculate

  i) the length of the perpendicular from B to AD,

  ii) the length of AD,

  iii) the area of ABCD, *giving your answers correct to two decimal places.*

c) ABCD is part of one side of a concrete pile 3 m thick, as shown.

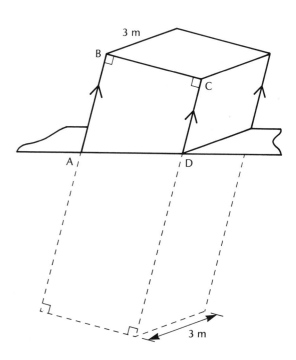

If 30% of the pile is above the ground calculate the total volume of the pile.

---

13 CIRCLES   Examination Questions (1)

1. The diagram shows a sector of a circle of radius 3 cm and arc length π cm. The diagram is not drawn to scale. Calculate angle XOY.

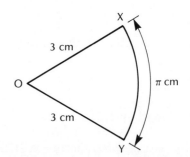

2.

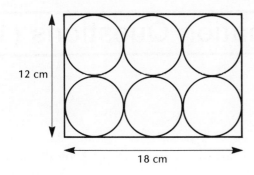

12 cm

18 cm

The diagram shows the plan of a box containing 6 tennis balls.

The internal dimensions of the box are 18 cm by 12 cm.

The balls just touch the bottom and top of the box.

a) i) What is the radius of each ball?

   ii) What is the internal depth of the box?

   iii) Calculate the volume of the box.

b) A sports shop has a stock of 50 boxes, two of which are on show in the window. If the rest are to be stored, calculate the minimum length of shelf space required, given that the depth of the shelf is 30 cm and it is 15 cm below the shelf above. A sketch of the shelf is shown below.

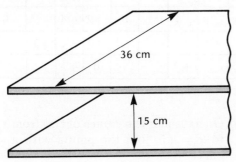

36 cm

15 cm

c) Boxes sell at £5.40 or individual tennis balls at £1 each. if the cost price per box to the shopkeeper is £4.50, calculate the total profit he makes if he sells 30 boxes complete and the remaining tennis balls individually.

3. *The diagrams in this question have not been drawn to scale.*

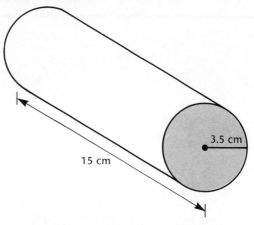

3.5 cm

15 cm

a) For the cylinder, shown above, of radius 3.5 cm and length 15 cm, calculate

   i) the area of the shaded face,
   ii) the volume of the cylinder.

   (Take $\pi = \frac{22}{7}$.)

b) The net of this cylinder is as shown.

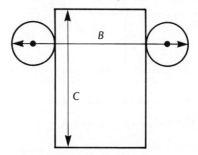

B

C

Calculate

   i) the length marked B,
   ii) the length marked C,
   iii) the total surface area of the cylinder.

c) The diagram below shows how the cylinders are stamped from a thin sheet of tin which measures 51 cm by 176 cm.

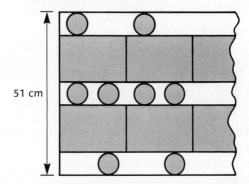

51 cm

   i) How many cylinders are stamped from the sheet?
   ii) How much metal is wasted?

1. The diagram shows a triangle ABC where A is (3, 3), B is (x, y) and C is (3, −2).

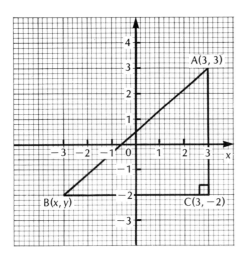

a) Write down the coordinates of B.

b) What is the value of tangent A.

2. For the line given, write down
   a) the gradient of the line,

   b) the value of y when $x = 0$,

   c) the equation of the line.

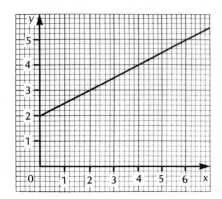

3. The cartesian coordinates of A are (2, 2).

   Calculate r and θ and hence state the polar coordinates of A (r, θ).

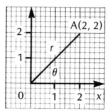

4. The points O (0, 0); A (5, 2); B (7, 5); C (x, y) are the vertices of a parallelogram OABC. Calculate the values of x and y.

5. a) Complete the table below for the function $x \rightarrow x^2 - 2x + 1$.

x	−3	−2	−1	0	1	2	3	4	5
x^2	+9			0	+1	+4			+25
$-2x$		+4		0	−2	−4		−8	−10
$+1$	+1	+1		+1	+1	+1	+1		
f(x)		+9			0	+1			+16

   b) On axes plot the values of f(x) from $x = -3$ to $x = +5$, join the points with a smooth curve.

   c) i) From your graph find the value of f(x) when $x = 1.8$.
      ii) From your graph find two values of x for which f$(x) = 6$.

   d) Using your graph or otherwise solve the equation $x^2 - 2x - 8 = 0$.

6. a) i) Complete the table for the values of x shown if $y = 3x - 4$.

x	-3	-1	0	1	3
y	-13				5

ii) Draw the line $y = 3x - 4$ on axes where $-6 \leqslant x \leqslant 6$ and $-14 \leqslant y \leqslant 10$.

b) The table below shows corresponding values of x and y on the line $3x + 5y = 16$. Draw the line $3x + 5y = 16$ on the same axes as in part a).

x	-5	0	5
y	6.2	3.2	0.2

c) What is the solution to the simultaneous equations $3x - y = 4$ *and* $3x + 5y = 16$?

d) The line $y = 3x - 4$ passes through the point $(0, h)$. State the value of h.

7. a) If $f(x) = (x - 3)(2 - x) + 10$, complete the table for values of x from -1 to $+6$.

b) Plot these points on a graph where $-1 \leqslant x \leqslant 7$ and $-2 \leqslant y \leqslant 11$.

c) Using your graph find for what values of x is $f(x) = 0$.

d) i) What is the maximum value of $f(x)$?
ii) Write down the value of x at which this occurs.

x	-1	0	1	2	3	4	5	6
$x - 3$	-4	-3	-2					
$2 - x$	3	2	1					
$+10$	10	10	10	10	10	10	10	10
$f(x)$	-2	4	8					

8. Points O, P and Q have polar coordinates $(0, 0°)$, $(2, 60°)$ and $(3, 150°)$ respectively.

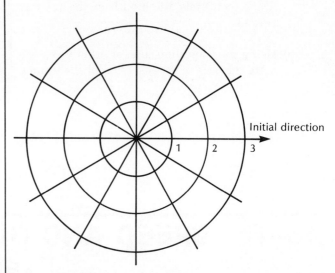

Initial direction

Radii are equally spaced

a) Plot O, P and Q on the axes and join to form a triangle OPQ.

b) Calculate the area of a triangle OPQ.

9.

A railway tunnel is cut through a mountain-side so that it is 6 m wide and its height varies according to the following table.

Distance from X (in metres)	0	1	2	3	4	5	6
Height of tunnel (in metres)	2.7	4.0	4.4	4.5	4.4	4.0	2.7

217

a) With a horizontal axis 'Distance from X' and a vertical axis 'Height of tunnel' draw accurately the mouth of the railway tunnel.

b) Using the trapezium rule, or otherwise, estimate the area of cross-section of the tunnel.

c) The tunnel is 150 m long. Estimate the volume of earth which has been removed.

d) A train which is 120 m in length passes completely through the tunnel in 9 seconds.

Given that speed = distance/time, calculate the speed of the train in $km\,h^{-1}$.

16–17 SPEED AND DISTANCE
Examination Questions (1)

1. A train travels from London to Birmingham, a distance of 100 miles, in $1\frac{1}{4}$ hours.
   a) Calculate the average speed of the train in mph.
   b) If the speed is reduced by 20 mph, how much longer would the journey take?

2. The diagram shows the speed-time graph for the first 60 s of a car journey.

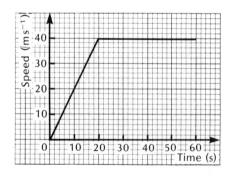

   a) What is the maximum speed reached?
   b) What is the acceleration during the first 20 s?
   c) What distance is travelled in the first 60 s?

3. The speed of a car from 0 to 10 seconds is shown in the graph below.

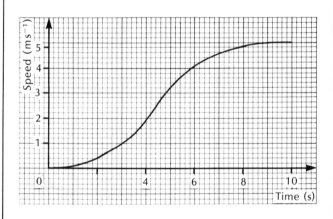

   a) Use the graph to complete Table A.

   b) By using the trapezium rule, applied to the readings in Table A only, estimate the distance travelled by the car in the 10 seconds,

   Table A

Time (s)	0	2	4	6	8	10
Speed ($m\,s^{-1}$)	0		1.9	4.1		5

4. A boat leaves a port A and sails to a buoy B, 5 km away on a bearing of 040°. It then leaves B on a bearing of 130° and travels at a speed of 24 kmph for a distance of 8 km to a mooring at C.

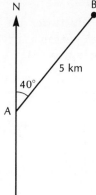

a) Complete the sketch to show the second part of the journey to the mooring C. (Your sketch does not have to be accurate but should show the bearing clearly.)

b) Calculate

   i) the time taken to sail from B to C,
   ii) the distance of the ship from A correct to decimal places.

c) Calculate the angle BAC and hence the bearing C from A.

18 STATISTICS Examination Questions (1)

1. Given the numbers 6.8, 7.2, 7.5, 6.7, 6.4, 7.2, 6.5.

   a) Write down

      i) the mode,
      ii) the median.

   b) Calculate the mean.

   b) After the bar graph had been drawn, two pupils who had scored 6 marks were found to have been marked incorrectly and so were given one extra mark each. state the mode, median and mean values after these two changes had been made.

2. The bar graph shows the marks scored out of 10 in a recent test.

   a) Use the graph to complete the following:

      i) Number of pupils
         taking test = ...
      ii) Modal score = ...
      iii) Median score = ...
      iv) Mean score = ...

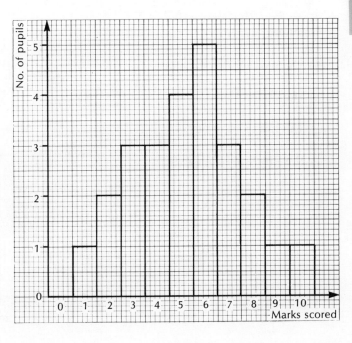

3. The pie chart represents the cost of making a colour television. The total cost is £270.

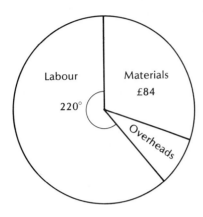

Calculate

a) the cost of labour,

b) the angle of the sector representing materials.

4. a, b, c, d and e are *five* numbers.

The mean of a, b and c is 9.
The mean of d and e is 3.

What is the mean of all *five* numbers?

5. Read from the cumulative frequency curve:

a) the median mark,

b) the upper quartile,

c) the lower quartile,

d) the interquartile range.

6. The mean of 3, 4, 7, x, and 5 is 4.

a) Calculate the value of x.

b) Write down the median.

7. The pie-chart illustrates the grouping of people who took part in a survey. The total number of people was 264.

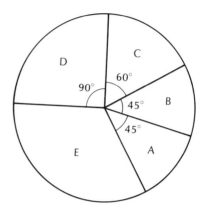

Calculate

a) the size of angle for sector, E,

b) the number of people who formed group E.

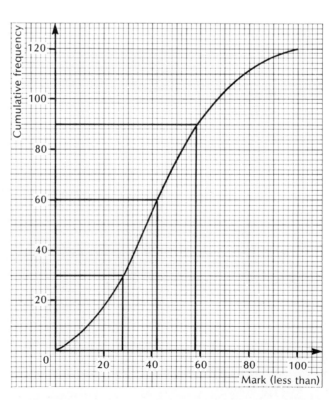

8. A group of children are given a statistics test and their results are graded as follows:

$\frac{1}{12}$ grade A,
$\frac{1}{6}$ grade B,
$\frac{1}{4}$ grade C,
$\frac{2}{9}$ grade D,

and an equal number are given either grade E or grade F.

a) This information is to be shown on a pie chart.

   i) Complete Table 1, to show the angle of each sector for each grade.

Table 1

Grade	Angle of sector
A	
B	
C	
D	
E	50°
F	50°

   ii) Draw accurately on a copy of the circle given a pie chart to represent the distribution of grades.

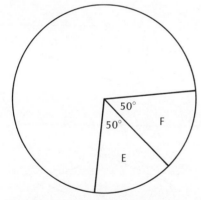

b) 6 children obtained a grade A.

   i) How many children took the test?
   ii) How many children obtained grade D?

c) Grades A, B, C and D represent pass grades State the ratio pass to fail in its simplest form.

d) The distribution of the boys, grades are shown in the bar chart following. On a copy of the axes given construct a bar chart to show the distribution of the girls, grades.

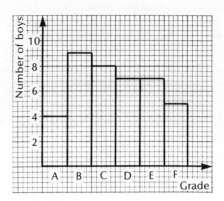

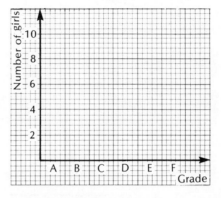

9. The chart below shows the frequency distribution of goals scored by a school football team. Use the chart to find:

a) the modal number of goals scored,
b) the total number of matches played,
c) the total number of goals scored,
d) the mean number of goals per match.

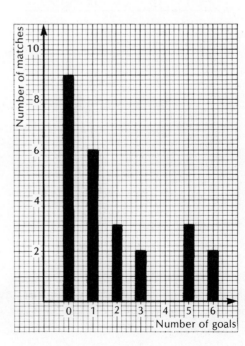

221

1. The following diagrams have not been drawn accurately.

Without using a protractor, work out the values of x, y and z.

a)

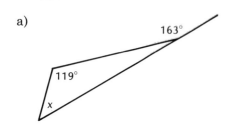

b)

c)

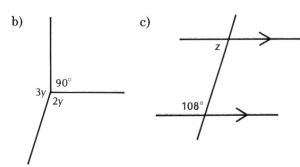

2. a)

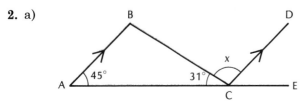

b)

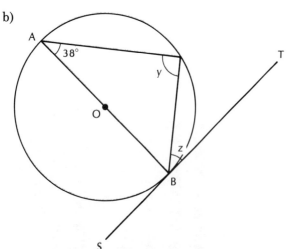

In the diagrams above calculate the angles marked x, y and z. In (b), AB is a diameter and ST a tangent to the circle.

3. The angles of a triangle are $x°$, $2x°$ and $3x°$. Calculate the size of the smallest angle.

4.

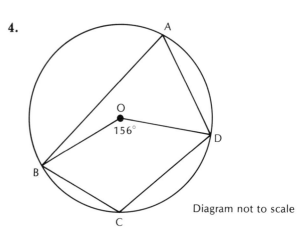

Diagram not to scale

A, B, C, D are points on the circumference of a circle, centre O. Angle BOD = 156°.

Calculate the size of each of these angles:

a) BAD   b) BCD.

5. Calculate the angles a and b in the figures shown.

ZY is parallel to WX.

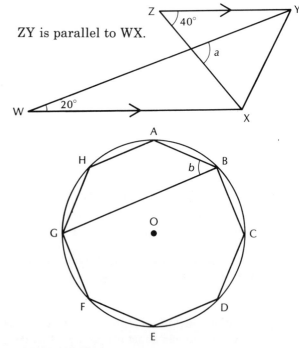

ABCDEFGH is a regular octagon.
O is the centre of the circle.

6. ABCDEFGH is a regular octagon with centre O.

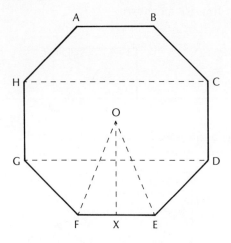

a)   i) What type of triangle is triangle EFO?
    ii) What name is given to the quadrilateral ABCD.
   iii) Calculate the size of angle ABC.

b) Given that angle FOE = 45° and FE = 4 cm calculate

   i) the length of OX,
   ii) the area of triangle EFO.
  iii) Using this result calculate the area of the octagon, giving your answer correct to 3 significant figures.

7. Without using a protractor, find the values of the angles a and b in the diagrams below:

a)

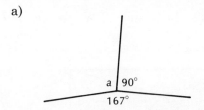

b)

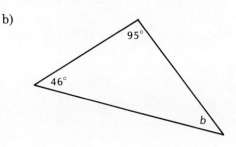

8. a) Complete the table for the regular polygons shown below.

Note: *In a regular polygon, the exterior angle = 360/number of sides.*

Regular Polygons	△	□	⬠	⬡
Number of sides	3	4	5	6
Name of polygon	Equilateral triangle	Square	i)	Hexagon
Size of each exterior angle	ii)	90°	72°	iii)
Size of each interior angle	60°	90°	iv)	120°
Sum of interior angles	180°	360°	v)	720°

b)   i) How many sides has a regular polygon with an exterior angle of 15°?

    ii) A regular polygon has 18 sides, what is the size of the interior angle?

   iii) What is the sum of the interior angles of a regular nine-sided polygon?

c) An equilateral triangle and a regular hexagon each have a perimeter of 24 cm. Calculate the ratio of their areas, giving your answer in its simplest form.

9. A ship sails from P on a course of 035° for 8 nautical miles to Q, then alters course to 165° for 13 nautical miles to R.

Use a scale of 1 cm to represent 1 nautical mile.

a) Make a scale drawing of the course of the ship from P to Q to R.

b) The ship travels at an average speed of 10 knots (1 knot = 1 nautical mile per hour).

If speed = distance/time, how long will the ship take to travel the distance of 21 nautical miles from P to R?

c) Measure the length PR on your diagram, and find the distance PR in nautical miles, correct to the nearest 0.1 nautical mile.

d) Find the course to be steered to go directly from R to P. Answer as a three figure bearing.

e) A lighthouse L is the same distance from P as it is from Q, and is on a bearing of 335° from R. Mark L on your diagram.

10. A rectangular piece of card is divided into two identical right-angled triangles, as shown:

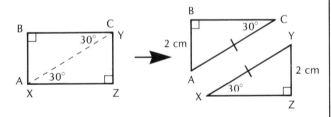

$$\angle B = \angle Z = 90°$$
$$\angle C = \angle X = 30°$$
$$AB = YZ = 2\,cm$$

a) The triangles ABC and XYZ are now re-arranged to form *four* different geometrical shapes:

　i) a parallelogram,
　ii) a kite,
　iii) an isosceles triangle (*which is not equilateral*), and
　iv) an equilateral triangle.

Draw a sketch of each shape, showing clearly how the triangles are placed together. *The triangles can be turned over, but they must not overlap.*

b) The triangles ABC and XYZ are again placed together to form a rectangle, with XZ on line ST as shown.

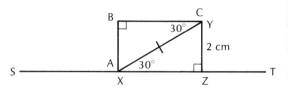

Triangle ABC is now rotated anticlockwise about A until AB lies on ST as shown below.

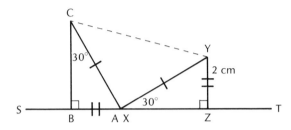

　i) Through how many degrees has AC moved?
　ii) Calculate the length of AC.
　iii) What name is given to quadrilateral BCYZ?
　iv) Calculate the length of CB.
　v) Calculate the area of quadrilateral BCYZ.

Give your answer correct to the nearest cm².

11. *The diagram is not drawn to scale.*

WXYZ is a square.

ABCD is a square of side 10 cm.

ADX, ABY, BCZ and CDW are equilateral triangles.

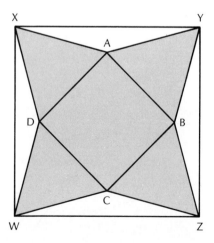

The shaded figure is the net of a solid which is to be cut from a square sheet of card WXYZ.

a) State the name of the solid.

b) How many i) edges, ii) vertices, has the solid?

c) Calculate i) angle XAY, ii) angle AXY.

d) Calculate
   i) the length XY, *giving your answer correct to two decimal places,*
   ii) the area of the net, *giving your answer correct to the nearest square centimetre.*

23–25 MATRICES AND TRANSFORMATIONS
Examination Questions (1)

1. M and **N** are matrices.

M has order 2 by 3, **N** has order 2 by 2.

If **NM** = **P**, state the order of matrix **P**.

2. a)

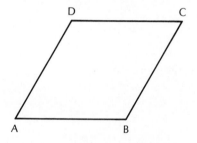

b)

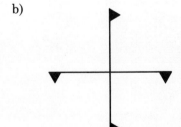

ABCD is a rhombus.

Draw in all the lines of symmetry in each of the diagrams above.

3. If $\begin{pmatrix} 1 & 2 \\ 3 & 4 \end{pmatrix} + \begin{pmatrix} p & -1 \\ -3 & 4 \end{pmatrix} + \begin{pmatrix} 2 & 3 \\ -6 & q \end{pmatrix} = \begin{pmatrix} -6 & r \\ -6 & 2 \end{pmatrix}$,

find the values of p, q, and r.

4. a) Find p and q if $\begin{pmatrix} p \\ -3 \end{pmatrix} = \begin{pmatrix} 3 & 4 \\ 1 & q \end{pmatrix}\begin{pmatrix} 1 \\ 2 \end{pmatrix}$.

b) r is a whole number, work out the value of r if $(r \ 1)\begin{pmatrix} r \\ 1 \end{pmatrix} = (10)$.

5. The matrix **M** shows the one stage routes between towns A and B.

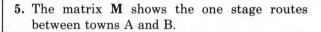

$$\mathbf{M} = \text{From } \begin{matrix} A \\ B \end{matrix}\begin{pmatrix} 1 & 2 \\ 1 & 1 \end{pmatrix}$$

a) Calculate $\mathbf{M}^2$.

b) State the number of ways of travelling from B to A in two stages.

6. a) The translation with vector

$$\begin{pmatrix} 2 \\ -1 \end{pmatrix}$$

maps S(3, 5) to the point T. Write down the coordinates of T.

b) Another translation maps X(2, 2) to Y(-2, -1).

  i) Write down the vector of this translation.

  ii) Calculate the distance XY.

7.

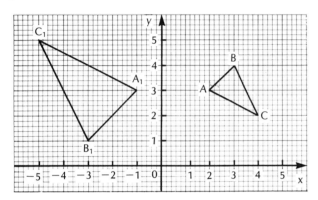

Triangle ABC is mapped to triangle $A_1B_1C_1$ by an enlargement.

Write

a) the scale factor of the enlargement,

b) the coordinates of the centre of enlargement.

8. a) How many i) arcs, ii) nodes, and iii) regions, are there in the diagram ABCD?

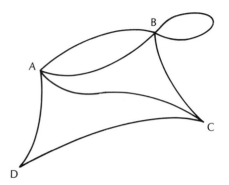

b) The diagram represents a network of roads connecting towns A, B, C and D. Complete the 'direct route' matrix'.

$$\text{From} \quad \begin{matrix} & & \text{To} \\ & & \text{A B C D} \\ A \\ B \\ C \\ D \end{matrix} \begin{pmatrix} 0 & 2 & 1 & 1 \\ & & & 1 \\ & & & \\ 1 & & & \end{pmatrix}$$

9. Describe fully the *single transformation* which maps the shaded figure on to

a) R, b) E, c) T

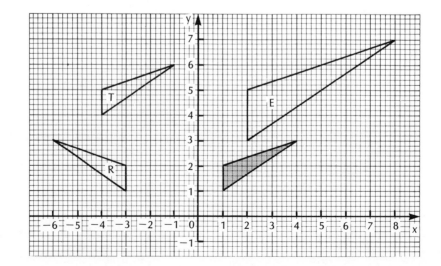

226

10. a) Work out the values

   i) of p if $(p - 1)\begin{pmatrix} p \\ 2 \end{pmatrix} = (14)$,

   ii) q and r if $\begin{pmatrix} 2 & 1 \\ 3 & 1 \end{pmatrix}\begin{pmatrix} q \\ r \end{pmatrix} = \begin{pmatrix} 1 \\ 0 \end{pmatrix}$.

   b) $\mathbf{M} = \begin{pmatrix} -1 & 0 \\ 0 & 1 \end{pmatrix}$, $\mathbf{T} = \begin{pmatrix} 0 & 1 \\ 1 & 0 \end{pmatrix}$.

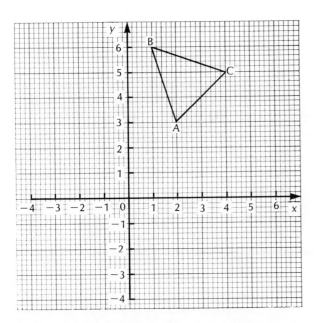

The triangle ABC shown in the diagram has vertices, A(2, 3), B(1, 6) and C(4, 5).

i) On the same axes, draw the image:
   1) $A_1B_1C_1$ if $\mathbf{M}(ABC) = A_1B_1C_1$,
   2) $A_2B_2C_2$ if $\mathbf{T}(ABC) = A_2B_2C_2$,
   3) $A_3B_3C_3$ if $\mathbf{TM}(ABC) = A_3B_3C_3$
   Label each image clearly.

ii) Describe fully the single transformation represented by
   1) $\mathbf{M}$ 2) $\mathbf{T}$ 3) $\mathbf{TM}$

11. The table below shows the daily sales of packets of crisps and peanuts by a school tuckshop for a particular week.

	Mon	Tues	Wed	Thur	Fri
Crisps	7	5	9	10	5
Peanuts	2	1	5	4	2

a) Write this information as a 2×5 matrix and call it **T**.

b) Crisps are sold at 8 p per packet and peanuts at 7 p per packet. Write this information as a 1×2 matrix and call it **S**.

c) Calculate **ST** and explain what this matrix represents.

d) What is the total value of sales of crisps and peanuts for the week?

e)   i) How many packets of crisps are sold?
    ii) How many packets of peanuts are sold?
    iii) Write this information as a 2×1 matrix and call it **R**.

f) The cost price of crisps and peanuts per packet is represented by a 1×2 matrix **C**, where **C** is $(6 \quad 4\frac{1}{2})$. Calculate **CR**.

g) How much profit did the shop make on crisps and peanuts for the week?

12. a) i) A quadrilateral ABCD has vertices A(1, 1), B(1, 3), C(3, 4), D(3, 3). Draw ABCD on squared paper.
       ii) What name do we give to quadrilateral ABCD?
       iii) What is the area of quadrilateral ABCD?

   b) i) Calculate
       $$\begin{pmatrix} 1 & 0 \\ 0 & -1 \end{pmatrix}\begin{pmatrix} A & B & C & D \\ 1 & 1 & 3 & 3 \\ 1 & 3 & 4 & 3 \end{pmatrix}$$
       ii) Hence, draw the image of ABCD under the transformation represented by $\begin{pmatrix} 1 & 0 \\ 0 & -1 \end{pmatrix}$. Label the image $A_1B_1C_1D_1$.
       iii) Describe this transformation.

   c) i) On the same axes draw the image $A_2B_2C_2D_2$ of ABCD under the transformation represented by the matrix $\begin{pmatrix} 0 & -1 \\ 1 & 0 \end{pmatrix}$.
       ii) Describe this transformation.

   d) i) Describe the single transformation which maps $A_1B_1C_1D_1$ to $A_2B_2C_2D_2$.
       ii) Write down the matrix for this transformation.

13.

$$\mathbf{T} = \text{from}\quad \begin{array}{c} \\ K \\ L \\ M \\ N \end{array} \overset{\text{to}}{\begin{pmatrix} K & L & M & N \\ 2 & 1 & 1 & 0 \\ 0 & 0 & 1 & 0 \\ 1 & 0 & 0 & 0 \\ 0 & 1 & 0 & 1 \end{pmatrix}}$$

a) **T** is the one-stage directed route matrix for a network of roads connecting towns K, L, M and N.

   i) Draw the network.

   ii) Is it possible to reach K from N? If it is possible describe the route.

   iii) Is it possible to reach N from M? If it is possible describe the route.

b) The diagram below shows four towns A, B, C, D, six roads u, v, w, x, y, z and four regions 1, 2, 3, 4.

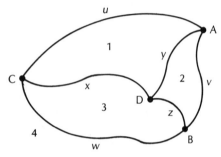

   i) Complete matrix **P**, showing the incidence of towns on roads.

$$\mathbf{P} = \begin{array}{c} A \\ B \\ C \\ D \end{array} \overset{\begin{array}{cccccc} u & v & w & x & y & z \end{array}}{\begin{pmatrix} 1 & 1 & 0 & 0 & & 0 \\ 0 & 1 & 1 & 0 & & 1 \\ & & & & & \\ 0 & 0 & 0 & 1 & & 1 \end{pmatrix}}$$

ii) Complete matrix **Q**, showing the incidence of roads on regions.

$$\mathbf{Q} = \begin{array}{c} u \\ v \\ w \\ x \\ y \\ z \end{array} \overset{\begin{array}{cccc} 1 & 2 & 3 & 4 \end{array}}{\begin{pmatrix} 1 & 0 & 0 \\ 0 & 1 & 0 \\ 0 & 0 & 1 \\ 1 & 0 & 1 \\ & & \\ & & \end{pmatrix}}$$

iii) Work out **PQ**.

iv) If matrix **R** shows the incidence of towns on regions what is the relation connecting **PQ** and **R**?

A salesman lives in town D and plans to visit shops in the three neighbouring towns A, B and C.

The distances u, v, w, x, y and z are 11, 8, 13, 5, 10 and 15 kilometres respectively:

v) Write down what route he should take in order to visit all three towns and return home if he is to keep his travelling distance to a minimum,

vi) Describe the shortest route if he has to start by visiting town B first. How much further does he travel by this route than by the minimum possible?

---

26   VECTORS   Examination Questions (1)

1. If $\mathbf{a} = \begin{pmatrix} -1 \\ 4 \end{pmatrix}$ and $\mathbf{b} = \begin{pmatrix} 2 \\ 2 \end{pmatrix}$, find the vectors

a) $\mathbf{a} + \mathbf{b}$,

b) $\frac{1}{2}\mathbf{a}$,

c) $\mathbf{a} - 2\mathbf{b}$.

2. $\overrightarrow{OA} = \mathbf{a}$, $\overrightarrow{OB} = \mathbf{b}$, OA = AC.
Write in terms of a and b:

a) $\overrightarrow{AC}$,

b) $\overrightarrow{AB}$,

c) $\overrightarrow{CB}$.

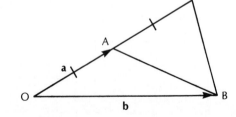

3. PQRS is a parallelogram with vertices at P(1, 1), Q(3, 5), R(x, y) and S(4, 3).

Q(3,5)
R(x,y)
S(4,3)
P(1,1)

The diagram is not drawn to scale.

a) Write down vector $\overrightarrow{PS}$.

b) Work out the coordinates of

   i) R,
   ii) the mid-point of PQ.

c) Calculate the length of PS.

4. X is the point (2, 4) and Y is the point (4, 3).

a) Work out

   i) the column vector $\overrightarrow{XY}$,
   ii) the distance XY.

b) Another vector $\overrightarrow{OZ}$, is equal to $2\overrightarrow{XY}$. Given O is the point (0, 0) state the coordinates of Z.

5.

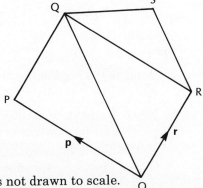

The diagram is not drawn to scale.
In the diagram OPQR is a rectangle.
OQ is parallel to RS.
$\overrightarrow{OP} = \mathbf{p}$ $\overrightarrow{OR} = \mathbf{r}$

a) Write in terms of vectors $\mathbf{p}$ and $\mathbf{r}$:
   i) $\overrightarrow{PQ}$,   ii) $\overrightarrow{QR}$,   iii) $\overrightarrow{OQ}$.
The diagram is to be drawn on squared paper with O at (0, 0).

b) $\mathbf{p} = \begin{pmatrix} -3 \\ 3 \end{pmatrix}$ and $\mathbf{r} = \begin{pmatrix} 2 \\ 2 \end{pmatrix}$,

   i) write as a column vector $\overrightarrow{OQ}$,
   ii) calculate the length of vector $\mathbf{p}$,
   iii) calculate the length of vector $\mathbf{r}$.

c) The ratio of RS : OQ is 1 : 2. Express
   i) $\overrightarrow{RS}$,
   ii) $\overrightarrow{QS}$, in terms of $\mathbf{p}$ and $\mathbf{r}$.

d) Calculate the length of $\overrightarrow{QS}$.

e) Write down the coordinates of
   i) Q,   ii) S.

6.

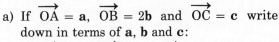

In the diagram shown
$$\overrightarrow{OA} = \overrightarrow{YB}$$
$$\overrightarrow{OC} = \overrightarrow{XB}$$

a) If $\overrightarrow{OA} = \mathbf{a}$, $\overrightarrow{OB} = 2\mathbf{b}$ and $\overrightarrow{OC} = \mathbf{c}$ write down in terms of $\mathbf{a}$, $\mathbf{b}$ and $\mathbf{c}$:

   i) $\overrightarrow{XB}$, $\overrightarrow{BY}$, $\overrightarrow{AX}$,
   iv) $\overrightarrow{AC}$, $\overrightarrow{XY}$, $\overrightarrow{CY}$.

b) i) What do your answers to a) iii) and vi) tell you about the lines AX and CY?
   ii) What do your answers to a) iv) and v) tell you about the lines AC and XY?
   iii) What name do we give to quadrilateral AXYC?

c) If OB is parallel to CY and twice its length, write down an equation in $\mathbf{a}$, $\mathbf{b}$ and $\mathbf{c}$.

d) The diagram is drawn on a cartesian graph with O at (0, 0) and C at (3, 2).
If $\mathbf{a} = \begin{pmatrix} -1 \\ 1 \end{pmatrix}$ and $\mathbf{b} = \begin{pmatrix} 2 \\ 3 \end{pmatrix}$ write down the coordinates of A, B, X and Y

27 PROBABILITY
Examination Questions (1)

1. A number is chosen at random from 3, 5, 7, 9, 11.

   What is the probability that it is

   a) odd,

   b) even,

   c) prime?

2. A random number selector is programmed to output, at random, one of the six numbers listed below.

       1   4   9   16   25   36

   What is the probability that it will output

   a) an even number,

   b) a multiple of 3,

   c) a factor of 36,

   d) an even multiple of 3, which is a factor of 36?

3. On a Pick the Straw stall at a school fete the pupils placed 100 red straws, 30 green straws, 23 yellow straws and 47 blue straws in a container. It was not possible to see the straws before choosing one.

   a) What was the probability of choosing a blue straw if you had the first pick at the fete?

   b) What was the probability of choosing a straw which was not blue if you had the first pick at the fete?

   c) They charged 5 p a straw and gave a 20 p prize to anyone who picked a blue straw. If all the straws were sold how much profit did the stall make?

4. A balloon salesman is holding the strings of 8 balloons; 4 red, 1 white and 3 blue. The strings are tangled together and each time somebody buys a balloon they choose a string and have whichever colour balloon is attached.

   a) What is the probability of a child buying one balloon and getting a balloon which is
      i) red,
      ii) white,
      iii) blue?

   b) If a child buys a balloon which is red, what is the probability that if he buys a second balloon it will also be red?

   c) What is the probability of a child buying two balloons and getting
      i) two red balloons,
      ii) two white balloons,
      iii) balloons of different colours?

   d) How many balloons must a child buy to be certain of buying a red balloon?

   e) A child buys 3 balloons and finds that they are all red.
      i) What is the probability of this happening?
      ii) How many more balloons would he need to buy to be certain of getting a balloon which is not red?

5. a box of 12 Christmas crackers were sold as 'seconds' because only 8 of them had novelties inside.

   a) What is the probability that if one cracker was pulled it would contain a novelty?

   b) What is the probability that the second cracker pulled contains a novelty, if
      i) the first cracker contains a novelty,
      ii) the first cracker does not contain a novelty?

   c) Use answers a) and b) to complete the tree diagram.

   d) If *two* crackers are pulled, use your tree diagram to find the probability that
      i) both crackers contain novelties,
      ii) at least one cracker contains a novelty.

   e) If three crackers are pulled, calculate the probability that

i) all three crackers contain novelties,

ii) no cracker contains a novelty.

f) How many crackers need to be pulled to be certain of getting a novelty?

g) One of the crackers contain a novelty ring.

What is the probability that one of the first three crackers pulled contains the ring?

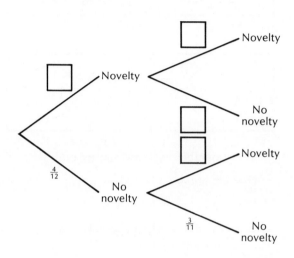

6. Three children Mary, Peter and Martin share a bag of sweets. The bag contains 12 sweets; 5 toffees (T), 4 chocolates (C) and 3 mints (M).

a) Mary takes a sweet from the bag, without looking, and eats it. What is the probability that Mary has eaten a chocolate?

b) Peter then takes a sweet from the bag, without looking, and eats it. Complete the tree diagram to show both Mary's and Peter's possible selections.

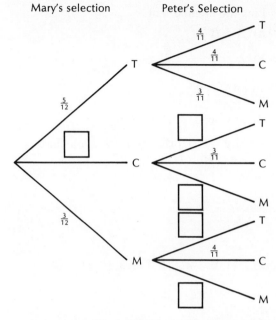

c) Use your tree diagram to determine the probability that they have both eaten

i) a toffee,

ii) sweets of the same type,

iii) different sweets.

d) Martin now takes a sweet, without looking, and eats it. What is the probability that all three children have eaten

i) a toffee,

ii) the same type of sweet?

28 SETS   Examination Questions (1)

1. $\mathscr{E} = \{2, 3, 5, 8, 13, 21\}$ $A = \{x : x > 5\}$

$B = \{x : x \leqslant 8\}$.

Write down the value of $n(A \cap B)$.

2. a) $\mathscr{E} = \{1, 2, 3, 4, 5, 6, 7\}$

$A = \{2, 3, 5, 7\}$

$B = \{2, 4, 6\}$

Work out

i) $n(A)$, ii) $A \cap B$, iii) A', iv) $A \triangle B$.

b) $\mathscr{E} = \{\text{all shoes}\}$

$X = \{\text{leather shoes}\}$

$Y = \{\text{black shoes}\}$

$Z = \{\text{lace-up shoes}\}$

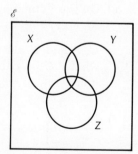

On a copy of the diagram given, shade the set of leather, lace-up shoes which are *not* black.

3. $\mathscr{E} = \{1, 2, 3, 4, 5, 6, 7\}$,

   $A = \{2, 4, 6\}$,

   and $B = \{3, 4, 5, 6\}$.

List the members of

a) $A \cap B$

b) A'

c) $(A')'$

d) any set C such that $B \cup C = \mathscr{E}$

e) any set D, other than $\varnothing$ such that $(A \cup B) \cap D = \varnothing$.

4. $\mathscr{E} = \{1, 2, 3, 4, 5, 6, 7, 8, 9, 10, 11, 12\}$

   $F = \{\text{factors of } 12\}$

   $P = \{\text{prime numbers}\}$

Note: 1 is not a prime number.

a) List i) F,   ii) P.

b) What is $n(F)$?

c) i) List $F \cap P$.
    ii) Describe this set in words.

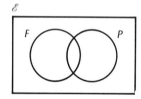   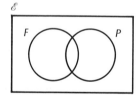

d) Express 12 as a product of prime factors.

e) On the Venn diagrams given shade i) $F' \cup P$, ii) $F \triangle P$.

   C, S and T are three further subsets of $\mathscr{E}$, where $C = \{\text{cube numbers}\}$, $S = \{\text{square numbers}\}$, $T = \{\text{triangle numbers}\}$.

f) List i) C, ii) S, iii) T, iv) $C \cap S \cap T$.

g) $\mathscr{E}$ is extended to include the set of all whole numbers from 1 to 100.
   State the next member of i) $C \cap S$, ii) $S \cap T$.

5. a) Use set notation to describe the shaded region in each of the following Venn diagrams:

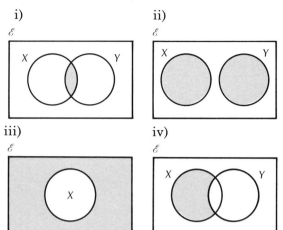

i)   ii)   iii)   iv)

b) $\mathscr{E} = \{\text{members of a swimming club}\}$

   $S = \{\text{members who can swim}\}$

   $D = \{\text{members who can dive}\}$

   $L = \{\text{members who have passed a life-saving test}\}$

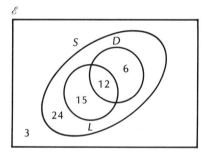

i) Write down

   1) $n(S)$,
   2) $n(S' \cap D)$,
   3) $n(S \cap D \cap L')$,
   4) $n(D \cup L \cap S)$.

ii) 1) How many members of the club cannot swim?
    2) Express this number is set notation.

iii) One member of the club is chosen at random, what is the probability that the member can

   1) swim,
   2) swim and dive, but has not passed a life-saving test?

iv) If a swimmer is chosen, what is the probability that he can also dive?

6. In order to investigate press reports that large numbers of cars with defective brakes, lights and tyres were being driven on the roads, a motoring organisation stopped and checked 100 cars. It was found that

10 had defective tyres,
7 had defective brakes,
7 had defective lights,
3 had defective lights and brakes,
5 had defective lights and tyres,
4 had defective tyres and brakes,
and 3 had all three defects.

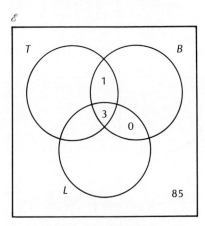

$T = \{\text{cars with defective tyres}\}$
$B = \{\text{cars with defective brakes}\}$
$L = \{\text{cars with defective lights}\}$

a) Represent this information on the Venn diagram.

b) How many cars had at least one defect?

c) Describe in words the set of cars $T \cap B \cap L'$.

d) What is the value of $n(T \cap B \cap L')$?

e) What percentage of cars checked had good tyres?

f) Assuming that this sample does accurately represent all cars in this country, find the probability that a car chosen at random has

  i) defective brakes,
  ii) no defects.

g) The press reports that '40% of all cars had at least one of these defects', is this statement justified from the sample checked?

29 RELATIONS, MAPPINGS AND FUNCTIONS Examination Questions (1)

1. Three arrows are missing from the diagram which partly shows the relation

'is greater than'

on four integers a, b, c and d.

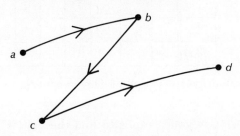

a) On the diagram draw the missing arrows.
b) Which is the smallest of the four integers?

2. $f(x) = 3x - 1 \qquad g(x) = x^2$

Work out
a) $f(2)$,   b) $g(\tfrac{1}{2})$,   c) $fg(-2)$.
  (fg means 'g followed by f'.)

3. For the mapping $x \mapsto \dfrac{12}{3-x}$ shown calculate the values of p and q.

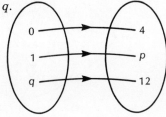

233

4. a) The diagram represents the function f which maps $x \to 2x - 1$.

Complete the diagram for $x = 3$ *and* $x = 4$.

f:x $\longmapsto$ 2x − 1

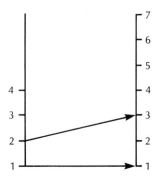

b) The following diagrams represent the functions g and h.

Complete the mappings.

g:x $\longmapsto$

h:x $\longmapsto$

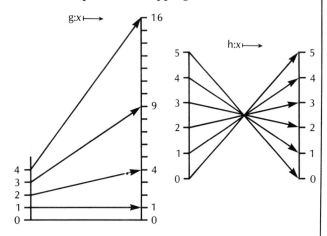

5. $f(x) = 2x + 2 \qquad g(x) = x^2 - 1$

a) Calculate

   i) $f(3)$,
   ii) $g(-1)$.

b) If $f(x) = g(x)$, find the values of x.

6. If $f:x \longmapsto mx + c$, $1 \longmapsto 3$, and $2 \longmapsto 7$, find the values of m and c.

7.

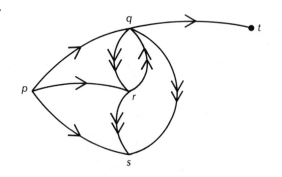

The relation $\longrightarrow$ represents 'is the father of'.

The relation $\longrightarrow\!\!\!\!\!\rightarrow$ represents 'is the brother of'.

Identify s and t as male, female or not known.

8. a) The graph of $g(x) = ax + b$ has been drawn on the axes.

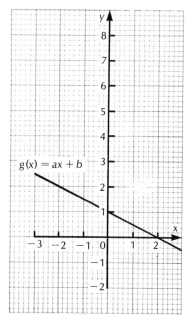

Use the graph to calculate the value of

   i) a,   ii) b.

b) Given $f(x) = x^2 + 2x$

   i) evalute   1) $f(1)$, 2) $ff(1)$,
   ii) if $f(x) = 15$, form an equation involving x and solve it to find *two* possible values of x,
   iii) complete the table of values for $f(x) = x^2 + 2x$,

x	-3	-2	-1	0	1	2
x^2			1	0		4
$2x$			-2	0		4
$f(x)$			-1	0		8

   iv) draw the graph of $f(x) = x^2 + 2x$ on the axes.

c) i) Use your graphs to find the values of x for which $f(x) = g(x)$.
   ii) Shade the region where $f(x) \geqslant x^2 + 2x$ and $g(x) \leqslant ax + b$.

234

9. The functions f and g are defined by

$$f(x) = 2x + 1 \quad \text{and} \quad g(x) = x^2 - 2$$

a) Calculate

   i) $f(1)$,　ii) $g(-2)$,　iii) $f[g(3)]$

b) If $g(x) = 23$, work out the values of x.

c) If $f(x) = g(x)$, work out the values of x.

d) The graph of $f(x) = 2x + 1$ has been drawn on the axes shown. Use the table of values below to draw the graph of $g(x) = x^2 - 2$ on the same axes.

x	-2	-1	0	1	2	3	4
$g(x)$	2	-1	-2	-1	2	7	14

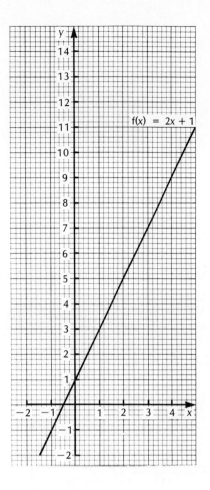

e) Read from your graphs

   i) a value of x for which $g(x) = 0$,
   ii) the range of values of x for which $g(x) < 0$,
   iii) the range of values of x for which $g(x) > f(x)$.

30　FLOW CHARTS
Examination Questions (1)

1. By following the instructions in the flow chart given complete Table B. Record the values of S, P, Q and D in the table as obtained at each stage in the flow chart.

Table B

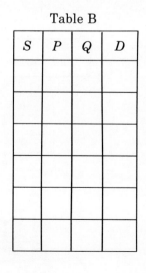

S	P	Q	D

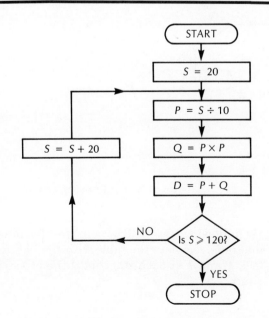

235

2. Use the flowchart to complete the table of values for x and n, after an input of $x = 3$.

x	n
3	0

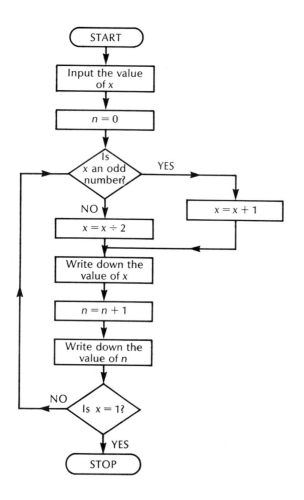

START

Input the value of x

$n = 0$

Is x an odd number? — YES

NO

$x = x + 1$

$x = x \div 2$

Write down the value of x

$n = n + 1$

Write down the value of n

NO ← Is $x = 1$?

YES

STOP

3. a) By following the instructions in the flow diagram, complete the table with the values of I, P and T at each stage until the process stops.

b) If £100 is invested at 10 per cent compound interest, the flow diagram can be used to estimate the increase in the investment P (£) over a time T (years).

  i) On axes plot values of P against T and draw a smooth curve through the points.

  ii) Use your graph to estimate the value of T when $P = £200$.

R	I	P	T
10	0	100	0

START

$P = 100$
$R = 10$
$I = 0$
$T = 0$

$I = P/R$
correct to one decimal place

$P = P + 1$

$T = T + 1$

Is $T = 10$? — NO

YES

STOP

236

4.

1   3   6   10   15

The first five triangle numbers are shown above.

a) i) Write down the next *two* numbers in this sequence.

   ii) The formula $T_n = \dfrac{n(n+1)}{2}$ may be used to find the nth triangle number.
Find the 25th triangle number (T_{25}).

b) A new set of numbers may be obtained by adding adjacent triangle numbers together, as shown below.

$$1 + 3 = 4$$
$$3 + 6 = 9$$

   i) Write down the next *four* numbers in this set.

   ii) What name do we give to this set of numbers?

c) The flow chart below produces a pattern of numbers.

   i) Follow the instructions in the flow chart and record in the table, each new value of P, Q, R, or C, as obtained, at each stage in the flow chart, until the process stops.

   ii) Which of the following, correctly describes the pattern of numbers in column R?

     A. Prime numbers.
     B. Rectangle numbers.
     C. Fibonacci sequence.
     D. Pascal's triangle.

P	Q	R	C
0	0	1	7

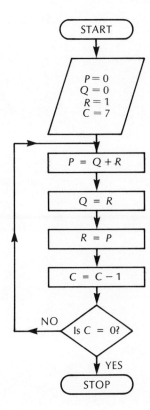

START

$P = 0$
$Q = 0$
$R = 1$
$C = 7$

$P = Q + R$

$Q = R$

$R = P$

$C = C - 1$

Is $C = 0$? NO

YES

STOP

SECTION V

EXAMINATION QUESTIONS (2)

1. Make b the subject of the formula

$$y = \frac{m(a - b)}{a + b}.$$

2. a) Solve the equation $x^2 + 4x = 0$.

   b) Solve the equation $x^2 + 4x + 1 = 0$, giving your answers correct to one decimal place.

3. a) Add together the two fractions

   $$\frac{2}{x - 5} \quad \text{and} \quad \frac{4}{3 - x}$$

   and simplify your answer.

   b) Solve the equation

   $$\frac{2x - 14}{8x - 15 - x^2} = 1,$$

   giving your answers correct to one decimal place.

   c) *Sketch* the graph of

   $$y = x^2 - 6x + 1$$

   Show clearly on your graph the coordinates of the points where the graph cuts the x-axis.

4. a) Given that $x - 3$ is a factor of the expression $x^3 + kx^2 - 5x + 6$, calculate the value of k. Hence determine the other factors of the expression.

   b) Solve for x and y the equations

   $$x - y = 4$$

   $$x^2 - 4x + y^2 - 2y = 0$$

5. a) Solve the following equations:

   i) $2 - 3x = 7$,
   ii) $y^2 + y - 6 = 36$,
   iii) $\begin{cases} p + q = 3, \\ 2p - q = -9, \end{cases}$
   iv) $2^{n+4} = 8^n$.

   b) Solve the following inequalities:

   i) $2 \leqslant 5 + x$,
   ii) $(x - 1)(x + 4) \geqslant 0$.

6. When a certain trainee, Alf, is being taught how to make a certain article, it is found that the time, t minutes, that he takes to make the nth article is given by the formula

   $$t = a + \frac{b}{n}$$

   where a and b are constants. If Alf takes 70 minutes to make the first article and 40 minutes to make the second, find the values of a and b and the time taken to make the third article.

   Find also how many articles Alf has to make before the time to make each one falls below 15 minutes.

   For another trainee, Bert, the formula is $t = 11 + \frac{40}{n}$. Find the least value of n for which Alf makes the nth article in a shorter time than Bert.

7. a) Give the solution sets of the following:

   i) $(x - 4)^2 = x^2 - 8x + 16$,
   ii) $(x - 4)^2 = x^2$,
   iii) $(x - 4)^2 = -8x$,
   iv) $(x - 4)^2 = 16$.

   b) Explain why the equation $(x - 4)^2 = -x^3$ cannot have a positive root.

   Given that this equation has a root which is a negative integer, find this root (by using the remainder theorem or otherwise).

8. a) Calculate the coordinates of the points of intersection of the line $x - y = 5$ and the curve $x^2 + y + 3 = 0$.

b)

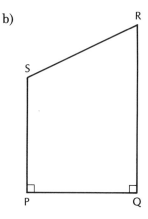

In the diagram, PQRS is a trapezium with PS = PQ and $\angle SPQ = \angle PQR = 90°$. Given that PQ is of length x cm and QR is 6 cm longer than PS, show that the area of the trapezium is $x(x + 3)\,\text{cm}^2$.

Given also that the area of the square drawn on the diagonal QS is 54 cm² greater than the area of the trapezium, calculate

i) the value of x,

ii) the area of the trapezium.

9. In January 1981 a traveller converted 320 American dollars into British money when the rate of exchange was x dollars to £1.

a) Write down an expression for the number of pounds he received.

In March 1981 the traveller converted a further 320 dollars to British money but the rate of exchange had now altered to $(x - 0.4)$ dollars to £1.

b) Write down an expression for the number of pounds he received in this second transaction.

c) Given that the traveller received £40 more in March than he did in January, write down an equation in x and solve it to obtain the rate of exchange in January.

2–5 NUMBER   Examination Questions (2)

1. The distances of the planets Mercury and Neptune from the Sun are approximately 6×10^7 km and 4.5×10^9 km respectively.

a) Find, in standard form, the value of

$$\frac{\text{distance of Neptune from the Sun}}{\text{distance of Mercury from the Sun}}$$

b) Given that the speed of light is 3×10^5 km/s, find, in minutes, the time taken for light to travel from the Sun to Neptune.

2. The mass of an atom of hydrogen is approximately 1.66×10^{-24} g, and that of an atom of oxygen is approximately 2.66×10^{-23} g.

a) Find, giving the answer in standard form to three significant figures, the mass of a molecule of water, which consists of two atoms of hydrogen and one of oxygen.

b) The given masses are correct to three significant figures. Find the maximum possible error in your answer to a), and show that this answer is not necessarily *correct* to three significant figures.

For parts c) and d), use your answer to a), approximating it to *two* significant figures.

c) Find, giving your answer in standard form, the approximate number of molecules in 1 g of water.

d) Find, to the nearest whole number, the percentage by mass of oxygen in water.

3.

The Venn diagram shows the set of all real numbers, which are either rational or irrational.

a) Copy the diagram and put into it both the set of integers, I, and the set of natural numbers, N.

b) For each of the following numbers, state *all* of the sets, using the letters I, N, P, Q, to which each belongs:

   i) π, ii) $3\frac{1}{7}$, iii) 4, iv) -4.

4. A game is played with counters. If there are n counters, the number of moves in which the game is completed is r, where

$$r = 2^n - 1$$

Find

a) how many moves are needed if there are four counters,

b) how many counters are used if 63 moves are needed,

c) the smallest number of counters that must be used if more than 200 moves are to be needed.

Given that for a certain number, say N, of counters, the number of moves needed is 8191, calculate the number of moves needed for

d) $N - 1$ counters,

e) $2N$ counters, giving the answer in standard form to two significant figures.

Given that the number of seconds in a year is approximately 3.15×10^7, show that with $2N$ counters, making one move a second, the game could not be completed in two years.

5. a) $\mathscr{E}$

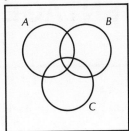

$\mathscr{E}$ is the set of positive integers from 1 to 25 inclusive.
A is the set of all even integers.
B is the set of all squares of positive integers.
C is the set of all positive integers which, after division by 10, leave a remainder of 6.

Copy the Venn diagram shown and write in, where possible, one positive integer in each region. Mark as empty any region which does not contain an element.

b) $\mathscr{E} = \{\text{Rational numbers}\}$,

   $P = \{x : x > 1\}$,

   $Q = \{x : -2 < x < 4\}$,

   $R = \{x : x < 3\}$.

Write, in the same form as above, the sets

   i) $P \cap R$, ii) P', iii) $P \cup Q'$, iv) $Q \cap R'$.

Describe, in terms of P, Q and the usual notation for sets,

   $\{x : 1 < x < 4\}$

6. Three children, A, B and C, are sharing a bowl of food. When the bowl is passed to A, he always takes one-sixth of whatever is in it, whereas B and C always take one-fifth and one-quarter respectively, of whatever is in the bowl when it is passed to them. If the bowl, which is full at the start, is passed round in the order A, B, C,

a) show that all the children receive equal amounts,

b) find what fraction of the food is left when each child has taken i) one helping, ii) two helpings.

If, on the other hand, the bowl is passed round in the order C, B, A,

c) show that the sizes of the helpings taken by C, B and A are in the ratio $5 : 3 : 2$,

d) find what fraction of the bowlful each child has eaten, and what fraction is left, after each child has taken two helpings.

1. An alloy of tin and aluminium contains 44% of tin by weight. Calculate the weight of tin which must be mixed with 84 kg of aluminium to produce a quantity of alloy.

2. A bank offers two schemes of investment. Scheme A pays tax-free interest of 8%. Scheme B pays interest of 12% on which tax at 30% has to be paid. A man has £1000 to invest. Calculate his income after tax, under the two different schemes.

3. A Mathematics examination consists of two papers and is marked out of 300 marks. Paper 1 carries one-third and Paper 2 two-thirds of these marks. Calculate the percentage of the maximum mark obtained by a candidate who scores 66% of the marks awarded to Paper 1 and 51% of the marks awarded to Paper 2.

4. A man bought a house for £24 000 and spent an additional £2500 on improvements and repairs. The rateable value of the house is £320 and the general rate for the first year was 72 p in the £ with an additional water rate of 26 p in the £. He decided to let the house at an annual rent to cover the rates, cost of maintenance, which he estimated at £100 per annum, and to give him a return of 8% for each year on his original outlay. He agreed to let the house at a rent of £50 per week for two years. Taking a year as 52 weeks, calculate

   a) his total outgoings for rates and maintenance in the first year,

   b) the amount by which he exceeds his target of an 8% return on his capital outlay for the first year.

   In the second year the general rate is increased by 15% and the water rate by 10%. His actual bills for maintenance over the two years total £260. Calculate

   c) his total outgoings for rates and maintenance for the two years,

   d) the amount by which he falls short of, or exceeds, his target of 8% return over the two year period.

5. In a mining operation during the early part of this century, ore was extracted which contained 2% tin, 0.05% zinc and 0.004% tungsten. Given that 20 000 tonnes of ore were extracted per week, and the plant was used for only 50 weeks in each year, calculate in tonnes per year

   a) the mass of ore extracted,

   b) the mass of each mineral present in the ore extracted.

   Because of the crude methods in use at the time, only 60% of the three minerals present could be recovered and used.

   c) Calculate, in tonnes, the mass of each mineral that could be recovered.

   If these minerals were used in making articles of an alloy using masses of tin, zinc and tungsten in the proportions 487 : 12 : 1, and such that 50 000 articles were made for each tonne of tungsten used, calculate

   d) the number of articles made in a year if all the tungsten recovered was used,

   e) the mass of tin and the mass of zinc recovered but not used.

6. To estimate the cost of providing windows, glazing suppliers measure the perimeter of the window space in millimetres and charge the following rates per mm:

   1.25 p per mm for glazing with a single piece of glass.

   1.5 p per mm for glazing with two sliding pieces of glass.

   1.75 p per mm for glazing with three sliding pieces of glass.

I have four windows which each measure 1200 mm by 1780 mm.

a) Calculate the perimeter of one window.

I decide to fit two sliding pieces of glass to each of two of the windows.

b) Calculate the cost of glazing these two windows.

I decide to fit three sliding pieces of glass to each of the other two windows.

c) Calculate the cost of glazing these two windows.

In addition, I decide that a single pane of glass will be adequate for the small hall window which measures 1050 mm by 840 mm.

d) Calculate the cost of glazing this window.

e) Find the total cost of all five windows.

An extra 10% is added to this total for fitting the windows.

f) Calculate the fitting charge.

A discount of 5% of the total price (including the fitting charge) is allowed for a cash payment.

g) Find, to the nearest penny, what saving this would represent on this order.

7. A certain radioactive body, P, has the property that at the end of any hour the number of units of radioactivity of P falls to three-quarters of its value at the beginning of that hour. If at a certain instant the radioactivity is 160 units, calculate the value of its radioactivity three hours later. Express this value as a percentage of the original value, i.e. of 160.

Find also the average rate of decrease of the radioactivity of P during the three hours, in units per hour.

The radioactivity of another body, Q, falls, after any hour, to a fraction m/n of its value at the beginning of that hour. At the end of 3 hours it has fallen to 21.6% of its value at the beginning of the 3 hours. Find the value of m/n. Find also after how many more complete hours the radioactivity of Q has fallen below 5% of its original value.

8. In a certain year a factory producing coats had a total wage bill of £1 500 000. Of this bill, 20% was paid for overtime and the remainder for normal working. The total amounts paid for normal working to each of three groups of employees, namely management, skilled workers and semi-skilled workers, were in the ratios 1:6:3. Calculate the yearly wages bill for normal working for each of the three groups of workers.

The average payments for normal work to employees in each of the three groups were in the ratios 5:3:2, and the factory employed 20 persons in the management group. Using the wages bill as calculated above, calculate

a) the average yearly wage, for normal working, for an employee in each of the three groups,

b) the total number of persons employed in the factory.

The payments for overtime were distributed between the three groups of employees in the ratios 0:3:2. Calculate the *total* average yearly wage of a person in the skilled worker group and express this as a percentage of the *total* average yearly wage of a person in the management group.

10 AREA AND VOLUME
Examination Questions (2)

1. The base of a rectangular tank measures 140 cm by 110 cm. Given that the tank holds 1386 litres, find its height, in cm.
   A cylindrical tank has the same height and the same capacity as the rectangular tank. Taking π as $\frac{22}{7}$, calculate the radius, in cm, of the cylindrical tank.

2. In a girl's pencil case there are three new un-sharpened pencils each of length 18 cm. The blue pencil has a circular cross-section of diameter 8 mm, the cross-section of the red pencil is an equilateral triangle of side 8 mm, and that of the green pencil is a regular hexagon of side 4 mm. Calculate the volume, to the nearest cm^3, of each pencil.

The girl sharpens the blue pencil, so that the end is a right circular cone of height 1.5 cm. The new length of the pencil from point to base is 17.5 cm. Calculate the reduction in volume, in cm^3 correct to 1 decimal place, of the blue pencil.

3.

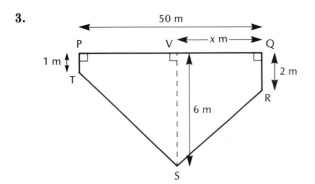

The diagram, not drawn to scale, shows the uniform vertical cross-section PQRST of a swimming pool of length 50 m and width 12 m. The deepest point S of the cross-section is vertically below the point V. The areas of the cross-sections PVST and VQRS are equal and PT = 1 m, VS = 6 m and QR = 2 m. Given that VQ = x m, show that $x = 23\frac{1}{2}$.

Calculate the volume of water in the pool

a) when it is completely full,

b) when the whole of the surface of the base of the pool is just covered with water.

The pool is empty and is then filled by water flowing at a rate of $2\frac{3}{4}$ m/s through a system of 10 cylindrical pipes. Given that the radius of the cross-section of each of the pipes is r cm, and taking π as $\frac{22}{7}$, write down an expression in terms of r for the volume, in m^3, of water flowing into the pool each hour through the system of pipes. Given that it takes 16 hours to fill the pool completely, calculate the value of r.

4.

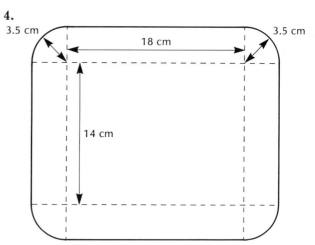

The diagram shows the uniform internal cross section of a container at right angles to its length. The straight sides of the cross section are 18 cm and 14 cm long and the rounded corners are arcs of quadrants of a circle of radius 3.5 cm.

The length of the container is 30 cm. Taking $\pi = \frac{22}{7}$, calculate

a) the area, in cm^2, of the cross section of the container,

b) the internal volume, in cm^3, of the container.

It is decided to replace the container with a cylindrical can with a conical top of the same base radius as the cylinder. The internal height of the cone is 9 cm and its base radius is 10.5 cm. Calculate, to the nearest mm, the overall internal height of the new container given that it has the same internal volume as the original container.

5. During a storm, the depth of the rainfall was 15.4 mm. The rain which fell on a horizontal roof measuring 7.5 m by 3.6 m was collected in a cylindrical tank of radius 35 cm which was empty before the storm began. Calculate

a) the area, in cm^2, of the roof,

b) the volume, in cm^3, of the rain which fell on the roof.

Taking π as $\frac{22}{7}$, find

c) the area, in cm^2, of the cross section of the tank,

d) the height, in cm, of the rain water in the tank.

Given that a watering can holds five litres, how many times could it be filled completely from the rain water?

6.

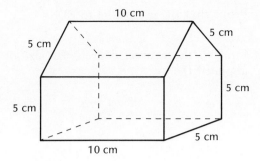

10 cm
5 cm
5 cm
5 cm
5 cm
10 cm
5 cm

The diagram shows a paper model house that can be made from a sheet of paper 20 cm square, by a certain method of folding, cutting, etc. There is no floor, but there are two vertical walls and two sloping roof-sections, all of which are rectangles 10 cm × 5 cm, and two end walls which are vertical pentagons. Write down the angle of slope of each roof-section, and calculate

a) the area of each end wall,

b) the total area of all the walls and roof-sections,

c) the answer to b) expressed as a percentage of the area of the sheet of paper from which the model was made,

d) the volume of the model.

State what would be the effect on your answers to b), c) and d) above, if the model were made from a sheet of paper 40 cm square, so that all the linear dimensions were doubled.

7. A hollow metal pipe of circular cross-section has internal radius 10 cm, external radius 11 cm.

Find

a) the area, in cm^2, of the cross-section of the metal,

b) the volume, in cm^3, of metal required to make a straight portion of pipe of length 2 m,

c) the weight, in kg, of this portion of pipe, given that 1 cm^3 of metal weighs 8.5 g.

Water passes along the pipe with a speed of 30 cm/s. This pipe is used to empty a swimming bath containing 500 m^3 of water.

d) Find, to the nearest hour, the time taken to empty the bath.
[The volume, V cm^3, of a circular cylinder of radius r cm and length l cm is given by $V = \pi r^2 l$.]

11 SIMILARITY Examination Questions (2)

1. A trophy in the form of a large circular plate weighs 5.4 kg. A scale miniature in the same material weighs 25 g.

Calculate the ratio of

a) the radius,

b) the surface area,

of the trophy to those of the miniature.

2. In a garden, there are two ornamental ponds which are similar in every respect. The perimeter of the surface of the larger is twice the perimeter of the surface of the smaller pond.

a) Write down the ratio of their surface areas.

b) Given that the smaller pond contains 420 litres of water, find how much water is contained in the larger pond.

3. A lump of metal is melted down and made into 1000 identical rectangular blocks each of length 3 cm. Assuming that in each case there is no wastage, calculate how many similar blocks each of length 5 cm could be made from the same lump of metal.

4. A bar of soap, of length 8 cm and of weight 160 g, was taken into use at the beginning of the first day of a month. At the end of the fifth day, the soap was the same shape as before, but its length had been reduced to 6 cm. Show that its weight was then 67.5 g, and calculate the percentage reduction in a) the length, and b) the weight of the bar of soap.

If the same weight of soap is used each day, calculate the weight of the bar at the end of the seventh day, and find on what day it was completely used up. (Assume that it could continue to be used until none at all was left.)

5.

The four triangles AOB, BOC, COD and DOE are all similar, and OA = 1 cm, OB = 2 cm.

a) Find, in cm², the area of the whole figure.

b) Find the length, in cm correct to one decimal place, of BE.

c) Prove that BC is parallel to ED.

d) Find, to the nearest degree, the size of the angle BED.

6.

Fig. a   Fig. b

Figure a shows a space capsule which consists of a portion of a cone whose parallel plane ends are circles of radii 2 metres and r metres, joined to a hemisphere of radius 2 metres. In Figure b, ACDEB is the cross-section of the complete cone of which the portion BCDE is the cross-section of the upper portion of the capsule. Given that the height of AX of the complete cone is 6 metres, find, by using similar triangles, the height AY, in terms of r, of the small cone whose cross-section is ABC.

Show that the volume of the portion of the cone whose cross-section is BCDE is $(8\pi - \pi r^3)\,\text{m}^3$.

Given that this volume is equal to the volume of the hemisphere, calculate the value of r correct to 2 decimal places.

Taking the value of r to be 1.4 and π as 3.14, find, in m^3 to 3 significant figures, the volume of the whole space capsule.

1. In the kite ABCD, where AB = AD, the diagonals BD and AC meet at E; P is the mid-point of AE and Q is the mid-point of CE.

   Given that BD = 12 cm, AC = 13 cm and AE = 4 cm,

   a) calculate AB and CB, in cm, giving your answers correct to two decimal places,

   b) prove that ∠ABC = 90°,

   c) calculate ∠EBC, to the nearest degree,

   d) calculate ∠PBQ, to the nearest degree.

2. A man stands on horizontal ground with his feet 50 m from the base of a vertical tower. He observes the angle of elevation of the top of the tower to be 12° and the angle of depression of the base of the tower to be 2°. Find, in metres correct to one decimal place, the height of the tower.

3.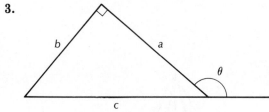

   Use the diagram to write down, in terms of a, b and c, the values of

   a) $\tan \theta$,   b) $\sin \theta$,   c) $\cos \theta$.

4.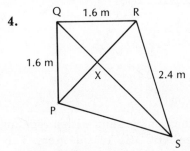

   The diagram shows a quadrilateral PQRS in which PQ = QR = 1.6 m, RS = 2.4 m, ∠PQR = 90° and ∠QRS = 120°. Calculate the lengths of PR and QS.

   The lines PR and QS intersect at X. By first obtaining ∠XQR, or otherwise, calculate the length of XR.

5. A ship sails from port A to port B, a distance of 5 km, on a bearing of 036°.

   a) Calculate, in km to 2 decimal places, the distance by which B is

      i) east of A,
      ii) north of A.

   The ship then sails to a point C, a further distance of 8 km, on a bearing of 138°.

   b) Calculate, in km to 2 decimal places, the distance by which C is

      i) east of A,
      ii) south of A.

   c) Calculate

      i) the bearing, to the nearest degree, of A from C,
      ii) the distance, in km to 2 decimal places, of A from C.

6. The points P, S, O are in the same horizontal plane and are at the base of the Post Office Tower, the base of St. Paul's Cathedral and at The Oval respectively.

   The bearings of O and P from S are 200° and 290° respectively and PS = 2.7 km, SO = 3.6 km.

   Calculate

   a) the length, in km, of OP,
   b) the bearing of O from P to the nearest degree,
   c) the area, in hectares, of △PSO.
      [1 hectare = 10 000 m².]

   The height of the Post Office Tower is 176 m and of St. Paul's Cathedral is 111 m. Calculate, to the nearest 0.1°, the angle of depression of the highest point of St. Paul's from the top of the Post Office Tower.

7.

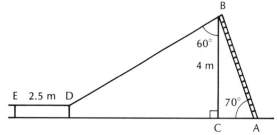

The diagram shows a children's playground slide. The highest point B is 4 m above the horizontal ground and the horizontal part DE is of length 2.5 m and is 0.5 m above the ground. The ladder AB makes an angle of 70° with the ground and the slope BD makes an angle of 60° with the main support BC which is vertical.

Calculate, in m correct to 1 decimal place,

a) the distance AC,

b) the perpendicular distance of D from BC,

c) the distance travelled by a child when going down the slide from B to E,

d) the length of the ladder.

This ladder is replaced by another of length 4.5 m. Calculate, to the nearest degree, the angle between the new ladder and the ground.

8.

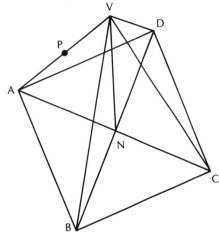

In the diagram, VABCD is a pyramid whose base ABCD is a square of side 6 cm. The vertex V is vertically above N, the centre of the base, and VN = 3 cm. Calculate the length of VA.

Calculate also

a) the angle between the line VA and the plane ABCD,

b) the angle between the plane VAB and the plane ABCD.

If P is the mid-point of VA, calculate the length of PN, giving your answer correct to two places of decimals.

9.

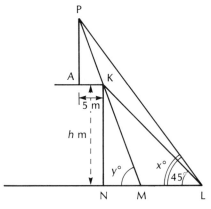

a) The diagram shows the vertical cross section of a tower of height h metres with a horizontal roof. A vertical flagpole, AP, stands at A on the roof 5 m from the edge K of the roof. KN is vertical and the points L, M and N are on horizontal ground through the base of the tower. The angles of elevation of P and K from L are $x°$ and 45° respectively and PKM is a straight line with $\angle\,PMN = y°$.

Given that $\tan x° = \frac{7}{6}$ and $\tan y° = 2$, calculate, in metres,

i) the height of flagpole, AP.

ii) the height h of the tower.

b)

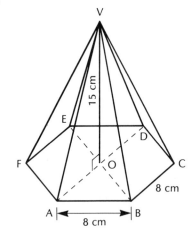

The diagram shows a pyramid with a regular hexagonal base ABCDEF of side 8 cm. The vertex of the pyramid, V, is vertically above the centre, O, of the hexagonal base and VO = 15 cm.

i) Write down the length of AO,

Calculate, correct to the nearest degree,

ii) $\angle\,VAO$,

iii) the angle between the face VAB and the base of the pyramid.

1. The radius of the chain-wheel of a bicycle is 9 cm. Given that the portion of chain in contact with the wheel is of length 33 cm calculate the angle subtended at the centre of the wheel by this portion of chain.

2. [In this question, take the value of π to be 3.14.]

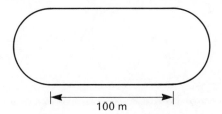

100 m

The figure shows a field which consists of a rectangle with a semicircle at each end. The length of each of the straight portions of the perimeter of the field is 100 m.

a) Given that the perimeter of the field is 400 m, find, to the nearest metre, the radius of one semicircular end.

Around the outside of this field is a running track consisting of eight "lanes", each of width 1 metre, and the inside line of each lane is used to measure the running distance.

b) Find the running distance in the outside lane.

c) What distance in front of the start line should a runner be placed in the outside lane if he is to run 400 m?

d) Find, in m² to the nearest 10 m², the area of grass occupied by the eight lanes.

3.

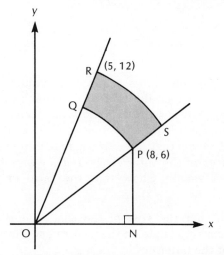

In the diagram P is the point (8, 6), R is the point (5, 12) and N is the foot of the perpendicular from P to the x-axis. If the unit of length on each axis represents 1 cm, calculate

a) OP,   b) $\angle$ PON.

The circle centre O and radius OP cuts OR at Q and the circle centre O radius OR cuts OP produced at S. Taking π as 3.142 and by first finding $\angle$ ROP, calculate, in cm², the area of the region PQRS (shown shaded). Correct your answer to two places of decimals.

4.

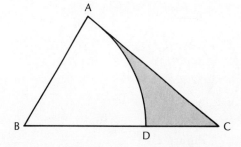

In the diagram, AB = 5 cm, BC = 8 cm and CA = 7 cm. AD is an arc of a circle drawn with centre B and radius BA. Show that cos ABC = $\frac{1}{2}$.

Calculate

a) the area of $\triangle$ABC,

b) the area of the shaded region ADC.
(Take π as 3.142.)

5.

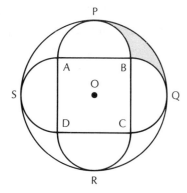

The diagram shows a circular window in a church. Semi-circles are drawn on each side of a square ABCD such that the semi-circles touch the circumference of the outer circle at P, Q, R and S. Given that AB = $2x$ cm, find, in terms of x, the area of the outer circle and the area of the shaded region. Show that the ratio of these areas is $8\pi : (\pi - 2)$.

Given that the area of the shaded portion is $3000\,\text{cm}^2$, calculate, to the nearest cm, the radius OP of the outer circle.

6.

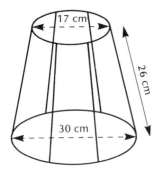

Figure 1

Figure 2

Figure 1 shows a wire frame which is to be constructed from a roll of wire of length 350 cm. The frame consists of two horizontal circles joined together by six equal straight wires, each of length 26 cm. The centre of the lower circle is vertically below the centre of the upper circle. The diameter of the upper circle is 17 cm and the diameter of the lower circle is 30 cm. Using π as

3.142 where required, calculate, giving your answers correct to three significant figures,

a) the perpendicular distance, in cm, between the two horizontal circles,

b) the total length, in cm, of the wire in the frame,

c) the percentage of the original roll of wire which is not used.

The frame is to be tightly covered by cloth with the plain ends remaining uncovered. Figure 2 is a *sketch* of the shape of the cloth. Copy the sketch and mark on it as many measurements as you can.

7.

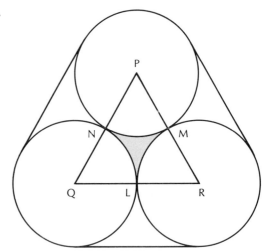

The diagram shows three equal discs, centres P, Q and R, each of radius 4 cm and resting on a horizontal plane. The discs are bound together by means of a string and L, M and N are the points of contact between the discs. Explain why the triangle PQR is equilateral.

Calculate, giving your answers correct to three significant figures,

a) the length, in cm, of PL,

b) the area, in cm^2, of the triangle PQR,

c) the area, in cm^2, of the sector PNM,

d) the shaded area, in cm^2, between the discs.

e) Explain why the length of the string in contact with the discs is $2 \times \pi \times 4$ cm.

f) Write down the total length, in cm, of the string.

1.

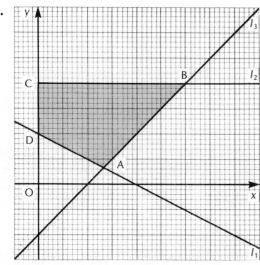

The equations of the lines l_1, l_2, l_3 are

$$l_1: \quad 2y + x = 20$$

$$l_2: \qquad y = 20$$

$$l_3: \qquad y = x - 10.$$

a) Find the coordinates of the points A, B, C, D, and the gradient of the line l_1.

b) Write down suitable inequalities to describe the shaded region ABCD (including the boundary).

c) If p and q are integers and the point (p, q) lies in the shaded region, find the least value of $3p + 10q$.

2.

x	0	1	2	3	4	5
y			1.6	5.4		

Three students Andrew, Barbara and Clare were each given a copy of the above table and asked to find a relationship between x and y, then sketch the graph $x \to y$.

a) Andrew assumed the relationship to be of the form $y = ax + b$. Calculate the values of a and b. Hence complete his table and sketch his graph.

b) Barbara assumed the relationship to be of the form $y = kx^3$. Calculate the value of k. Hence complete her table and sketch her graph.

c) Clare assumed the relationship to be of the form $y = pq^x$. Show that $q = \frac{27}{8}$ and calculate the value of p correct to 2 significant figures. Do not sketch her graph.

3.

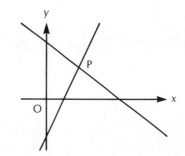

The diagram shows the two lines

$$3x + 4y = 12$$

$$2x - y = 2$$

Sketch a copy of this diagram and mark clearly which equation belongs to which line.

Calculate the coordinates of P, the point of intersection of the two lines.

Shade on your diagram the region defined by

$\{(x, y): y > 0\} \cap \{(x, y): 3x + 4y < 12\} \cap \{(x, y): 2x - y > 2\}.$

SECTION V

4.

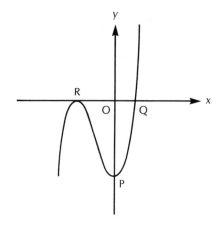

The diagram shows the graph of

$$y = x^3 + 3x^2 - 4$$

The graph cuts the y-axis at P, cuts the x-axis at Q and touches the x-axis at R.

a) Find the coordinates of P.

b) Given that Q is the point (1, 0), find the coordinates of R.

c) If T is the point (0, −9), find the area of △QTR.

5. Copy and complete the following table for

$$y = 2x^3 + x^2 - 8x$$

x	-2	$-1\frac{1}{2}$	-1	$-\frac{1}{2}$	0	$\frac{1}{2}$	1	$1\frac{1}{2}$	2
$2x^3$		$-6\frac{3}{4}$	-2	$-\frac{1}{4}$				$6\frac{3}{4}$	16
x^2		$2\frac{1}{4}$	1	$\frac{1}{4}$				$2\frac{1}{4}$	4
$-8x$		12	8	4				-12	-16
y		$7\frac{1}{2}$	7	4				-3	4

Draw the graph of $y = 2x^3 + x^2 - 8x$, using a scale of 4 cm to 1 unit on the x-axis and 1 cm to 1 unit on the y-axis.

Use your graph to estimate

a) the positive root of the equation

$$2x^3 + x^2 - 8x = 0,$$

b) the set of negative values of x for which $y \geqslant 4$.

Using the same axes draw the straight line $y = x$ and hence estimate the positive root of the equation

$$2x^3 + x^2 - 8x = x$$

6. The weights of certain British coins were taken as being as follows:

'Silver' coins		'Copper' coins	
Value	Weight	Value	Weight
10 p	11 g	2 p	7 g
5 p	5.5 g	1 p	3.5 g
		$\frac{1}{2}$ p	1.75 g

a) Show that the combined weight of 'silver' coins, value x pence, and 'copper' coins, value y pence, is

$$(1.1x + 3.5y) \text{ g}$$

b) A sealed collecting box is found to contain 770 g of coins which are known to be of the above kinds. Show that, if the values of the 'silver' and 'copper' coins in the box are x pence and y pence respectively, then $11x + 35y = 7700$. On graph-paper, with a scale of 1 cm to 50 units, draw the line with this equation.

c) Find inequalities in x and y to express the following conditions:

   i) the value of the 'silver' coins is not less than that of the 'copper' coins,
   ii) the weight of the 'copper' coins is not less than that of the 'silver' coins.

d) Draw the appropriate lines and shade the areas containing points representing pairs of values of x and y ruled out by these inequalities.

e) Find the largest possible sum of money in the box, consistent with conditions i) and ii).

1. A particle moves along a straight line so that, t seconds after observations are commenced, its distance,

s metres, from a fixed point O in the line is given by

$$s = 8 - 6t + 2t^3$$

Calculate

a) the values of t when $s = 8$,

b) the distance travelled by the particle in the first second after observations are commenced.

2. The distance by rail from Bournemouth to Southampton is 49 km. A train leaves Bournemouth at 08 40 and arrives at Southampton at 09 08. Calculate the average speed, in km/h, of the train.

The same train leaves Southampton at 09 10 and travels a distance of 128 km to London at an average speed of 112 km/h. Find, to the nearest minute, the time of arrival of the train in London.

Giving your answer to the nearest whole number, calculate the average speed, in km/h, for the journey from Bournemouth to London.

3. The speed of a motor boat in still water is x km/h. A river is flowing at 6 km/h. Write down expressions for the times, in hours, taken by the motor boat to travel a distance of 5 km in the river

a) upstream,   b) downstream.

If the total time taken by the boat to travel 5 km upstream and immediately back to its starting point is 2 hours, form an equation for x and solve it.

Hence calculate the time taken by the boat to travel the 5 km upstream.

4.

Time (s)	0	1	2	3	4	5	6	7	8
Speed (m/s)	0	6	12	16	19	21	22	22	22

The table shows the speeds, in m/s, of a car starting from rest and moving along a straight road. Using a scale of 2 cm to represent 1 second and 1 cm to represent 2 m/s draw the time-speed graph for the car for the first 8 seconds of its motion.

a) Explain carefully how to use the graph to estimate the distance moved by the car in a given time.

b) Use your graph to estimate the distance moved by the car in the first 6 seconds of its motion.

A lorry is travelling at a steady speed of 16 m/s along the same road and in the same direction as the car. Calculate the distance moved by the lorry in 6 seconds.

Draw, on your graph, the time-speed graph of the lorry. Given that the lorry passes the car at the moment at which the car starts, calculate

c) the distance between the lorry and the car after 6 seconds,

d) the further time taken for the car to overtake the lorry.

5. A car A travels 63 km in t hours at a uniform speed.

a) Write down an expression for the car's speed.

b) Write down an expression for the speed of a second car B which can cover the 63 km in 15 minutes less time than A.

c) It is known that the second car travels 6 km/h faster than the first. Write down an equation to show this fact.

d) Simplify and solve your equation, stating clearly which of the two answers you obtain is the relevant answer.

1.

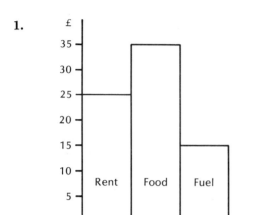

The bar chart illustrates the weekly expenditure of a family on rent, food and fuel. Sketch a pie chart to represent this information, marking the size of the angle in each sector.

2. A count was made of the numbers of occupants of 100 cars passing a certain point, with the results shown below:

Number of occupants	1	2	3	4	5	6
Number of cars	23	35	22	11	6	3

a) Write down the number of cars with 4 or more occupants.

b) Calculate the number of people travelling in cars with 4 or more occupants.

c) Calculate the mean number of occupants per car in all the 100 cars.

It was also noted that exactly 27 of the cars were driven by women. Find the largest and smallest possible numbers of cars which were driven by women and had fewer than 4 occupants each.

3. Eighty pupils ran 100 m. Their times, to the nearest 0.1 second, are given in the table.

Time in s	13.3	13.4	13.5	13.6	13.7	13.8	13.9
No. of pupils	10	14	24	21	7	2	2

a) Estimate, in seconds to one decimal place, the mean time.

b) Plotting values over the range 13.25 seconds to 13.95 seconds and using a scale of 2 cm to represent 0.1 second and a scale of 2 cm to represent 10 pupils, draw a cumulative frequency diagram to illustrate these data.

Use your diagram to answer parts c) and d) of this question and mark clearly on your diagram any points which you use.

Estimate

c) the number of pupils who took longer than 13.60 seconds,

d) the percentage who achieved a time of 13.50 seconds or better.

4. A manufacturer of electric light bulbs tested 100 bulbs to find the number of hours, to the nearest hour, which they burned before failing.

No. of hours before failure	0 to 199	200 to 399	400 to 599	600 to 799	800 to 999	1000 to 1199	1200 to 1399
No. of bulbs failing	1	6	13	25	34	18	3

a) On graph paper, using a scale of 1 cm to represent 100 hours across the page and 4 cm to represent 10 bulbs up the page, draw a histogram to display this information.

b) Estimate the mean life of a bulb. (Take the mid-interval values to be 100, 300, 500, ... hours.)

c) Find the probability that a bulb chosen at random had a life of 1000 or more hours.

d) Find the probability that 2 bulbs chosen at random both had a life of 800 or more hours.

5.

Marks	10	20	30	40	50	60	70	80	90	100
Number of candidates who gained this mark or less than this mark	5	19	58	120	209	348	540	712	787	800

The table shows the distribution of marks gained by a group of 800 candidates in an examination. Using a scale of 2 cm to represent 10 marks and 2 cm to represent 100 candidates, plot these values and draw a smooth curve through your points.

75% of the candidates obtain a grade A, B or C and of these candidates 7% obtain grade A. Calculate

a) the number of candidates who obtain grades A, B or C,

b) the number of candidates who obtain grade A.

c) Express, as a percentage of the 800 candidates, the number who obtain grades B or C.

Use your graph to estimate

d) the lowest mark which will obtain a grade C,

e) the lowest mark which will obtain a grade A,

f) the median mark.

6. a) Find the mean and the median of the seven numbers in the set A, where $A = \{1, 3, 7, 13, 21, 31, 43\}$.

b) The set B consists of five different even integers whose mean is 12. Find the mean of the members of $A \cup B$.

c) The median of the members of set B is 12. If a member of B is chosen at random, show that the probability that it is less than 12 is $\frac{2}{5}$.

d) A member of A and a member of B are both chosen at random. Find the probability that
   i) both are less than 12,
   ii) either both are less than 12, or both are more than 12.

19–22 GEOMETRY
Examination Questions (2)

1. Describe the locus in a plane of a point P equidistant from two fixed points, X and Y, of the plane.

Using ruler and compasses only construct

a) △BKC such that BC = 10 cm, BK = 13 cm and ∠KBC = 45°.

b) On the same diagram construct a point A on BK such that AC = AK.

2.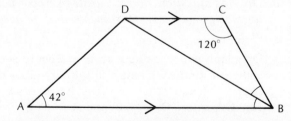

In the diagram, AB is parallel to DC and DB bisects ∠ABC. Given that ∠BAD = 42° and ∠BCD = 120°, calculate ∠ABC and ∠ADB.

3.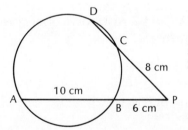

The chords AB and DC of a circle are produced to intersect at P outside the circle ABCD. Given that AB = 10 cm, BP = 6 cm, and PC = 8 cm, calculate

a) CD,

b) the ratio BC : DA.

257

4.

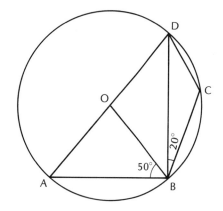

In the diagram, A, B, C and D are four points on a circle centre O and AD is a diameter. Given that $\angle OBA = 50°$ and $\angle CBD = 20°$, calculate $\angle BCD$ and $\angle ADC$.

5.

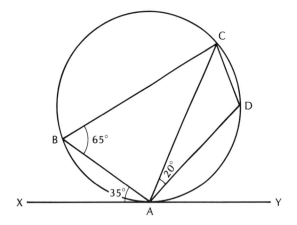

XAY is the tangent at A to the circle ABCD. Given that $\angle XAB = 35°$, $\angle ABC = 65°$ and $\angle CAD = 20°$, calculate the size, in degrees, of $\angle BCA$, $\angle BAC$ and $\angle ACD$. Give brief reasons for your answers.

6. State the locus in two dimensions of the centre of a variable circle

a) which touches a given line at a given point,

b) which touches both of two fixed parallel lines.

On graph paper draw the rectangle ABYX in which AB = 10 cm, BY = 8 cm. Draw also the line LM where L is the mid-point of AX and M is the mid-point of BY.

Determine, by construction, the point P lying inside the rectangle ABYX, such that it is equidistant from AB and LM, and AP = 5 cm.

Construct a circle which passes through P touching AB and XY.

Construct a further circle which touches the circle you have drawn and also the lines LM and XY. Label its centre R and measure and write down the length of PR.

7.

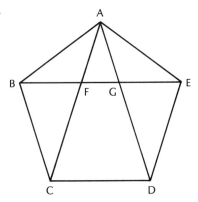

ABCDE is a regular pentagon.

a) Write down the size in degrees of $\angle BAE$.

The diagonals AC, AD cut the diagonal BE at F and G respectively.

b) Calculate the size in degrees of $\angle BAC$, $\angle ABE$, $\angle CBF$ and $\angle CFB$.

c) Show that BGDC is a rhombus.

d) Taking each side of the pentagon to be of length one centimetre, find the length, in cm, of FC.

e) Taking AF to be of length x cm, find, in terms of x, the length, in cm, of FG.

f) Show that $\triangle AFG$ is similar to $\triangle ACD$ and hence that $AF \times CD = AC \times FG$.

g) By substituting the lengths in terms of x in this equation, form and simplify an equation in x but do not solve it.

8. (*In this question any accurate method using normal geometrical instruments will be acceptable.*)

On graph paper, using a scale of 2 cm to represent 1 unit on each axis and taking values of x from 0 to 9 and values of y from 0 to 6, draw the line OA where O = (0, 0) and A = (8, 6).

Draw the locus of points which are equidistant from the x-axis OX and from the line OA, and which lie within the acute angle XOA.

Taking as centre the point P at which $x = 3$ on this locus, construct a circle to touch OX and OA.

Mark the point B(4, 2). Join OB to cut the circle at C and D, where C lies between O and D. Draw the line BQ, which is an enlargement of the line CP from centre O.

Hence construct a circle which passes through B and touches OX and OA.

9.

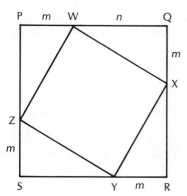

The side of the square PQRS is of length $m + n$. Points W, X, Y, Z are taken on the sides PQ, QR, RS, SP respectively such that

$$PW = QX = RY = SZ = m.$$

a) Prove that $\triangle QXW$ is congruent to $\triangle RYX$.

b) Prove that $\angle WXY$ is a right angle.

c) Give reasons why WXYZ is a square.

d) Write down, in terms of m and n, the areas of square PQRS and of $\triangle PWZ$.

By considering the areas of the squares and the triangles, verify that $WX^2 = m^2 + n^2$.

e) Given that $WY = 4m$, calculate the value of the ratio $n : m$.

10.

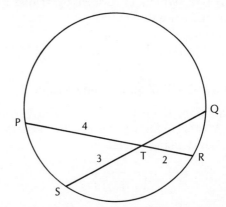

In the diagram, T is the point of intersection of the chords PR and SQ of a circle. PT = 4 cm, TR = 2 cm and TS = 3 cm.

a) Prove that the length of TQ is $2\frac{2}{3}$ cm.

b) Prove that $\triangle PTS$ is similar to $\triangle QTR$.

c) Given that the area of $\triangle PTS$ is 3 cm², find the area of $\triangle QTR$.

d) Find the value of the ratio

$$\frac{\text{area of } \triangle PTQ}{\text{area of } \triangle RTS}$$

23–25 MATRICES AND TRANSFORMATIONS
Examination Questions (2)

1. Anne, Brenda and Clare compare the prices of apples, plums and damsons in two shops X and Y. The prices, in pence per kg, are shown in matrix **Q**. The weights, in kg, which they wish to buy of each type of fruit are shown in matrix **P**.

	P				Q	
	kg	kg	kg		price p per kg	
	Apples	Plums	Damsons		X	Y
Anne	3	2	4	Apples	40	44
Brenda	1	1	2	Plums	31	28
Clare	$\frac{1}{2}$	1	1	Damsons	35	30

Form the matrix product **PQ** and use it to answer the following questions.

a) How much would Anne have spent in shop X?

b) How much would Brenda have spent in shop Y?

c) How much would Clare have saved by shopping at shop Y?

d) If all three shopped at shop Y, calculate
   i) the total amount spent at shop Y,
   ii) the average cost, to the nearest p per kg, of the fruit purchased.

2. The points A(1, 1), B(5, 1) and C(3, 2) are joined to form △ABC.

a) On graph paper, using 1 cm to a unit, and putting the origin in the lower left corner of the paper, draw △ABC.

b) Calculate the coordinates of the vertices of △A′B′C′, which is formed by transforming △ABC using the matrix

$$\begin{pmatrix} 1 & -1 \\ 1 & 2 \end{pmatrix}.$$

c) Draw △A′B′C′ on the same graph.

d) Calculate the coordinates of the vertices of △A″B″C″, which is formed by transforming △A′B′C′ using the matrix

$$\begin{pmatrix} 2 & 1 \\ -1 & 1 \end{pmatrix}.$$

e) Draw △A″B″C″ on the same graph and state the scale factor of the enlargement from △ABC to △A″B″C″.

f) State the ratios of the areas of the three triangles.

3. On graph paper, taking the origin near to the centre of the page, draw two perpendicular axes. Label both axes with equal scales from −6 to +6. On your diagram draw and label the triangle T, with vertices at the points (2, 1), (6, 1) and (6, 3).

A is the image of T after a rotation of 180° about the origin.
B is the image of T after a rotation of 180° about the point (4, 0).
C is the image of T after a reflection in the y-axis.
D is the image of T after a reflection in the line x + y = 0.

On your diagram draw the four images A, B, C and D, clearly identifying each.

Describe fully

a) the transformation which maps A onto B,

b) the transformation which maps A onto C,

c) the transformation which maps C onto D.

4. A set of positive integers in sequence is called

$$P = \{1, 2, 3, 4, \ldots\}$$

Another sequence of integers is called

$$Q = \{5, 8, 11, 14, \ldots\}.$$

The sequences are connected by the matrix

$$\mathbf{M} = \begin{pmatrix} 1 & -2 \\ 2 & 5 \end{pmatrix}, \text{ such that } (1\ \ 2)\mathbf{M} = (5\ \ 8) \text{ and}$$

(2 3)**M** = (8 11) and so on: that is, two consecutive members of P are trannsformed by **M** into the two corresponding consecutive members of Q. Let this be represented by P ∗ **M** = Q.

a) Evaluate (3 4)**M** and (4 5)**M**.

b) Write down the fifth and sixth members of Q.

c) The sequence R is similarly defined, so that Q ∗ **M** = R. Write down the first two members of R.

d) Find, in terms of **M**, a matrix **N** such that P ∗ **N** = R.

e) Find, in terms of **M**, a matrix **X** such that Q ∗ **X** = P.

5. a) On graph paper, with axes and scales (the same scale on both axes) chosen so that x can range at least from −4 to +4 and y at least from −8 to +8, plot the points (1, 0), (3, 1) and (4, 0) and join them to form the triangle T.

b) Form the matrix product $\mathbf{M} \begin{pmatrix} 1 & 3 & 4 \\ 0 & 1 & 0 \end{pmatrix}$,

where **M** is the matrix $\begin{pmatrix} -1 & 1 \\ -1 & -1 \end{pmatrix}$.

c) Use the result of b) to draw the image of T under the transformation whose matrix is **M**.

d) Form the matrix **M**², and draw the image of T under the transformation whose matrix is **M**².

e) The transformation whose matrix is **M**² consists of a rotation combined with an enlargement. Find the angle of the rotation and the scale factor of the enlargement.

f) Describe completely the transformation whose matrix is **M**.

6.

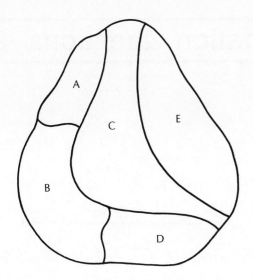

The figure is a map of a country which is divided into five regions, A, B, C, D and E. The matrix **M**, the first row of which is given below, shows which regions border on which others; thus, the 1s show that A borders on B and C, the 0s that it does not border on itself or D or E.

$$\text{A} \begin{pmatrix} \text{A} & \text{B} & \text{C} & \text{D} & \text{E} \\ 0 & 1 & 1 & 0 & 0 \end{pmatrix}.$$

Complete the matrix **M**.

Form the matrix $\mathbf{M}^2$ and interpret

a) the leading diagonal elements,

b) the other elements.

Explain also the special significance of the zero elements.

As a result of reorganization, a small area is transferred from one region to another, and the first row of the matrix **M** now becomes

$$\text{A} \begin{pmatrix} \text{A} & \text{B} & \text{C} & \text{D} & \text{E} \\ 0 & 1 & 1 & 0 & 1 \end{pmatrix}$$

the other rows being unchanged except for the first element in the last row. Draw a map of the country showing the borders of the regions as they might be after the reorganization.

7. On graph paper, using a scale of 1 cm to represent 1 unit on each axis and taking values of x from -8 to 10 and values of y from 0 to 16, draw $\triangle$ABC with vertices A(5, 5), B(10, 0) and C(10, 10).

Calculate the coordinates of the points D, E and F which are the images of A, B, C respectively under the reflection R, whose matrix is **R** where

$$\mathbf{R} = \begin{pmatrix} -\frac{3}{5} & \frac{4}{5} \\ \frac{4}{5} & \frac{3}{5} \end{pmatrix}$$

On the same diagram draw the triangle DEF and hence draw the mirror line of the reflection R.

Calculate the coordinates of the points G, H and J which are the images of D, E, F respectively under a second reflection S whose matrix is **S**, where

$$\mathbf{S} = \begin{pmatrix} -1 & 0 \\ 0 & 1 \end{pmatrix}.$$

Draw the triangle GHJ and describe fully the single transformation T which is equivalent to the combined transformation SR.

8. Given that S is the set of all non-singular 2×2 matrices of the form $\begin{pmatrix} a & b \\ c & d \end{pmatrix}$ with $c = b$ and $d = a + b$, write down the matrix **M** which is the member of S with $a = 0$ and $b = 1$. Show that

$$\mathbf{M}^2 = \begin{pmatrix} 1 & 1 \\ 1 & 2 \end{pmatrix}.$$

Calculate the following matrices:

a) $\mathbf{M}^3$, b) $\mathbf{M}^4$, c) $\mathbf{M}^{-1}$, d) $2\mathbf{M}$, and show that they are all members of S. Given that $\mathbf{M}^n = \begin{pmatrix} 8 & 13 \\ 13 & 21 \end{pmatrix}$ where n is an integer, find the value of n.

The matrix $\mathbf{A} = \begin{pmatrix} p & q \\ r & s \end{pmatrix}$ is a member of S. Show that the determinant of **A** can be written in the form $p^2 + pq - q^2$. When $q = 7$, the value of this determinant is 11. Find the corresponding positive value of p.

261

26 VECTORS   Examination Questions (2)

1. Two straight lines, PQ and RS, intersect at T, where PT = 2TQ and ST = 2TR.

   Given that $\overrightarrow{TR} = \mathbf{a}$ and $\overrightarrow{TQ} = \mathbf{b}$, express, in terms of $\mathbf{a}$ and $\mathbf{b}$ the vectors $\overrightarrow{PT}$, $\overrightarrow{TS}$, $\overrightarrow{PS}$ and $\overrightarrow{RQ}$. State two distinct geometrical facts relating PS and RQ.

2. In the regular hexagon OPQRST, $\overrightarrow{OP} = \mathbf{p}$ and $\overrightarrow{OT} = \mathbf{t}$.

   Express $\overrightarrow{PT}$ in terms of $\mathbf{p}$ and $\mathbf{t}$ and show that
   a) $\overrightarrow{PS} = 2\mathbf{t}$.

   b) $\overrightarrow{OS} = \mathbf{p} + 2\mathbf{t}$.
   Given that $\overrightarrow{PX} = \frac{2}{3}\overrightarrow{PT}$, show that X lies on OS and find the value of $\dfrac{OX}{XS}$.

3. The points O, A, B, not in the same straight line, are such that $\overrightarrow{OA} = \mathbf{a}$, $\overrightarrow{OB} = \mathbf{b}$. Points C and D are such that $\overrightarrow{OC} = 4\mathbf{a}$ and $\overrightarrow{OD} = 4\mathbf{b}$.

   a) Express $\overrightarrow{AD}$ and $\overrightarrow{BC}$ in terms of $\mathbf{a}$ and $\mathbf{b}$.

   Given that P is the point on AD such that AP = $\frac{1}{5}$AD,

   b) express $\overrightarrow{AP}$, $\overrightarrow{OP}$ and $\overrightarrow{BP}$ in terms of $\mathbf{a}$ and $\mathbf{b}$, and show that P divides BC in the ratio $1:4$.

   Given also that the figure OCED is a parallelogram,

   c) express $\overrightarrow{OE}$ in terms of $\mathbf{a}$ and $\mathbf{b}$.

   d) State in words what this result shows about
      i) the points O, P, E,
      ii) the lengths of OP and OE.

4.

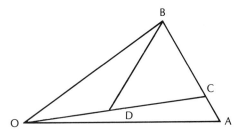

   $\overrightarrow{OA} = \mathbf{a}$, $\overrightarrow{OB} = \mathbf{b}$, $\overrightarrow{BC} = 3\overrightarrow{CA}$ and $\overrightarrow{OD} = \overrightarrow{DC}$.

   Express the following vectors in terms of $\mathbf{a}$ and $\mathbf{b}$:
   a) $\overrightarrow{AB}$, b) $\overrightarrow{AC}$, c) $\overrightarrow{OC}$, d) $\overrightarrow{OD}$.
   Show that $\overrightarrow{BD} = \frac{1}{8}(3\mathbf{a} - 7\mathbf{b})$.

   Given that BD is produced to E so that BD = 7DE, express $\overrightarrow{OE}$ in terms of $\mathbf{a}$, or $\mathbf{b}$, or $\mathbf{a}$ and $\mathbf{b}$.

   Deduce that E lies on the line OA.

5. In a quadrilateral ABCD, $\overrightarrow{AB} = .\ \overrightarrow{DC} = 3\mathbf{a}$ and $\overrightarrow{AC} = \mathbf{b}$.

   The point P on AC is such that AP : PC = 2 : 3. Express $\overrightarrow{AP}$ in terms of $\mathbf{b}$, and $\overrightarrow{AD}$ and $\overrightarrow{DP}$ in terms of $\mathbf{a}$ and $\mathbf{b}$.

   Given that Q is a point on AB produced such that $\overrightarrow{AQ} = h\,\overrightarrow{AB}$ and $\overrightarrow{DQ} = k\,\overrightarrow{DP}$, write down two expressions for $\overrightarrow{DQ}$ in terms of $\mathbf{a}$, $\mathbf{b}$, h and k. Find values for h and k, and hence find the ratios AB : AQ and DP : PQ.

6. In the parallelogram OACB, $\overrightarrow{OA} = \overrightarrow{BC} = \mathbf{a}$ and $\overrightarrow{OB} = \overrightarrow{AC} = \mathbf{b}$.

   a) Write down vectors, in terms of $\mathbf{a}$ and $\mathbf{b}$, which represent $\overrightarrow{BA}$ and $\overrightarrow{OC}$.

   b) Define what is meant by the modulus $|\mathbf{a}|$ of the vector $\mathbf{a}$.

   c) If $|\mathbf{a}| = |\mathbf{b}|$, what kind of special shape is the parallelogram OACB?

   d) If $|\mathbf{a}| = |\mathbf{b}|$, find the angle between the lines represented by $\mathbf{a} - \mathbf{b}$ and $\mathbf{a} + \mathbf{b}$.

   e) Points D and E are defined by $\overrightarrow{OD} = 2\mathbf{a}$ and $\overrightarrow{OE} = 2\mathbf{b}$. Prove that DCE is a straight line.

27 PROBABILITY
Examination Questions (2)

1. A 'spinner' is constructed so that at the end of a spin it has an equal chance of pointing to any one of the numbers 1, 2, 3, 4, 5, 6, 7. Write down the probabilities that, after one spin, the spinner points to

a) 3,

b) an even number.

Two identical spinners are spun at the same time. Calculate the probability that

c) they both point to 3,

d) the total of the two scores is 13,

e) the total of the two scores is less than 13,

f) the total of the two scores is an odd number.

2.

	4	5	6	7	8	9	10	11	

The diagram shows part of a board for a game. A player throws a die and then moves a counter on the board subject to the following rules. A player's counter always starts from square 6. If an *odd* number is thrown, the counter is moved 1 space to the *left*. If an *even* number is thrown, the counter is moved 2 spaces to the *right*. If the even number is a *six*, then the counter is moved 2 spaces to the *right* and the die is thrown again for the second and final time, the player's counter is moved a second time and the player's turn is at an end. Write down the probability that, after one turn, the counter will be on

a) square 5,

b) square 8,

c) square 7,

d) square 10.

A possible combination for reaching or passing square 10 in two turns is

first turn	second turn
6 and (1 or 3 or 5)	6 and (2 or 4 or 6)

e) Calculate the probability that this will occur.

f) Write down, in a similar way, a second different combination in two turns to reach or pass square 10 and calculate the probability that this will occur.

3. A student is supposed to attend a course of six lectures. He is sure to attend the first lecture, and the probability that he will attend the second one is $\frac{3}{4}$. If he ever misses a lecture, he is sure to attend the next one, and the probability that he will attend the one after that is $\frac{3}{4}$. If he has attended two or more lectures in succession, the probability that he will attend the next one is $\frac{1}{2}$. Find the probability that he will attend

a) the first three lectures,

b) the first and third, but not the second,

c) the third lecture, whether or not he attends the second,

d) all six lectures.

Find e) the smallest number of lectures he can attend, and the probability that he will attend this smallest number.

4. A family of 2 children can be represented by one of the following codes

BB, BG, GB, GG

where *BG* means that the elder child is a boy and the younger child is a girl, etc.

a) Write down the 8 possible codes for a family of 3 children.

Given that in all these families the probabilities of any child being a boy or a girl are equal, find the probability that

b) a family of 2 children will consist of one boy and one girl (in any order),

c) a family of 3 children will consist of 2 boys and one girl

   i) in that order,
   ii) in any order,

d) a family of 3 children will contain at least one girl.

Two neighbouring families, the Smiths and the Browns, contain 3 children and 2 children respectively. Find the probability that there will be exactly 3 boys in the two families.

5. In an election, with just 2 candidates, x voters voted for candidate A and 30 voted for candidate B. If a voter is to be picked at random, write down an expression for the probability that a voter will be picked who voted for candidate A.

In a second election, with the same 2 candidates, there were 30 more voters altogether but 4 fewer voted for candidate A. If, again, a voter is to be picked at random, write down an expression for the probability that a voter will be picked who voted for candidate A.

Given that the first probability is twice the second probability, form a quadratic equation in x.

Hence find the value of x.

6. A motorist turns left with probability $\frac{1}{2}$ and turns right with probability $\frac{1}{2}$ whenever he comes to a T-junction. The motorist sets off from town A in the following road system so that the probability he will go to B is $\frac{1}{2}$ and the probability he will go to C is $\frac{1}{2}$, as shown.

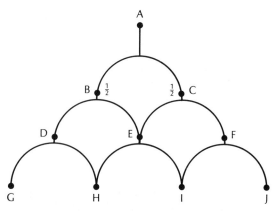

a) Make a copy of the diagram, and mark on it the probabilities that he will reach D, E, F. G, H, I and J.

b) Explain why the sum of the last four probabilities in a) should be 1.

c) Another motorist turns left with probability q and turns right with probability p, so that on the same road system, we would write p by B and q by C.

   State the probabilities that this second motorist reaches i) D, ii) E, iii) F.

d) Work out $(p + q)^2$ and show that this is the same as the sum of your three answers to c).

---

28 SETS Examination Questions (2)

1.

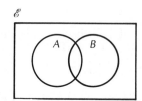

a) Make 4 copies of the above and indicate on them, by shading, the sets A', B', $A \cup B'$, $(A' \cup B')'$.

Write down a simpler expression for $(A' \cup B')'$, not using the symbol for complement.

b) One hundred office workers use various combinations of travel by bus, train and car to reach their offices. Of these one hundred workers, 42 use buses, 43 use cars and 66 use trains; 18 use both bus and train but not car, and 23 use train and car but not bus. There are no workers who use bus and car but not train. Every worker uses at least one of bus, train and car.

Draw a Venn diagram to illustrate this data, denoting by x the number of workers who use all three means of transport. Mark in your diagram the numbers, in terms of x where necessary, of workers in the subsets represented by each region.

Hence calculate x.

2. In a village a survey was made of the possibility of supplying gas, electricity, water and drainage to all the houses, none of which had any of these services. It was found that each house could be supplied with water and electricity only, or water and drainage only, or gas and drainage only. Given that

$\mathscr{E}$ = {all the houses in the village}

G = {houses which can be supplied with gas},

E = {houses which can be supplied with electricity},

W = {houses which can be connected to a main water supply},

D = {houses which can be connected to the main drainage system},

state which one of the sets $\mathscr{E}$, G, E, W, D, $\varnothing$ is equal to each of

a) E', b) G', c) $G \cap E$, d) $W \cup D$, e) $E \cap W$.

It is impossible to supply more than 70 houses with water or to connect more than 80 houses to the drainage system.

If the water and drainage supplies are to be fully used, find

f) the largest possible number of houses there could be in the village,

g) the smallest possible number of houses there could be in the village.

State in each case the number of houses which could be supplied with electricity and the number which could be supplied with gas.

3. Sets are defined as follows:

$\mathscr{E}$ = {cars in a certain car park},

R = {red cars},

F = {cars not made in Great Britain},

A = {cars with automatic transmission},

H = {cars with a rear door ('hatchbacks')},

M = {cars with engines of more than 2 litres capacity},

S = {cars with sunshine roofs}.

Write sentences, *not* using set language, to express the following statements:

a) $F' \cap H = \varnothing$,

b) $H \cap R = H$,

c) $A \cup M = A$.

Express the following statements in set language:

d) None of the red cars has *both* automatic transmission and a sunshine roof.

e) Only cars made in Great Britain have engines of more than 2 litres.

f) All the cars not made in Great Britain have sunshine roofs.

4. If $\mathscr{E}$ = {men}, S = {Scotsmen}, R = {red-haired men}, M = {male members of clan MacMathics}, express the following symbolic statements in normal English, not using technical words like 'set'. (You are not concerned at this stage with the truth of the statements.)

a) $S \subset R$,   b) $S \cap R \neq \varnothing$.

Write symbolic statements, using some or all of the symbols $'$, $\cap$, $\subset$, $=$, $\neq$, $\varnothing$, to express the meanings of the following sentences:

c) All red-haired men are Scotsmen.

d) Some Scotsmen are not red-haired.

Statement e) is 'Male members of clan Mac-Mathics are all Scotsmen, and they all have black hair', and this is known to be true. For each of the statements a), b), c) and d), write down whether it is proved, disproved or unaffected by statement e).

Using the fact that statement e) is true, and assuming that all other statements which have not been disproved are true, draw a Venn diagram to illustrate the relations between sets $\mathscr{E}$, S, R and M.

5. $\mathscr{E}$ is the set of the first twenty natural numbers, so that

$\mathscr{E} = \{1, 2, 3, 4, 5, 6, 7, 8, 9, 10, 11, 12, 13, 14, 15, 16, 17, 18, 19, 20\}$

List the members of the following subsets:

a) $A = \{x: 11 < 4x - 5 \leqslant 43\}$,

b) $B = \{x: x$ is a prime number, $x > 1\}$,

c) $C = \{x: x$ is a factor of 20, $x > 1\}$.

Draw a Venn diagram showing the relationship between $\mathscr{E}$, A, B and C, writing each of the members of $\mathscr{E}$ in the appropriate region.

List the members of the following sets:

d) $A' \cap B$,

e) $(A \cup B)'$,

f) $B' \cap C'$

g) $(A \cup B) \cap C$.

6. In this question

$\mathscr{E} = \{$quadrilaterals$\}$,

$A = \{$quadrilaterals with all four sides equal$\}$,

$B = \{$quadrilaterals with at least three sides equal$\}$,

$C = \{$quadrilaterials with no axes of symmetry$\}$

Marking any equal sides and showing any axes of symmetry, sketch a member of each of the following sets:

a) $A \cap C'$,   b) $B \cap A' \cap C$,   c) $B \cap A' \cap C'$.

d) $C' \cap B'$.

Express in symbolic form the following statements:

e) There are no quadrilaterals with all four sides equal but no axes of symmetry.

f) There are some quadrilaterals with three sides equal and no axes of symmetry.

Draw a Venn diagram to illustrate the relation between $\mathscr{E}$, A, B and C.

29 FUNCTIONS Examination Questions (2)

1. Given that f: $x \mapsto x + 3$ and g: $x \mapsto x^2 - 1$, express the composite functions fg and gf in the forms

fg: $x \mapsto \ldots$ and   gf: $x \mapsto \ldots$.

Find the value of x for which fg$(x) = $ gf(x).

2. The mappings f, g and h are defined as follows:

f: $x \mapsto 3x$,
g: $x \mapsto x - 2$,
h: $x \mapsto x^2$.

a) Express in the form $x \mapsto$

    i) fg,   ii) fh,   iii) hg,
    iv) the inverse mapping f^{-1},
    v) the inverse mapping g^{-1},
    vi) $g^{-1} f^{-1}$.

b) Find the number a such that
$$fg(a) = g^{-1}f^{-1}(a).$$

c) show that, if $fh(x) = hg(x)$, then
$$x^2 + 2x - 2 = 0.$$

Hence, or otherwise, solve the equation
$$x^2 + 2x - 2 = 0,$$

giving each answer correct to two decimal places.

3. Two functions f and g are defined by
$$f: x \mapsto \frac{3}{x}, \quad g: x \mapsto 4 - x.$$

a) State the inverses of f and g, in the forms $f^{-1}: x \mapsto \ldots$ and $g^{-1}: x \mapsto \ldots$.

b) Given that $h = fg$, write down the function h in the form $h: x \mapsto \ldots$.
Find, in similar form, the function h^{-1}.

c) Find the two values of x for which $gf = h$.

d) Given that $f(a) = b$, show that $f(b) = a$. State a similar relationship for the function g.

4. The functions f, g and h are defined by
$$f: x \mapsto 2x, \quad g: x \mapsto x - 3 \quad \text{and} \quad h: x \mapsto x^2$$

a) Using the same notation, complete the definitions
$$gf: x \mapsto \ldots, \quad fg: x \mapsto \ldots, \quad hgf: x \mapsto \ldots,$$
$$fgh: x \mapsto \ldots.$$

b) Find the values of x which satisfy the equation
$$fgh(x) = hgf(x)$$
giving your answers to 2 decimal places.

c) Find the values of x which satisfy the equation
$$fgh(x) = hgf(x) + 1.$$

5. The function f is defined as follows for any positive integer n:

if n is even, $f(n) = \frac{1}{2}n$,
if n is odd, $f(n) = n + 1$.

a) Write down the values of $f(9)$, $ff(9)$ and $fff(9)$.

b) Find the value of n for which $f(n) = 7$, and two values of n for which $f(n) = 8$.

c) Name the set of values of n for which $f^{-1}(n)$ has two values, and the set for which it has only one value.

d) Explain why, for any value of n except 1 or 2, $ff(n) < n$.

e) A computer is programmed so that when any positive integer n is set into it, it finds and prints $f(n)$, then sets $f(n)$ into itself, finds and prints $ff(n)$, then sets $ff(n)$ into itself, and so on indefinitely. Show that if $n = 9$ the computer will eventually print 2, and describe what happens after that.

6. The functions f and g are defined as follows:
$$f: x \to x^2$$
$$g: x \to 9x + 1$$

a) Write down the values of $f(-1)$ and $gf(-1)$.

b) Express in the form $f: x \to \ldots$ the functions
   i) gf,   ii) fg.

c) Find the values of x for which
$$gf(x) = fg(x).$$

d) Show that the inequality
$$fg(x) - gf(x) < 54$$
simplifies to
$$4x^2 + x - 3 < 0,$$
and find the set of values of x for which this is satisfied.

267

30 FLOW CHARTS
Examination Questions (2)

(The questions in this chapter are all original authors' questions.)

1. Use the flow chart to complete the table to calculate the amount, £A, and the accumulated compound interest, £C, on £7200, at the end of each year for 5 years, at a rate of interest of 9.75% (*You are expected to use a calculator.*)

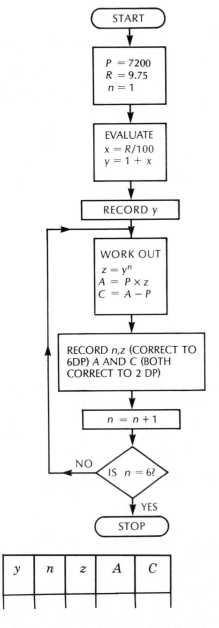

y	n	z	A	C

Suggest a way of improving the flow chart to make the calculation of z easier.

2. The area A under part of the graph of $y = 5x^3$ is calculated using a method shown by the flow-chart below.

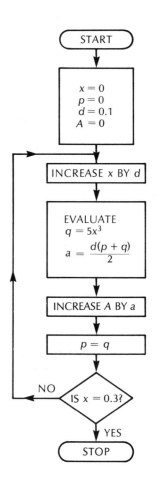

Copy and complete the table using your calculator to work out the required values:

d	p	q	a	A	x
0.1	— 0	—	—	0	0 0.1

It is known that $A = 1.25x^4$. Calculate the value of A when $x = 0.3$ and work out the percentage error involved when using the flowchart method.

3. An approximate solution which satisfies the equation $x = 10 - \dfrac{3}{x}$ can be found using the following iterative method:

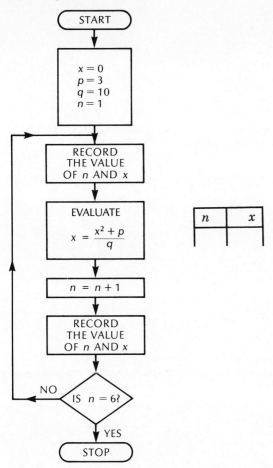

n	x

State the solution you have found correct to 4 d.p.

Starting with $x_1 = 10$ and using the formula

$$x_{n+1} = 10 - \frac{3}{x_n}$$

and recording the values x_2, x_3, x_4 and x_5, find a second solution correct to 4 decimal places.

4. A shop estimates it has an increase in takings of 20% each year with an estimated fixed loss of £40 000 through shop-lifting, depreciation of building and fittings, damaged stock, etc.

The flow chart is used to calculate the expected takings, T, at the end of each year, Y from 1985 to 1989.

a) If the takings are £220 000 on Dec. 31st 1985 calculate the takings on Dec. 31st 1986 through till Dec. 31st 1989.

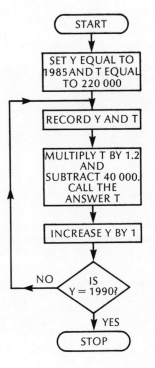

b) Plot the annual takings against the years 1985–1989 on a graph and join the points with a smooth curve.

c) Repeat on the same graph, assuming the takings on Dec. 31st 1985 were £180 000 instead.

d) Comment on your results and use your calculator to find what the takings must be on Dec. 31st 1985 in order to ensure they stay the same each year.

SECTION VI

EXAMINATION QUESTIONS (3)

PAPER 1   MENTAL ARITHMETIC

The questions should be read twice. Write down only the answers.

TEST A

1. $25 + 26$
2. 0.4×6
3. $5 - 1\frac{1}{2}$
4. $£2.90 \div 2$
5. $74\,p + 36\,p$
6. 25% of 84 cm
7. $3 \times 14 - 2 \times 7$
8. Change 1.7 m to cm
9. $6 \div \frac{1}{2}$
10. $\frac{4}{9} + \frac{2}{9}$

11. $3 - 0.9$
12. Write $\frac{9}{7}$ as a mixed number
13. $9 - (2 + 11)$
14. $\sqrt{64}$
15. It is $17:30$. What time will it be in 45 minutes?
16. $10.3 + 0.8$
17. Cancel $\frac{18}{27}$
18. One cake costs 26 p. What do 3 cost?
19. What is 18.48 cm to the nearest cm?
20. Write in figures 'One pound and seven pence'.

TEST B

1. $18 - 11$
2. 20×20
3. $£5 - £1.50$
4. Change 6000 m to km
5. $(8 - 2) \div 2$
6. How many minutes between $08:50$ and $09:10$?
7. $145 \div 5$
8. Write $\frac{9}{20}$ as a decimal
9. $1000 + 11 + 101$

10. $60 \div 3 \div 4$
11. 3^3
12. How many degrees has it fallen if the temperature drops from $8°C$ to $-4°C$?
13. Write £7293 to the nearest £100
14. 15% of £200
15. 0.3×0.2
16. How many in $2\frac{1}{2}$ dozen?

17. Take 42 from 51
18. $\frac{3}{8} + \frac{1}{4}$
19. Divide $\frac{1}{4}$ of 24 by $\frac{1}{2}$ of 12
20. $0.2 - 0.15$

TEST C

1. How many grams are there in one and a half kilograms?
2. Take thirty-two pence from one pound.
3. A piece of wood seventy-two centimetres long is divided into nine equal pieces. How long is each piece?
4. How many feet are there in two yards?
5. Write down ten per cent of two pounds eighty.
6. Add one and a quarter to two and a half.
7. What is the cost of ten stamps at seventeen pence plus two stamps at twelve pence?
8. Subtract thirty-five centimetres from one metre ten centimetres.
9. Multiply nought point eight by six.
10. How many faces are there on a cube?
11. Add three point one kilograms to two point nine kilograms.
12. Take twenty-seven from fifty-five.
13. What is the cost of an eighteen minute phone call if three minutes cost eight pence?
14. Write down the square root of one hundred and forty-four.
15. Give the name of the plane shape with eight sides.
16. Multiply nought point two by nought point three.
17. Find the average speed if a car travels 200 miles in 4 hours.
18. How many cubic centimetres are there in half a litre?
19. What is the change from five pounds for three items costing one pound fifteen each?

20. How many twenty-fives are there in three hundred?

21. Thirty-seven per cent of a class are boys. What percentage are girls?

22. If two similar articles cost £5.50 how much would six similar articles cost?

23. Write down the average of eight, twelve and sixteen.

24. How many seven centimetre lengths of steel could be cut from a rod which is eighty-four centimetres long?

25. What is the name of the solid figure with twenty regular faces?

26. How many pounds are there in two and a half stone?

27. Take seven-eighths of a yard from one and a quarter yards.

28. A rectangle has an area of thirty-six square millimetres. What is its length if its width is four millimetres?

29. A quarter of a pound of sweets costs thirty-one pence. How much would one pound cost?

30. What is the time eighteen minutes after seven fifty-five?

TEST D

1. Write down the sum of twenty-eight and thirty-seven.

2. Change one fifth into a percentage.

3. A clock gives the time as 8 : 50. If it is twenty-eight minutes slow, what is the correct time?

4. How much change is given when a five pound note is used to pay a bill of one pound, ninety-two pence?

5. What is the square of fourteen?

6. A rectangle has an area of one hundred and ninety-two square metres. If it is six metres wide, how long is it?

7. What number is two point seven less than three point four?

8. A right-angled triangle contains an angle of forty-eight degrees. What is the size of the third angle?

9. Change one hundred and eight centimetres into metres.

10. How many edges does a cube have?

11. Cancel eighteen twenty-fourths to its simplest form.

12. If one cinema ticket costs two pounds fifty, how much would five tickets cost?

13. A television set costing £300 is reduced by ten per cent in a sale. What is its sale price?

14. What is one quarter of three fifths?

15. If one hundred pounds is shared in the ratio two to eight, how much is the larger share?

16. A number is four more than half of eighteen. What is the number?

17. Calculate the mean of twenty, seventy and ninety.

18. What is the probability of selecting the letter, D from the word MAD if a letter is selected at random?

19. If x is worth negative three, what is the value of x squared minus two?

20. By how much is half of twenty-four greater than one third of twenty-four?

TEST E

1. Write in figures the number one million, seven thousand and three.

2. What is one third of one half of thirty?

3. How many cubic centimetres are there in one litre?

4. Calculate the total cost of a dozen cakes costing fifteen pence each.

5. A boy is one point two seven metres tall and his sister is one point three two metres tall. What is the difference in their heights?

6. A square has an area of eighty-one square centimetres. What is the perimeter of the square?

7. A train journey lasting forty minutes is delayed by ten minutes at the start. It ends at seven thirty, when should it have started?

8. Calculate the value of eight times twenty-five times twelve.

9. Write two thousand five hundred in standard form.

10. Square nought point four.

11. A number is doubled and the result is two less than three times the number. What is the number?

12. Only ninety per cent of a packet of fifty seeds grow. What is the probability of a seed in the packet not growing?

13. A photograph is enlarged with a scale factor of two. If the area of the small photograph is 30 square centimetres, what is the area of the enlarged photograph?

14. Five miles are approximately equivalent to eight kilometres. How many kilometres are roughly equivalent to forty miles?

15. What is the product of twenty and ninety?

16. Calculate the total cost of two items costing twenty-seven pence each and two items costing one pound forty each.

17. Shampoo costs sixty pence for a five hundred millilitre bottle and eighty pence for a seven hundred and fifty millilitre bottle. How much would be saved by buying two large bottles?

18. Express eleven twentieths as a decimal.

19. A radio costing twenty-five pounds is reduced to twenty pounds in a sale. What is the percentage reduction?

20. A three-hour video tape is used to record a programme starting at 16:50 and ending at 19:10. How long is left on the tape?

PAPER 2   MULTIPLE CHOICE

Select the correct answer from the 5 given.

TEST A

1. The area of a square of side 6 cm is

   A $12 \, \text{cm}^2$ B $36 \, \text{cm}^2$ C $24 \, \text{cm}^2$
   D $30 \, \text{cm}^2$ E $216 \, \text{cm}^2$

2. 29.4 is 1.37 less than

   A 30.77   B 28.17   C 31.03
   D 43.1   E 15.7

3.

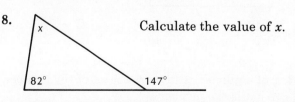

   The shaded area is described as

   A $y \geqslant 2$ B $x \geqslant 2$ C $y \leqslant 2$
   D $x \leqslant 2$ E none of these

4. $3(x + 2) - (x + 2) =$

   A 3   B $2x + 8$ C $4(x + 2)$
   D $4x + 4$ E $2(x + 2)$

5. The weekly wage of a man earning £6000 per annum is approximately

   A £100   B £200   C £125
   D £115   E £150

6. Find the next number in this sequence.

   $$4, 7, 13, \underline{\quad}$$

   A 10   B 12   C 19
   D 25   E 30

7. Express 492 cm in metres.

   A 49 200 m   B 0.0492 m   C 49.2 m
   D 4.92 m   E 0.004 92 m

8. Calculate the value of x.

   A 82°   B 75°   C 65°
   D 108°   E 147°

9. This table shows the marks of a French test given to a class. Which pie chart represents this information?

Mark	Frequency
2	4
3	15
4	9
5	2

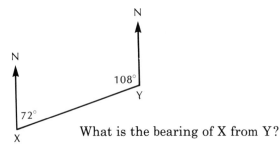

10. 10.798 47 expressed to 2 decimal places =

A 10.7   B 10.79   C 10.80
D 11.0   E 10.89

11.

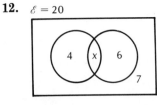

What is the bearing of X from Y?

A 258°   B 288°   C 072°
D 252°   E 108°

12. $\mathscr{E} = 20$

The value of x is

A 12   B 3   C 7
D 9   E 10

13. $\frac{3}{4}$ of a number is 12 more than $\frac{1}{4}$ of the number. What is the number?

A 24   B 9   C 16
D 6   E 18

14. $3 \times 4 + 7 \times 4 =$

A 76   B 132   C 77
D 23   E 40

15. A television programme starts at 8:45 and ends at twenty to 10. How long does it last?

A 1 hr 5 min   B 55 min   C 1 hr 25 min
D 105 min   E 40 min

16. If $x = 3$ and $y = 2$, find the value of $x^2 y$.

A 12   B 8   C 25
D 36   E 18

17. Which is the largest fraction?

A $\frac{2}{5}$ B $\frac{7}{10}$ C $\frac{1}{2}$
D $\frac{3}{30}$ E $\frac{1}{4}$

18.

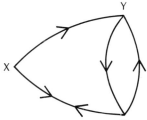

Describe this network.

A $\begin{pmatrix} 0 & 1 & 1 \\ 0 & 1 & 0 \\ 1 & 1 & 0 \end{pmatrix}$ B $\begin{pmatrix} 0 & 1 & 1 \\ 0 & 0 & 1 \\ 1 & 1 & 0 \end{pmatrix}$ C $\begin{pmatrix} 1 & 0 & 1 \\ 0 & 1 & 0 \\ 1 & 1 & 0 \end{pmatrix}$

D $\begin{pmatrix} 1 & 0 & 1 \\ 0 & 1 & 0 \\ 1 & 0 & 1 \end{pmatrix}$ E $\begin{pmatrix} 1 & 1 & 1 \\ 0 & 1 & 0 \\ 1 & 1 & 1 \end{pmatrix}$

19. The net of this polyhedron is

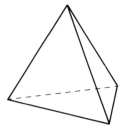

A   B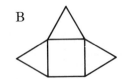

C 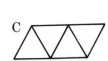   D   E

20. A train travels at 120 km/h for 45 minutes. How far does it travel in this time?

A $2\frac{2}{3}$ km   B 100 km   C 90 km
D 5400 km   E 1200 km

21. Find the total cost of 2 tins of soup at 26 p each and $\frac{1}{2}$ lb of meat at £2.20 per lb.

A £6.30   B £4.80   C £1.62
D £4.92   E £1.46

22. If 25% of the sweets in a packet are toffees, then the probability of a toffee being selected at random is

A $\frac{1}{2}$ B $\frac{3}{4}$ C $\frac{1}{25}$
D 2   E $\frac{1}{4}$

23. Which quadrilateral has only one line of symmetry and two pairs of sides of equal length?

A a rectangle   B a rhombus   C a kite
D a parallelogram   E a square

24. What is the perimeter of a regular hexagon of side 5 cm?

A 40 cm   B 30 cm   C 25 cm
D 50 cm   E 20 cm

25.

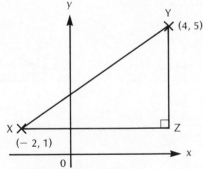

The coordinates of Z are

A (5, 2)   B (4, 1)   C (−2, 5)
D (4, −2)   E (1, 1)

TEST B

1. When $x = -2$ and $y = -3$, the value of $x^2(2 - y)$ is

A 4   B 1   C 20
D −4   E −20

2. The network with five regions, six arcs and three vertices is

A   B   C

D   E

3. In a sale, all furniture is to be reduced by 20%. Calculate the full price of a settee on sale for £320.

A £384   B £300   C £256
D £400   E £640

4. The gradient of $2y + 3x = 4$ is

A 3   B $-\frac{3}{2}$ C −3
D $\frac{2}{3}$ E 4

5. Calculate the area of $\triangle$XYZ.

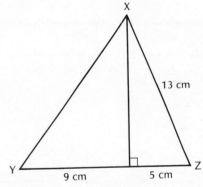

A 91 cm^2 B 65 cm^2 C 84 cm^2
D 168 cm^2 E 117 cm^2

6. $\{x : -2 < x \leqslant 1\}$ describes

A 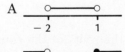   B

C   D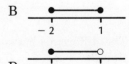

E

7. Simplify $\dfrac{4.8 \times 10^{-2}}{16 \times 10^{-5}}$ giving the answer in standard form.

A 3×10^{-3} B 0.3×10^{-3} C 30×10^{-7}
D 0.3×10^{-7} E 3×10^2

8. Two business partners share profits in the ratio of $7:4$. If one receives £42 000 more than the other, how much were the total profits?

   A £24 000   B £154 000   C £73 500
   D £14 000   E £2 400 000

9. Which one of the following is *not* equal to $\sqrt{512}$.

   A $8\sqrt{16}$ B $4\sqrt{32}$ C $16\sqrt{2}$
   D $2\sqrt{128}$ E $8\sqrt{8}$

10. $\mathbf{M} = \begin{pmatrix} 2 & 3 \\ -1 & 2 \end{pmatrix}$, so $\mathbf{M}^2 = 5$

    A $\begin{pmatrix} 1 & 12 \\ -4 & 1 \end{pmatrix}$ B $\begin{pmatrix} 4 & 9 \\ 1 & 4 \end{pmatrix}$ C $\begin{pmatrix} 4 & 6 \\ -2 & 6 \end{pmatrix}$

    D $\begin{pmatrix} 4 & 9 \\ -1 & 4 \end{pmatrix}$ E $\begin{pmatrix} 1 & 12 \\ 4 & 1 \end{pmatrix}$

11. A carpenter measures a length of wood as 45.9 cm instead of the correct length of 45 cm. What is his percentage error?

    A 20%   B 5%   C 10%
    D 2%   E 25%

12. If $\quad X = $, $\quad Y = $

    and $Z = $.

    What is $(X \cap Z) \cup Y$?

    A   B   C

    D   E

13. The difference between the roots of the equation $2x^2 + x - 6 = 0$ is

    A -1 B -5 C $3\frac{1}{2}$
    D 1   E $\frac{1}{2}$

14. Two concentric circles have radii of 3 cm and 4 cm. Calculate the area of the ring between the circles.

    A $\pi\,\text{cm}^2$ B $\pi^2\,\text{cm}^2$ C $2\pi\,\text{cm}^2$
    D $7\pi\,\text{cm}^2$ E $7\pi^2\,\text{cm}^2$

15. $\sin\theta = \frac{2}{3}$ and θ is acute. $\tan\theta =$

    A $\dfrac{2}{\sqrt{5}}$ B $-\frac{3}{2}$ C $-\frac{2}{5}$

    D $\dfrac{3}{\sqrt{5}}$ E $\dfrac{\sqrt{3}}{[5]}$

16. The mean of five numbers is 6, the mode is 3 and the median is 5. The numbers could be

    A 3, 3, 5, 6, 6   B 3, 5, 5, 6, 9   C 1, 2, 3, 5, 7
    D 3, 5, 6, 9, 12   E 3, 3, 5, 9, 10

17.

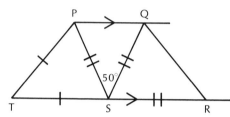

    Given the information in the diagram, which of these statements *must* be correct.

    i) PT//QS   ii) $P\hat{T}S = 50°$ iii) PT = QR
    iv) $S\hat{Q}R = 65°$

    A i) and iv)   B ii) and iii)   C iv) only
    D ii) only   E all of them

18. The graph of $y = 2^x$ is

    A   B

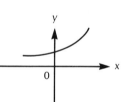

    C   D

    E

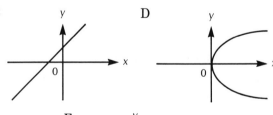

19. $F = \{2, 3, 4, 7, 9, 11\}$. How many prime factors of 198 are contained in F?

    A 0   B 1   C 2
    D 3   E 4

20. $f(x) = (x - 3)$ and $g(x) = (2x + 3)$
So $gf(x)$ is

A x B $2x - 3$ C $3x$
D $2x - 2$ E $2x$

21. The image of the point $(2, -3)$ after reflection in a mirror line is $(2, 5)$. What is the equation of the mirror line?

A $x = 2$ B $y = 2$ C $y = 1$
D $y = x$ E $x = 1$

22. A shopkeeper found that out of a box of oranges, $\frac{1}{6}$ of them were bad and that of the remainder $\frac{3}{5}$ were large enough to be sold for 15 p each while the rest were small so could only be sold for 10 p each. How many oranges were in the box altogether if all the small ones sold for a total of £4.80?

A 160   B 120   C 100
D 96   E 144

23. Calculate the value of x.

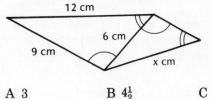

A 3   B $4\frac{1}{2}$ C 8
D 6   E 9

24. An express train travels for 150 km at 100 km/h and for 75 km at 150 km/h. The average speed of the journey is

A $112\frac{1}{2}$ km/h   B 125 km/h   C 120 km/h
D $62\frac{1}{2}$ km/h   E 100 km/h

25. If $2x + 3y = 0$ and $x + y = 2$ then

A $x = 6$ and $y = -4$ B $x = 6$ and $y = 4$
C $x = 4$ and $y = -6$ D $x = 6$ and $y = 6$
E $x = -4$ and $y = 6$

PAPER 3   NATIONAL CRITERIA

TEST A:

NATIONAL CRITERIA LEVEL 1

Topics in list 1 of the G.C.S.E. National Criteria are included in all mathematics syllabuses.

1. Write down

  a) an odd number less than 10,

  b) $\sqrt{25}$,

  c) a multiple of 6 less than 20,

  d) a factor of 15,

  e) the square of 7.

2. Work out

  a) $-1 - 3$,

  b) the drop in temperature from 10 °C to -3°C,

  c) $\frac{3}{7} + \frac{6}{7}$.

3. a) Express 20% as a fraction.

  b) Change 0.6 into a fraction.

  c) Write $\frac{1}{4}$ as a decimal.

4. Use your calculator to work out

  a) £2.72 × 12,

  b) £348.60 ÷ 15,

  c) $\frac{7}{8}$ as a decimal,

  d) the area of a rectangle 4.23 cm long and 1.4 cm wide,

  e) 8π,

  f) the change given if a £20 note is used to pay a bill for items costing 82 p, 7 p, £1.36, 29 p, £8.29, 73 p, 62 p.

5. A clerk earning £90 per week is given an increase of 6%. What is his new wage?

His stoppages each week total 36% of his earnings. How much did he actually take home when he earned £90 each week?

6. A father and his son have ages in the ratio 7 : 1. If the son is 5 years old, how old is his father?

7. a) 8 km is approximately 5 miles. A tourist travels 976 km while on holiday in Germany. Roughly how many miles is this?

b) While in Germany he sees a pair of jeans, which would cost £15 at home, costing 92 DM. If there are 4.78 DM to the £, how much, approximately, would he save by buying the jeans at home?

8. a) What meal would you have at 18 : 30?

b) A train journey starts at 14 : 15 and ends at 15 : 00. How long has it taken?

c) What time does it say on a 24-hour clock at ten minutes past midnight?

9.

Write down the reading on this electricity meter.

The Electricity Board charges 5.20 p per unit plus a standing charge of £8.72 per quarter.

How much would the quarterly bill be for a family that use 435 units?

10.

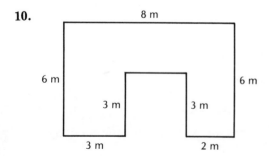

This is a plan—*not* drawn to scale—of a patio which is to be covered with paving stones 1 m square.

How many stones are needed?

11. You have three choices as to how to pay for a new washing machine costing £240. These are:

a) to pay the cash price of £240 by cheque,

b) to pay a 20% deposit and then 12 monthly payments of £18,

c) to borrow £240 from the bank and pay back £23 each month for a year.

What is the total cost of each method?

Which would you choose, and why would you choose it?

12.

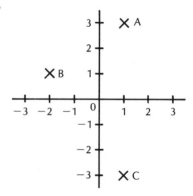

What are the coordinates of A, B, and C?

On a copy of the graph, plot the points D(0, 3) and E(−2, −3).

13. A train travels at 80 km/h for 2 hours, 110 km/h for $1\frac{1}{2}$ hours and 190 km/h for $\frac{1}{2}$ hour. What is its average speed for the whole journey?

14. a) The area of a rectangle, $A = l \times b$. If $l = 7$ cm and $b = 2$ cm, what is A?

b) A cookery book says that meat should be cooked for 20 minutes per lb plus 40 minutes. How long should you cook a 4 lb joint of meat?

c) What is the perimeter of this rectangle?

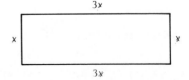

15. a)

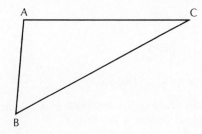

Measure all the sides and angles of this triangle as accurately as possible.

b) Draw an angle of 82°.

16. Calculate but *do not measure* the lettered angles.

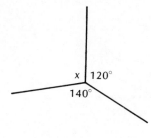

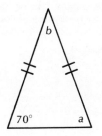

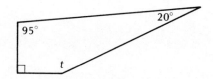

17. Draw one example of each of the following:

a) perpendicular lines,

b) a parallelogram,

c) a segment of a circle,

d) an obtuse angle,

e) a square based pyramid.

18.

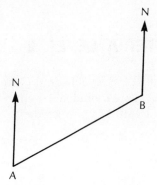

a) What is the actual distance between A and B?

b) What is the bearing of B from A?

c) What is the bearing of A from B?

d) How far North is B from A?

19. Calculate the volume of this cuboid.

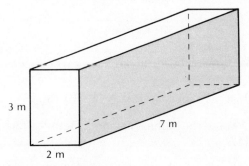

Scale 1 cm : 5 km.

This is a scale diagram showing the position of two towns, A and B.

What is the area of the shaded face?

If the cuboid was made of a wire frame, what total length of wire would be needed?

20. In a long jump competition, the eight competitors jumped

5.6 m, 4.9 m, 5.8 m, 4.8 m, 5.2 m, 5.9 m, 5.0 m, 5.2 m.

a) What is the median length of jump?

b) Calculate the mean of the lengths.

c) What is the probability that a competitor chosen at random jumped over 5.5 m?

TEST B:

NATIONAL CRITERIA LEVEL 2

Topics on List 2 of the G.C.S.E. National Criteria, as well as those on List 1, are included in syllabuses which can lead to an award of up to grade C.

1. Correct

   a) 1.732 to 2 decimal places,

   b) 8746 to 1 significant figure,

   c) 29 761 to the nearest hundred,

   d) 2.97 × 8.63 to 1 significant figure,

   e) £43.87 to the nearest £.

2. a) Write

   i) 270 000 in standard form,
   ii) 0.000 036 in standard form.

   b) Calculate

   i) 0.03 ÷ 0.5,
   ii) 0.2 × 1.02

3. a) List all the factors of i) 12,   ii) 15.

   b) What is the highest common factor of 12 and 15?

   c) What is the lowest common multiple of 12 and 15?

   d) Write down the prime factors of 66.

4. a) $\frac{3}{4} + 2\frac{1}{2}$.

   b) $1\frac{1}{3} \times 2\frac{5}{8}$.

   c) How many lengths of wire $\frac{4}{5}$ m long can be cut from a piece of wire 20 m long?

5. a) Increase 150 by 30%.

   b) At a football match there are 700 spectators of whom 168 are women.

   i) What percentage are women?
   ii) If 60% are men, how many of the spectators are men?

6. a) Share £750 in the ratio 2:3.

   b) A map scale is 20 cm : 4 km. Cancel this to its simplest form.

7. $y = 2x - 1$
   Complete this table.

x	-3	-2	-1	0	1	2	3
y		-5		-1			

   Draw the graph of $y = 2x - 1$ for $-3 \leqslant x \leqslant 3$.

8.

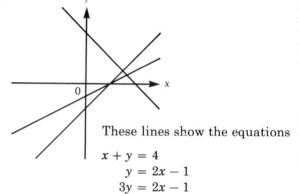

   These lines show the equations

   $$x + y = 4$$
   $$y = 2x - 1$$
   $$3y = 2x - 1$$

   Which is which?

9. Simplify

   a) $4(2 - 7) - 3(8 - 6)$,

   b) $2^3 \times 3^2 \times 4^{-1}$,

   c) $x^7 \times x^{-3} \times x^2$,

   d) $\dfrac{y^4}{y^7}$.

10. a) If $y = mx + c$, express x in terms of y, m and c.

    b) Solve

    i) $5x = 30$ ii) $2y - 1 = 4$

    iii) $\dfrac{2t}{3} = 4$ iv) $3(a + 2) = 12$

11. a) Factorise   i) $5x + 10y$,   ii) $8de + 12e^2$.

    b) Expand $2t(3 - 4t)$.

    c) Simplify $3(2x + 4) + 2(1 - x)$.

282

12.

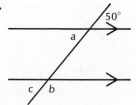

Find the values of a, b and c.

13. a) Calculate the values of the lettered angles.

i)

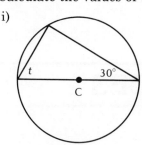

(C is the centre of the circle)

ii)

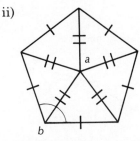

b) What is the size of each interior angle of a regular 12 sided polygon?

14. a)

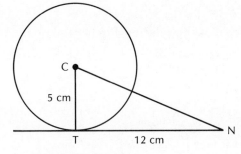

C is the centre of the circle and TN is a tangent.

Calculate CN.

b)

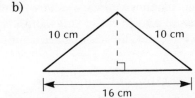

Find the perpendicular height of this triangle and use it to calculate the area of the triangle.

15. Work out the areas of

a)

b) a circle of radius 8 cm. Give the answer correct to 2 decimal places.

16. Find the volume of a cylindrical pipe with a diameter of 3 m and a length of 50 m.

17. What are the values of x and y?

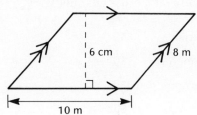

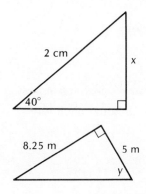

18. A P.E. teacher records the times that 50 junior pupils take to run 100 metres, measured to the nearest second.

Time (seconds)	Tally	Frequency
15	~~llll~~ 1	6
16	~~llll~~ ~~llll~~ 11	
17	~~llll~~ 111	
18	111	
19	~~llll~~ ~~llll~~ 1111	14
20	~~llll~~ 11	

a) Fill in the missing numbers in the frequency column.

b) Show this information on a histogram.

c) What is the modal time taken?

19. Draw a pie chart to show the nationality of 720 passengers on a cross-channel ferry.

British	340
French	210
German	110
Others	60

20. There are 10 cars in a car park. 4 of them are red, 2 blue, 1 black and 3 white.

What is the probability that

a) the first car to leave is black,

b) the first car to leave is black and the second is red,

c) the blue cars leave before all the others?

PAPER 4   GCSE MIDDLE GRADES

1. A man is paid £5 per hour for a basic 35 hour week and then overtime rate of time and a half for evenings and Saturdays and double time for Sundays.

How much is he paid for

a) a basic week?

b) ten hours evening overtime?

c) a seven day week of 8 hours each day?

2. a) On a set of axes draw a parallelogram with vertices (0, 4), (3, 4),)5, 6), (2, 6). Reflect the figure in the line $y = x$ and also in the line $y = 2$.

b) Draw a regular pentagon of side 3 cm and show all its lines of symmetry.

3. a) Simplify

i) $\dfrac{3}{2x} + \dfrac{4}{x}$,

ii) $6(x^2 + 3) - (x + 1)(x + 2)$.

b) $(x - 1)$ is a factor of $x^2 + ax - 3$. What is the value of a?

c) Solve the equation $2x^2 = 5x - 3$.

4. a)

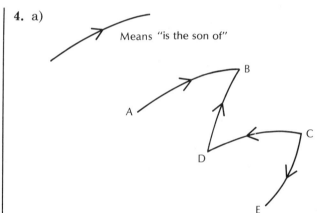

Means "is the son of"

What is the relationship between

i) A and D?

ii) C and A?

iii) D and E?

b) $\mathbf{R} = \begin{array}{c} \\ X \\ Y \\ Z \end{array}\begin{array}{c} \begin{array}{ccc} X & Y & Z \end{array} \\ \begin{pmatrix} 0 & 0 & 1 \\ 1 & 1 & 0 \\ 1 & 0 & 1 \end{pmatrix} \end{array}$

Matrix $\mathbf{R}$ represents a road system connecting X, Y, Z. Draw the network.

Calculate $\mathbf{R}^2$ and explain its meaning.

5. Two business partners always share their monthly profits in a fixed ratio. One month the profits were £1800 and the senior partner took £1080.

a) What is the ratio of their shares in its simplest form?

b) If the profits are £2400, how much will the junior partner take?

6.

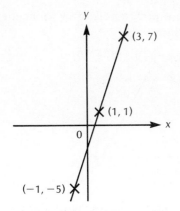

a) What is y when $x = 0$?

b) Calculate the gradient of the line.

c) Write down the equation of the line.

d) For a point on the line, what is x when $y = 2\frac{1}{2}$?

7.

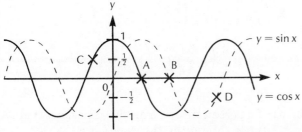

a) What are the coordinates of A, B, C and D?

b) If $\sin x = \dfrac{\sqrt{3}}{2}$, what are the possible values of x within the limits of the graph?

8. Each edge of a cuboid has a length which is a one digit number of metres. If no two dimensions are the same,

a) what is the largest possible volume of the cuboid if each length is a prime number?

b) what is the largest volume of the cuboid if one side is a triangle number, one is a factor of 35 and the other is a common factor of 54 and 72?

9. In selling a car for £6327 a garage makes a profit of 11%. By how much would they have to increase the price to make a profit of 13%?

10. Evaluate

a) $f(-2)$ if $f(x) = 3(2 - x)$,

b) $gg(x)$ if $g(x) = \dfrac{3}{x}$.

Solve $g(x) = f(x)$.

11. a) What is the value of $0.042\,73 \times 1000$ correct to one significant figure.

b) Evaluate
   i) $\sqrt{18} \times \sqrt{50}$ ii) $\sqrt{490\,000}$

c) Express in standard form $0.000\,05 \times 40\,000\,000$.

12.

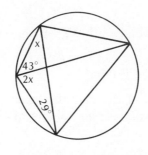

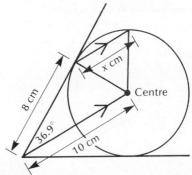

Calculate the value of x in each diagram.

13. A supermarket has special offers on its own brand of soap and shampoo.

125 g bars of soap are on sale at 19 p a bar, 35 p for a 2-bar pack and 54 p for a 3-bar pack. Shampoo is on sale at 56 p for a 125 ml bottle and £1.37 for a 300 ml bottle.

Which soap and shampoo would you choose and why?

A bar of soap measures 9 cm by 6 cm by 3 cm. If it is wrapped in one piece of paper, folded and stuck down, show by means of a diagram the measurements of a suitable piece of paper and where the paper would have to be folded.

14. a) Solve $3x^2 + x - 2 \geqslant 0$.

b) In a school of 1200 pupils, there are 214 more boys than girls. Form an equation and use it to find the number of boys.

c) After being reduced by 20%. £x becomes £56. What is the value of x?

15. An engineer designing a machine part draws

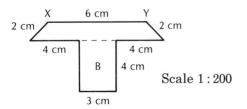

Scale 1 : 200

a) What would be the length XY on the machine?

b) What is the area of B in m²?

c) If the diagram is of the end of a prism of volume 28 cm³, what is the volume of the machine part in

i) cm³?
ii) m³?

16.

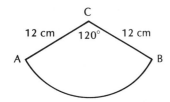

ABC is a sector of a circle of centre C.

a) Calculate the length of the arc AB.

b) If this shape is made into a cone by joining AC to CB, what would be the radius of the base of the cone?

17. Without using a protractor, draw an accurate copy of this triangle.

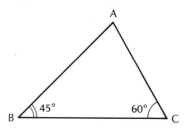

Measure AB and AC.

On the same diagram, find any points which are equidistant from B and C and 3 cm from A.

18. a) A train travels at 100 km/h for $\frac{1}{4}$ hour and 80 km/h for $\frac{1}{2}$ hour. What is its average speed in km/h?

b) Convert 180 000 000 cm/s into km/h.

19. Calculate the values of a, b, x, y, w if

$$2\begin{pmatrix} a \\ b \end{pmatrix} - \begin{pmatrix} 4 \\ -1 \end{pmatrix} = \begin{pmatrix} 6 \\ 7 \end{pmatrix}$$

and $\begin{pmatrix} x & 0 \\ x & y \end{pmatrix}\begin{pmatrix} 2 & 3 \\ -2 & 4 \end{pmatrix} = \begin{pmatrix} 6 & 9 \\ 8 & w \end{pmatrix}$.

20. a) If a person throws a die 300 times, how many times should the thrower score

i) an even number?
ii) more than 2?
iii) a 6?

b) In a bag there are 6 toffees and 9 chocolates. How many would have to be taken to make sure of selecting

i) 2 of the same kind?
ii) 3 toffees?

What is the probability of selecting a toffee and then a chocolate?

PAPER 5   GCSE HIGHER GRADES

1.

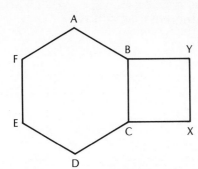

ABCDEF is a regular hexagon and BCXY is a square.

a) Calculate the size of $\hat{ABE}$.

b) If AB = 10 cm, what is the length of BE?

c) What type of figure is ABEF?

d) Calculate the area of ABCDEF (to 2 d.p.).

e) Sketch a net of a hexagonal-based prism.

f) If ABCDEF is the base, and BCXY is one side of a hexagonal-based prism, find the total surface area of the prism.

2. a) A video shop hires out 280 videos on a day when the takings total £360. They hire out x videos at £2, y at £1.50 and $x + 2y$ at £1. How many of each type were hired out?

b) A number of friends pay £96 to book seats for a concert. When two decide that they cannot afford to go their friends have to pay an extra £4 each for their share of the cost. Find the number that actually went to the concert.

3. A plane which can seat 198 passengers is full when it takes off to fly from Heathrow to Germany.

a) If G = {German passengers}, M = {male passengers} and $n(M) = 124$, copy and complete this Venn diagram.

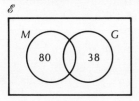

b) Use your diagram to find how many

   i) male passengers were German,
   ii) female passengers were not German.

c) Only 12 of the 47 men travelling for business reasons were German but all the eight business women were German.

If B = {passengers travelling on business}, copy and complete this diagram.

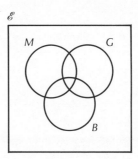

d) i) What is the ratio of men to women on the plane?
   ii) What percentage of passengers were German?

e) Paying the fare in Germany costs 555 DM and in Britain it costs £151.50. How much would a firm save by paying the cheapest fare for its 20 representatives if the exchange rate is 3.75 DM to the £?

4. a) A sailor has to navigate around an island to reach the harbour. He calculates that he has to sail either on a bearing of 063° for 9.5 nautical miles or else 047° for 6 nautical miles to a buoy B where he will have to change direction. Calculate the bearing and the distance of the harbour from B.

b) An air traffic controller sitting in a tower 800 ft high calculates that, at exactly one o'clock, a plane is 5000 ft above the ground at a point 5600 ft away from the foot of the tower.

   i) What is the angle of elevation of the plane, as seen by the air traffic controller, at one o'clock?

   ii) If the plane continues flying away from the tower at this height at a speed of 100 ft/s for $1\frac{1}{4}$ minutes, what will then be its angle of elevation from the foot of the control tower?

5.
$$y = 2x^2 - x + 1$$

a) Copy and complete this table.

x	-3	-2	-1	0	1	2
$2x^2$	18			0		
$-x$		$+2$			-1	
$+1$			$+1$	$+1$		
y						

b) Draw the graph of $y = 2x^2 - x + 1$ for $-3 \leqslant x \leqslant 2$.

c) On the graph, shade the area where $y \geqslant 0$, $-2 \leqslant x \leqslant 2$ and $y \leqslant 2x^2 - x + 1$.

d) Calculate this area approximately.

e) Find the equation of the tangent to the curve at the point where $x = 2$.

6. a) When the mortgage rate is 9%, Mr Kennedy's interest payments are £171 per month. How much does he pay when it is increased to 13%?

b) If he paid £38 500 for his house when he bought it three years ago and house prices have increased by 10% per year, what is it worth now?

c) The rateable value of his house is £400 and the rates due for this year are 87 p in the £. What will be the cost of the half yearly rates bill?

d) Mr Kennedy earns £17 500 per year, but after stoppages takes home only 72% of this. He spends $\frac{1}{2}$ of his money on household expenses, $\frac{1}{3}$ on entertainment and clothing and puts the rest in the building society. Calculate his savings for a year.

e) He calculates that, taking everything into account, the running costs for his new car are 12.5 p per mile for the first 1000 miles, 8 p per mile for the next 2000 miles and 6.5 p per mile for any additional mileage. What are his running costs for this year if he has driven a total of 6850 miles?

7.

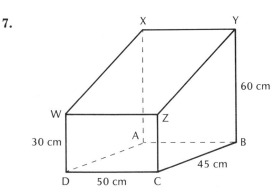

This diagram shows a display cabinet made with wooden sides and base and a rectangular glass top.

ABCD is the horizontal base and WD, ZC, YB and XA are vertical.

a) Calculate the dimensions of the glass top.

b) Find the size of $Y\hat{Z}C$.

c) The sides for eight of these cabinets have to be cut out of a 180 cm square of wood so that there is no wastage. Show two different ways in which this can be done.

d) Calculate the volume of the cabinet.

8. a) A darts player records his scores on a tally chart.

Score	Tally	Frequency
0–10	11	
11–20	111	
21–30	~~1111~~	
31–40	1111	
41–50	~~1111~~ 1	
51–60	~~1111~~	

   i) Complete the frequency column.

   ii) How many darts did he throw altogether?

   iii) Estimate his mean score.

   iv) Draw a cumulative frequency curve and use it to find an approximate value for his median score.

b) He calculates that the probability of one of his darts hitting a two digit number is $\frac{3}{5}$ and assumes that all the other darts hit a one digit number. The probability of any dart hitting a treble is $\frac{1}{10}$ and a double is $\frac{2}{10}$.

Calculate the probability of a dart hitting

 i) a two digit treble,
 ii) a one digit double,
 iii) a one digit single score followed by a two digit double.

c) What is the probability that his last dart hits either a two digit treble or a one digit double?

9. ABCD is a parallelogram with $\overrightarrow{AB} = \mathbf{a}$ and $\overrightarrow{BC} = \mathbf{b}$. BC is produced to E so that $\overrightarrow{CE} = 2\overrightarrow{BC}$ and AE meets DC at F.

a) Express in terms of a and b
  i) $\overrightarrow{AD}$, ii) $\overrightarrow{DB}$, iii) $\overrightarrow{CE}$, iv) $\overrightarrow{AE}$

b) What is the relationship between $\triangle$ADF and $\triangle$CEF?

c) Express $\overrightarrow{FC}$ and $\overrightarrow{FE}$ in terms of **a** and **b**.

If A = (3, 2), $\mathbf{a} = \begin{pmatrix} 3 \\ 0 \end{pmatrix}$ and $\mathbf{b} = \begin{pmatrix} -3 \\ -4 \end{pmatrix}$

d) What are the coordinates of B, C, D and F?

e) Prove that $\triangle$ABC is right-angled.

f) Calculate the area of $\triangle$AEC.

10. a) In an athletics match between three teams the results were: Team A, 3 first, 4 second and 9 third places; team B, 6 first and 1 third place and team C, 3 first, 8 second and 2 third places. Points were 5 for a first, 3 for a second and 2 for a third place.

  i) Express the results in a 3 by 3 matrix.
  ii) Write the points for the placings in a 3 by 1 matrix.
  iii) Use a matrix product to calculate the points scored by each team.

b) On a set of axes with $-10 \leqslant x \leqslant 10$ and $-8 \leqslant y \leqslant 8$, draw the triangle with vertices P(2, 1), Q(5, 1), R(3, 4).

  i) Transform $\triangle$PQR by the matrix $\begin{pmatrix} 0 & 1 \\ 1 & 0 \end{pmatrix}$ to $P_1Q_1R_1$. Plot P_1, Q_1 and R_1. What are the coordinates of P_1, Q_1 and R_1?

  Describe the transformation represented by $\begin{pmatrix} 0 & 1 \\ 1 & 0 \end{pmatrix}$.

  ii) Translate $\triangle$PQR by $\begin{pmatrix} -4 \\ -2 \end{pmatrix}$ to $P_2Q_2R_2$.

  Plot $\triangle P_2Q_2R_2$. What are the coordinates of P_2, Q_2 and R_2?

  iii) $\triangle$PQR is enlarged from the origin with a scale factor of -2. Show the enlarged figure on the axes.
  What matrix represents this transformation?
  Write down the inverse of this matrix.

11. Ken leaves home at 7:30 one morning to jog to work 5 km away. After jogging the first 2 km in 10 minutes, he stops for 3 minutes to wait for his wife who left home after him. They continue jogging together and reach work at 7:55.

a) Show Ken's journey on a distance/time graph.

b) If his wife jogs the whole journey at a constant speed, show her journey on the same axes. What time did she leave home?

c) Calculate
  i) Ken's average speed,
  ii) his wife's average speed for the whole journey.

d) A friend, who lives 3 km further away from work than Ken, cycles to work at an average speed of 20 km/h. What time must he leave home in order to arrive at work at exactly 8 o'clock?

12. An orange juice carton is 6 cm by 8 cm by 16 cm. On the side it says

> CONTENTS   0.75 LITRES

a) If it is full right up to the top, what is the percentage error in the amount of juice that the carton contains? (Take the contents to be 0.75 litres.)

b) The juice is emptied, half into each of two cylindrical glasses of diameter 7 cm. Calculate the height of juice in each glass (to 1 decimal place).

c) How much profit is made if a carton costs 48 p but a cafe charges 15 p per glass for a cylindrical glass which has only half the diameter of the glasses in b) and which is filled to only half the height?

d) Orange juice can be bought in cylindrical tins containing 2.2 litres. If the height of the tins is 28 cm, what is the radius?

e) What would be the cost of a tin if its cost is directly proportional to the cost of a carton (to the nearest 1 p)?

ANSWERS

Unless the question is specific, answers have been given to a suitable approximation.

SECTION III

1. ALGEBRA

1. a) $6x + 5y$ b) $8def + 3ef$ c) $60a^2$

d) $3b$ e) $4x^2 + x$ f) $\dfrac{3y^2}{x^4}$

g) $\dfrac{2}{3}$ h) $\dfrac{ax}{2}$ i) $\dfrac{x+3}{x+4}$

j) $\dfrac{2x}{y^5}$

2. a) 75 b) 8 c) 85
d) 1 e) 59 f) 8
g) 10 h) $2\frac{1}{4}$ i) 3
j) -19

3. a) $8a + 12b$ b) $6x^2 - 12xy$
c) $x^2 + 8x + 15$ d) $x^2 - 5x + 6$
e) $2x^2 + 7x + 3$ f) $x^2 - 16$
g) $-6d + 3g$ h) $6 + 14y + 4y^2$
i) $10a^2 + 21a - 10$ j) $4f^2 - 9$

4. a) $6(y + t)$
b) $3y(3x + 2a)$
c) $4a(3b - 2a)$
d) $(x + 4)(x + 3)$
e) $(x - 5)(x + 2)$
f) $(2y + 3)(y + 4)$
g) $-4(4x + 3y)$
h) $8(a - 2g)(a + 2g)$
i) $(x + y)(3 + x - y)$
j) $(4t + 3y)(2 - x)$
k) $5(x - 2)(x - 1)$
l) $(x - 8)^2$

5. a) 4 b) 2.5 c) 3
d) 18 e) $4\frac{2}{3}$ f) $-\frac{7}{9}$
g) -1.2 h) $1\frac{1}{7}$ i) -2
j) $\frac{1}{2}$ k) $\frac{1}{4}$ l) 20

6. a) $x = 3, y = 2$
b) $x = 3, y = -1$
c) $x = \frac{1}{2}, y = -1$
d) $x = \frac{3}{4}, y = 2\frac{3}{4}$

e) $x = 1\frac{9}{23}, y = -\frac{1}{23}$
f) $x = 1, y = 1$
g) $x = 2, y = 4$ or $x = -3, y = 9$
h) $x = 2, y = 0$ or $x = -7, y = -6$
i) $x = 0.9, y = 0.7$

7. a) -4 or -2 b) 7 or 2
c) 10 or -2 d) 0 or 3
e) 3 f) 3 or -3
g) 2 or -8 h) 5.12 or -3.12
i) 5.16 or -1.16 j) 2.52 or 0.08
k) -0.85 or 2.35 l) 1.14 or -2.64
m) 7.46 or 0.54 n) 0.90 or -2.23

8. a) i) $x \geqslant -1$ ii) $-1 < x \leqslant 1$
iii) $0 < x < 4$

b) i)

ii)

iii)

c) $x \geqslant 8$ d) $x > -4$
e) $x \geqslant 6$ f) $x > 1$
g) $x \leqslant -1$ or $x \geqslant 3$ h) $-1 < x < 3$
i) $-4 < x < -3$ j) $x > 2$ or $x < -4$

9. a) $\dfrac{t}{a}$ b) $\dfrac{p - ey}{d}$

c) $\sqrt{\dfrac{y}{3}}$ d) $\dfrac{y(d - 7)}{3 - a}$

e) $\dfrac{a}{t^2}$ f) $\dfrac{dy + at}{a + d}$

g) $\dfrac{t(4y - 1)}{1 - 4t}$ h) $\sqrt{\dfrac{t + 4y}{3}}$

i) $\sqrt{\dfrac{y - t}{a}}$ j) $\sqrt{\dfrac{ay - t}{a}}$

10. a) $\dfrac{12}{y}$ b) $\dfrac{2}{x}$

c) $\dfrac{t+p}{y}$ d) $\dfrac{3b-2a}{ab}$

e) $\dfrac{16y-27t}{6ty}$ f) $\dfrac{8xt+15y^2}{12yt}$

g) $\dfrac{10x-6t}{(x-t)(x+t)}$ h) $\dfrac{a(a-3)}{(a+3)(a+1)}$

i) $\dfrac{2tx-7t}{(2x-1)(2x+1)}$ j) $\dfrac{3y^2+4y+6}{y(y+1)}$

11. a) $100x$ b) t c) $2x^2$

d) $A=\dfrac{L(L-2)}{2},\ P=3L-2$

e) 20 f) $3s=f-12$

g) $\frac{5}{6}$ h) $60-x+y$

i) $8x+9y$ pence   j) $2\left(\dfrac{x}{3}+4\right)=10,\ x=3$

12. a) $(24-4)\div 5=4$
b) $(16-2)\div(5-3)=7$
c) $4+12\div 3=8$
d) $8\times 2-(4\times 2)=8$
e) $(14-2)\times 3=26$
f) $2\times(4+5)=18$
g) $36\div 4-2=7$
h) $36\div(4-2)=18$
i) $180-51-62=67$
j) $[(1+1)\div(1+1)]\times 3=3$

13. a) 1 b) 11
c) 3 d) 8
e) -1 f) $3\frac{1}{8}$

14. a) $(x+1)(x+2)(x+4)$
b) $(x-1)(x+2)(x+4)$
c) $(x-2)(x+2)(x+5)$
d) $(x+1)(x-3)(x-4)$
e) $(x-1)(x+1)(2x-1)$
f) $(x+2)(x-1)(3x+2)$

2. NUMBERS

1. a) $\frac{1}{4},\frac{1}{8}$ b) $0.1, 0.01$
c) $8, 160$ d) $36, 49$
e) $52, 65$

2. a) 9 or 16
b) any two from 7, 11, 13, 17
c) 10 or 15
d) one from 8, 12 or 16
e) 12 and 15
f) 6, 10, 15

3. a) 1, 2, 3, 4, 6, 9, 12, 18, 36
b) 1, 7, 49
c) 1, 2, 4, 5, 10, 20, 25, 50, 100
d) 1, 2, 4, 7, 8, 14, 28, 56

4. a) $2\times 2\times 3=2^2\times 3$
b) $2\times 3\times 3=2\times 3^2$
c) 5×7
d) $2\times 2\times 2\times 2\times 5=2^4\times 5$
e) $2\times 2\times 2\times 2\times 3\times 3=2^4\times 3^2$

5. a) i) 60   ii) 18   iii) 462
b) i) 4   ii) 15   iii) 14

6. a) 4×10^4 b) 2.9×10^2
c) 3×10^{-4} d) 4.2×10^{-1}
e) 3.42×10^3 f) 2.06×10^{-2}
g) 9.5×10^7 h) 9×10^{-7}
i) 5.702×10^{-2} j) 6.31×10^1

7. a) 300   b) 42
c) 0.013   d) 0.000 005 6
e) 0.8   f) 7030
g) 0.21   h) 64
i) 820 000 000   j) 0.000 000 039

8. a) 6×10^5 b) 3.2×10^3
c) 6×10^0 d) 2×10^{-4}
e) 6×10^1 f) 4×10^3
g) 1.2×10^{-2} h) 1.65×10^{-6}
i) 5×10^5 j) 2.4×10^0

9. a) $6\times 10^1=60$
b) $6\times 10^{-2}=0.06$
c) $1.08\times 10^1=10.8$
d) $2\times 10^4=20\,000$
e) $6\times 10^{-3}=0.006$
f) $4\times 10^1=40$
g) $1.2\times 10^4=12\,000$
h) $2\times 10^3=2000$
i) $1.6\times 10^3=1600$
j) $5\times 10^0=5$

10. a) 16   b) 27   c) -1
d) 0.25   e) 11   f) 2
g) $\frac{2}{3}$ h) 8   i) 25
j) 9

3. DIRECTED NUMBERS

1. a) $2 > -1$ b) $-7 < 3$
c) $-2 > -9$ d) $-47 < 0$
e) $-294 > -295$ f) $-1\frac{1}{2} < -1\frac{1}{4}$

2. a) -3 b) -12
c) 2 d) 3
e) -70 f) -43
g) -3 h) 102
i) 1 j) 147

3. a) -12 b) 56
c) -8 d) 1
e) 4 f) 6
g) 6 h) -24
i) -12.5 j) -12

4. a) 7 b) 4
c) -8 d) 110
e) 81 f) 125

5. a) -2 b) 6
c) -9 d) 3
e) 13

6. a) 4 b) 16
c) -80 d) 4
e) 96

7. a) 5 b) -4
c) 13 d) 5
e) 16

8. a) x b) $-5a - 2y$
c) $12xy$ d) $-8 + 16a$
e) $-6a + 18y$ f) $-3x - 2y$

4. DECIMALS

1. a) 2.3 b) 0.42 c) 6.02
d) 497.014 e) 10.101

2. a) i) 2.4 ii) 0.6 iii) 65.0
iv) 10037.3 v) 10.0
b) i) 4.33 ii) 28.21 iii) 0.01
iv) 1.10 v) 0.00

3. a) 60.472 b) £93.71 c) 24.75
d) £67.66 e) 106.19

4. a) 12.8 b) 0.91 c) 0.36
d) 8.61 e) 9.92 f) 0.024
g) 3 h) 24 i) 36.8
j) 0.7855

5. a) 3.2 b) 0.005 c) 400
d) 16 e) 20 f) 0.3
g) 4000 h) $10\,000$ i) 4.8
j) $10\,000$

6. a) $2\,\text{km}$ b) $3000\,\text{g}$ c) $4000\,\text{mg}$
d) $8.47\,\text{m}$ e) $327\,\text{cm}$ f) $2.946\,\text{kg}$
g) $0.005\,\text{m}$ h) $47\,\text{m}$ i) $2980\,\text{cm}^3$
j) $0.001\,48\,\text{km}$

7. a) 2.8 b) 20 c) $0.005\,876$
d) 4000 e) 10 f) 0.807
g) 2.0 h) 800 i) 29
j) 0.0321

5. FRACTIONS

1. a) $\frac{1}{2}$ b) $\frac{2}{3}$ c) $\frac{2}{3}$
d) $\frac{3}{17}$ e) $\frac{2}{3}$ f) $\frac{3}{4}$
g) $\frac{4}{5}$ h) $\frac{1}{3}$ i) $\frac{3}{8}$
j) $\frac{2}{3}$

2. a) $\frac{10}{11}$ b) 1 c) $\frac{9}{10}$
d) $\frac{1}{2}$ e) $\frac{2}{21}$ f) $\frac{13}{30}$
g) $\frac{13}{20}$ h) $31\frac{5}{16}$ i) $3\frac{1}{4}$
j) $6\frac{1}{14}$

3. a) $1\frac{1}{3}$ b) $4\frac{3}{5}$ c) $11\frac{1}{4}$
d) $2\frac{1}{2}$ e) $2\frac{5}{19}$ f) $9\frac{3}{5}$
g) $2\frac{5}{7}$ h) $11\frac{1}{2}$ i) 48
j) $1\frac{11}{17}$

4. a) $\frac{5}{3}$ b) $\frac{17}{6}$ c) $\frac{69}{10}$
d) $\frac{35}{19}$ e) $\frac{67}{13}$ f) $\frac{59}{53}$
g) $\frac{10}{3}$ h) $\frac{103}{11}$ i) $\frac{87}{4}$
j) $\frac{34}{7}$

5. a) $\frac{12}{35}$ b) $\frac{2}{3}$ c) $\frac{11}{15}$
d) $\frac{3}{10}$ e) 6 f) $3\frac{3}{4}$
g) $32\frac{2}{3}$ h) $14\frac{2}{3}$

6. a) $\frac{14}{15}$ b) $\frac{5}{6}$ c) $2\frac{10}{11}$
d) $\frac{8}{25}$ e) $\frac{2}{15}$ f) $\frac{10}{27}$
g) $\frac{6}{11}$ h) $1\frac{5}{6}$

7. a) 0.8   b) 0.875   c) 0.95
d) 0.75   e) 1.375   f) 2.54
g) 0.4375   h) 0.76   i) 0.667
j) 0.917

6. PERCENTAGES

1. a) $\frac{2}{5}$ b) $\frac{13}{20}$ c) $\frac{3}{25}$
d) $\frac{1}{12}$ e) $1\frac{9}{20}$ f) $\frac{5}{8}$
g) $2\frac{3}{4}$ h) $\frac{19}{20}$ i) $\frac{1}{40}$
j) $\frac{11}{25}$

2. a) 80%   b) 35%   c) 76%
d) $57\frac{1}{7}$%   e) 700%   f) $55\frac{5}{9}$%
g) 650%   h) 94%   i) 290%
j) $87\frac{1}{2}$%

3. a) 36 g   b) £160   c) 96 p
d) 22 p   e) 672 cm   f) 63 litres
g) £12.02   h) £4.75   i) $1\frac{3}{4}$ m
j) £7.36

4. a) 25%   b) $12\frac{1}{2}$%   c) 16%
d) 20%   e) 80%   f) 150%
g) 64%   h) $66\frac{2}{3}$%   i) 30%
j) $12\frac{1}{2}$%

5. a) £100, 25%   b) £3, 60%   c) £300, £312
d) £6, 60 p   e) £7.50, £9   f) £43.26, £1.26
g) £250, £37.50   h) 12 p, $8\frac{1}{3}$%

6. a)   i) £99   ii) £240   iii) £4.10
    iv) £5760
b)   i) £75.24   ii) £129.52   iii) £22.51
    iv) £108.75

7. a) £7.50   b) £1.10   c) £120
d) £187.50   e) £1.80   f) 18 p

8. a) £1350   b) £2475   c) £1935
d) £3421.50   e) £757.80

9. a) £480, £336, £288, £240, £192
b) £360, £252, £216, £180, £144
c) £600, £420, £360, £300, £240
d) £252, £176.40, £151.20, £126, £100.80
e) £575, £402.50, £345, £287.50, £230.

7. RATIO

1. a) 3 : 4   b) 3 : 2   c) 5 : 1
d) 2 : 3   e) 3 : 2 : 5   f) 2 : 4 : 1
g) 3 : 1   h) 2 : 3   i) 1 : 3
j) 4 : 5   k) 1 : 4 : 2   l) 1 : 10
m) 2 : 1   n) 1 : 5 : 8   o) 6 : 5

2. a) $\frac{1}{2}$ b) $\frac{5}{6}$ c) $\frac{2}{5}$
d) $\frac{2}{5}$ e) $\frac{1}{2}$ f) 2
g) $\frac{3}{5}$ h) $\frac{1}{40}$ i) $\frac{1}{5}$
j) $\frac{5}{6}$

3. a) £30 : £70   b) £96 : £48
c) £3400 : £600   d) £35 : £15 : £10
e) 55 km : 45 km : 20 km   f) 16 p : 32 p : 48 p

4. a) £6   b) £1400   c) £144
d) £1.76   e) £31.50

5. a) 2 m   b) 3 m   c) 100 m
d) 6 cm   e) 1 : 5   f) 500 m
g) 1 : 200 000   h) 10 cm   i) 800 cm
j) 1 : 5000

8. ERROR

1. a) 5.5 cm, 6.5 cm   b) 35.55 m, 35.65 m
c) 865 km, 875 km   d) 0.725 m, 0.735 m
e) 7950 mm, 8050 mm   f) 3.405 m, 3.415 m
g) 4365 cm, 4375 cm   h) 1.5 km, 2.5 km
i) 0.0035 km, 0.0045 km   j) 9.05 cm, 9.15 cm

2. a) 1.6675 cm^2, 1.9375 cm^2
b) 1125 mm^2, 2125 mm^2
c) 0.014 525 m^2, 0.019 125 m^2
d) 0.375 km^2, 0.875 km^2
e) 89.25 m^2, 109.25 m^2

3. a) 0.05 cm   b) £50   c) 0.005 kg
d) 0.005   e) 0.5 p

4. a) 9.09%   b) 3.45%   c) 4.76%
d) 6.25%   e) 2.99%   f) 3.10%

9. EVERYDAY ARITHMETIC

1. 2 × 20 p, 5 p, 2 p;   2 × 20 p, 5 p, 2 × 1 p;
2 × 20 p, 7 × 1 p;   2 × 20 p, 2 × 2 p, 3 × 1 p;
2 × 20 p, 3 × 2 p, 1 p;   4 × 10 p, 5 p, 2 p;
4 × 10 p, 5 p, 2 × 1 p;   20 p, 10 p, 3 × 5 p, 2 p;
9 × 5 p, 2 p;   3 × 10 p, 2 × 5 p, 7 × 1 p, etc.

2. 2 coffees @ 36 p each   £
   - 2 coffees @ 36 p each — 0.72
   - 4 rolls & butter @ 25 p each — 1.00
   - 4 soups @ 35 p each — 1.40
   - 3 ham salads @ £1.45 each — 4.35
   - 1 chicken salad @ £1.20 — 1.20
   - Total (without VAT) — 8.67
   - VAT @ 15% — 1.30
   - Total including VAT — 9.97

3. 7th August, 5 p.m., £10.53

4. Registration   9.10
   - Lesson (1)   9.15
   - (2)   9.50
   - Break   10.25
   - (3)   10.55
   - (4)   11.30
   - Lunch   12.05
   - (5)   01.25
   - (6)   2.05
   - (7)   2.45
   - End   3.25
   - a) 12.05 p.m.   b) 3.25 p.m.

5. graph b)

6. £45.50 (dials read 97596 and 98475)

7. a) i) £771   ii) £195   iii) £782.25
   b) i) 8900 pesetas ii) 150 miles iii) 360 pesetas
   iv) £1.80   v) £54.10

8. a) i) £1740   ii) £145
   b) i) £39   ii) £312   iii) £351   iv) £26
   c) 8%

9. a) i) £72   ii) 200 gallons
   iii) £410   iv) £934.55
   b) £89.74
   c) £5616

10. a) i) 3204   ii) £172.05   iii) £180.80
    b) i) £266.60   ii) £88.87

10. AREA AND VOLUME

1. a) 28 cm^2 b) 48 cm^2 c) 18 cm^2
   d) 93.5 cm^2 e) 50.2 cm^2 f) 48 cm^2
   g) 60 cm^2

2. a) 140 cm^3 b) 64 cm^3 c) 502 m^3
   d) 452 cm^3 e) 33.5 m^3

3. a) 126 cm^2 b) 113 cm^2 c) 62 cm^2
   d) 75.4 cm^2

4. a) i) 2000 cm^2 ii) 0.2 m^2
   b) 40 000 cm^2
   c) i) 6 000 000 cm^3 ii) 6 m^3
   d) 60 m^2
   e) 120 000 m^3
   f) i) 600 mm^2 ii) 50 cm^3 iii) 0.08 mm^2

11. SIMILARITY

1. a) and c), b) and e)

2. b) and d), c) and e)

3. a) $b = 12$ cm, $c = 10$ cm b) $b = 4$ cm, $y = 6$ cm
   c) $x = 12$ m, $y = 13\frac{1}{2}$ m d) $y = 7$ cm, $c = 1\frac{2}{3}$ cm
   e) $z = \frac{2}{5}$ m, $x = \frac{3}{5}$ m

4. a) 16 cm^2 b) 78.55 cm^2
   c) 216 cm^3 d) 1.25 m^3
   e) i) 6 m^2 ii) $1\frac{1}{3}$ m   iii) 45 cm^2

12. TRIGONOMETRY

1. a) 10 cm   b) 8.06 cm   c) 3.62 cm
   d) 13.0 cm   e) 41.0 cm   f) 34.7 cm

2. a) 2.27 cm   b) 9.83 cm   c) 1.53 cm
   d) 3.35 cm   e) 22.0 cm   f) 3.25 cm
   g) $x = 3.63$ cm, $y = 7.13$ cm
   h) $a = 13.2$ cm, $b = 13.9$ cm

3. a) 26.3°   b) 78.3°   c) 51.1°
   d) t = 47.7°, p = 42.3°   e) 36.9°

4. a) i) 2.4   ii) $\frac{12}{13}$ iii) $\frac{5}{13}$
   b) i) $\frac{15}{17}$ ii) $\frac{8}{15}$ iii) $\frac{8}{17}$
   c) i) $\dfrac{1}{\sqrt{3}}$ ii) $\dfrac{1}{2}$ iii) $\dfrac{\sqrt{3}}{2}$
   d) i) $\frac{3}{4}$ ii) $\frac{3}{5}$

5. a) $\dfrac{1}{2}$ b) $-\dfrac{1}{\sqrt{3}}$ c) $-\dfrac{1}{2}$

d) -1 e) $-\sqrt{3}$ f) $-\dfrac{\sqrt{3}}{2}$

g) $-\dfrac{1}{\sqrt{2}}$ h) $\sqrt{3}$ i) $-\dfrac{\sqrt{3}}{2}$

j) $-\dfrac{1}{2}$

6. a) i) $31.6°$ ii) $9.54\,\text{cm}$
b) i) $27.3\,\text{m}$ ii) $38°$ iii) $17.9\,\text{m}$
c) $d = 6.43\,\text{cm}, f = 10.2\,\text{cm}$
d) i) $29.9°$ ii) $93.8°$ iii) $56.3°$
e) i) $8.28\,\text{cm}$ ii) $117°$

7. a) $4.73\,\text{cm}^2$ b) $19.9\,\text{cm}^2$ c) $3.20\,\text{m}^2$
d) $10.8\,\text{cm}^2$

8. a) i) $7.2\,\text{cm}$ ii) $8.9\,\text{cm}$
iii) $10.8\,\text{cm}$
b) i) $29.1°$ ii) $68.2°$

9. a)  b)   c)
170°   290°   20°

d)   e) 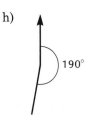 f)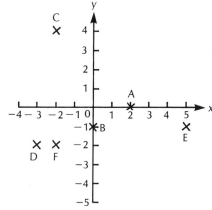
350°   255°

g) 100° h) 190°

10. a) $6.25\,\text{cm}$ b) $297.5°$

11. a) $69.4°$ b) $63.4°$

12. $2.81\,\text{km}, 26.9\,\text{km}$

298

13. CIRCLES

1. a) $31.4\,\text{cm}$ b) $18.8\,\text{cm}$ c) $44\,\text{m}$
d) $66\,\text{cm}$ e) $62.8\,\text{cm}$

2. a) $78.5\,\text{cm}^2$ b) $28.3\,\text{cm}^2$ c) $154\,\text{m}^2$
d) 346 or $347\,\text{cm}^2$ e) $314\,\text{cm}^2$

3. a) $15.7\,\text{cm}$
b) $14.1\,\text{cm}^2$
c) i) $4.71\,\text{cm}^2$ ii) $9.14\,\text{cm}$
d) $30.9\,\text{cm}, 52.3\,\text{cm}^2$
e) $9.42\,\text{m}^2$

4. a) $125.7\,\text{cm}^2\ (40\pi)$ b) $3.77\,\text{cm}^2\ (1.2\pi)$
c) $37.7\,\text{m}^2\ (12\pi)$ d) $20\pi\,\text{cm}^2$
e) $80\pi\,\text{cm}^2$

14. GRAPHS

1.

2. a) 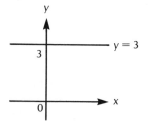 b)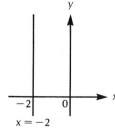
$y = 3$ $x = -2$

c) 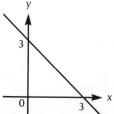 d)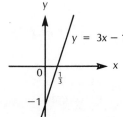
$x + y = 3$ $y = 3x - 1$

e)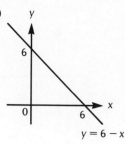
$y = 6 - x$

f)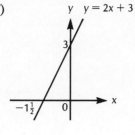
$y = 2x + 3$

g)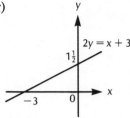
$2y = x + 3$

h)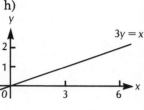
$3y = x$

i)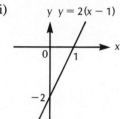
$y = 2(x - 1)$

j)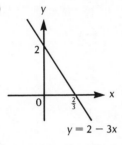
$y = 2 - 3x$

3.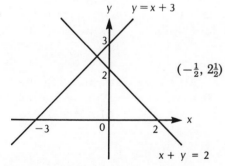
$y = x + 3$
$x + y = 2$
$(-\frac{1}{2}, 2\frac{1}{2})$

4. a)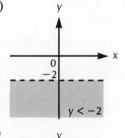
$y < -2$

b)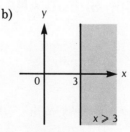
$x \geqslant 3$

c)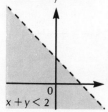
$x + y < 2$

d)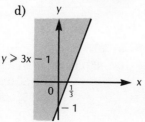
$y \geqslant 3x - 1$

e)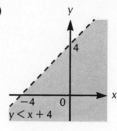
$y < x + 4$

f)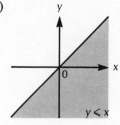
$y < x$

g)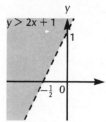
$y > 2x + 1$

h)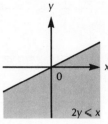
$2y < x$

i)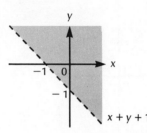
$x + y + 1 > 0$

j)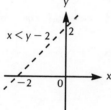
$x < y - 2$

5. a) $8x + 10y$ b) $12x + 4y$
c) $8x + 10y \leqslant 120$,
$12x + 4y \leqslant 96$
e) £18, $x = 5$, $y = 8$ or $x = 6$, $y = 6$

6. a) $8x + 5y \leqslant 40$, $6x + 9y \leqslant 36$
b)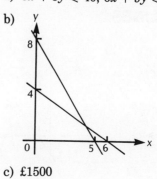

c) £1500

299

7. f(x) = 20 12 6 2 0 0 2
  a) 2 or 3   b) 4 or 1

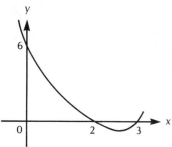

8. y = 6 0 −4 −6 −6 −4 0 6
  a) −4 or 1   b) −3.3 or 0.3

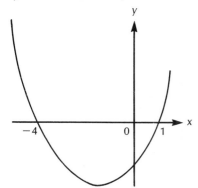

9. a) $71\frac{2}{3}$ b) 78

10.

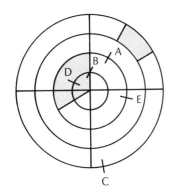

11. a) i) 18 DM   ii) £7.10   iii) 22.5 DM
    b) i) 24 DM   ii) £5.30   iii) 30 DM

15. STRAIGHT LINES

1. a)

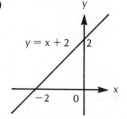

b)

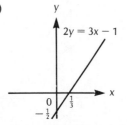

c)

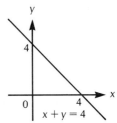

d)

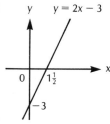

e)

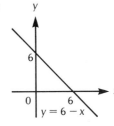

2. a) 4   b) $\frac{4}{5}$ c) −3
    d) $-\frac{6}{5}$ e) 1   f) $-\frac{1}{2}$
    g) $-\frac{1}{6}$ h) 0

3. a) 7, −4   b) 2, 3   c) 2, $\frac{3}{2}$
    d) −2, 4   e) $-\frac{3}{2}, -\frac{5}{2}$ f) 0, 6
    g) −1, 9   h) $\frac{2}{5}, \frac{3}{5}$ i) $\frac{2}{3}$, 0
    j) 1, −4

4. a) y = 2x + 3   b) 4y + 3x + 8 = 0
    c) 2y + x = 10   d) 2y = 12x + 1
    e) 6y = 2x − 1   f) y = 3x − 3
    g) 2y = 5x + 3   h) 8y = 5x − 18

5. a) y = 4x − 7   b) 2y + x = 3
    c) y = x + 8   d) 3y + 2x = 0
    e) 4y = 3x + 2   f) 6y = 5x + 32
    g) y = x   h) x = −2

16. SPEED AND DISTANCE

1. a) 49.5 mph   b) 4.5 h   c) 24 cm
    d) 10 min   e) 6 cm   f) 20 km/s

2. a) 43.75 km/h   b) $33\frac{1}{3}$ mph   c) $91\frac{2}{3}$ km/h
    d) $\frac{1}{3}$ cm/s

3. a) $10\,\text{mh}^{-1}$ b) 150 km
    c) 490 cm,   i) 8 cm/s²
          ii) 20 cm/s²
          iii) $6\frac{2}{3}$ cm/s²

d)

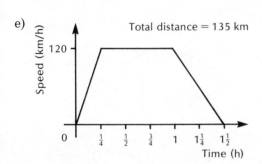

e)

Total distance = 135 km

(Speed (km/h) vs Time (h) graph: rises to 120, stays at 120 from ¼ to 1, then falls to 0 at 1½)

17. VARIATION

1. a) $y = \frac{1}{4}x$ b) $y = 12x$ c) $y = 3x^2$
d) $y = 4x$ e) $y = 3x^3$ f) $y = \frac{1}{2}x$
g) $y = 5x$ h) $y = \frac{2}{3}x$

2. a) $y = \dfrac{6}{x}$ b) $y = \dfrac{5}{x}$ c) $y = \dfrac{24}{x}$
d) $y = \dfrac{1}{x}$ e) $y = \dfrac{2}{x}$ f) $y = \dfrac{1}{x}$
g) $y = \dfrac{1}{8x}$ h) $y = \dfrac{9}{x}$

3. a) 18   b) 3
c) 2   d) 72
e) Multiplied by 4

4. a) 3   b) $x = \frac{36}{15}$ c) $\frac{3}{2}$

18. STATISTICS

1. a) i) 3   ii) 2   iii) $4\frac{1}{3}$
b) i) 82   ii) 82   iii) 83
c) i) 17.2   ii) 17.2   iii) 17.3
d) i) 1043.5   ii) 1040   iii) 1044
e) i) 100   ii) none   iii) 100

2. a) $\dfrac{1\ 2\ 3\ 4\ 5\ 6\ 7\ 8}{4\ 2\ 3\ 4\ 3\ 2\ 0\ 2}$

i) 1 and 4   ii) 4   iii) 3.8

b) $\dfrac{0\ \ 1\ \ 2\ 3\ 4\ 5}{7\ 11\ 7\ 5\ 6\ 4}$

i) 1   ii) 2   iii) 2.1

c) $\dfrac{50\ 51\ 52\ 53\ 54\ 55}{5\ \ \ 5\ \ \ 3\ \ \ 5\ \ \ 4\ \ \ 3}$

i) 50, 51 and 53   ii) 52   iii) 52.3

3.

Age	Frequency
1	6
2	7
3	7
4	8
5	2

a) 4 years   b) 3 years
c) $2\frac{23}{30}$ years per child

4. a) $1\frac{1}{2}$ b) 70 children   c) 1.82 per child

5.

Mark	Frequency
0–10	2
11–20	6
21–30	17
31–40	15
41–50	9
51–60	14
61–70	11
71–80	10
81–90	7
91–100	9

mean = 51.89

6. a) 29.4 years   c) 28 years

7. b) 9640 spectators per match
d) i) 10 000   ii) 5300

8. a)

Score	1	2	3	4	5	6
Angle	30°	50°	100°	40°	80°	60°

b)

Rent	Food	Ent.	Others
90°	45°	60°	165°

9. a) c b)

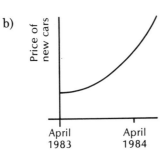

April 1983   April 1984

e)

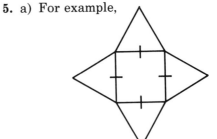

19. GEOMETRY

1. a) $d = 23°$
   b) $g = 154°$
   c) $122°$
   d) $m = p = t = 117°,\ q = n = 63°$
   e) $a = 109°,\ b = 71°,\ c = 38°,\ d = 109°$
   f) $l = 37°,\ f = 65°,\ k = 78°,\ w = 78°,\ t = 65°$
   g) $x = 63°,\ z = 43°,\ y = 47°$
   h) $a = b = 63°,\ c = 54°$
   i) $g = 105°$
   j) $w = 44°,\ z = 68°,\ y = 68°,\ x = 68°$

5. a) For example,

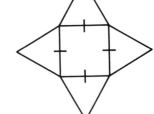

2. a) $540°$ b) $135°$ c) $360°$
   d) $25\frac{5}{7}°$ e) $162°$

b)

3. a) $8.06\,\text{cm}$ b) $10.9\,\text{m}$ c) $7.85\,\text{cm}$
   d) $15.9\,\text{m}$ e) $93.8\,\text{m}$

c)

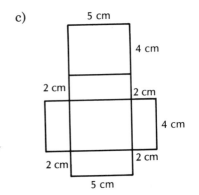

5 cm

4 cm

2 cm   2 cm

4 cm

2 cm   2 cm

5 cm

4. a)

b)

c)

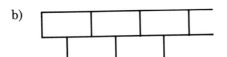

6. There are eleven different nets.

7. a) 6, 12, 8   b) 5, 8, 5   c) 8, 18, 12
   d) 20, 30, 12   e) 12, 30, 20

d)

8. a) 4   b) 20
   c) octagonal prism

20. CIRCLE GEOMETRY

1. $17°$ 2. $24°$
3. $a = 24°$, $b = 36°$, $c = 70°$
4. a) $90°$ b) $32°$ c) $90°$ d) $73°$
5. $27°$, $78°$, $75°$
6. $f = 96°$, $g = 37°$, $h = 72°$
7. $a = 122°$, $b = 119°$ 8. $5\,\text{cm}$
9. $24\,\text{cm}$ 10. $4\,\text{cm}$
11. $6\,\text{cm}$ 12. $7\,\text{m}$

21. CONSTRUCTIONS

2. $40°$, $125°$, $310°$, $25°$, $112°$, $43°$, $131°$, $126°$, $225°$

3. a) $75°$
   b) $DE = 4.1\,\text{cm}$, $DF = 7.4\,\text{cm}$
   c) $87°$
   d) $4.3\,\text{cm}$
   e) $RQ = 47\,\text{mm}$, $PR = 38\,\text{mm}$

22. LOCI

1.
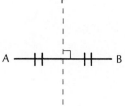

2.
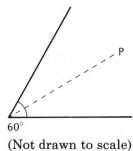

(Not drawn to scale)

3.
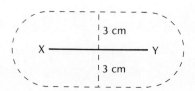

4.

5.
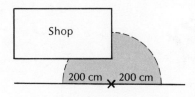

6.
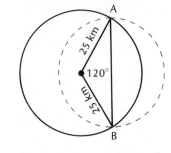

Except A & B
$AB = 43.3\,\text{km}$

7. Sphere (AB a diameter)

8. Cone (vertex at C)   9. Cylinder

23. SYMMETRY

1. a)   b)
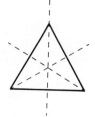 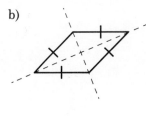

c)   d)
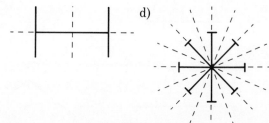

e)   f)
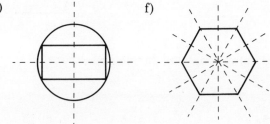

2. a)    b)

c)

d)

e)

f)

3. a) 2   b) 1   c) 4
d) 3   e) 2   f) 4

4. a) For example,   b)

c)   d)

e) not possible in two dimensions

5. a) 4   b) 4   c) 13

---

24. MATRICES

1. a) 1×3 b) 2×2 c) 2×3
d) 3×1 e) 2×2 f) 3×4

2. a) $\begin{pmatrix} 8 & 5 \\ 8 & 9 \end{pmatrix}$ b) $\begin{pmatrix} 7 \\ 7 \end{pmatrix}$

c) $(7 \; -5)$ d) $\begin{pmatrix} 1 & 3 & 2 \\ 0 & 2 & 2 \end{pmatrix}$

e) impossible   f) $\begin{pmatrix} 1 & -4 \\ 2 & 7 \end{pmatrix}$

g) $\begin{pmatrix} 5 & 3 \\ 4 & -5 \end{pmatrix}$ h) $\begin{pmatrix} -2 & 1 & -3 \\ 4 & 14 & 46 \\ -1 & 0 & 9 \end{pmatrix}$

3. a) $\begin{pmatrix} 11 & 16 \\ 16 & 28 \end{pmatrix}$ b) $\begin{pmatrix} -2 & -6 \\ 4 & 12 \end{pmatrix}$

c) (10) d) $\begin{pmatrix} 13 & 5 & 6 \\ 26 & 12 & 4 \end{pmatrix}$

e) $\begin{pmatrix} 2 & 10 \\ 3 & 9 \end{pmatrix}$ f) $\begin{pmatrix} -1 & 0 \\ 9 & 12 \end{pmatrix}$

g) $\begin{pmatrix} 16 & 9 \\ 15 & 19 \end{pmatrix}$ h) impossible

i) impossible   j) impossible

k) $\begin{pmatrix} 4 & 10 \\ 13 & 8 \end{pmatrix}$ l) $\begin{pmatrix} 1 & 5 \\ 3 & 1 \end{pmatrix}$

4. a) 4   b) 40   c) 5
d) -18 e) -10 f) -1

5. a) $\dfrac{1}{7}\begin{pmatrix} 5 & -4 \\ -2 & 3 \end{pmatrix}$ b) $\dfrac{1}{3}\begin{pmatrix} 5 & -2 \\ -1 & 1 \end{pmatrix}$ c) $\dfrac{1}{4}\begin{pmatrix} 5 & 3 \\ 2 & 2 \end{pmatrix}$

d) $\begin{pmatrix} -1 & 0 \\ 0 & -1 \end{pmatrix}$ e) $\dfrac{1}{25}\begin{pmatrix} 5 & 0 \\ 0 & 5 \end{pmatrix}$ f) $\dfrac{1}{3}\begin{pmatrix} 0 & -3 \\ 1 & -4 \end{pmatrix}$

6. a) $(2 \; 7)$ b) $\begin{pmatrix} 6 & 2 \\ 9 & 1 \end{pmatrix}$ c) $\begin{pmatrix} 4 & -1 \\ 2 & 3 \\ 6 & 4 \end{pmatrix}$

d) $\begin{pmatrix} 8 \\ 2 \\ 7 \\ -1 \end{pmatrix}$ e) $\begin{pmatrix} 0 & 3 \\ 3 & 0 \end{pmatrix}$ f) $\begin{pmatrix} 2 & -1 & 3 \\ -3 & 0 & -4 \end{pmatrix}$

7. a) 1, 2, 3
b) 5, 7, 4 or 3, 5, 4
c) 4, 7, 5
d) 8, 11, 5 or 4, 7, 5
e) 8, 13, 7
f) 7, 12, 7
g) 10, 16, 8
h) 6, 7, 3

8. a) $\begin{pmatrix} 0 & 1 & 1 & 0 \\ 1 & 0 & 2 & 0 \\ 1 & 2 & 0 & 2 \\ 0 & 0 & 2 & 0 \end{pmatrix}$
b) $\begin{pmatrix} 2 & 2 & 2 & 2 \\ 2 & 5 & 1 & 4 \\ 2 & 1 & 9 & 0 \\ 2 & 4 & 0 & 4 \end{pmatrix}$
c) 42

9. a) i) $\begin{pmatrix} 0 & 1 & 1 \\ 2 & 0 & 1 \\ 1 & 0 & 2 \end{pmatrix}$
ii) $\begin{pmatrix} 3 & 0 & 3 \\ 1 & 2 & 4 \\ 2 & 1 & 5 \end{pmatrix}$
iii) 21

b) i) $\begin{pmatrix} 0 & 3 & 0 \\ 3 & 0 & 0 \\ 1 & 0 & 0 \end{pmatrix}$
ii) $\begin{pmatrix} 9 & 0 & 0 \\ 0 & 9 & 0 \\ 0 & 3 & 0 \end{pmatrix}$
iii) 21

c) i) $\begin{pmatrix} 0 & 1 & 2 \\ 1 & 2 & 0 \\ 2 & 1 & 1 \end{pmatrix}$
ii) $\begin{pmatrix} 5 & 4 & 2 \\ 2 & 5 & 2 \\ 3 & 5 & 5 \end{pmatrix}$
iii) 33

10. *Answers will vary with the labelling of the diagram.*

a)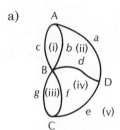

i)

	i	ii	iii	iv	v
A	1	1	0	0	1
B	1	1	1	1	1
C	0	0	1	1	1
D	0	1	0	1	1

ii)

	A	B	C	D
a	1	0	0	1
b	1	1	0	0
c	1	1	0	0
d	0	1	0	1
e	0	0	1	1
f	0	1	1	0
g	0	1	1	0

iii)

	i	ii	iii	iv	v
a	0	1	0	0	1
b	1	1	0	0	0
c	1	0	0	0	1
d	0	1	0	1	0
e	0	0	0	1	1
f	0	0	1	1	0
g	0	0	1	0	1

b)

i)

	A	B	C	D	E
i	1	0	0	1	1
ii	1	1	0	0	1
iii	0	1	1	0	1
iv	0	0	1	1	1
v	1	1	1	1	0

ii)

	i	ii	iii	iv	v
a	1	0	0	0	1
b	0	1	0	0	1
c	1	1	0	0	0
d	1	0	0	1	0
e	0	0	0	1	1
f	0	1	1	0	0
g	0	0	1	1	0
h	0	0	1	0	1

iii)

	a	b	c	d	e	f	g	h
A	1	1	1	0	0	0	0	0
B	0	1	0	0	0	1	0	1
C	0	0	0	0	1	0	1	1
D	1	0	0	1	1	0	0	0
E	0	0	1	1	0	1	1	0

11. a) $\begin{pmatrix} 2 & 2 & 4 & 4 \\ -1 & -4 & -4 & -1 \end{pmatrix}$

c) Rotation of $+90°$ about $(0, 0)$

d) $\begin{pmatrix} 0 & -1 \\ 1 & 0 \end{pmatrix}$

12. b) $\begin{pmatrix} 3 & 2 & 7 & 5 \\ -5 & -3 & -3 & -5 \end{pmatrix}$

c) $\begin{pmatrix} -3 & -2 & -7 & -5 \\ 5 & 3 & 3 & 5 \end{pmatrix}$

d) $\begin{pmatrix} 5 & 3 & 3 & 5 \\ 3 & 2 & 7 & 5 \end{pmatrix}$

13. a) $\begin{pmatrix} -1 & -6 & -2 \\ -1 & -2 & -4 \end{pmatrix}$

b) $\begin{pmatrix} -1 & 0 \\ 0 & -1 \end{pmatrix}$

d) Rotation of $+90°$ about $(0, 0)$

25. TRANSFORMATIONS

1.

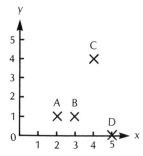

a) $\begin{pmatrix} 1 \\ 3 \end{pmatrix}$

b) $\begin{pmatrix} -3 \\ 1 \end{pmatrix}$

c) $\begin{pmatrix} 1 \\ 0 \end{pmatrix}$

d) $\begin{pmatrix} 1 \\ -4 \end{pmatrix}$

e) $\begin{pmatrix} -2 \\ -3 \end{pmatrix}$

2.

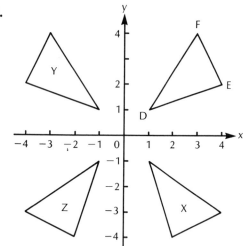

3. a) $x = 2$ b) $y = x$

4. a)

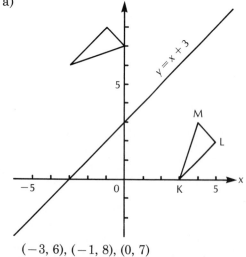

$(-3, 6), (-1, 8), (0, 7)$

b) $(0, -3), (-2, -5), (-3, -4)$

5.

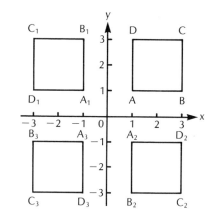

6. (Not drawn to scale)

a)

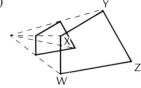

b)

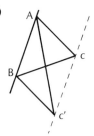

c)

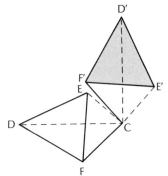

d)

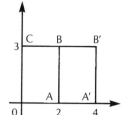

e)

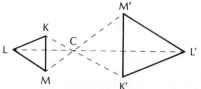

f) $80°$

g) on the perpendicular bisector of DD′, etc.

7. a) $24\,\text{cm}^2$ b) $7\tfrac{1}{2}\,\text{cm}^2$ c) 140

8. a) i) $\begin{pmatrix} 4 & 10 \\ 6 & 16 \end{pmatrix}$ ii) $\dfrac{1}{4}\begin{pmatrix} 16 & -10 \\ -6 & 4 \end{pmatrix}$

b) $\dfrac{1}{3}\begin{pmatrix} 1 & -1 \\ 2 & 1 \end{pmatrix}$

c) i) $\dfrac{1}{4}\begin{pmatrix} 0 & -2 \\ 2 & 0 \end{pmatrix}$ ii) $\dfrac{1}{4}\begin{pmatrix} 0 & -2 \\ 2 & 0 \end{pmatrix}$

iii) Rotation of $+90°$ about $(0, 0)$ and enlargement scale factor of $\tfrac{1}{2}$.

26. VECTORS

1. a) $\begin{pmatrix} -4 \\ -1 \end{pmatrix}$ b) $\begin{pmatrix} 6 \\ 3 \end{pmatrix}$ c) $\begin{pmatrix} 2 \\ 0 \end{pmatrix}$

d) $\begin{pmatrix} 1 \\ -5 \end{pmatrix}$ e) $\begin{pmatrix} -1 \\ 5 \end{pmatrix}$ f) $\begin{pmatrix} 3 \\ -3 \end{pmatrix}$

g) $\begin{pmatrix} -1 \\ -6 \end{pmatrix}$ h) $\begin{pmatrix} 0 \\ 0 \end{pmatrix}$

2. a) 5 b) 10 c) 13
d) 3.60 e) 7.21

3. a) $45°$ b) $36.9°$ c) $135°$
d) $341.6°$ e) $198.4°$

4. a) yes $AB = 3CD$ b) yes $XY = 2PQ$
c) no d) yes $ST = \tfrac{1}{8}MN$
e) yes $CD = \tfrac{1}{2}FE$ (but they are opposite in direction)

5. a) $\mathbf{r} - \mathbf{k} - \mathbf{f}$ b) $2\mathbf{b} + \mathbf{a}$
c) i) $-\mathbf{a} + 5\mathbf{b}$ ii) $-5\mathbf{b} + 3\mathbf{a}$ iii) $-3\mathbf{b} + 3\mathbf{a}$
d) $\mathbf{a} + \mathbf{t} + \mathbf{b}, \mathbf{a} + 3\mathbf{y}, 3\mathbf{x} + \mathbf{b}, \mathbf{x} + 2\mathbf{y}$

6. a) $\mathbf{x} + \mathbf{b}$ b) $\mathbf{x} + \mathbf{b} - \mathbf{a}$ c) $\mathbf{a} - \mathbf{x}$
d) $\mathbf{a} + \mathbf{b}$ e) $-\tfrac{1}{2}\mathbf{b} + \mathbf{a} - \mathbf{x}$

7. a) $2\mathbf{a} + 4\mathbf{b}, 2\mathbf{a} + 2\mathbf{b}, -4\mathbf{b} + 2\mathbf{a}, -4\mathbf{b} + \mathbf{a}$
b) $\overrightarrow{AC} = 2\mathbf{a} + 4\mathbf{b}, \overrightarrow{MN} = \mathbf{a} + 2\mathbf{b}$
AC is parallel to MN and twice its length

8. $-\mathbf{b} + \mathbf{a}, -\mathbf{a} + 3\mathbf{b}, -\tfrac{1}{2}\mathbf{a} + 3\mathbf{b}, -\tfrac{1}{2}\mathbf{a} + \mathbf{b}$

9. a) $2\mathbf{a}$ b) $2\mathbf{b} + \mathbf{a}$ c) $-3\mathbf{b} + \mathbf{a}$
d) $\mathbf{a} + 3\mathbf{b}$ e) $-5\mathbf{b}$

27. PROBABILITY

1. a) $\tfrac{1}{2}$ b) $\tfrac{3}{5}$ c) $\tfrac{4}{7}$
d) $\tfrac{7}{16}$ e) $\tfrac{63}{240} = \tfrac{21}{80}$ f) $\tfrac{16}{52} = \tfrac{4}{13}$
g) $\tfrac{2}{6} = \tfrac{1}{3}$ h) $\tfrac{1}{12}$ i) $\tfrac{1}{36}$
j) $\tfrac{1}{8}$ k) $\tfrac{3}{36} = \tfrac{1}{12}$ l) $\tfrac{18}{42} = \tfrac{3}{7}$

2. $\tfrac{54}{110}$

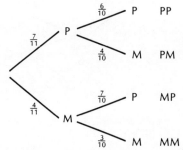

3. $\tfrac{4}{10}$

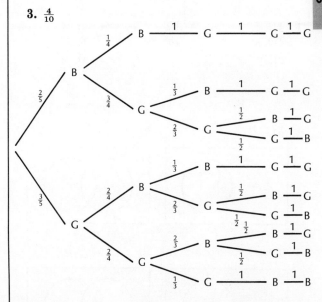

4.

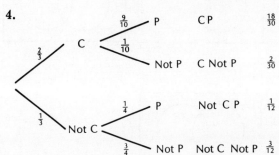

5. a) $\frac{54}{125}$

b) $\frac{27}{125}$

c) $\frac{44}{125}$

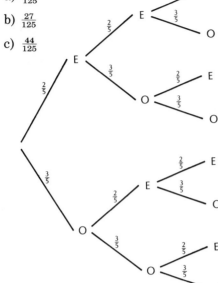

28. SETS

1. a) $\subset$ b) $\in$ c) $\not\subset$

d) $\cup$ e) $\cap$ f) $\notin$

g) $\subset$ h) $\cap$ i) $\varnothing$

j) $\cap$

2. a)   b)

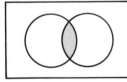 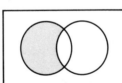

c)   d)

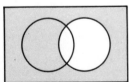 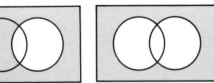

e)

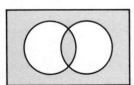

3. a) $A \cap B \cap C$

b) $A \cap C$

c) C

d) $A' \cap B \cap C'$

e) $A \cap B \cap C'$

f) $(A \cap B \cap C') \cup (A' \cap B \cap C)$

g) $(A \cup B \cup C)'$

h) $A \cup B$

4. a) $\{c, f, g, h, p\}$

b) $\{c, n\}$

c) $\{a, b, c, f, g, h, n, p\}$

d) $\{d\}$

e) $\{c, f, p\}$

f) $\{e, g, h, k, m, n\}$

g) $\{c, f, n, p\}$

h) $\{c\}$

i) $\{a, b, d, e, f, g, h, k, m, n, p\}$

j) $\{a, b, d, g, h\}$

5. a) 32   b) 7   c) 3

d) 11   e) 1   f) 8

g) 12   h) 8   i) 20

j) 2

6. a)

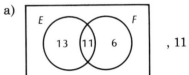 , 11

b)

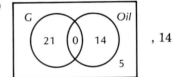 , 14

c)

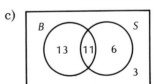 , 33

d)

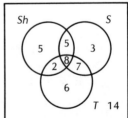 , 7

e)

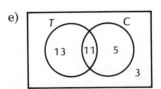 , 11

7. a)

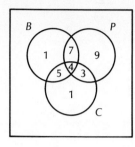

b)

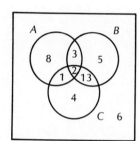

$n(C) = 13$

8.

$n(A' \cap B \cap C') = 5$

29. RELATIONS, MAPPINGS AND FUNCTIONS

1. a) $2 \longrightarrow 3$
$3 \longrightarrow 4$
$4 \longrightarrow 5$
$5 \longrightarrow 6$

b) $2 \longrightarrow 1$
$4 \longrightarrow 2$
$6 \longrightarrow 3$
$8 \longrightarrow 4$

c) $13 \longrightarrow 11$
$14 \longrightarrow 12$
$15 \longrightarrow 13$
$16 \longrightarrow 14$
$17 \longrightarrow 15$

d) $-2 \qquad 0$
$-1 \qquad 1$
$0 \qquad 2$
$1 \qquad 3$
$2 \longrightarrow 4$

e) $2 \qquad 8$
$3 \qquad 9$
$4 \qquad 10$
$5 \qquad 11$
$\qquad 12$

f) $1 \longrightarrow 4$
$2 \longrightarrow 6$
$3 \longrightarrow 8$
$4 \longrightarrow 10$

g) $15 \longrightarrow 4$
$8 \longrightarrow 3$
$3 \longrightarrow 2$

h) $1 \longrightarrow 2$
$3 \longrightarrow 8$
$5 \longrightarrow 14$
$10 \longrightarrow 29$

i) $3 \longrightarrow 2$
$2 \longrightarrow 3$
$1 \longrightarrow 4$
$0 \longrightarrow 5$
$-1 \longrightarrow 6$

j) $-2 \longrightarrow -10$
$-1 \longrightarrow -5$
$0 \longrightarrow 0$
$1 \longrightarrow 5$
$2 \longrightarrow 10$

k) $-2 \longrightarrow -4$
$-\frac{1}{2} \longrightarrow -1$
$2 \longrightarrow 4$
$16 \longrightarrow 32$

l) $4 \longrightarrow 3$
$3 \longrightarrow 4$
$2 \longrightarrow 6$
$1 \longrightarrow 12$
$-1 \longrightarrow -12$
$-2 \longrightarrow -6$

2. a) $\{4, 2, 0, -2, -4\}$ b) $\{-1, 1, 3, 5\}$

3. a) i) 5   ii) -1 iii) -7
b) i) $\frac{2}{3}$ ii) -2 iii) 14
c) i) 3   ii) 10   iii) 12
d) i) 2   ii) 36   iii) 1
e) i) 42   ii) $(y + 3)(y + 2)$ iii) 90
f) i) 8   ii) 8   iii) $4a^2 - 1$
g) i) 3   ii) -3 iii) $\frac{3(2 + t)}{4}$
h) i) 1   ii) $-\frac{1}{9}$ iii) $-\frac{1}{9}$
i) i) $\frac{2}{7}$ ii) -2 iii) $\frac{2}{43}$
j) i) 8   ii) 72   iii) $18y^2$

4. a) $x + 2$ b) $\dfrac{x}{6}$ c) $\dfrac{x + 1}{3}$

d) $\dfrac{1}{x}$ e) $\dfrac{1}{3}\left(\dfrac{x}{2} - 4\right)$ f) $3 - x$

g) $\dfrac{3}{2}(x - 1)$ h) $3x - 2$ i) $\dfrac{1}{2 - x}$

j) $\frac{1}{2}(3 - 4x)$ k) $\sqrt{x} - 1$ l) $\dfrac{1}{2}\left(4 - \dfrac{x}{3}\right)$

5. a) i) 5   ii) 8   iii) 14
b) i) 6   ii) -2 iii) 14
c) i) 14   ii) 11.5   iii) $\frac{1}{2}(9a - 1)$
d) i) $\frac{1}{11}$ ii) $\frac{1}{4}$ iii) 1
e) i) 3   ii) 0   iii) 1

6. a) i) $2(x + 3)$ ii) $2x + 3$ iii) $x + 6$
iv) $4x$
b) i) $(x - 1)^2$ ii) x^4 iii) $x^2 - 1$
c) i) $x - 4$ ii) $\dfrac{3x}{2}$ iii) $2(3x - 2)$
iv) $9x$ v) $4x - 12$ vi) $6(x - 2)$
d) i) $\dfrac{2}{1 - x}$ ii) $1 - \dfrac{2}{x}$ iii) x
iv) x

7. a)

x	-2	-1	0	1	2	3	4
y	$\frac{1}{25}$	$\frac{1}{5}$	1	5	25	125	625

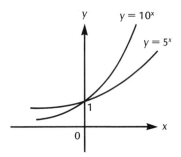

b)

x	-2	-1	0	1	2	3	4
y	$\frac{1}{100}$	$\frac{1}{10}$	1	10	100	1000	10 000

30. FLOW CHARTS

1.

A	B	C	D	E
2	3	4	7	14
3	4	5	9	27
4	5	6	11	44
5	6	7	13	65

2. 45

3. 128

4. 7, 7.2, 7.4, 7.6

SECTION IV

'The Southern Regional Examinations Board accept no responsibility whatever for the accuracy of method or working in the answers given'.

1. ALGEBRA

1. a) 0   b) 2

2. a) 8   b) 5 or -5
    c) 1 or -4 d) $x \leqslant -1$

3. a) $x \geqslant -1$ b) $x + y \leqslant 3$

4. a) 2   b) $(3x + 2)(x - 3)$

5. $x = 3, y = -1$

6. a) $1\frac{1}{4}$ b) $\dfrac{3k - 7}{k}$

7. a) 14
   b) i) $(x - 1)(x + 4)$
   c) 1, -4

8. a) $2x - 4$ b) $5x - 7$ c) 8

9. a) $x(x + 2)$
   b) i) $(x + 3), (x + 1)$ ii) $(x + 3)(x + 1)$
   c) i) $7\,m^2$ ii) £52.50

10. a) $3x + 2y = 24$ and $2x + 3y = 31$
    b) $8\,p$

11. a)   i) $3x + 1$ ii) $x - 3$ iii) $x + 1$
       iv) $x + 3$ v) $x + 3$
   b) i) $4x$ ii) x^2
   c) $(x + 2)(x - 1)$
   d) $x = 2$

2.–5. NUMBER

1. a) i) 4321   ii) 1243   iii) 4312
   b) 6

2. a) 45.678
   b) i) 627.06   ii) 630

3. 81 p

4. a) 0.14   b) 30   c) $\frac{17}{20}$ d) $\frac{2}{3}$

5. a) 5.84×10^5 b) 498 000

6. a) 2   b) 0   c) -2

7. 1.16×10^2

8. a) £100
   b) i) 8 hours   ii) £130

9. a) 17   b) 9

10. £43.92

11. a) 28   b) 3   c) 21   d) 3, 6, 15

12. a) 3   b) 4   c) 4

13. a) $\frac{11}{12}$ b) $1\frac{2}{7}$

14. a) 24, 35
   b) 36, 49
   c) 28
   d) i) $2S$ ii) $7S$ iii) $28S$ or S^2
   e) 28 or S

6.–9. PERCENTAGES

1. a) $\frac{2}{5}$ b) 4%

2. a) £150, £200   b) £128

3. a) £1.04   b) 25%

4. 18 ml

5. a) i) £28.75   ii) £257.40   iii) £286.15
   b) i) £46   ii) £276   iii) £23
   c) £30
   d) £28.50

6. a) £500   b) 4%

7. a) i) £1 154 760   ii) £180.80   iii) £195
      iv) 65%
   b) i) £9000   ii) £3690   iii) £2790
      iv) 41%

8. a) £400, £600
   b) £27
   c) i) £29.43   ii) £32.08   iii) £388.51

9. a) £240
   b) 3 : 1
   c) 25%
   d) i) £30   iii) £270
   e) i) £81   ii) £52.65   iii) £403.65
   f) 15%

10. a) 60, 144   b) 86   c) 54
   d) 30° No change

10. AREA AND VOLUME

1. 36 cm   **2.** 125   **3.** 1.3 m^3 **4.** 168 cm^3

5. 3080 cm^3

6. a) 20.14 m   b) 547.1 m^2 c) £984.78
   d) 750 m^3 e) 750 000 kg

7. a) 162 cm^3 b) 60°   c) 5.2 cm
   d) 187.2 cm^2 e) $P = Q$

11. SIMILARITY

1. a) 16 cm   b) 36 cm

2. 80 cm^3 **3.** 4

4. a) 1.5 m   b) 800 m^3 c) 16

5. $\frac{1}{4}$

6. 8 cm

7. a) 1.5 cm^2
   b) i)    ii)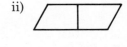
   iii)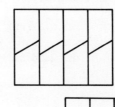
   c)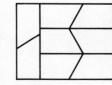

   d) 6
   e) i) 4   ii) 6 cm^2
   f) 72

12. TRIGONOMETRY

1. a) i) $\frac{15}{25} = 0.6$ ii) $36.9°$
   b) $20\,\text{cm}$

2. $36.9°$

3. $5\,\text{cm}$

4. $10.47\,\text{m}$

5. b) $9.17\,\text{cm}$
   c) i) $\frac{2}{5}$ ii) $66.4°$

6. a) $2x + 8$ b) $\dfrac{7x}{2}$ c) $x^2 + 7^2$, $x = 24$

7. a) i) $6\,\text{cm}$ ii) $8\,\text{cm}$
   b) $10\,\text{cm}$
   c) $104\,\text{cm}^2$
   d) $53°$
   e) $4.8\,\text{cm}$

8. a) $9.54\,\text{cm}$ b) $14.3\,\text{cm}^2$

9. a) $45°$ b) $30\,\text{m}$ c) $19.7°$
   d) $10.7\,\text{m}$ e) $26.6°$

10. a) $104°$
   b) i) $3.88\,\text{m}$ ii) $4.12\,\text{m}$ iii) $14\,\text{m}^2$
   c) $140\,\text{m}^3$

13. CIRCLES

1. $60°$

2. a) i) $3\,\text{cm}$ ii) $6\,\text{cm}$ iii) $1296\,\text{cm}^3$
   b) $144\,\text{cm}$
   c) £52.20

3. a) i) $38.5\,\text{cm}^2$ ii) $577.5\,\text{cm}^3$
   b) i) $29\,\text{cm}$ ii) $22\,\text{cm}$ iii) $407\,\text{cm}^2$
   c) i) 16 ii) $2464\,\text{cm}^2$

14.–15. GRAPHS

1. a) $(-3, -2)$ b) $\frac{6}{5}$

2. a) $\frac{1}{2}$ b) 2 c) $y = \frac{1}{2}x + 2$

3. $(2.83, 45°)$

4. $(2, 3)$

5. a) $f(x) = 16, 9, 4, 1, 0, 1, 4, 9, 16$
   c) i) 0.6 ii) $-1.5, 3.5$
   d) $4, -2$

6. a) i) $y = -13, -7, -4, -1, 5$
   c) $(2, 2)$
   d) -4

7. a) $f(x) = -2, 4, 8, 10, 10, 8, 4, -2$
   c) $0.7, 5.7$
   d) i) 10.25 ii) 2.5

8. b) 3 units.

9. b) $24\,\text{m}^2$ c) $3600\,\text{m}^3$ d) $108\,\text{km}\,\text{h}^{-1}$

16.–17. SPEED AND DISTANCE

1. a) $80\,\text{mph}$ b) 25 minutes

2. a) $40\,\text{m}\,\text{s}^{-1}$ b) $2\,\text{m}\,\text{s}^{-2}$ c) $2000\,\text{m}$

3. a) $0.4, 4.8$ b) $27.4\,\text{m}$

4. a)

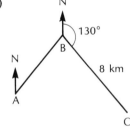

   b) i) 20 minutes   ii) $9.43\,\text{km}$
   c) $58°, 058°$

18. STATISTICS

1. a) i) 7.2 ii) 6.8
   b) 6.9

2. a) i) 25 ii) 6 iii) 5 iv) $5\frac{7}{25}$
   b) $7, 5, 5\frac{9}{25}$

3. a) £165   b) $112°$

4. 6.6

5. a) 42 b) 58 c) 28 d) 30

6. a) 1 b) 4

7. a) $120°$ b) 88

8. a) $30°, 60°, 90°, 80°$
   b) i) 72   ii) 16   c) $13:5$

9. a) 0   b) 25   c) 45
   d) 1.8

19.–22. GEOMETRY

1. a) $44°$ b) $54°$ c) $72°$

2. a) $104°$ b) i) $90°$ ii) $38°$

3. $30°$

4. a) $78°$ b) $102°$

5. $a = 60°, b = 45°$

6. a) i) isosceles   ii) trapezium   iii) $135°$
   b) i) $4.83\,\text{cm}$ ii) $9.66\,\text{cm}^2$ iii) $77.3\,\text{cm}^2$

7. a) $103°$ b) $39°$

8. a) i) pentagon   ii) $120°$ iii) $60°$
    iv) $108°$ v) $540°$
   b) i) 24   ii) $160°$ iii) $1260°$
   c) $2:3$

9. b) $2\frac{1}{10}$ hours   c) 10 n. miles   d) $307°$

10. a) i)

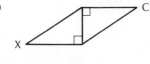 or

    ii)

    iii) 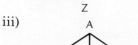   iv)

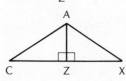 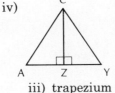

   b) i) $90°$ ii) $4\,\text{cm}$ iii) trapezium
     iv) $3.46\,\text{cm}$ v) $15\,\text{cm}^2$

11. a) square-based pyramid
   b) i) 8   ii) 5
   c) i) $150°$ ii) $15°$
   d) i) $19.32\,\text{cm}$ ii) $273\,\text{cm}^2$

23.–25. MATRICES AND TRANSFORMATIONS

1. 2×3

2.

3. $-9, -6, 4$

4. a) $11, -2$ b) ± 3

5. a) $\begin{pmatrix} 3 & 4 \\ 2 & 3 \end{pmatrix}$ b) 2

6. a) $(5, 4)$
   b) i) $\begin{pmatrix} -4 \\ -3 \end{pmatrix}$ ii) 5

7. a) -2 b) $(1, 3)$

8. a) i) 7   ii) 4   iii) 5
   b) $\begin{pmatrix} 0 & 2 & 1 & 1 \\ 2 & 2 & 1 & 0 \\ 1 & 1 & 0 & 1 \\ 1 & 0 & 1 & 0 \end{pmatrix}$

9. a) reflection in $x = -1$
   b) enlargement centre $(0, -1)$, scale factor 2
   c) translation of $\begin{pmatrix} -5 \\ 3 \end{pmatrix}$

10. a) i) ± 4 ii) $2, -3$
   b) i) $\begin{pmatrix} -2 & -1 & -4 \\ 3 & 6 & 5 \end{pmatrix} \begin{pmatrix} 3 & 6 & 5 \\ 2 & 1 & 4 \end{pmatrix} \begin{pmatrix} 3 & 6 & 5 \\ -2 & -1 & -4 \end{pmatrix}$
    ii) reflection in the y axis, reflection in $y = x$,
     rotation about $(0, 0)$ of $-90°$

11. a) $\begin{pmatrix} 7 & 5 & 9 & 10 & 5 \\ 2 & 1 & 5 & 4 & 2 \end{pmatrix}$
   b) $(8 \quad 7)$
   c) $(70 \ 47 \ 107 \ 108 \ 54)$ Total taken per day
   d) £3.86
   e) i) 36   ii) 14   iii) $\begin{pmatrix} 36 \\ 14 \end{pmatrix}$
   f) 279
   g) £1.07

12. a) ii) trapezium   iii) $3\,\text{cm}^2$

    b) i) $\begin{pmatrix} 1 & 1 & 3 & 3 \\ -1 & -3 & -4 & -3 \end{pmatrix}$

       iii) reflection in x-axis

    c) i) $\begin{pmatrix} -1 & -3 & -4 & -3 \\ 1 & 1 & 3 & 3 \end{pmatrix}$

       ii) rotation about $(0, 0)$ of $+90°$

    d) i) reflection in $y = x$

       ii) $\begin{pmatrix} 0 & 1 \\ 1 & 0 \end{pmatrix}$

13. a) i)

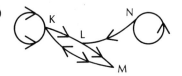

       ii) N to L to M to K   iii) no

    b) i) $\mathbf{P} = \begin{pmatrix} 1 \\ 0 \\ 1 \ 0 \ 1 \ 1 \ 0 \ 0 \\ 1 \end{pmatrix}$

       ii) $\mathbf{Q} = \begin{pmatrix} 1 \\ 1 \\ 1 \\ 0 \\ 1 \ 1 \ 0 \ 0 \\ 0 \ 1 \ 1 \ 0 \end{pmatrix}$

       iii) $\begin{pmatrix} 2 & 2 & 0 & 2 \\ 0 & 2 & 2 & 2 \\ 2 & 0 & 2 & 2 \\ 2 & 2 & 2 & 0 \end{pmatrix}$

       iv) $\mathbf{PQ} = 2\mathbf{R}$
       v) D to A to B to C to D or D to C to B to A
         to D
       vi) D to B to A to C to D, $3\,\text{km}$

26. VECTORS

1. a) $\begin{pmatrix} 1 \\ 7 \end{pmatrix}$ **b)** $\begin{pmatrix} -\frac{1}{2} \\ 2 \end{pmatrix}$ **c)** $\begin{pmatrix} -5 \\ -2 \end{pmatrix}$

2. a) $\mathbf{a}$ **b)** $\mathbf{b} - \mathbf{a}$ **c)** $\mathbf{b} - 2\mathbf{a}$

3. a) $\begin{pmatrix} 3 \\ 2 \end{pmatrix}$ **b)** i) $(6, 7)$ ii) $(2, 3)$

    c) $\sqrt{13}$

4. a) i) $\begin{pmatrix} 2 \\ -1 \end{pmatrix}$ ii) $\sqrt{5}$

    b) $(4, -2)$

5. a) i) $\mathbf{r}$ ii) $-\mathbf{p}$ iii) $\mathbf{p} + \mathbf{r}$

    b) i) $\begin{pmatrix} -1 \\ 5 \end{pmatrix}$ ii) $\sqrt{18}$ iii) $\sqrt{8}$

    c) i) $\frac{1}{2}(\mathbf{p} + \mathbf{r})$ ii) $\frac{1}{2}(\mathbf{r} - \mathbf{p})$

    d) $\sqrt{\frac{13}{2}}$

    e) i) $(-1, 5)$ ii) $(1\frac{1}{2}, 4\frac{1}{2})$

6. a) i) $\mathbf{c}$ ii) $-\mathbf{a}$ iii) $2\mathbf{b} - \mathbf{a} - \mathbf{c}$
       iv) $\mathbf{c} - \mathbf{a}$ v) $\mathbf{c} - \mathbf{a}$ vi) $2\mathbf{b} - \mathbf{a} - \mathbf{c}$

    b) i) AX = CY and AX∥CY
       ii) AC = XY and AC∥XY
       iii) parallelogram

    c) $\mathbf{a} + \mathbf{c} = \mathbf{b}$
    d) $(-1, 1), (4, 6), (1, 4), (5, 5)$.

27. PROBABILITY

1. a) 1   **b)** 0   **c)** $\frac{4}{5}$

2. a) $\frac{1}{2}$ **b)** $\frac{1}{3}$ **c)** $\frac{2}{3}$
    d) $\frac{1}{6}$

3. a) $\frac{47}{200}$ **b)** $\frac{153}{200}$ **c)** 60 p

4. a) i) $\frac{1}{2}$ ii) $\frac{1}{8}$ iii) $\frac{3}{8}$
    b) $\frac{3}{7}$
    c) i) $\frac{3}{14}$ ii) 0   iii) $\frac{19}{28}$
    d) 5
    e) i) $\frac{1}{14}$ ii) 2

5. a) $\frac{2}{3}$
    b) i) $\frac{7}{11}$ ii) $\frac{8}{11}$
    c) $\frac{8}{12}, \frac{7}{11}, \frac{4}{11}, \frac{8}{11}$
    d) i) $\frac{14}{33}$ ii) $\frac{10}{11}$
    e) i) $\frac{14}{55}$ ii) $\frac{1}{55}$
    f) 5
    g) $\frac{1}{4}$

6. a) $\frac{1}{3}$
   b) $\frac{1}{3}, \frac{5}{11}, \frac{3}{11}, \frac{5}{11}, \frac{2}{11}$
   c) i) $\frac{5}{33}$ ii) $\frac{19}{66}$ iii) $\frac{47}{66}$
   d) i) $\frac{1}{22}$ ii) $\frac{3}{44}$

28. SETS

1. 1

2. a) i) 4   ii) {2}   iii) {1, 4, 6}
   iv) {3, 4, 5, 6, 7}

   b)
   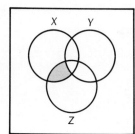

3. a) {4, 6}   b) {1, 3, 5, 7}   c) {2, 4, 6}
   d) {1, 2, 7}   e) {1, 7}

4. a) i) {1, 2, 3, 4, 6, 12}   ii) {2, 3, 5, 7, 11}
   b) 6
   c) i) {2, 3}   ii) prime factors of 12
   d) $2^2 \times 3$
   e) i)
   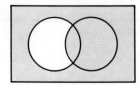

   ii)
   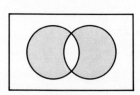

   f) i) {1, 8}   ii) {1, 4, 9}   iii) {1, 3, 6, 10}
   iv) {1}

   g) i) 64   ii) 36

5. a) i) $X \cap Y$ ii) $X \cup Y$ iii) X'
   iv) $X \cap Y'$
   b) i) 57, 0, 6, 33   ii) 3, $n(S')$
   iii) $\frac{19}{20}, \frac{1}{10}$ iv) $\frac{6}{19}$

6. a)
   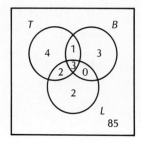

   b) 15
   c) cars with good lights and defective brakes and tyres.
   d) 1
   e) 90%
   f) i) $\frac{7}{100}$ ii) $\frac{17}{20}$
   g) no

29. RELATIONS, MAPPINGS AND FUNCTIONS

1. a)
   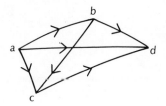

   b) d

2. a) 5   b) $\frac{1}{4}$ c) 11

3. $p = 6, q = 2$

4. a) $3 \rightarrow 5, 4 \rightarrow 7$
   b) i) x^2 ii) $5 - x$

5. a) i) 8   ii) 0
   b) -1 or 3

6. 4, -1

7. female, not known.

8. a) i) $-\frac{1}{2}$ ii) 1
   b) i) 3, 15   ii) 3 or -5 iii) f(x) = 3, 0, 3
   c) i) $-2.85, 0.35$ ii)
   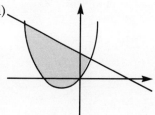

315

9. a) i) 3 ii) 2 iii) 15
b) ± 5
c) -1 or 3
e) i) ± 1.4 ii) $-1.4 < x < 1.4$
iii) $x < -1$ or $x > 3$

30. FLOW CHARTS

1.

S	P	Q	D
20	2	4	6
40	4	16	20
60	6	36	42
80	8	64	72
100	10	100	110
120	12	144	156

2.

x	n
4	1
2	2
1	3

3. a)

I	P	T
10	110	1
11	121	2
12.1	133.1	3
13.3	146.4	4
14.6	161.0	5
16.1	177.1	6
17.7	194.8	7
19.5	214.3	8
21.4	235.7	9
23.6	259.3	10

b) 7 years 3 months

4. a) i) 21, 28 ii) 325
b) i) 16, 25, 36, 49
ii) square numbers

c) i)

1	1	1	6
2	1	2	5
3	2	3	4
5	3	5	3
8	5	8	2
13	8	13	1
21	13	21	0

ii) C

SECTION V

'The University of London School Examinations Board accepts no responsibility whatever for the accuracy of method or working in the answers given'.

1. ALGEBRA

1. $b = \dfrac{(m - y)a}{(m + y)}$

2. a) 0, -4 b) 0.3, -3.7

3. a) $\dfrac{2x - 14}{(x - 5)(3 - x)}$ b) 5.8, 0.2

c)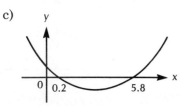

4. a) $k = -2, (x + 2)(x - 1)$
b) 4, 0 or 3, -1

5. a) i) $-1\frac{2}{3}$ ii) 6, -7
iii) $-2, 5$ iv) 2
b) i) $x \geqslant -3$
ii) $x \geqslant 1$ or $x \leqslant -4$

6. $a = 10, b = 60$, 30 minutes, 12 articles, 20 articles

7. a) i) all values of x ii) 2
iii) no values of x iv) 0 or 8
b) $(x - 4)^2$ is always positive, -4

316

8. a) $(-2, -7)$ and $(1, -4)$
b) i) 9   ii) $108\,\text{cm}^2$

9. a) £$\dfrac{320}{x}$ b) £$\dfrac{320}{x - 0.4}$

c) $x = 2$

2.–5. NUMBER

1. a) 7.5×10^1 b) 250 minutes

2. a) 2.99×10^{-23} b) 6×10^{-26} c) 3.3×10^{22}
d) 89%

3. a)

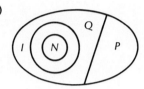

b) i) $\pi \in P$
ii) $3\frac{1}{7} \in Q$
iii) $4 \in I, N, Q$
iv) $-4 \in I, Q$

4. a) 15
b) 6
c) 8
d) 4095
e) Number of moves $= 6.7 \times 10^7$

5. a)

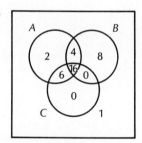

b) i) $\{x : 1 < x < 3\}$
ii) $\{x : x \leqslant 1\}$
iii) $\{x : x > 1 \text{ or } x \leqslant -2\}$
iv) $\{x : 3 < x < 4\}, P \cap Q$

6. a) $\frac{1}{6}$
b) i) $\frac{5}{6}, \frac{4}{6}, \frac{3}{6}$ ii) $\frac{5}{12}, \frac{1}{3}, \frac{1}{4}$
d) left $\frac{3}{8}, \frac{3}{10}, \frac{1}{4}$

6.–9. PERCENTAGE

1. 66 kg   **2.** £80, £84   **3.** 56%

4. a) £413.60   b) £66.40   c) £930.08
d) exceeds by £30

5. a) 10^6 tonnes
b) tin 20 000, zinc 500, tungsten 40 (tonnes)
c) tin 12 000, zinc 300, tungsten 24 (tonnes)
d) 1 200 000 articles
e) tin 312, zinc 12 (tonnes)

6. a) 5960 mm   b) £178.80   c) £208.60
d) £47.25   e) £434.65   f) £43.47
g) £23.91

7. 67.5 units, 42.2%, 30.83 units per hour

$\dfrac{m}{n} = 0.6$, 6 hours

8. £120 000; £720 000; £360 000
a) £6000, £3600, £2400
b) 370
c) £4500, 75%

10. AREA AND VOLUME

1. 90 cm, 70 cm

2. $9\,\text{cm}^3$, $5\,\text{cm}^3$, $7\,\text{cm}^3$, $0.8\,\text{cm}^3$

3. a) $2240\,\text{m}^3$
b) $1640\,\text{m}^3$, $r = 2.12\,\text{cm}$.

4. a) $514.5\,\text{cm}^2$
b) $15\,435\,\text{cm}^3$, $h = 50.5\,\text{cm}$

5. a) $270\,000\,\text{cm}^2$ b) $415\,800\,\text{cm}^3$ c) $3850\,\text{cm}^2$
d) 108 cm, 83

6. 60°
a) $35.8\,\text{cm}^2$ b) $271.6\,\text{cm}^2$ c) 68%
d) $358\,\text{cm}^3$

lengths $\times 2$, area $\times 4$, volume $\times 8$, answer to c) the same

7. a) $66\,\text{cm}^2$ b) $13\,200\,\text{cm}^3$ c) 112.2 kg
d) 15 hours

11. SIMILARITY

1. a) $6:1$ b) $36:1$

2. a) $1:4$ b) 3360 litres

3. 216

4. a) 25%
b) 57.8%, 30.5 g, 9th day

5. a) 85 cm²   b) 16.1 cm   d) 34°

6. $3r$, $r = 1.69$, 22.2 m³

12. TRIGONOMETRY

1. a) 7.21 cm   b) 10.82 cm   c) 56°
d) 55°

2. 12.4 m

3. a) $-\dfrac{b}{a}$ b) $\dfrac{b}{c}$ c) $-\dfrac{a}{c}$

4. 2.26 m, 3.49 m, 0.96 m

5. a) i) 2.94 km   ii) 4.04 km
b) i) 8.29 km   ii) 1.90 km
c) i) 283°   ii) 8.50 km

6. a) 4.5 km   b) 163°   c) 486 ha
    1.4°

7. a) 1.5 m   b) 6.1 m   c) 9.5 m
d) 4.3 m
    63°

8. 5.2 cm
a) 35.3°   b) 45°
    3.35°

9. a) i) 10 m   ii) 25 m
b) i) 8 cm   ii) 62°   iii) 65°

13. CIRCLES

1. 210°

2. a) 32 m   b) 445 m   c) 45 m
d) 3410 m²

3. a) 10 cm
b) 36.9°, Area = 45 cm²

4. a) 17.32 cm²   b) 4.22 cm²

5. $4\pi x^2$, $\dfrac{x^2}{2}(\pi - 2)$, 145 cm

6. a) 25.2 cm   b) 304 cm   c) 13.2%

7. a) 6.93 cm   b) 27.7 cm²   c) 8.38 cm²
d) 2.57 cm²   f) 49.1 cm

14.–15. GRAPHS

1. a) $(13\frac{1}{3}, 3\frac{1}{3})$, (30, 20), (0, 20), (0, 10), $-\frac{1}{2}$
b) $x \geqslant 0$, $y \leqslant 20$, $2y + x \geqslant 20$ and $y \geqslant x - 10$
c) 72

2. a) 3.8, -6 b) 0.2   c) 0.14

3. $\left(\dfrac{20}{11}, \dfrac{18}{11}\right)$

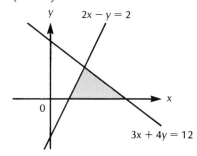

4. a) $(0, -4)$ b) $(-2, 0)$
c) $13\frac{1}{2}$ cm²

5. $y = 4$, $7\frac{1}{2}$, 7, 4, 0, $-3\frac{1}{2}$, -5, -3, 4
a) 1.75
b) $-2 \leqslant x \leqslant -\frac{1}{2}$, $x = 1.9$

6. c) i) $x \geqslant y$ ii) $3.5y \geqslant 1.1x$
e) £4.60

16.–17. SPEED AND DISTANCE

1. a) 0, $\sqrt{3}$ b) 4 m

2. 105 km h^{-1}, 10:19, 109 km h^{-1}

3. a) $\dfrac{5}{x - 6}$

b) $\dfrac{5}{x + 6}$, $1\frac{2}{3}$ h

4. a) Area under the curve above the x-axis
b) 84 m
c) 12 m
d) 2 s

5. a) $\dfrac{63}{t}$ km/h

b) $\dfrac{63}{t-\frac{1}{4}}$ km/h

c) $\dfrac{63}{t} + 6 = \dfrac{63}{t-\frac{1}{4}}$

d) $1\frac{3}{4}$ h

18. STATISTICS

1. $120°, 168°, 72°$

2. a) 20   b) 92   c) 2.51; 27, 7

3. a) 13.5   c) 19   d) 42.5%

4. b) 802   c) $\frac{21}{100}$ d) $\frac{3}{10}$

5. a) 600   b) 42   c) 69.75%
d) 49.5%   e) 86.5%   f) 63.5%

6. a) mean = 17, median = 13.
b) $14\frac{11}{12}$
d) i) $\frac{6}{35}$ ii) $\frac{14}{35}$

19.–22. GEOMETRY

1. On the perpendicular bisector of the line joining the points.

2. $60°, 108°$

3. a) 4 cm   b) 1 : 2

4. $130°, 70°$

5. $35°, 80°, 45°$

6. a) Line passing through the given point and perpendicular to the given line
b) The perpendicular bisector of the perpendicular between the parallel lines
PR = 4.6 cm

7. a) $108°$ b) $36°, 36°, 72°, 72°$
d) 1 cm   e) $2x \sin 18° \approx 0.618x$
g) $x = 1 - x^2$

8.

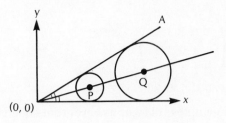

9. d) $(m+n)^2, \frac{1}{2}mn$ e) $\sqrt{7}:1$

10. c) $\frac{4}{3}$ cm^2 d) $\frac{16}{9}$

23.–25. MATRICES AND TRANSFORMATIONS

1. $\begin{pmatrix} 322 & 308 \\ 141 & 132 \\ 86 & 80 \end{pmatrix}$

a) £3.22   b) £1.32   c) 6 p
d) i) £5.20   ii) 34 p/kg

2. b) (0, 3), (4, 7), (1, 7)
d) (3, 3), (15, 3), (9, 6)
f) 1 : 3 : 9

3. a) translation of $\begin{pmatrix} 8 \\ 0 \end{pmatrix}$

b) reflection in the x-axis
c) rotation of $+90°$ about (0, 0)

4. a) (11 14), (14 17)   b) 17, 20
c) 21, 30   d) $\mathbf{M}^2$
e) $\mathbf{M}^{-1}$

5. b) $\begin{pmatrix} -1 & -2 & -4 \\ -1 & -4 & -4 \end{pmatrix}$

d) $\begin{pmatrix} 0 & -2 \\ 2 & 0 \end{pmatrix}, \begin{pmatrix} 0 & -2 & 0 \\ 2 & 6 & 8 \end{pmatrix}$

e) $90°, 2$
f) centre (0, 0), rotation $225°$ and enlargement scale factor $\sqrt{2}$

6. $\mathbf{M} = \begin{pmatrix} 0 & 1 & 1 & 0 & 0 \\ 1 & 0 & 1 & 1 & 0 \\ 1 & 1 & 0 & 1 & 1 \\ 0 & 1 & 1 & 0 & 0 \\ 0 & 0 & 1 & 0 & 0 \end{pmatrix}$

a) The number of regions bordering each region

b) The number of regions bordering both the given regions

Zero shows that no region borders on both.

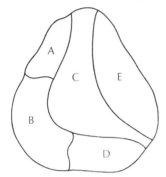

7. $(1, 7)$, $(-6, 8)$, $(2, 14)$, mirror line $y = 2x$
$(-1, 7)$, $(6, 8)$, $(-2, 14)$, rotation of $53°$ about $(0, 0)$

8. $\mathbf{M} = \begin{pmatrix} 0 & 1 \\ 1 & 1 \end{pmatrix}$

a) $\begin{pmatrix} 1 & 2 \\ 2 & 3 \end{pmatrix}$
b) $\begin{pmatrix} 2 & 3 \\ 3 & 5 \end{pmatrix}$
c) $\begin{pmatrix} -1 & 1 \\ 1 & 0 \end{pmatrix}$

d) $\begin{pmatrix} 0 & 2 \\ 2 & 2 \end{pmatrix}$

$n = 7 \qquad p = 5$

26. VECTORS

1. $2\mathbf{b}$, $-2\mathbf{a}$, $2\mathbf{b} - 2\mathbf{a}$, $\mathbf{b} - \mathbf{a}$; $PS = 2RQ$ and $PS \parallel RQ$.

2. $\overrightarrow{PT} = \mathbf{t} - \mathbf{p}$. $\dfrac{OX}{XS} = \dfrac{1}{2}$

3. a) $4\mathbf{b} - \mathbf{a}$, $4\mathbf{a} - \mathbf{b}$
b) $\frac{4}{5}\mathbf{b} - \frac{1}{5}\mathbf{a}$, $\frac{4}{5}(\mathbf{a} + \mathbf{b})$, $\frac{1}{5}(4\mathbf{a} - \mathbf{b})$
c) $4(\mathbf{a} + \mathbf{b})$
d) P lies on OE, OE = 5OP.

4. a) $\mathbf{b} - \mathbf{a}$
b) $\frac{1}{4}(\mathbf{b} - \mathbf{a})$
c) $\frac{1}{4}(\mathbf{b} + 3\mathbf{a})$
d) $\frac{1}{8}(\mathbf{b} + 3\mathbf{a})$
$\overrightarrow{OE} = \frac{11}{28}\mathbf{a}$

5. $\overrightarrow{AP} = \frac{2}{5}\mathbf{b}$, $\overrightarrow{AD} = \mathbf{b} - 3\mathbf{a}$, $\overrightarrow{DP} = 3\mathbf{a} - \frac{3}{5}\mathbf{b}$
$\overrightarrow{DQ} = k(3\mathbf{a} - \frac{3}{5}\mathbf{b}) = (3 + h)\mathbf{a} - \mathbf{b}$
$h = 2$, $k = \frac{5}{3}$, $1:2$, $3:2$

6. a) $\mathbf{a} - \mathbf{b}$, $\mathbf{a} + \mathbf{b}$
b) magnitude or length
c) rhombus
d) $90°$

27. PROBABILITY

1. a) $\frac{1}{7}$ b) $\frac{3}{7}$ c) $\frac{1}{49}$
d) $\frac{2}{49}$ e) $\frac{46}{49}$ f) $\frac{24}{49}$

2. a) $\frac{1}{2}$ b) $\frac{1}{3}$ c) $\frac{1}{12}$
d) $\frac{1}{12}$ e) $\frac{1}{144}$ f) $\frac{1}{36}$

3. a) $\frac{3}{8}$ b) $\frac{1}{4}$ c) $\frac{5}{8}$
d) $\frac{3}{64}$ e) $3, \frac{1}{64}$

4. a) BBB/BBG/BGB/GBB/GGG/GGB/GBG/BGG
b) $\frac{1}{2}$
c) i) $\frac{1}{8}$ ii) $\frac{3}{8}$
d) $\frac{7}{8}$, $\frac{10}{32}$

5. $\dfrac{x}{x + 30}$, $\dfrac{x - 4}{x + 60}$, $x = 20$

6. a)

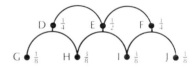

b) must go to one of them
c) i) p^2 ii) $2pq$ iii) q^2
d) $p^2 + 2pq + q^2$

28. SETS

1. a)

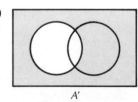

A'

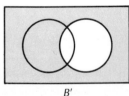

B'

$A' \cup B'$

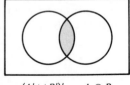

$(A' \cup B')' = A \cap B$

320

b)

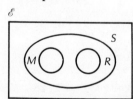

$x = 5$

2. a) D b) W c) $\emptyset$ d) $\mathscr{E}$ e) E

f) $n\,(\text{Houses}) = 150,\ n(E) = 70,\ n(G) = 80$

g) $n\,(\text{Houses}) = 80,\ n(E) = 0,\ n(G) = 10$

3. a) No hatchbacks are made in Britain.

b) All hatchbacks are red.

c) All cars with engines of more than 2 litres have automatic transmission.

d) $R \cap A \cap S = \emptyset$

e) $M \subset F'$ or $M \cap F' = M$ or $M \cup F' = F'$

f) $F \subset S$ or $F \cap S = F$ or $F \cup S = S$

4. a) All Scotsmen have red hair.

b) There are some Scotsmen with red hair.

c) $R \subset S$

d) $S \cap R' \neq \emptyset$

e) a is disproved, b is unaffected, c is unaffected, d is proved.

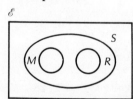

5. a) $A = \{5, 6, 7, 8, 9, 10, 11, 12\}$

b) $B = \{2, 3, 5, 7, 11, 13, 17, 19\}$

c) $C = \{2, 4, 5, 10, 20\}$

d) $\{2, 3, 13, 17, 19\}$

e) $\{1, 4, 14, 15, 16, 18, 20\}$

f) $\{1, 6, 8, 9, 12, 14, 15, 16, 18\}$

g) $\{2, 5, 10\}$

6. a) 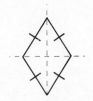 b)

d)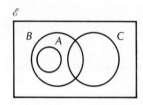

c)

e) $A \cap C = \emptyset$

f) $B \cap A' \cap C \neq \emptyset$

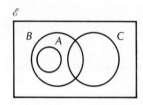

29. FUNCTIONS

1. $x^2 + 2,\ (x + 3)^2 - 1,\ x = -1$

2. a) i) $3(x - 2)$ ii) $3x^2$ iii) $(x - 2)^2$

iv) $\dfrac{x}{3}$ v) $x + 2$ vi) $\dfrac{x}{3} + 2$

b) $a = 3$ c) 0.73 or -2.73

3. a) $\dfrac{3}{x},\ (4 - x)$ b) $\dfrac{3}{4 - x},\ 4 - \dfrac{3}{x}$

c) 3 or 1 d) $g(c) = d \Rightarrow g(d) = c$

4. a) $2x - 3,\ 2(x - 3),\ (2x - 3)^2,\ 2(x^2 - 3)$

b) $4.22,\ 1.78$ c) $2, 4$

5. a) $10, 5, 6$

b) $n = 14,\ n = 7$ or 16

c) n is even, n is odd.

e) $9 \to 10 \to 5 \to 6 \to 3 \to 4 \to 2 \to 1 \to 2 \to 1$, etc.

6. a) $1, 10$

b) i) $9x^2 + 1$ ii) $(9x + 1)^2$

c) $0, -\frac{1}{4}$

d) $-1 < x < \frac{3}{4}$

30. FLOW CHARTS

1.

y	n	z	A	C
1.0975	1	1.097 500	7902	702
	2	1.204 506	8672.45	1472.45
	3	1.321 946	9518.01	2318.01
	4	1.450 835	10 446.01	3246.01
	5	1.592 292	11 464.50	4264.50

$z = 1$ in first box and $z = z \times y$ in place of $z = y^n$

2.

d	p	q	a	A	x
0.1	—	—	—	0	0
0	0.005	0.000 25	0.000 25	0.1	
0.005	0.04	0.002 25	0.002 5	0.2	
0.04	0.135	0.008 75	0.011 25	0.3	
0.135					

$A = 0.010\,125$, 11.1%

3.

n	1	2	3	4	5	6
x	0	0.3	0.309	0.309 548 1	0.309 582 002	0.309 584 101

0.3096 (to 4 d.p.)

$x_2 = 9.7$, $x_3 = 9.690\,721\,65$, $x_4 = 9.690\,425\,532$, $x_5 = 9.690\,416\,07$

9.6904 (to 4 d.p.)

4. a)

1985	220 000	c)	1985	180 000
1986	224 000		1986	176 000
1987	228 800		1987	171 200
1988	234 560		1988	165 440
1989	241 472		1989	158 528

d) For £220 000 the shop increases its takings. For £180 000 the takings decrease $200 000.

SECTION VI

PAPER 1: MENTAL ARITHMETIC

Test A

1. 51
2. 2.4
3. $3\frac{1}{2}$
4. £1.45
5. £1.10
6. 21 cm
7. 28
8. 170 cm
9. 12
10. $\frac{6}{9}$
11. 2.1
12. $1\frac{2}{7}$
13. -4
14. 8
15. 18 : 15
16. 11.1
17. $\frac{2}{3}$
18. 84 p
19. 18 cm
20. £1.07

Test B

1. 7
2. 400
3. £3.50
4. 6 km
5. 3
6. 20 min
7. 29
8. 0.45
9. 1112
10. 5
11. 27
12. $12°$
13. £7300
14. £30
15. 0.06
16. 30
17. 9
18. $\frac{5}{8}$
19. 1
20. 0.05

Test C

1. 1500 g
2. 68 p
3. 8 cm
4. 6 ft
5. 28 p
6. $3\frac{3}{4}$
7. £1.94
8. 75 cm
9. 4.8
10. 6
11. 6 kg
12. 28
13. 48 p
14. 12
15. octagon
16. 0.06
17. 50 m/h
18. $500\,\text{cm}^3$
19. £1.55
20. 12
21. 63%
22. £16.50
23. 12
24. 12
25. icosahedron
26. 35 lb
27. $\frac{3}{8}$ yd
28. 9 mm
29. £1.24
30. 8 : 13

Test D

1. 65
2. 20%
3. 9:18
4. £3.08
5. 196
6. 32 m
7. 0.7
8. 42°
9. 1.8 m
10. 12
11. $\frac{3}{4}$
12. £12.50
13. £270
14. $\frac{3}{20}$
15. £80
16. 13
17. 60
18. $\frac{1}{3}$
19. 7
20. 4

Test E

1. 1 007 003
2. 5
3. 1000
4. £1.80
5. 0.05 m
6. 36 cm
7. 6:40
8. 2400
9. 2.5×10^3
10. 0.16
11. 2
12. $\frac{1}{10}$
13. 120 cm²
14. 64 km
15. 1800
16. £3.34
17. 20 p
18. 0.55
19. 20%
20. 40 min

PAPER 2: MULTIPLE CHOICE

Test A

1. B
2. A
3. B
4. E
5. D
6. D
7. D
8. C
9. A
10. C
11. D
12. B
13. A
14. E
15. B
16. E
17. B
18. A
19. D
20. C
21. C
22. E
23. C
24. B
25. B

Test B

1. C
2. B
3. D
4. B
5. C
6. E
7. E
8. B
9. A
10. A
11. D
12. A
13. C
14. D
15. A
16. E
17. D
18. B
19. D
20. B
21. C
22. E
23. C
24. A
25. A

PAPER 3: NATIONAL CRITERIA

Test A: National Criteria Level 1

1. a) 1 or 3 or 5 or 7 or 9   b) 5
   c) 6 or 12 or 18   d) 1 or 3 or 5 or 15
   e) 49

2. a) -4 b) 13°C   c) $\frac{9}{7} = 1\frac{2}{7}$

3. a) $\frac{20}{100} = \frac{1}{5}$ b) $\frac{6}{10} = \frac{3}{5}$ c) 0.25

4. a) £32.64   b) £23.24   c) 0.875
   d) 5.922   e) 25.132 741 f) £7.82

5. £95.40; £57.60

6. 35 years

7. a) 610 miles   b) £3 (approx)

8. a) evening meal   b) 45 minutes
   c) 00:10

9. 4714; £31.34

10. 39 stones

11. a) £240   b) £264   c) £276

12. A(1, 3), B(-2, 1), C(1, -3)

13. 105 km/h

14. a) A = 14 cm²   b) 120 min = 2 hrs
    c) $8x$

15. AB = 2.5 cm, AC = 4.5 cm,
BC = 5.3 cm, A = 95°,
B = 57°, C = 28°

16. $x = 100°$, $a = 70°$, $b = 40°$, $t = 155°$

17. a) b)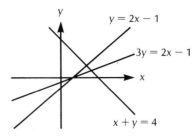

c) 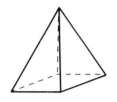 d)

e)

18. a) 20 km   b) 060°   c) 240°
d) 10 km

19. 42 m³, 21 m², 48 m

20. a) 5.2 m   b) 5.3 m   c) $\frac{3}{8}$

Test B: National Criteria Level 2

1. a) 1.73   b) 9000   c) 29 800
d) 30   e) £44

2. a) i) 2.7×10^5 ii) 3.6×10^{-5}
b) i) 0.06   ii) 0.204

3. a) i) 1, 2, 3, 4, 6, 12   ii) 1, 3, 5, 15
b) 3
c) 60
d) 2, 3, 11

4. a) $3\frac{1}{4}$ b) $3\frac{1}{2}$ c) 25

5. a) 195   b) 24%   c) 420 men

6. a) £300 : £450   b) 1 : 20 000

7. −7, −3, 1, 3, 5

8.

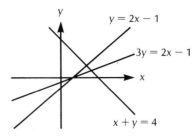

9. a) −26   b) 18
c) x^6 d) $\frac{1}{y^3} = y^{-3}$

10. a) $x = \dfrac{y - c}{m}$
b) i) 6   ii) $2\frac{1}{2}$ iii) 6
iv) 2

11. a) i) $5(x + 2y)$ ii) $4e(2d + 3e)$
b) $6t - 8t^2$
c) $4x + 14$

12. $a = 50°$, $b = 130°$, $c = 50°$

13. a) i) $t = 60°$ ii) $a = 72°$; $b = 108°$
b) 150°

14. a) 13 cm   b) 6 cm; Area = 48 cm²

15. a) 60 m²   b) 201.06 cm²

16. 112.5π m³ ≈ 353.43 m³

17. $x ≈ 1.29$ cm, $y ≈ 58.8°$

18. a) 12, 8, 3, 7   c) 19 seconds

19. British 170°, French 105°, German 55°, Others 30°

20. a) $\frac{1}{10}$ b) $\frac{1}{10} \times \frac{4}{9} = \frac{2}{45}$ c) $\frac{2}{10} \times \frac{1}{9} = \frac{1}{45}$

PAPER 4: GCSE MIDDLE GRADES

1. a) £175   b) £75   c) £352.50

2. a) (4, 0), (4, 3), (6, 5), (6, 2); (0, 0), (3, 0), (5, −2), (2, −2)
5 lines of symmetry

3. a) i) $\dfrac{11}{2x}$ ii) $5x^2 - 3x + 16$
b) 2
c) $x = 1$ or $1\frac{1}{2}$

4. a) i) brothers   ii) uncle/nephew
    iii) husband/wife

b)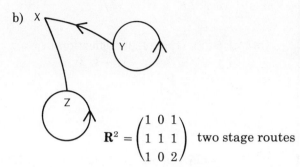
$$\mathbf{R}^2 = \begin{pmatrix} 1 & 0 & 1 \\ 1 & 1 & 1 \\ 1 & 0 & 2 \end{pmatrix} \text{ two stage routes}$$

5. a) $3:2$ b) £960

6. a) -2 b) 3 c) $y = 3x - 2$
d) $1\frac{1}{2}$

7. a) $(90°, 0)$ $(180°, 0)$ $(-60°, \frac{1}{2})$ $(330°, -\frac{1}{2})$
b) $-300°, -240°, 60°, 120°, 420°$

8. a) $3 \times 5 \times 7 = 105$
b) $6 \times 7 \times 9 = 378$

9. £6441

10. a) 12 b) $x; x = 1$

11. a) 40
b) i) 30 ii) 700
c) 2×10^3

12. $x = 36°; x \approx 7.2\,\text{cm}$

13. a) 2-bar pack and 125 ml bottle
b) For example, a rectangle 19 cm by 13 cm (to allow for overlap to glue)

14. a) $x \leqslant -1$ or $x \geqslant \frac{2}{3}$
b) 707
c) £70

15. a) $12\,\text{m}$ b) $48\,\text{m}^2$
c) i) $224\,000\,000\,\text{cm}^3$ ii) $224\,\text{m}^3$

16. a) $8\pi \approx 25.13\,\text{cm}$ b) $4\,\text{cm}$

17. $AC = 5.9\,\text{cm}$, $AB = 7.2\,\text{cm}$
2 points

18. a) $86\frac{2}{3}\,\text{km/h}$ b) $\frac{1}{2}\,\text{km/h}$

19. $a = 5, b = 3, x = 3, y = -1, w = 5$

20. a) i) 150   ii) 200   iii) 50
b) i) 3
ii) 12 $\frac{6}{15} \times \frac{9}{14} = \frac{9}{35}$

PAPER 5: GCSE HIGHER GRADES

1. a) $60°$ b) $20\,\text{cm}$ c) isosceles trapezium
d) $259.81\,\text{cm}^2$ e) e.g.

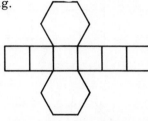

f) $1119.62\,\text{cm}^2$

2. a) 50 at £2, 60 at £1.50, 170 at £1
b) 6

3. a)

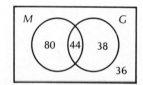

b) i) 44   ii) 36
c)

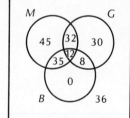

d) i) $124:74 = 62:37$ ii) 41.4%
e) £70 (or 262.5 DM)

4. a) 4.08 nautical miles, $086.9°$
b) i) $36.9°$ ii) $20.9°$

5. a) $y = 22, 11, 4, 1, 2, 7$
c)

d) $14\frac{2}{3}$ sq. units
e) $y = 7x - 7$

6. a) £247
  b) £51 243.50 ≈ £51 250
  c) £174
  d) £2100
  e) £535.25

7. a) 50 cm × 54.1 cm
  b) 123.7°
  c)
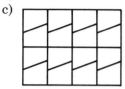 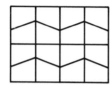
  d) 101 250 cm³

8. a) i) 2, 3, 5, 4, 6, 5   ii) 25   iii) 35
     iv) 36
  b) i) $\frac{3}{50}$ ii) $\frac{4}{50}$ iii) $\frac{84}{2500}$
     iv) $\frac{7}{50}$

9. a) i) **b**   ii) **a** − **b**   iii) 2**b**
     iv) **a** + 3**b**
  b) similar, scale factor 2
  c) $\frac{2}{3}$**a**, $\frac{2}{3}$(**a** + 3**b**)
  d) (6, 2), (3, −2), (0, −2) (1, −2)
  e) Â = 90°
  f) 12

10. a) i) $\begin{pmatrix} 3 & 4 & 9 \\ 6 & 0 & 1 \\ 3 & 8 & 2 \end{pmatrix}$ ii) $\begin{pmatrix} 5 \\ 3 \\ 2 \end{pmatrix}$ iii) $\begin{pmatrix} 45 \\ 32 \\ 43 \end{pmatrix}$

  b) i) (1, 2), (1, 5) (4, 3), reflection in $y = x$
     ii) (−2, −1), (1, −1)(−1, 2)
     iii) $\begin{pmatrix} -2 & 0 \\ 0 & -2 \end{pmatrix}$

       $\begin{pmatrix} -\frac{1}{2} & 0 \\ 0 & -\frac{1}{2} \end{pmatrix}$

       enlarged figure (−4, −2), (−10, −2), (−6, −8)

11. a)
```
5 km ┤                           ●
     │                        ╱
     │                     ╱
   2 ┤        ____      ╱
     │      ╱    ·   ╱
     │   ╱    ·  ·╱
     └──┬──────────┬──────
      7.30       7.55
```
  b) 7:35
  c) i) 12 km/h   ii) 15 km/h
  d) 7:36

12. a) 2.4%   b) 10.0 cm   c) £1.92
  d) 5.0 cm   e) £1.41